THE MILITARY ORDERS, VOLUME 3

The Military Orders, Volume 3
History and Heritage

Edited by

VICTOR MALLIA-MILANES
University of Malta, Malta

editorial committee
Malcolm Barber, Peter Edbury, Anthony Luttrell,
Jonathan Phillips, Jonathan Riley-Smith

ASHGATE

Published by
Ashgate Publishing Limited
Gower House
Croft Road
Aldershot
Hampshire GU11 3HR
England

Ashgate Publishing Company
Suite 420
101 Cherry Street
Burlington, VT 05401-4405
USA

Ashgate website: http://www.ashgate.com

British Library Cataloguing in Publication Data
The Military Orders
  Vol. 3: History and Heritage
  1. Knights of Malta – Congresses. 2. Templars – Congresses. 3. Military religious orders – Europe – History – Congresses. 4. Hospitallers – History – Congresses.
  I. Mallia-Milanes, Victor, 1940– .
  271.7'91

Library of Congress Cataloging-in-Publication Data
The Military Orders. Volume 3 History and Heritage
  1. Military religious orders – History – Congresses. 2. Hospitallers – History – Congresses. 3. Templars – History – Congresses. 4. Teutonic Knights – History – Congresses. I. Mallia-Milanes, Victor.
  CR4701.M55 1994
  271'.05–dc20

ISBN 978-0-7546-6290-7

This volume has been printed on acid-free paper.

Printed and bound in Great Britain by TJ International Ltd, Padstow.

Contents

List of Illustrations   ix
Abbreviations   xi
Notes on Contributors   xiii
Editor's Preface   xix
Introduction   xxi
Jonathan Riley-Smith

PART I: Historiography   **1**

1   Hospitaller Historiography: Heritages and Heresies   3
      Anthony T. Luttrell
2   A Survey of Research on the History of the Military Orders
      in Poland in the Middle Ages   13
      Maria Starnawska
3   Historiography and History: Medieval Studies on the
      Military Orders in Spain since 1975   23
      Luis García-Guijarro Ramos
4   The Knights Templar between Theatre and History:
      Raynouard's works on the Templars (1805–1813)   45
      Alain Demurger

PART II: Liturgy and Fiction, Heraldry and Piety   **53**

5   Sad Stories of the Death of Kings: Last Illnesses and
      Funerary Rites of the Grand Masters of the Order of St John
      from Aubusson to the Cotoners   55
      Ann Williams
6   The Liturgical Policies of the Hospitallers between the Invention
      of Printing and the Council of Trent: The Evidence of the Early
      Printed Breviaries and Missals   63
      Cristina Dondi
7   Hospitallers, Mysticism, and Reform in Late-Medieval Strasburg   73
      Karl Borchardt
8   Heraldry in Medieval Rhodes: Hospitallers and Others   79
      Anna-Maria Kasdagli
9   The Fictional Hospitaller: Images and Stories of the Knights
      of Malta in Count Jan Potocki's *Manuscript Found in Saragossa*   87
      Yuri Stoyanov

PART III: Templars, Teutonic Knights, and Other Military Orders   **93**

10   The Templar Order in North-Western Italy:
A General Picture (1142–1312)   95
Elena Bellomo

11   The Templar James of Garrigans: Illuminator and Deserter   107
Alan Forey

12   The University of Paris and the Trial of the Templars   115
Paul F. Crawford

13   A Look through the Keyhole: Templars in Italy from the
Trial Testimony   123
Anne Gilmour-Bryson

14   Teutonic Castles in Cilician Armenia: A Reappraisal   131
Kristian Molin

15   The Use of Indulgences by the Teutonic Order in the Middle Ages   139
Axel Ehlers

16   Innocent III and the Origins of the Order of Sword Brothers   147
Barbara Bombi

17   The Military Orders and Papal Crusading Propaganda   155
Rudolf Hiestand

18   The Hospitaller and Templar Houses of Périgord:
Some Observations   167
David Bryson

19   The Battle of Tannenberg-Grunwald-Žalgiris (1410)
as Reflected in Twentieth-Century Monuments   175
Sven Ekdahl

PART IV: Hospitallers   **195**

20   The Decree of 1262: A Glimpse into the Economic
Decision-Making of the Hospitallers   197
Judith Bronstein

21   The Hospitaller Order in Acre and Manueth: The Ceramic Evidence   203
Edna J. Stern

22   Bioarchaeological Analysis of the Latrine Soil from the
Thirteenth-Century Hospital of St John at Acre, Israel   213
Piers D. Mitchell, Jacqui P. Huntley, and Eliezer Stern

23   The Hospitallers and the 'Peasants' Revolt' of 1381 Revisited   225
Helen J. Nicholson

24   The Hospitallers and the Kings of Castile in the Fourteenth
and Fifteenth Centuries   235
Carlos Barquero Goñi

25   The Visit of the Emperor Manuel II Palaeologus at the Priory
of St John in 1401   241
Julian Chrysostomides

26   John Kaye, the 'Dread Turk', and the Siege of Rhodes   245
       Theresa M. Vann
27   The Hospitaller Fraternity of St John at SS Johan and
       Cordula in Cologne   253
       Klaus Militzer
28   Hospitaller Commanderies in the Kingdom of
       Hungary (*c.*1150–*c.*1330)   257
       Zsolt Hunyadi
29   Frisians and Foreigners in the Hospitaller House of Sneek:
       Origins and Careers   269
       Johannes Adriaan Mol
30   Hospitaller Baroque Culture: The Order of St John's Legacy
       to Early Modern Malta   279
       Victor Mallia-Milanes
Select Bibliography   289
Index   297

List of Illustrations

Illustrations

8.1	Tomb slab of Ioannes Pitzos, d.1306	82
8.2	Civic heraldry from the house at 2, Gavalas Street, Old Town of Rhodes	84
8.3	Heraldry from the east wall, Chapel of St George on the Collachio Wall	86
18.1	Hospitaller and Templar Houses of Périgord	168
19.1	Tannenberg-Grunwald. Foundation walls of the Teutonic Order's Mary chapel of 1411, with the vestry in front. View from the north-east in the direction of Grunwald village (Grünfelde) (Photo S. Ekdahl, 1985)	176
19.2	Tannenberg-Grunwald. The German commemorative stone tablet of 1901. The inscription *Im Kampf für deutsches Wesen, deutsches Recht starb hier der Hochmeister Ulrich von Jungingen am 15. Juli 1410 den Heldentod* was chiselled away in 1960 by order of a Communist functionary. Cf. Figure 19.10 (Photo S. Ekdahl, 1977)	178
19.3	Kraków: The rider statue of King Władyslaw Jagiełło (1910). (Polish pre-war postcard)	180
19.4	Kaunas: The statue of Vytautas the Great at its present site on Freedom Avenue (Photo S. Ekdahl, 1995)	182
19.5	New York: 'King Jagiello' with two raised and crossed swords at the 1939 World's Fair. The statue was later moved to Central Park.	184
19.6	Tannenberg-Grunwald: The obelisk of 1960 (Photo D. Heckmann, 2005)	187
19.7	Vilnius: Stone tablet commemorating the battle of Žalgiris-Grjunval'd, now lost. (Photo S. Ekdahl, 1991)	189
19.8	Tannenberg-Grunwald: Władysław Gomułka, First Secretary of the Polish United Workers Party, was the main personality during the Grunwald celebrations in 1960 (Courtesy Trybuna Ludu)	190
19.9	Tannenberg-Grunwald: Sixteen Ilyushin bombers and 64 MIG fighters demonstrated Polish military effectiveness during the celebrations of 1960 (Courtesy Trybuna Ludu)	191
19.10	Tannenberg-Grunwald: In 1984, the German memorial stone tablet of 1901 was laid, face down, outside the ruins of Mary chapel. Next to it lay a smaller tablet with an explanatory text.	193
21.1	Location of Acre and Manueth.	204

21.2	Simple unglazed closed-shaped vessels and 'Acre Bowls' from the Hospitaller compound	206
21.3	A drawing of sugar vessels	209
21.4	Sugar pots in storage in the Hospitaller compound at Acre	209
22.1	Fly Puparia from the Latrines (each approximately 2mm long)	215
22.2	Cutting meadow grass with a scythe. An illustration for June, from the calendar of an English psalter, c.1250–75 (parchment). Corpus Christi College, Oxford, UK/Bridgeman Art Library. MS CCC 285, fol.5v. (Reproduced by permission of the President and Fellows of Corpus Christi College, Oxford)	217
22.3	Charred cereal grain, probably Triticum sp. (wheat). Left ventral view (7mm long)	218
22.4	Ova of whipworm (Trichuris trichuria) from the Latrines of St John's.	219
23.1	The City of London and its environs in 1381	226
28.1	Hospitaller commanderies in the Hungarian-Slavonian priory, 1200–1250	261
28.2	Hospitaller commanderies in the Hungarian-Slavonian priory, 1250–1300	265
28.3	Hospitaller commanderies in the Hungarian-Slavonian priory, 1300–c.1350	266

List of Tables

8.1	Arms of the Grand Masters in Rhodes, 1319–1522	79
8.2	Heraldry on the Fortifications of Rhodes, 1377–1522	80
22.1	Pollen analysis of samples from the latrines	222
22.2	Dietary components recovered from the complex of St John	223
26.1	The Siege of Rhodes (1480) in Caoursin, Kay, and d'Aubusson	247
29.1	Frisians and Foreigners in the Hospitaller House of Sneek	275

Abbreviations

ACA	Archivo de la Corona de Aragón, Barcelona
ACB	Archivo Capitular, Barcelona
AD	Archaiologikon Deltion, Athens
ADPA	Archives départementales des Pyrénées-Atlantiques, Pau
AOM	Archives of the Order of St John, National Library of Malta
ÁUO	*Árpádkori új okmánytár. Codex diplomaticus Arpadianus continuatus*, ed. G. Wenzel, 12 vols (Pest, 1860-74)
CCR	Calendar of the Close Rolls, PRO
CEPRGI	Calendar of Entries in the Papal Registers Relating to Great Britain and Ireland
CH	*Cartulaire général de l'Ordre des Hospitaliers de Saint-Jean de Jérusalem, 1000-1310*, ed J. Delaville Le Roulx, 4 vols (Paris, 1894-1906)
CP	Court of Common Pleas
CPR	Calendar of the Patent Rolls, PRO
CRD	Cartas reales diplomáticas
Fejér CD	*Codex diplomaticus Hungariae ecclesiasticus ac civilis*, ed. G. Fejér, 11 vols (Buda, 1829–44)
ISTC	*Incunabula Short-Title Catalogue*
JBS	*Journal of Baltic Studies*
KB	King's Bench Records
MES	*Monumenta Ecclesiae Strigoniensis*, ed. F. Knauz *et al.*, 4 vols (Esztergom–Budapest, 1874-1999)
MGH SS	*Monumenta Germaniae historica. Scriptores*
MO, i	*The Military Orders*, [i]: *Fighting for the Faith and Caring for the Sick*, ed. M. Barber (Aldershot, 1994)
MO, ii	*The Military Orders*, ii: *Welfare and Warfare*, ed. Helen Nicholson (Aldershot, 1998)
MonWesp	*Veszprémi püspökség római oklevéltára, Monumenta romana episcopatus Wesprimiensis, 1103–1526*, ed. V. Fraknói, 3 vols (Budapest, 1896-1907)
PL	*Patrologia Latina*
PRO	Public Record Office, Kew
PRT	*A pannonhalmi Szent-Benedek-rend története* [History of the Benedictine Order of Pannonhalma], ed. L. Erdélyi and P. Sörös, 12 vols (Budapest, 1902–16)
RHC	*Recueil des Historiens des Croisades*
DArm	*Documents arméniens*

RHGF	*Recueil des Historiens des Gaules et de la France*
RRH	*Regesta Regni Hierosolymitani* and *Additamentum*, ed. R. Röhricht (Innsbruck, 1893-1904).
Smičiklas	*Codex diplomaticus regni Croatiae, Dalmatiae ac Slavoniae, Diplomatički zbornik kraljevine Hrvatske, Dalmacije i Slavonije*, ed. M. Kostrenčić and T. Smičiklas, 18 vols (Zagreb, 1904-90)
SRP	*Scriptores Rerum Prussicarum*, ed. T. Hirsch *et al.* (Leipzig, 1861)
Theiner	*Vetera Monumenta Historica Hungariam Sacram Illustrantia, 1216-1352*, ed. A. Theiner, 2 vols (Rome, 1859–60)
TNA	The National Archives
TTPSA	*The Trial of the Templars in the Papal State and the Abruzzi*, ed. A. Gilmour-Bryson (Vatican City, 1982)
UB	*Urkundenbuch*

Notes on Contributors

Carlos Barquero Goñi holds a doctorate in Medieval History from the Universidad Autónoma of Madrid. His research field is the Order of Saint John in Medieval Spain. At present, he holds a post-doctoral grant from the Caja Madrid Foundation. His most recent book is *Los caballeros hospitalarios durante la Edad Media en España* (Burgos, 2003).

Elena Bellomo graduated at the Università Cattolica del Sacro Cuore (Milan), where she also received a PhD in medieval history. Subsequently she held a two-year post-doctoral fellowship at the Department of History of the University of Padua. Her research interests concern the military orders in Italy and the Italian participation in the crusades. Her main publications include *A servizio di Dio e del Santo Sepolcro. Caffaro e L'Oriente latino* (Padua, 2003) and *Cronache genovesi di crociata (secoli XII-XIII)*, forthcoming.

Barbara Bombi is a Lecturer in Medieval History at the University of Kent, Canterbury. Her publications include a forthcoming book on the Mission and Crusade in Livonia at the beginning of the thirteenth century and a number of articles on the representatives of the Teutonic Knights at the papal curia in the thirteenth and fourteenth centuries.

Karl Borchardt teaches at the History Department of the University of Würzburg and works as archivist in Rothenburg ob der Tauber, Germany. He has published a number of articles on the Hospitallers in central Europe and is editor of the Bulletin of the Society for the Study of the Crusades and the Latin East.

Judith Bronstein graduated PhD from the University of Cambridge and is currently teaching at the Department of General History at the University of Haifa. Her research interests are particularly concerned with the history of the Order of St John. Her several publications include *The Hospitallers and the Holy Land, Financing the Latin East, 1187-1274*, which appeared in 2005.

David Bryson has taught at the University of Melbourne, the Royal Melbourne Institute of Technology and Trinity Western University. He is a Fellow of the History Department of the University of Melbourne. His work on the Hospitallers and Templars is focused on the part they played in the medieval and early modern history of southwestern France.

Julian Chrysostomides is Director of the Hellenic Institute, Royal Holloway College, University of London. She has edited Manuel II Palaeologus's Funeral Oration on His Brother Theodore. Her other major publications include *Monumenta*

Peloponnesiaca. Documents for the History of the Peloponnese in the Fourteenth and Fifteenth Centuries (1995) and *The Letter of the Three Patriarchs to Emperor Theophilos*, ed. with J.A. Munitiz *et al.* (1997).

Paul F. Crawford is Assistant Professor of ancient and medieval history at California University of Pennsylvania. He is the translator of *The Templar of Tyre*, and the author of several articles on the crusades and the military orders. He specializes in the history of the Templars and Hospitallers in the thirteenth and fourteenth centuries.

Alain Demurger is 'Maître de conférences' at the University Paris 1, Panthéon-Sorbonne. Publications include *Vie et mort de l'ordre du Temple* (1985); *Temps de crises, temps d'espoirs, XIVe-XVe siècles*, Nouvelle histoire de la France médiévale, vol. V (1990); *La croisade au Moyen Age. Idée et pratiques* (1998); and *Les ordres religieux-militaires au Moyen Age (1129-1530)*, forthcoming.

Cristina Dondi is J. P. R. Lyell Research Fellow in the History of the Early Modern Printed Book at the University of Oxford and a Fellow of Lincoln College.

Axel Ehlers studied History and Theology at the Universities of Göttingen (Staatsexamen) and Cambridge (MPhil). His PhD (University of Göttingen) dealt with the use of indulgences by the Teutonic Order in the Middle Ages. He is currently teaching at a grammar school in Hanover. His research interests include the crusades in the Baltic region, the military orders, and medieval piety.

Sven Ekdahl is Research Professor of Medieval History at the Instytut Polsko-Skandynawski (Polish-Scandianavian Research Institute), Copenhagen, Honorary PhD at the University of Vilnius, and Foreign Member of the Lithuanian Academy of Sciences. He has published extensively on the history of the Teutonic Order in Prussia, and has also treated Polish, Baltic, and Scandinavian themes.

Alan Forey has taught at the universities of Oxford, St Andrews, and Durham. He has published extensively on the crusades and the military orders. His publications include *The Templars in the Corona de Aragón*, *The Military Orders: From the Twelfth to the Early Fourteenth Centuries*, and *Military Orders and Crusades*.

Luis García-Guijarro Ramos lectures in Medieval History at the University of Zaragoza, campus of Huesca. He has researched into various aspects of military and monastic orders in medieval Spain, especially into the Order of Montesa and into the history of the pre-Gregorian Catalan and Aragonese monasteries. He has also done work on crusader historiography. His publications include *Papado, Cruzadas y Órdenes Militares, siglos XI-XIII* (1995), a comparative analysis of the structure of the international military orders and the role they played in the Latin Church.

Anne Gilmour-Bryson completed her MA and PhD at the University of Montreal, Institute of Medieval Studies. She led the programme in Medieval Studies at the

University of Melbourne, Australia, returning to Canada to teach at Trinity Western University. She edited the trial of the Templars in the Abruzzi and the Papal State as well as the trial in Cyprus. She is a Principal Fellow of the Department of History, University of Melbourne.

Rudolf Hiestand is Emeritus Professor of Medieval History at the Heinrich-Heine-Universität, Düsseldorf, and has published extensively on the Latin East and the military orders.

Jacqui P. Huntley graduated from Cambridge with a Natural Sciences degree (Honours Botany) and went on to research in palaeoecology at Lancaster University. This was followed by a return to Cambridge working on the National Vegetation Classification, after which she moved to Durham University. She worked as the English Heritage Archaeobotanist in Durham for some thirteen years and then took up post as the English Heritage Regional Science Advisor for the North-East Region, where she continues today.

Zsolt Hunyadi teaches in the Department of Medieval and Early Modern Hungarian History, University of Szeged, Hungary. His doctoral thesis deals with the history of the Hospitallers in the medieval kingdom of Hungary (*c*.1150–1387).

Anna-Maria Kasdagli graduated BA Honours in Ancient and Medieval History from the University of Birmingham. Currently employed by the Ministry for Culture, 4th Ephorate of Byzantine Antiquities, she has been working in Rhodes as an archaeologist since 1986. She has published articles both in Greek and English on topics ranging from numismatics and heraldry to military architecture.

Anthony T. Luttrell has held lectureships at Edinburgh and Malta and is a former Assistant Director of the British School at Rome. He is a leading authority on the occupation of Rhodes by the Order of St John (1306-1522) and has also published extensively on the order's European possessions and on other Western settlements in Greece in the later Middle Ages.

Victor Mallia-Milanes is Professor of Early Modern History at the University of Malta, where he served for several years as Head of the History Department and Dean of the Faculty of Arts. His special research interest is Venice, the Order of St John, and Malta in the early modern period, on which he has published extensively. His most recent work is *In the Service of the Venetian Republic: Massimiliano Buzzaccarini Gonzaga's Letters to Venice's Magistracy of Trade 1754-1776* (Malta, PEG, 2008).

Klaus Militzer is Professor of Medieval History at the University of Bochum. His publications on the military orders centre particularly upon the history of the Teutonic Order in Germany, Prussia, and Livonia, and include *Die Entstehung der Deutschordensballeien im Deutschen Reich* (1981), *Ritterbrüder im livländischen*

Zweig des Deutschen Ordens (1993) (with Lutz Fenske), and *Von Akkon zur Marienburg* (1999).

Piers D. Mitchell is a palaeopathologist, a medical historian, and is also qualified in medicine. He is a lecturer in the Faculty of Medicine at Imperial College London, where he runs a course on health and disease in the past. He uses archaeological and textual evidence from the medieval period to investigate disease and its treatment at the time of the crusades.

Johannes Adriaan Mol is Research Fellow at the Fryske Akademy in Leeuwarden. He has published several books and articles on Frisian medieval history and on the history of the military orders in the Netherlands.

Kristian Molin is a part-time Lecturer in Medieval History at the universities of Keele and Nottingham. He has published a monograph on crusader castles in the eastern Mediterranean and various related papers and articles. He is currently working on an English translation of the Old French version of the Chronicle of Morea.

Helen J. Nicholson is Lecturer in Medieval History at the University of Wales, Cardiff. Her extensive publications on the military orders and other related subjects include *Templars, Hospitallers and Teutonic Knights. Images of the Military Orders 1128-1291* (1993) and *Chronicle of the Third Crusade: a Translation of the Itinerarium Peregrinorum et Gesta Regis Ricardi* (1997).

Jonathan Riley-Smith has been until very recently Dixie Professor of Ecclesiastical History at the University of Cambridge. He is President of the Society for the Study of the Crusades and the Latin East. He is the author of many books and articles on the military orders, the Western settlements in Palestine, and the crusades, including *The Knights of St John in Jerusalem and Cyprus c. 1050-1310* (1967).

Maria Starnawska lectures on medieval history at the University of Podlasie in Siedlec, Poland. She is the author of several works on the history of the military orders. She is currently working on the cult of the relics of the saints in medieval Poland.

Edna J. Stern is a medieval archaeologist and ceramic specialist in the Israel Antiquities Authority (IAA). She is currently studying the crusader pottery from the IAA excavations in Acre ('Akko), and from other sites in northern Israel. She recently completed her PhD dissertation titled 'Trade and Redistribution of Pottery Types in the Mediterranean during the twelfth and thirteenth centuries as Reflected in the Excavations of Crusader Acre'. Her MA dissertation dealt with the sugar industry in Palestine during the Crusader, Ayyubid, and Mamluk periods in the light of archaeological remains.

Eliezer Stern has studied Archaeology and World History at the Hebrew University, Jerusalem. He is currently the District Archaeologist of the Western Galilee for the Israel Antiquities Authority and has been in charge of Acre for the last two decades, excavating and studying mainly the remains from the crusader period.

Yuri Stoyanov graduated B.A. and M.A. from the University of Sofia and M.Phil. and Ph.D. in Combined Historical Studies from the Warburg Institute of the University of London. He is currently Director of the Kenyon Institute in Jerusalem (incorporating the British School of Archaeology in Jerusalem), part of the British Academy's Council for British Research in the Levant. His publications include *The Hidden Tradition in Europe* (1994) and *The Other God. Dualist Religions from Antiquity to the Cathar Heresy* (2000). He has also been assistant editor and translator of *Christian Dualist Heresies in the Byzantine World c.650-c.1450*, ed. Bernard Hamilton and Janet Hamilton (1998).

Theresa M.Vann is the Joseph S. Micallef Curator of the Malta Study Center, Hill Monastic Manuscript Library, Saint John's University in Collegeville, Minnesota. She is currently working on a new edition of Guillaume Caoursin's *Obsidionis Rhodiae urbis descriptio*.

Ann Williams is Senior Lecturer in Mediterranean History at the University of Exeter. She is a specialist in the hospital and charitable work of the Order of St John in the early modern period, and is about to publish *Servants of the Sick: The Convent of the Order of St John 1309-1631*.

Editor's Preface

What follows is a collection of thirty papers read at the third international conference on the military orders organized by the London Centre for the Study of the Crusades, the Military Orders, and the East Mediterranean Region in the Middle Ages. The conference, focusing on the general theme of 'History and Heritage', was held on 7-10 September 2000 at the Museum of the Order of St John, St John's Gate, Clerkenwell, London. It is regretted that the present volume of proceedings has had to take so long to appear in print – seven full years after the event. However, to seek a rational explanation for this prolonged delay would be an exercise both futile and unnecessary: the reasons lay beyond my control as editor and that of the editorial committee, and were indeed entirely out of our reach. What should be pointed out here, of course, is that as a result of this unhappy interlude all the papers have had to be brought up to date by including references to more recent publications, while certain conclusions have had to be reconsidered in the light of further research and a continuous exchange of ideas. In all modesty, it can safely be claimed, first, that, like the other prestigious volumes in the series, this one provides the most recent scholarship on the history of the military orders, and, secondly, that the contributors to it, like those of previous volumes, are among the most highly distinguished scholars in the field.

There can be no doubt that in fairly recent years the study of the military orders has developed into an enormous topic and remains a vital area of historical research; their relevance has withstood the most convulsive impact of the passage of time, with the Hospitallers, in particular, being rightly considered as a powerful force of continuity in European history. Within the wider framework of the general theme of the conference, the chapters collected in this volume reflect different interests and include wide-ranging studies, in-depth research papers, and surveys, with each providing a clear picture of the current state of research in the particular theme or aspect it deals with. There are contributions on such fascinating topics as the state of historiography on the military orders in Poland and Spain; liturgy, fiction, and funerary rites of Hospitaller grand masters; heraldry, mysticism; and piety; the trial of the Templars; indulgences; Hospitaller commanderies and Teutonic castles; and indeed aspects of the history of other military orders. It has been perhaps one of the great merits of the conference to have provided an international team of eminent historians with an opportunity to reflect on the state of their discipline and profession in their own country, on historical methodology, on the nature of heritage, and on what is currently being done and what can or ought to be done in the future.

The literally massive amount of inedited resources on the military orders that lie scattered all over Europe and beyond, in manuscript form or in stone, awaiting scrutiny or excavation, prompts me to make one final observation. There is a growing need to have an international conference, similar to these four-yearly ones, organized in the immediate future round the theme 'The Military Orders: Archival and Archaeological Evidence'.

It is both a pleasure and a privilege, indeed a great honour, to thank all those friends and colleagues without whose generous help, expert advice, and constant encouragement, the publication of this volume would have had to wait for another year or so. These will have to remain anonymous because I fear that in trying to identify them individually I would run the risk of leaving one or two names out. To all of them, I must confess, I owe debts of gratitude. I would also like to thank all the contributors to this book for their patience. Special thanks should go to Dr John Smedley, of Ashgate, for his tolerance, understanding, and collaboration. To Professor Jonathan Riley-Smith in particular I owe much, much more than my poor and feeble words can express.

Introduction

Jonathan Riley-Smith

The regular conferences on the military orders held at Clerkenwell in London – together with others which meet in Italy, France, and Poland – are expressions of a remarkable growth in interest in the subject throughout the world. Fifty years ago R.C. Smail wrote that 'research on the military orders of knighthood has been almost at a standstill since the far-off days of Prutz and Delaville Le Roulx', but the first signs of a revival of the subject were already apparent at about the time he wrote. Lionel Butler was beginning work on the Knights Hospitallers on Rhodes and he was soon to be followed by Anthony Luttrell. Alan Forey and Derek Lomax were students in Spain, studying the Orders of the Temple and Santiago respectively. And in 1960 Smail himself suggested the topic of the Hospitallers in the Levant as a subject for my doctoral research. Why post-war England should have been the scene of the first stirrings of an interest in the history of the military orders remains a mystery, but from relatively small beginnings the subject has grown into a major one, involving not only historians of the crusades, but also those engaged in the study of Europe's economic and cultural past. The articles in this volume, a selection of the papers read at the third London conference, testify to its health and to the quality of the work being done.

It is not easy to explain why the orders had been neglected for so long. Perhaps they suffered from a general malaise afflicting crusade studies between the two World Wars, which must have been a consequence of the association of crusading with the imperial ideal, now in decline and attracting hostility and derision. Ranging from tiny national bodies to great international organizations, the military orders should always have been of exceptional interest to historians of the church, warfare, and military and naval institutions, theories of violence, hospitals and medicine, art and architecture, the management of estates and agriculture, trade and banking, and Europe overseas. They foreshadowed the State orders of chivalry – indeed some of them were secularized and were transformed into such orders – but they were originally, and two of them remain, interesting and unusual orders of the church. The Hospital of St John of Jerusalem and the Teutonic Order, which survive today, evolved unique polities in their order-states of Prussia, Rhodes, and Malta. Elements of them grew non-Catholic offshoots, which were, like the Spanish and Portuguese orders in the early modern period, Christian orders of chivalry, to be distinguished from military orders proper, in that they were legitimized by secular authorities and their members were not professed religious, and from State orders by the fact that their membership continued to entail public, as opposed to private, obligations with respect to the defence and fostering of the Christian Faith. Today the heirs of the military orders remain very significant charitable institutions. It is not generally known that the Sovereign Military Order of Malta and the four non-Catholic Orders of St John, engaged in 150 countries, can collectively put into the field up to 450,000 volunteers.

Of the thirty papers published in this collection, two deal with the orders in general, while eighteen concentrate on the Hospital of St John, four on the Temple, and three on the Teutonic Order, together with another on the Order of the Sword Brothers which it absorbed. The preponderance of works on the Hospitallers is not, I think, typical of world-wide research. On the other hand, the fact that most of the papers relate to provincial life, rather than to the headquarters in the east, Prussia, or Malta, accurately reflects modern concerns, as do the contributions on historiography, the papacy, cultural history, and religious life. Examples of new research interests are the paper on bioarchaeology and the two on liturgy.

The conference takes place in and around the gatehouse of the medieval Hospitaller Priory of England, built in 1504 by Prior Thomas Docwra after his return from Rhodes, where he had been captain of Bodrum and Turcopolier. Participants have often told me how inspired they are by the historical associations of the place and, as always, we owe more than we can say to The Most Venerable Order of St John, its curator Pamela Willis and her staff, and Rosemary Bailey and Helen Gribble and their team of helpers. The fact that so much of the assistance is provided free of charge or on a voluntary basis means that the conference is much more affordable to young scholars than would otherwise be the case. And we owe an especial debt of gratitude to Victor Mallia-Milanes, who took over the responsibility for editing the collection and seeing it through the press when it looked as though it was foundering.

PART I
Historiography

Chapter 1

Hospitaller Historiography: Heritages and Heresies

Anthony T. Luttrell

The so-called heritage movement encourages and often exploits a wide public interest in the past, in its monuments, and in other survivals. Some heritage enterprises are merely businesses which are inspired by tourist statistics while operating heritage centres through audio-visual aids, guide tapes, and so forth; even for respectable bodies, concern for conservation sometimes amounts to little more than a face-saving exercise in damage limitation. The disadvantages involved have been debated extensively.[1] Much tourism-conditioned activity is evidently irreversible, but the dangers and deficiencies could perhaps be reduced. Ludicrous mythologies have perverted the history of the Templars, and the heritage of other military-religious orders has been distorted in many, sometimes gruesome, ways.[2] However, the various branches of the Hospital of Saint John enjoy a special position in that they are still active, useful charitable institutions as well as possessing a military-religious past which forms an essential component of their present heritage.

Unscientific history has no validity, and the importance of the religious and medical concerns of the Hospital's modern branches cannot justify any falsification of their own past. Yet existing welfare states face increasing difficulties in caring directly for the sick, for the elderly, and for others, so that in consequence society evidently needs to mobilize alternative machinery to provide effective non-state welfare care; good examples are the St John's Ambulance Brigade in Britain and the Malteser Hilfdienst and the Johanniter in Germany. Such bodies are well aware that they can attract funds and volunteers through the glamour of their past and on the strength of their traditions: 'The peculiar achievement of the Knights of Malta is the conjuring trick by which they turn titles and ceremonies into hospitals, ambulances, medical supplies, transport of goods for the needy, and services of all kinds – a conjuring trick the more singular because its ingredients are fantasy and its product

---

[1] The bibliography, including numerous scientific studies concerning conservation techniques, has become extremely extensive: P. Ucko, 'Enlivening a "Dead" Past,' *Conservation and Management of Archaeological Sites*, iv, 2 (2000), provides a wide selection of references.

[2] The worst examples of interference in the history of a military order are undoubtedly the wholesale distortions promoted by Heinrich Himmler and others who exploited the history of the Teutonic Order to propagate a series of Nazi myths: 'Zwischenkreigzeit, Nationalsozialismus und Zweiter Weltkreig,' in *800 Jahr Deutscher Orden*, ed. U. Arnold *et al.* (Munich, 1990).

substance.'[3] The risk is that well-intentioned attempts to foster public relations may somehow distort Hospitaller historiography.

Arguably the strictest regard for accuracy must in the long term be the most effective media weapon. The Hospital's material heritage cannot be claimed exclusively by any single body. What now survives is dispersed in differing ways between the Order of Malta, other Orders of Saint John, national States with their commissions for the classification and protection of monuments, various official bodies administering Hospitaller sites, and private persons owning, for example, a former commandery that has been converted into a hotel. Action may originate outside the orders, as in the case of the Council of Europe, which in 1970 produced a major exhibition on the Hospital with an excellent catalogue and an important bibliography,[4] or from the orders themselves, as for example when the Protestant Johanniter-Orden and the Catholic Malteser-Orden collaborated in an extensive collective volume on the Hospital in Germany.[5] No single institution can be wholly responsible for promoting the Hospital's history or for opposing self-styled 'unrecognized' orders, though the five legitimate orders have a False Orders Committee which meets regularly.[6] Many monuments once belonging to the Hospital actually lie outside the Christian world. Thus there was a threat in 2000 that the Hospitallers' former German church in Jerusalem would be handed over to an ultra-Orthodox Jewish group.[7] The astonishing excavations of the great Hospitaller palace at Acre in Israel are financed, and its restoration to some extent constrained, by a tourist development company, and in such a case the archaeologists' natural desire publicly to display the results of their investigations may be frustrated by economic and political considerations.[8] There are rumours about the future utilization of the Hospital's fortified commandery at Kolossi on Cyprus, while its great castle at Bodrum in Turkey, which has been adapted for various museums and is overrun by tourists, faces a degree of degradation.

On Rhodes, where the tourist influx and the profits from it are immense, the problem is extreme. After 1912 the Italians extensively restored the medieval town and fortifications; they invented an Italian *auberge* and rebuilt the Master's palace

[3]   H. Sire, *The Knights of Malta* (New Haven, 1994), 275–76; though sometimes uncertain on points of detail, this is — despite its title — one of the best major works on the complete span of the Hospital's history.

[4]   *The Order of St. John in Malta*, ed. Government of Malta and Council of Europe (Malta, 1970); this work provides the last attempt at a systematic Hospitaller bibliography, a task which has since become virtually impossible.

[5]   *Der Johanniter-Orden/Der Malteser-Orden*, ed. A. Wienand (3rd ed: Cologne, 1988).

[6]   P. Kurrild-Klitgaard, *Knights of Fantasy: an Overview, History and Critique of the Self-styled "Orders" called "of Saint John" or "of Malta", in Denmark and other Nordic Countries* (Turku, 2002), documents an astonishing scenario.

[7]   'Kreuzfahrerruine soll Jeschiwa werden: Proteste in Jerusalem gegen die Pläne, "St. Maria Alemannorum" zu einer Talmudschule umzubauen,' *Frankfurter Allgemeine Zeitung* (28 January 2000), 10.

[8]   E. Stern, 'Excavations in Crusader Acre (1990-1999)', in *Il Cammino I Gerusalemme*, ed. M.S. Calò Mariani (Bari, 2002).

in horrendous Fascist taste. Their motives were largely colonial, that is political.[9] After 1947 the newly-installed Greek authorities sought at first to emphasize the Byzantine aspects of the Rhodian heritage, but the pressures of Western tourism led the Greek archaeological service to make extraordinary efforts to preserve the Hospitallers' Latin town, so that much has been excavated or restored and a fine new museum is now open there.[10] On Malta there is much to be saved. The problem of whether parts of the heritage, such as the former conventual church or Caravaggio's masterpiece, belong morally to the Order or to the Maltese people can still arouse debate, especially as some Maltese regard the Hospital's presence as that of a former occupying power.

Governments have profited from mass tourism while investing minimally in the heritage. Recently, however, the Order of Malta has itself leased its old conventual headquarters in Fort Saint Angelo and partially restored it, though not without provoking discussion, while there is now an official Valletta Rehabilitation Project. Furthermore, the heritage and archaeological establishment on Malta has recently been restructured, improving prospects for future conservation.[11]

Similar dilemmas arise in Western Europe, where commanderies and churches are sometimes destroyed or clumsily restored, but where many associations and historical societies devoted to the Hospitallers' contemporary activities seek to defend and conserve their monuments, sometimes putting them to modern use and attracting tourists or creating museums. The priory buildings, museum, and library at Clerkenwell and the great medieval barns at Temple Cressing are obvious English examples of excellent heritage management. There is a renewed museum at the Swiss commandery of Bubikon;[12] an English archaeologist has purchased, restored, excavated, and published the Aragonese commandery at Ambel;[13] the

---

[9]   L. Ciacci, *Rodi 1912–1923: Come si inventa una città* (Venice, 1991); cf. M. Petricoli, *Archeologia e "Mare Nostrum": le Missioni archeologiche nella Politica mediterranea dell'Italia 1898–1943* (Rome, 1990); *La Presenza italiana nel Dodecaneso tra il 1912 e il 1948: la Ricerca archeologica, la Conservazione, le Scelte progettuali*, ed. M. Livadotti - G. Rocco (Catania, 1996).

[10]   Recent surveys and bibliographies in E. Kollias, *The Medieval City of Rhodes and the Palace of the Grand Master* (2nd English edn.: Athens, 1998); K. Manoussou-Della, *Medieval Town of Rhodes: Restoration Works (1985–2000)* (Rhodes, 2001); A. Luttrell, *Rhodes Town: 1306–1356* (Rhodes, 2003). Possibilities for collaborative research between the UNESCO Heritage sites of Valletta and Rhodes were discussed at a colloquium held on Rhodes in 2003: *From Rhodes to Malta: the End of an Era, the Birth of a New One*.

[11]   A. Caruana, 'Heritage Malta', *Vigilo*, xxiv (October 2003), 20–21; this journal, the organ of Din l-Art Helwa/National Trust of Malta, documents ongoing Maltese developments in detail.

[12]   *Johanniterkommende Bubikon "Kreuz und Quer": Museumsführer*, ed. M. Brühlmeier - M. Tomaschett (Bubikon, 2000).

[13]   C. Gerrard, 'Opposing Identity: Muslims, Christians, and the Military Orders in Rural Aragon,' *Medieval Archaeology*, xliii (1999); id., *Paisaje y señorío: la Casa conventual de Ambel (Zaragoza): Arqueología, Arquitectura e Historia de las Ordenes Militares del Temple y del Hospital* (Saragossa, 2003).

frescoes in the church of San Bevignate in Perugia[14] and the commandery buildings at Poggibonsi[15] have been protected and published; the ancient house and church at Asti have been excavated and studied;[16] a volunteer group has restored the French commandery at Coulommiers;[17] and there are many other examples of such salvage operations. Scientific investigation and publication can in fact be an effective way of safeguarding a monument.

The rural landscape itself may sometimes be considered as part of the heritage. An entire region can be approached through its Hospitaller buildings and art,[18] and it may be possible to reconstitute the past of an abandoned commandery and its estates by supplementing written texts with topographical surveys, place-name information, aerial photographs, early-modern estate books, and so forth.[19] The outstanding study of the Hospital's impact on the development of the countryside is undoubtedly the one made in Normandy,[20] and elsewhere there are good arguments for the complete investigation of the settlement, economy, and exploitation of an area once controlled by a military order using sophisticated archaeological techniques; this possibility is especially attractive in Spain, where castles, irrigation systems, mills, and sheep tracks were important elements in the military orders' activities.[21] An ambitious approach to regional heritage is provided by the Centre Larzac Templier et Hospitalier, which works to protect three impressive fortified villages in Southern France which are under threat from a new motorway. It seeks to do so by developing and preserving them as a coordinated enterprise that is oriented towards an advantageous absorption of the mass tourist and is designed to improve the region's economy; the aim is to mobilize support through educational events designed for the general public and by

---

[14] *Templari e Ospitalieri in Italia: la Chiesa di San Bevignate a Perugia*, ed. M. Roncetti *et al.* (Perugia, 1987).

[15] *La Chiesa di San Giovanni in Jerusalem alla Magione di Poggibonsi*, ed. L. de Filla *et al.* (Siena, 1986).

[16] *L'Antico San Pietro in Asti: Storia, Architettura, Archeologia*, ed. R. Bordone *et al.*(Turin, 2000).

[17] *La Commanderie des Templiers sur Coulommiers*, ed. J. Schelstraete *et al.* (Coulommiers, 1970).

[18] Excellent examples are A.-M. Legras, *Les Commanderies des Templiers et Hospitaliers de Saint-Jean de Jerusalem en Saintonge et en Aunis* (Paris, 1983); L. Jan - V. Jesensky, 'Hospitaller and Templar Commanderies in Bohemia and Moravia: their Structure and Architectural Forms,' in *MO*, ii; O. Pérez Monzón, *Arte Sanjuanista en Castilla y Léon: las Encomiendas de la Guareña y su entorno geo-histórico* (Madrid, 1999).

[19] A. Luttrell, 'Two Hospitaller-Templar Preceptories North of Tuscania,' *Papers of the British School at Rome*, xxxix (1971).

[20] M. Miguet, *Templiers et Hospitaliers en Normandie* (Paris, 1995).

[21] R. Izquierdo Benito, 'El Espacio de las Ordenes Militares: Plantemientos para un Análisis arqueológico,' in *Las Ordenes Militares en la Península Ibérica*, ed. R. Izquierdo Benito - F. Ruiz Gómez, i (Cuenca, 2000): these valuable proposals should not be discounted on account of the current Spanish tendency to regard the military orders as essentially 'feudal,' with confusing references to the 'archaeology of feudalism', the 'space-feudal power relationship' and so forth.

a programme of conservation and research.[22] An initial colloquium held in the late-medieval commandery at Sainte-Eulalie de Larzac in 2000 contains many studies[23] and a monograph series is under way.[24]

In addition to those seeking to raise support for charitable causes, other schemes plan to attract visitors or simply to profit financially from film-shows and walk-around presentations with videos, sounds, and smells. A plethora of such tourist attractions has developed on Malta. There is a 'Malta Experience' in the Hospitallers' great infirmary in Valletta and a 'Great Siege of Malta and Knights of St. John' experience which is actually located beneath the Order's archives; the latter is primarily devoted not to Malta but to the history of the Hospital from its origins until the present day. Much more scientific, and with genuine objects accurately labelled, is the new museum in the Master's palace at Rhodes. Some initiatives come from the orders themselves, as for example through certain television programmes shown in Germany or by means of the comic-strip history of the Hospital produced by the Oeuvres Hospitalières françaises de l'Ordre de Malte; the latter contains some rather bizarre and inaccurate items, but its overall presentation of developments is not unreasonable.[25] Various branches of the Hospital do not always resist the temptation to manipulate the past and to make propaganda through unjustifiable claims. Thus several branches chose, somewhat controversially, to celebrate the ninth centenary of the original 'foundation' of the Hospital in 1999, nine centuries after the Latin conquest of Jerusalem.

Hospitaller history can undoubtedly be publicized in ways that are both accurate and attractive, despite the possibility of over-simplifications or even of errors on the part of those who present it. It seems essential to combat fundamental heresies: Hospitallers were not Templars, they were religious but not monks, they were not technically crusaders nor, in many cases, were they nobles or knights; some were priests and others women. Popular misunderstandings of such matters can be extensive, and confusions concerning the Templars are a special obstacle to a correct presentation of Hospitaller history. The extremely productive excavations at Clerkenwell raise different, more complex problems, such as, for example, the question of whether the priory buildings constituted a secular palace or a type of monastery without a cloister.[26] The public needs to understand such historical distinctions in order to appreciate the significance of the archaeological finds when they are displayed in museum surroundings.

---

[22]   Cf. D. Lapeyre, 'Sainte-Eulalie's Commandery: a Templar and Hospitaller Establishment in Larzac', is not published in the present volume.

[23]   *La Commanderie: Institution des Ordres Militaires dans l'Occident Médiéval*, ed. A. Luttrell - L. Pressouyre (Paris, 2002).

[24]   R. Hyacinthe, *L'Ordre de Saint-Lazare de Jérusalem au Moyen Age* (Millau, 2003), a work which throws light on aspects of Hospitaller history; P. Bonneaud, *Le Prieuré de Catalogne, le Couvent de Rhodes et la Couronne d'Aragon: 1415–1447* (Millau, 2004).

[25]   G. d'Aubigny - B. Capo, *Les Hospitaliers de Malte: Neuf Siècles au Service des Autres* (Paris, 1999).

[26]   B. Sloane - G. Malcolm, *Excavations at the Priory of the Order of the Hospital of St John of Jerusalem, Clerkenwell, London* (London, 2004).

One striking form of propaganda has been a series of exhibitions of Hospitaller paintings, frescoes, armour, tombs, coins, and suchlike. The two most recent major examples are those that were mounted in Venice[27] and Turin[28]. As with other such displays, these were accompanied by a catalogue containing a selection of historical essays. The resulting publications naturally include much that is valuable; yet there is a danger that the visual approach may serve as an over-facile substitute for more serious historical understanding. The general essays may be the work of scholars who are not expert in the Order's history; the artistic comments may be the contribution of art historians who employ methodologies of their own, who sometimes work without access to a proper historical library, and who may create an imbalance by concentrating on the aesthetic rather than on the historical aspects of the works exhibited.[29] Behind such problems lie others; they include the virtual absence in some countries of university teachers capable of directing students in Hospitaller research and the lack of bibliographical tools in the face of a great proliferation of interest and publication on the Hospital. There have recently been a number of important publications, especially in Italy and Spain, yet the current trend in work produced in academic institutions is towards quantity rather than quality.[30]

At a different level are misunderstandings fostered in part, and across many centuries, by the Hospitallers themselves. The Order's first papal privilege of 1113 mentioned seven European hospices, most of which apparently did not exist at that time;[31] before 1187 a series of myths or *miracula* concerning the supposed Biblical origins of the Hospital had been elaborated and had even been translated into Anglo-Norman verse;[32] by 1493 the Hospital's original twelfth-century Rule, which did not mention either nobility or military activities, had had the military-sounding phrase *tuitio Fidei* added to it;[33] various Hospitaller saints were invented in the sixteenth and early-seventeenth centuries;[34] and so on. Much later, in the nineteenth century,

---

[27]   *Lungo il Tragitto Crociato della Vita*, ed. L. Corti (Venice, 2000).

[28]   *"Gentilhuomini Christiani e Religiosi Cavalieri": Nove Secoli dell'Ordine di Malta in Piemonte*, ed. T. Ricardi di Netro - L. Gentile (Milan, 2000).

[29]   Critical remarks and extensive bibliography in A. Luttrell, 'Iconography and Historiography : the Italian Hospitallers before 1530,' *Sacra Militia*, iii (2002).

[30]   Id., 'Gli Ospedalieri italiani: Storia e Storiografia,' *Studi Melitensi*, vi (1998); L. García-Guijarro Ramos, 'Historiography and History: The Study of the Military Orders in Spain since 1975', *infra*.

[31]   A. Luttrell, 'The Earliest Hospitallers,' in *Montjoie: Studies in Crusade History in Honour of Hans Eberhard Mayer*, ed. B. Kedar *et al.* (Aldershot, 1997).

[32]   *The Hospitallers' "Riwle": (Miracula et Regula Hospitalis Sancti Johannis Jerosolimitani)*, ed. K. Sinclair (London, 1984); A. Luttrell, 'Préface,' in *Les Légendes de l'Hôpital de Saint-Jean de Jérusalem*, ed. A. Calvet (Paris, 2000).

[33]   The phrase *tuitio Fidei* apparently appeared only in 1493: Guillaume Caorsin, *Volumen Stabilimentorum Rhodiorum Militum Sacri Ordinis Hospitalis Sancti Johannis Jerosolimitani* (Ulm, 1496), f. 23r; Sire, 212, wrongly ascribes 'the addition of *tuitio Fidei*' to the Master Raymund *de Podio* who died in 1158/60.

[34]   Invaluable survey in L. Corti, 'Santi ed Eroe: l'Immaginario dei Cavalieri Gerosolimitani,' in *Lungo il Tragitto*; add especially R. Rex, 'Blessed Adrian Fortescue: a Martyr without a Cause,' *Analecta Bollandiana*, cxv (1997), 341–49.

the military orders were romanticized and reinterpreted by Sir Walter Scott and others, including some groups which sought to revive the Order as a military force designed to intervene in the Levant.[35] Other confusions have different roots. For example, the visitor to Vittoriosa on Malta finds in the main square a large board purportedly showing the exact whereabouts of the post-1530 *auberges* of the eight *langues* though, with only one exception, they cannot be located or assigned with any probability to a particular *langue*; the English brethren clearly did not build an *auberge* and there is no evidence to suggest that they could have lived in the place officially indicated to the public as the *Auberge* of England.[36]

The solution to such misconceptions is for good history to chase out bad heritage and heresy. Yet there are many gaps in Hospitaller historiography. For example, until the recent major works of Nicolas Vatin, Zacharias Tsirpanlis, and Jürgen Sarnowsky,[37] the only comprehensive archive-based coverage of the fifteenth-century Hospital, that of Giacomo Bosio, had been published as long ago as 1630, while the statutes for the period from 1310 to 1493 still await a proper published edition.[38] Much of the Malta period is yet to be explored, and for the nineteenth and twentieth centuries there is little reliable work in print; the dramatic events of the 1950s, which seriously threatened the Order of Malta, are generally known almost exclusively through a novel.[39] The various authorities may, understandably, be reluctant to open their archives, but for that they could pay a price.

The worst historiographical-heritage problem facing the various legitimate branches of the Hospital is the extremely serious one of the false or 'unrecognized' orders. In the long run, the most likely antidote is an ever-widening dispersal of the truth. People who know the difference between Templars and Hospitallers or between monastic, mendicant, and military orders, who understand correctly the distinction between a crusade and the holy war of a military order, are less likely to be misled by unreliable claims. All Hospitaller publications and presentations, however popular in intention, should reflect historical truth, and their promoters need to ensure that this is the case by consulting reputable authorities and by seeking

---

[35]   E. Clay, 'Rhodes: Sir William to Sir Walter — Notes to Save Sir Walter Scott the Trouble of Looking Out Information about Rhodes: W. Gell, 1832,' *Journal of the Warburg and Courtauld Institutes*, xxxiii (1970): E. Siberry, 'Victorian Perceptions of the Military Orders,' in *MO*, i, 370–72; id., *The New Crusaders: Images of the Crusades in the 19th and Early 20th Centuries* (Aldershot, 2000), 73–82, 115, 121.

[36]   A. Luttrell, 'Hospitaller Birgu: 1530–1536,' *Crusades*, ii (2003).

[37]   N. Vatin, *L'Ordre de Saint-Jean-de-Jérusalem, l'Empire ottoman et la Méditerranée orientale entre les deux Sièges de Rhodes: 1480–1522* (Louvain, 1994); Z. Tsirpanlis, *Anekdota eggrapha gia te Rodo kai tis Noties Sporades apo to Archeio Ioanniton Ippoton: 1421–1453* (Rhodes, 1995); J. Sarnowsky, *Macht und Herrschaft im Johanniterorden des 15. Jahrhunderts: Verfassung und Verwaltung der Johanniter auf Rhodos (1421–1522)* (Münster, 2001).

[38]   Problems discussed in A. Luttrell, 'The Hospitallers' Early Statutes,' *Revue Mabillon* lxxv (2003), with cautionary remarks on R. Cierbide Martinena, *Estatutois antiguos de la Orden de San Juan de Jerusalén: Versión original occitana y su Traducción al Español según el Códice navarro del AHN de Madrid (1314)* (Pamplona, 1999).

[39]   Sire, 258-67.

more seriously to reflect sound scholarship. The Larzac centre has set an admirable example not just by instituting an international scientific advisory committee, but also by listening to its advice.

There are institutions devoted to the Order's history. In Italy these are the Hospitaller publication centres in Rome, at Perugia, in Liguria, and above all at Taranto, where a Centro Studi Melitensi has established the journal *Studi Melitensi*; all have produced a good number of monographs. An Accademia Internazionale Melitense set up in Fort Saint Angelo on Malta has also sponsored several meetings.[40] In Madrid, Paris, London, and elsewhere are a number of centres and societies, while a new journal *Sacra Militia* is dedicated to all the military orders.[41] With one exception, however, no coordinated historiographical programme exists and it is difficult to see how one could.[42] The military orders certainly care for their history and they do provide some funds for it, but their members, mostly not trained scholars with a proper understanding of their own order's past, are sometimes anxious to express opinions which are not always based on a thorough study of the bibliography or on archive research. Publications tend to cling to certain themes while ignoring other, often important, subjects. The Clerkenwell collection apart, satisfactorily specialized libraries are lacking. The microfilm copy of the Hospital's central archives from Malta deposited in the Hill Monastic Manuscript Library of St John's University at Collegeville, Minnesota provides a valuable safety precaution,[43] but the central archive itself is isolated on Malta, where it remains incompletely catalogued and where researchers face various obstacles. Many scholars are content to study Hospitaller history without working on its central records. Those documents, a vital part of the Hospital's heritage, themselves require conservation; a useful pilot project recently demonstrated the problems and the possible solutions.[44]

Some of these drawbacks might well be overcome through the Internet, which may offer the chance of cultural 'portals' or 'doorways' which could help to avoid frictions between the different branches of the Hospital, but while such possibilities exist for published works, bibliographies, and prosopographies, and in particular for listing and describing museum holdings, the Internet can scarcely provide a satisfactory substitute for basic archival research. A considerable public is eager for information about the Hospitallers, and some kind of general agreement to promote Hospitaller history in a coherent collaborative way or to create a coordinating international or inter-order body is clearly desirable, even if the obstacles appear formidable. If composed of genuine experts functioning in independence, such a body could perhaps do something to eliminate the duplication of effort and to

---

[40]   *Peregrinationes: Acta et Documenta*, i – (Perugia, 2000–).

[41]   *Sacra Militia*, i – (2000–).

[42]   N. Beriou, 'Le Programme de Recherches Milord: Université Lyon 2, CNRS, EHESS', *Revue Mabillon*, lxxv (2003), 261-63.

[43]   T. Vann, 'Hospitaller Record Keeping and Archival Practice,' in *MO*, ii, discusses possibilities and limitations in the use of the microfilms; some films are virtually illegible.

[44]   H. Szczepanowska, 'The Conservation of 14th-Century Parchment Documents with Pendant Seals,' *The Paper Conservator*, xvi (1992), and H. Szczepanowska - E. West FitzHugh, 'Fourteenth-Century Documents of the Knights of St. John of Jerusalem: Analysis of Inks, Parchment and Seals,' ibid., xxiii (1999); the historical data given is somewhat unreliable.

further important studies. Future projects might include annotations and corrections to Delaville le Roulx' *Cartulaire*, which remains invaluable but contains many inaccuracies; reliable prosopographical data and lists of officers; guides to select literatures rather than full bibliographical lists; and the publication of select texts. Some part of work which is in progress can be followed in the annual bulletin of the Society for the Study of the Crusades and the Latin East, but many of those who write about the Hospitallers are unfortunately ignorant of existing studies on their particular subject, and a more systematic guide would be useful for both medieval and modern topics. Meanwhile societies, editors, librarians, curators, and individual scholars must continue to do their best to salvage monuments and to promote an accurate understanding of the Hospital's history and heritage.

Chapter 2

A Survey of Research on the History of the Military Orders in Poland in the Middle Ages

Maria Starnawska

The negligible number of Polish crusaders to the Holy Land and the problems with access to historical sources concerning Palestine have often discouraged Polish historians from a systematic approach to the phenomenon of the crusades. Among outstanding studies by Polish historians, there are the works by Aleksander Gieysztor on the false encyclical appeal to free the Holy Sepulchre, attributed to Sergius IV, and the works by Jerzy Hauziński on the assassins' sect and Orient politics of Frederick II Hohenstauf.[1] The Polish contribution to the crusades has been discussed by several scholars at various levels of historical expertise.[2] Mikołaj Gładysz has fairly recently published his doctoral thesis on the reception of the idea of the crusade among the upper social milieu in Poland.[3] As Gładysz shows, the propaganda campaign launched prior to the Second Crusade resulted in a few dukes and magnates actually going on a pilgrimage to the Holy Land. Indirect forms of participation in the crusading movement were much more visible. These included: proclaiming the wars against the heathen Pomeranians and, since the twelfth century, against the Pruthenians, as crusades; and the transplantation of the military and hospitaller orders into Poland.[4] Polish researchers of the crusading movement have usually focused on these two points.

The progress of this research and its scope in Polish historiography vary from one order to another, depending on their prospective significance in the history of Poland. From the mid-twelfth century the Hospitallers, Templars, Teutonic Knights, Knights of Calatrava, and a local order of Knights of Christ (better known as Knights of Dobrzyń), were setting up their centres on Polish soil. The Knights of Calatrava

---

[1]   A. Gieysztor, *Ze studiów nad genezą wypraw krzyżowych. Encyklika Sergiusza IV (1009-1012)* (Warszawa, 1948); J. Hauziński, *Muzułmańska sekta asasynów w europejskim piśmiennictwie wieków średnich* (Poznań, 1978); id., *Polityka orientalna Fryderyka II Hohenstaufa* (Poznań, 1978); Z. Pentek, *Geoffroy de Villehardouin. Rycerz i kronikarz IV wyprawy krzyżowej* (Poznań, 1996).

[2]   See Bibliography.

[3]   M. Gładysz, *Zapomniani krzyżowcy. Polska wobec ruchu krucjatowego w XII-XIII wieku* (Warszawa, 2002).

[4]   R. Grodecki, 'Polska wobec idei wypraw krzyżowych', *Przegląd Współczesny*, vii (1923), 107-109.

and of Dobrzyń were only incidentally active on the Prussian borderland in the third and fourth decades of the thirteenth century; the Templars and Hospitallers founded a network of centres, mainly in Silesia and Pomerania. Following the dissolution of the Temple, the Hospitallers acquired most of the Templar commanderies. Their houses belonged to the Czech priory and the Brandenburg bailiwick.[5] Teutonic Knights, however, who were settled in 1226-28 by Konrad, duke of Mazovia, on the lands bordering with Prussia, made those lands and the annexed Prussia into a sovereign state. From the mid-thirteenth century, and particularly from 1308, that state was in constant political conflict with the Polish dukes and Polish kingdom (revived in 1320). The main items of discord included East Pomerania, seized by the Teutonic Order in 1308 and retrieved by Poland in 1466, and the Order's expansion into Lithuania, which was pagan until 1386, when it was christened by, and united with, Poland. The question of the Teutonic Order became one of the key issues of Polish foreign policy in the late Middle Ages.

The Teutonic Order differed from other communities not only in its significance and political impact, but also in its structure. While the houses of the Templars and Hospitallers were monastic convents and belonged, as the convents of other orders did, to the regular Catholic Church structure, the Teutonic commanderies were also administrative centres of the State apparatus.[6] Teutonic Prussia was initially a province governed by a local master, subordinate to the Grand Master residing in Acre, and after 1291 in Venice. In 1309 the Grand Master moved his seat to Malbork in Prussia, and those lands formed the core of the Teutonic State. The Grand Master and other executive bodies of the Order not only controlled the life of the community; above all they pursued political goals and administered the State. The latter was divided into districts governed by the commanders of individual commanderies. These districts were also called commanderies.

Consequently, the Teutonic Order greatly attracted the interest of Polish historians from the end of the nineteenth century, and its history has always been the subject of scholarly research; other military orders appear to have been less popular. At present the University of Toruń is the main Polish centre of research on the history of the Teutonic Order. Researchers tend to focus on the political and military aspects of its activity. In this sense, the Order is studied as being more like any other State organism rather than as a religious community. Systematic studies,

---

    5   M. Starnawska, *Między Jerozolimą a Łukowem. Zakony krzyżowe na ziemiach polskich w średniowieczu* (Warsaw, 1999), 25-72, 107-117; id., 'Crusade Orders on Polish Lands during the Middle Ages. Adaptation in a Peripheral Environment', *Quaestiones Medii Aevi Novae*, ii (1997), 137-42; id., 'Der Johanniterorden und Schlesien im Mittelalter', Würzburger medizinhistorische Mitteilungen, xxii (2003), 405-18; K. Dola, 'Zakon joannitów na Śląsku do poł. XIV w.', *Studia Teologiczno-Historyczne Śląska Opolskiego*, iii (1973), 46-51, 79-86; W. Polkowska-Markowska, 'Dzieje Zakonu Dobrzyńskiego', *Roczniki Historyczne* ii (1926), 150-62, 205 ; R. Frydrychowicz, 'Die Ritterorden von Calatrava im Tymau bei Mewe', *Altpreussische Monatschrift*, xvii (1890), 315-20; M. Goliński, 'Uposażenie i organizacja zakonu templariuszy w Polsce do 1241 roku', *Kwartalnik Historyczny*, xcviii, 3 (1991), 3-15.
    6   M. Biskup, *G. Labuda, Dzieje Zakonu Krzyżackiego w Prusach* (Gdańsk 1986), 162-74.

initiated in the interwar period, have resulted in a meticulous analysis of the major political and military aspects of Polish-Teutonic relations.[7] Nor have the economy and administration of the Teutonic Order been ignored in any way.[8] Research on a military order cannot exclude the history of the armament of brethren-knights. Andrzej Nadolski and Andrzej Nowakowski, who pursue this line of research, have inquired, among other things, into how the local environment determined the choice of Teutonic weapons.[9]

Since the 1960s Polish historians have been underscoring the need for the study of the Teutonic Order from a religious perspective, including its organization, and the social, cultural, and religious roles it played.[10] This widening scope of Hospitaller research has been encouraged by joint meetings and symposia of Polish and German scholars, which began in the 1970s and were intended to harmonize the history curriculum in the schools of both countries. Since 1981, conferences on the *Ordines Militares* have been regularly organized by the University of Toruń every other year, attracting participants not only from Germany and Poland, but also from Britain, Denmark, and the former Soviet Union. The main theme of such conferences has

---

[7]   Id., 'Zakon Krzyżacki i jego państwo w Prusach w polskiej historiografii lat trzydziestych XX wieku', *Komunikaty Mazursko-Warmińskie* ii-iii (1994), 155-69; id., 'Stan i potrzeby badań nad państwem krzyżackim w Prusach (w. XIII – początek XVI)', *Zapiski Historyczne*, xli (1976), 30-33; id., 'Polish Research Work on the History of the Teutonic Order State Organization in Prussia (1945-1959)', *Acta Poloniae Historica*, iii (1960), 89-113; id., 'Pomorze Zachodnie i Wschodnie jako problem w stosunkach niemiecko-polskich w XIV i XV w.', in *Śląsk i Pomorze e historii stosunków polsko-niemieckich w średniowieczu*, ed. M. Biskup (Wrocław, 1983), 132-41; id., 'Rola Zakonu Krzyżackiego w wiekach XIII-XV', in *Stosunki polsko-niemieckie w historiografii, i: Studia z dziejów historiografii polskiej i niemieckiej*, ed. J. Krasuski, G. Labuda, A.W. Walczak (Poznań, 1974), 335-61.

[8]   For example, M. Dygo, *Die Münzpolitik des Deutschen Ordens in Preußen in der ersten Hälfte des 15. Jahrhunderts* (Warsaw, 1987); Z.H. Nowak, 'Die Vorburg als Wirschaftszenturm des Deutschen Ordens in Preußen', *Quellen und Studien zur Geschichte des Deutschen Ordens*, xxxviii (1989), 148-62; id., 'Zamki krzyżackie jako ośrodku gospodarki w Prusach około 1400 r.', in *Średniowieczne zamki Polski Północnej. Wybór materiałów z sesji* (Malbork, 1983), 58-71; H. Samsonowicz, 'Europejski handel Krzyżaków w XIV-XV wieku', *Komunikaty Mazursko-Warmińskie* (Olsztyn, 1994), 137-45.

[9]   For example, A. Nowakowski, *Uzbrojenie wojsk krzyżackich w Prusach w XIV w. i na początku XV w* (Warsaw, 1980); id., 'Some Remarks about Weapons stored in the Arsenals of the Teutonic Order's Castles in Prussia by the end of the fourteenth and early fifteenth centuries', in *Das Kriegswesen der Ritterorden im Mittelalter*, ed. Z. H. Nowak (Toruń, 1991), 75-88; A. Nadolski, 'Remarques sur l'art. Militaire de l'Ordre Teutonique aux temps de la bataille de Grunwald (Tannenberg)', in *Das Kriegswesen* , 19-27.

[10]   M. Pollakówna,' O nowe spojrzenie na dzieje Zakonu Niemieckiego' in *Wieki średnie. Medium aevum. Prace ofiarowane Tadeuszowi Manteufflowi w 60 rocznicę urodzin*, ed. A. Gieysztor, M. H. Serejski, S. Trawkowski (Warsaw, 1962), 167-68; K. Górski, 'Nowe spojrzenie na Krzyżaków', *Zapiski Historyczne*, xxviii (1963), 39-46; id., 'L'Ordre Teutonique. Un nouveau point de vue', *Revue historique*, 468 (1963), 285; M. Biskup, 'W sprawie planów reformy Zakonu Krzyżackiego w Prusach w połowie XV wieku', in *Społeczeństwo – gospodarka – kultura. Studia ofiarowane Marianowi Małowistowi w czterdziestolecie pracy naukowej*, ed. S. Herbst et al. (Warsaw, 1974), p.31.

been the history of the Teutonic Order as a religious community within the wider context of the activity of other military-religious orders.[11]

In fact, even before the Second World War, some Polish researchers have regarded the Teutonic Order as a religious community, as evidenced, for example, by the work of Karol Górski, a distinguished specialist on spiritual history, on the inner life of the Teutonic Order. Referring mainly to the conventual rules and statutes governing the Order, Górski endeavoured to understand why the Teutonic Knights turned away from ascetic monasticism and towards a more mundane political life conducted by means hardly consistent with the Christian spirit. He sought to explain this phenomenon by defining the religious formation of the Teutonic Order as an eclectic blend of the collective experiences of the other orders and of the superficial religious attitudes of its increasingly illiterate and spiritually unrefined brethren-knights. The relatively high level of religious sensitivity in the first half of the thirteenth century eventually declined, owing to the too liberal selection of candidates admitted into the Order to replace the brethren killed in the wars in c.1250; consequently, in the fourteenth and fifteenth centuries, the Order acquired a character of a corporation with almost exclusively secular goals. The definite decline in religiosity is claimed to have resulted in the Teutonic insensibility to war atrocities.[12]

On the other hand, Polish historians have identified reformatory efforts of several Grand Masters of the Order in the fourteenth and fifteenth centuries.[13] The history of

---

[11]   Z. H. Nowak, 'Zehn Konferenzen „Ordines militares – Colloquia Torunensia Historica 1981-1999', in *Vergangenheit und Gegenwart der Ritterorden. Die Rezeption der Idee und die Wirklichkeit*, ed. Z. H. Nowak, R. Czaja (Toruń, 2001), 7-9; *Ordines militares*, i: *Die Rolle der Ritterorden in der Christanisierung und Kolonisierung des Ostseegebietes*, ed. Z. H. Nowak (Toruń, 1983); ibid., ii: *Prace z dziejów państwa i zakonu krzyżackiego*, ed. A. Czacharowski (Toruń, 1984); ibid., iii: *Die Rolle der Ritterorden in der mittelalterlichen Kultur*, ed. Z. H. Nowak (Toruń, 1985); ibid., iv: *Werkstatt des Historikers der mittelalterlichen Ritterorden: Probleme und Forschungsmethoden*, ed. Z. H. Nowak (Toruń, 1987); ibid., v: *Die Ritterorden zwischen geistlicher und weltlicher Macht im Mittelalter*, ed. Z. H. Nowak (Toruń, 1900); ibid., vi: *Das Kriegswesen der Ritterorden im Mittelalter*, ed. Z. H. Nowak (Toruń, 1991); ibid., vii: *Die Spiritualität der Ritterorden im Mittelalter*, ed. Z. H. Nowak (Toruń, 1993); ibid., viii: *Ritterorden und Region – politische, soziale und wirtschaftliche Verbindungen im Mittelalter*, ed. Z. H. Nowak (Toruń, 1995); ibid., ix: *Ritterorden und Kirche im Mittelalter*, ed. Z. H. Nowak (Toruń, 1997); ibid., x: *Der Deutsche Orden in der Zeit der Kalmarer Union 1937-1521*, ed. R. Czaja, Z. H. Nowak (Toruń, 1999); ibid., xi: *Vergangenheit und Gegenwart der Ritterorden. Die Rezeption der Idee und die Wirklichkeit*, ed. Z. H. Nowak, R. Czaja (Toruń, 2001).

[12]   M. Biskup, 'Zakon Krzyżacki i jego państwo', 162; K. Górski, 'O życiu wewnętrznym zakonu krzyżackiego', *Przegląd Powszechny*, ccvi (1935), 63-83, 360-83; a second edition appeared in K. Górski, *Studia i materiały z dziejów duchowości* (Warsaw, 1980), 193-215.

[13]   M. Pollakówna, 'Sprawa ocenzurowania Kroniki Piotra z Dusburga', in *Europa-Słowiańszczyzna-Polska. Studia ku uczczeniu profesora Kazimierza Tymienieckiego*, ed. J. Bardach et al. (Poznań, 1970), 127-34; M. Biskup, 'Plany reformy Zakonu Krzyżackiego w Prusach z 1492 roku', in *Prusy – Polska – Europa, Studia z dziejów średniowiecza i czasów wczesnonowożytnych*, ed. A. Radzimiński, J. Tandecki (Toruń, 1999), 277-85; id., 'W sprawie planów reformy', 31-43; id., 'Wizytacja zamków Zakonu Krzyżackiego w Inflantach z 1488 roku', *Zapiski Historyczne*, xlix (1984), 119-28; id., 'Warunki przyjmowania kandydatów

reform within the Teutonic Order, however, demands a more systematic approach. In order to evaluate the Order's performance, including its religious dimension, it is necessary to examine its reputation as reflected in medieval non-Teutonic documents. An example of such an approach is the recent dissertation of Wojciech Polak on the image of the Teutonic Order as revealed in the writings of the celebrated fifteenth-century Polish chronicler, Jan Długosz. Polak has underscored the fact that Długosz, himself a cleric, had consciously approved of the crusading mission of the Order so long as it did not interfere with the affairs of the Polish State. For the chronicler, Poland remained his main concern. A diplomat in the Polish-Teutonic negotiations during the 1454-66 war, Długosz viewed the conflict between the two institutions in terms of a feud between the Church and the heirs of its patron and benefactor – Konrad, the Duke of Mazovia.[14]

Nevertheless, the main focus of Polish historians with respect to the Teutonic Order is not entirely the evaluation of its religious life;[15] it is rather its ideology, as expressed in the literature and works of art sponsored by the Order itself. Detailed monographs published by Polish scholars on the Teutonic State art – painting, goldsmithery, architecture, carving, and chronicles[16] – provide a good basis for such studies. Such works include, for instance, Stefan Kwiatkowski's interpretation of the Teutonic version of St. Augustine's philosophy, referred to in debates to justify the conquest of the lands of the heathen Balts,[17] and the research carried out by Marian Dygo on the cult of the Virgin Mary, the patron of the Order and sovereign of Pruthenia.[18] Inquiry into the reception of the crusade ideology by the Teutonic Order has indicated few direct parallels to the Holy Land. These have been limited to the

---

do zakonu krzyżackiego w Rzeszy Niemieckiej na przełomie XV-XVI wieku', *Zapiski Historyczne*, xlix (1984), 535-38.

[14]   W. Polak, *Aprobata i spór. Zakon krzyżacki jako instytucja kościelna w dziełach Jana Długosza* (Lublin, 1999), 157-251.

[15]   K. Górski, 'Religijność Krzyżaków a klimat kulturalny', *Przegląd Historyczny*, lxxv (1984), 249-58; H. Piwoński, 'Kult świętych w zabytkach liturgicznych Krzyżaków w Polsce', *Archiwa, Biblioteki i Muzea Kościelne*, xlvii (1983), 313-62; id., 'Indeks sekwencji w zabytkach liturgicznych Krzyżaków w Polsce', *Archiwa, Biblioteki i Muzea Kościelne,* xlix (1984), 221-44.

[16]   M. Pollakówna, *Kronika Piotra z Dusburga* (Wrocław, 1968); S. Zonenberg, *Kronika Wiganda z Marburga* (Bydgoszcz, 1994); J. Wenta, *Kierunki rozwoju rocznikarstwa w państwie Zakonu Niemieckiego w XIII-XIV w* (Toruń, 1990), 16-29; J. Trupinda, *Ideologia krucjatowa w Kronice Piotra z Dusburga* (Gdańsk, 1999). For works on art, notes 20-22 below.

[17]   S. Kwiatkowski, *Zakon niemiecki w Prusach a umysłowość średniowieczna. Scholastyczne rozumienie prawa natury a etyczna i religijna świadomość Krzyżaków do około 1420 roku* (Toruń, 1998); id., '*Devotio antiqua*, ihr Niedergang und die geistigen Ursachen der religiösen Krise des Deutschen Ordens im Spätmittelalter', in *Deutscher Orden 1190-1990*, ed. U. Arnold (Lüneburg, 1997), 107-130.

[18]   M. Dygo, 'O kulcie maryjnym w Prusach Krzyżackich w XIV-XV wieku', *Zapiski Historyczne*, lii (1987), 5-38; id., 'The political role of the cult of the Virgin Mary in Teutonic Prussia in the fourteenth and fifteenth centuries', *Journal of Medieval History*, xv (1989), 63-81.

liturgy adopted by the Canons of the Holy Sepulchre before 1244[19] and, possibly, the symbolic design of the Chapel in Malbork.[20] The distinction becomes even sharper when compared to the way the invasion of Prussia has been presented as a holy war waged by Christian knights on the infidel, illustrated by the images of knights in liturgical codices and architectural carvings, and the emphasis on their saintliness in the chronicle of Peter of Dusburg.[21] Works published in the last twenty-five years on the art of painting in the Teutonic State and on the chronicle of Wigand of Marburg, show some secular motifs of the knightly culture within the Teutonic Order,[22] motifs unrelated to the crusade. The subject of the social status of the Teutonic Order within the wider structure of society has been undertaken by Henryk Samsonowicz, an eminent Polish historian who specializes in urban history. In a noteworthy article, he demonstrated analogies and contrasts in the positions of two groups accepted by the Church in the late Middle Ages – the Teutonic Knights and the burghers.[23]

The interest of Polish scholars in the history of Teutonic houses outside Pruthenia (Frankonia, Sicily, the Reich) is limited to problems of access to archival material, to fragmentary papers, and very often to the publication of documentary sources with a running commentary.[24] Karol Polejowski (Gdańsk) has been working on the history

---

[19] K. Górski, 'O życiu wewnętrznym' (1980), p. 94.

[20] S. Skibiński, *Kaplica na Zamku Wysokim w Malborku* (Poznań, 1982), 200; M. Dygo, 'Nowe spojrzenie na zamek w Malborku', *Komunikaty Mazursko-Warmińskie* (1983), 487-97.

[21] For example, B. Jakubowska, *Złota Brama w Malborku* (Malbork, 1989), 134-39; T. Jurkowlaniec, *Gotycka rzeźba architektoniczna w Prusach* (Wrocław, 1989), 51, 69; J. Domasłowski, 'Malerei im Deutschordensland Preußen', in *Deutscher Orden 1190-1990*, ed. U. Arnold (Lüneburg, 1997), p.138; A. Karłowska-Kamzowa, 'Ilustrowane apokalispy krzyżackie z XIV w', in *Studia o działalności i zbiorach Biblioteki Uniwersytetu Mikołaja Kopernika*, vi, ed. B. Ryszewski (Toruń, 1991), p.126; L. Pudłowski, 'Czternastowieczne przedstawienie krzyżowców z katedry w Królewcu', in *Portret. Funkcja – Forma – Symbol*, (Warsaw, 1990), 351-63; M. Dygo, 'Mnich i rycerz. Ideologiczne modele postaw w zakonie krzyżackim w Prusach w XIV-XV wieku', *Zapiski Historyczne*, xl (1990), 9-15.

[22] J. Domasłowski, 'Malerei im Deutschordensland'; A. Karłowska-Kamzowa, 'Gotyckie rękopisy iluminowane na Pomorzu Wschodnim. Problemy badawcze', *Zeszyty Naukowe KUL*, xxvii, 2 (1984), p. 43-44; Zonenberg, 73-95.

[23] H. Samsonowicz, 'Der Deutsche Orden und die Städte in Preußen. Verknüpfungen und Unterschiede im kulturellen Leben' in *Die Rolle der Ritterorden in der mittelalterlichen Kultur*, ed. Z. H. Nowak (Toruń, 1985), 7-22.

[24] M. Arszyński Marian, 'Konferencja Międzynarodowej Komisji Historycznej do Badań nad Zakonem Krzyżackim w Bolzano (Bozen)', *Zapiski Historyczne*, lxi (1996), 143-45; M. Biskup, 'Echa bitwy grunwaldzkiej i oblężenia Malborka w niemieckiej gałęzi Zakonu Krzyżackiego w lecie 1410', *Komunikaty Mazursko-Warmińskie* (1983), 455-60; id., 'Warunki przyjmowania kandydatów do zakonu krzyżackiego w Rzeszy Niemieckiej na przełomie XV-XVI wieku', *Zapiski Historyczne*, xlix (1984), 535-38.

of the Teutonic Order in France.[25] Polish research has, however, produced several useful syntheses of Teutonic activities in Pruthenia.[26]

The study of other military orders has been outside the main focus of Polish medievalists, although their interest in the subject has increased in the last twenty years. The short-lived Knights of Christ attracted scholarly attention out of all proportion to their historical significance, as one element of the situation on the Prussian borderland at the time when the Teutonic Knights were established there.[27] Stanislaw Kujot and Wanda Polkowska-Markowska have both determined (the latter in much more detail) the extent of the land ceded to the Teutonic Knights by Konrad of Mazovia in the Dobrzyń area and on the border with Pruthenia.[28] The analogy between the Knights of the Sword, who acted in Livonia as a military arm of the Cistercians, and the Knights of Christ, established by the Cistercian missionary bishop of Pruthenia, has led Tadeusz Manteuffel to assume that the Cistercians also attempted to constitute a State similar to the one in Livonia.[29] The origin of the establishment of this community is still a matter of academic controversy. Despite a first mention dating it back to 1228, the Knights of Christ could have emerged earlier, by the side of the Cistercian missionaries who were already active in Pruthenia at the very beginning of the thirteenth century.[30] Research on the other orders' participation

---

[25] K. Polejowski, 'Stan i potrzeby badań nad posiadłościami Zakonu Krzyżackiego w krajach romańskojęzycznych w średniowieczu (ze szczególnym uwzględnieniem królestwa Francji) in *Szlachta, starostowie, zaciężni*, ed. B. Śliwiński (Gdańsk-Koszalin, 1998), 147-156; id., '*Beauvoir* czy *Beaufort*? O pochodzeniu przydomka wielkiego mistrza Zakonu Krzyżackiego Karola z Trewiru' in *Książęta, urzędnicy, złoczyńcy*, ed. B. Śliwiński (Gdańsk, 1999), 147-55; id., 'Geneza i rola kultu św. Elżbiety węgierskiej w posiadłościach francuskich zakonu krzyżackiego', *Zapiski Historyczne*, lxiii (1998), 7-14.

[26] K. Górski, *Państwo krzyżackie w Prusach* (Gdańsk-Bydgoszcz, 1946); M. Biskup, G. Labuda, *Dzieje Zakonu Krzyżackiego w Prusach* (Gdańsk, 1986), recently translated into German as *Die Geschichte des Deutschen Ordens in Preußen. Wirtschaft-Gesellschaft-Staat-Ideologie* (Osnabrück, 2000).

[27] Z. H. Nowak, 'Der Anteil der Ritterorden an dr preussischen Mission (mit Ausnahme des Deutschen Ordens)' in *Die Rolle der Ritterorden in der Christianisierung und Kolonisierung des Ostseegebietes*, ed. Z. H. Nowak (Toruń, 1983), 90; id., 'Milites Christi de Prussia. Der Orden zu Dobrin und seine Stellung in der preussischen Mission', in *Die geistlichen Ritterorden Europas*, ed. J. Fleckenstein, M. Hellmann (Sigmaringen, 1980), 339-52; Polkowska-Markowska, 145-210; J. Powierski, *Prusowie, Mazowsze i sprowadzenie Krzyżaków do Polski* (Malbork, 1996), 12-16; G. Labuda, 'O nadaniu biskupa Chrystiana dla dobrzyńców z roku 1228', *Roczniki Humanistyczne*, xx, 2 (1972), 43-49.

[28] S. Kujot, ' ... usque in Pruciam. Studium nad dokumentami kawalerów dobrzyńskich z roku 1228', *Roczniki Towarzystwa Naukowego w Toruniu*, xvi (1909), 3-8; Polkowska-Markowska, 179-91.

[29] T. Manteuffel, 'Próba stworzenia cysterskiego państwa biskupiego w Prusach' *Zapiski Towarzystwa Naukowego w Toruniu*, xviii (1953), 157-74; id., *Papiestwo i cystersi ze szczególnym uwzględnieniem ich roli w Polsce na przełomie XII i XIII w* (Warsaw, 1955), 97-106.

[30] W. Polkowska-Markowska, 178, 193-94; Powierski, *Prusowie*, 14-16; Manteuffel, *Papiestwo*, 92-96, 102-103; G. Labuda, 'O nadaniu biskupa Chrystiana', 43-49; Nowak, 'Milites Christi', 342-48; A. Gieysztor, 'Trzy stulecia najdawniejszego Mazowsza (połowa

in the Prussian campaign is even less extensive. It has, nevertheless, confirmed the endowments of land on the Prussian border by numerous patrons on behalf of various military orders – the Hospitallers received one in Starogard, the Knights of Calatrava in Tymawa in East Pomerania, the Templars in Mazovia and Łuków (Little Poland), the Knights of Christ in Dobrzyń and Drohiczyn on the border of Mazovia, Pruthenia, and Sudovia. On the other hand, traces of their contribution to the Prussian campaign are scarce.[31]

In the case of the Templars and the Hospitallers, who owned a wide network of convents on Polish soil, the primary tasks for historians has been to investigate how these were founded, their numbers, their affiliations both to one another and to their provinces. Thanks to the pioneering work of Antoni Małecki in the late nineteenth century and to the more recent studies by Kazimierz Dola, the present writer, and others,[32] it would appear that the emerging picture is nearing completion, although the scarcity of sources has not allowed certain arguable issues to be clarified,

X – połowa XIII w.)', in *Dzieje Mazowsza do 1526 roku*, ed. A. Gieysztor, H. Samsonowicz (Warsaw, 1994), 24; Starnawska, *Między Jerozolimą*, 107-111; id., 'Military Orders and the Beginning of Crusade in Prussia', in *The Crusades and the Military Orders. Expanding the Frontiers of Medieval Latin Christianity*, ed. Zs. Hunyadi , J. Laszlovsky (Budapest, 2001), 420-21.

[31] Frydrychowicz, 319; Nowak, 'Der Anteil', 79-91; Starnawska, 'Military Orders', passim; id., *Między Jerozolimą*, 188-203; id., 'Templariusze nad Bugiem i w Łukowie', *Zeszyty Naukowe Wyższej Szkoły Rolniczo-Pedagogicznej w Siedlcach*, seria: *Nauki Humanistyczne. No 45, Historia*, ii (1996), 7-11; J. Powierski, *Stosunki polsko-pruskie do 1230 r. ze szczególnym uwzględnieniem roli Pomorza Gdańskiego* (Toruń, 1968), 129-30, 167-68; T. W. Lange, 'Joannici na Pomorzu Gdańskim. Stan badań – interpretacje – próba syntezy', *Zapiski Historyczne*, xlix (1994), 11, 12; H. Łowmiański, 'Początki i rola polityczna zakonów rycerskich nad Bałtykiem w wieku XIII i XIV', in H. Łowmiański, *Prusy-Litwa-Krzyżacy*, (Warsaw, 1989), 408-36; Goliński, 'Uposażenie', 16-17; J. Karwasińska, 'Sąsiedztwo kujawsko-krzyżackie 1235-1343', in J. Karwasińska, *Kujawy i Mazowsze* (Warsaw, 1997), 61, 70; B. Zientara, *Henryk Brodaty i jego czasy* (Warsaw, 1975), 207.

[32] J. Knopek, 'Zakon templariuszy na Pomorzu Zachodnim w najnowszej historiografii polskiej i obcej', *Przegląd Zachodniopomorski*, xi (1996), 184-90; A. Małecki, 'Klasztory i zakony w Polsce w obrębie wieków średnich', *Przewodnik Naukowy i Literacki*, iii (1875); and the revised edition in A. Małecki, *Z dziejów i literatury* (Lwów-Petersburg, 1896), 332-46; K. Dola, 'Zakon'; Starnawska, *Między Jerozolimą*; id., 'Der Johanniterorden und Schlesien in Mittelaleter', *passim*; id., 'Die Ritter- und Hospitaliterorden in der Diözese Breslau im Mittelalter. Der Forschungsstand', in *Geschichte des christlichen Lebens im schlesischen Raum*, ed. J. Köhler, R. Bendel, i (Münster, 2002), 283-97; K. Gancarczyk, 'Fundacja komendy joannickiej Bożego Ciała we Wrocławiu', *Acta Universitatis Wratislaviensis* nr 1112, *Historia*, lxxvi (1989), 155-63; id., 'W kwestii początków zakonu joannitów na Śląsku', *Sobótka,* xl (1985), 191-201; M. Goliński, 'Krzyżacy czy joannici? W sprawie rzekomej obecności joannitów pod Wrocławiem w 1273 r.', *Sobótka*, xlvi (1991), 341-44; P. Hope, 'Curia Militaie Templi in Liceniz. Z dziejów templariuszy na zaodrzańskim obszarze diecezji lubuskiej', *Poznański Rocznik Archiwalno-Historyczny*, ii-iii (1994-95), 11-18; P. Hope, 'Kwestia sprowadzenie templariuszy do Polski. Rozwój uposażenia zakonu w Wielkopolsce', *Poznański Rocznik Archiwalno-Historyczny*, i (1993), 15-40; D. Wybranowski, 'Fundacja komandorii joannitów w Goleniowie na tle stosunków księcia Bogusława IV z zakonami rycerskimi w latach 1280-1291', *Przegląd Zachodniopomorski*, xliii (1999), 9-22.

particularly those concerning the circumstances in which the Templar houses were founded.[33] For several years now, experts in the history of the military orders have been showing increasing interest in the role these orders played within a society so indifferent to the crusading ideal. The present writer has suggested a process of adaptation in the peripheral environment as providing a new perspective in the history of the military orders on Polish lands.[34] Research on the military orders has pointed to a wide variety of themes, ranging from their meagre, though evident, participation in the propaganda of the crusades, to their religious practices,[35] and their role in defending the borders, not only in the case of Pruthenia, but also in the case of various regional principalities;[36] from the transformation of some Hospitaller houses into semi-secular fraternities for the sons of knights,[37] to the Hospitallers' minor social contribution (and a marginal one in the case of the Templars); from the founding and administration of hospitals[38] to the remarkable phenomenon of the Hospitallers assuming the parochial ministry in Silesia, which resulted in the almost definite clericalization of the local branch of the Order.[39] The architecture of the military orders on Polish lands is the subject of some monographs on the history of

---

[33]   J. Hauziński, 'Templariusze w Małopolsce – legenda czy rzeczywistość?' in *Polska-Prusy-Ruś*, ed. B. Śliwiński (Gdańsk, 1995), 71-83; M. Starnawska, 'Wiadomości Długosza o templariuszach i joannitach' in *Kultura średniowieczna i staropolska*, ed. D. Gawinowa *et al.* (Warsaw, 1991), 474-76; A. Tomaszewski, '*Sub habitu templariorum – porta occidentalis ecclesiae Oppatoviensis*', in ibid., 295-303; E. Rymar, 'Powstanie i stan posiadania pomorskich komend templariuszy w Chwarszczanach i Myśliborzu w XIII wieku', *Przegląd Zachodniopomorski*, ii (1987), 192-204; J. Spors, 'Początki i stan posiadania templariuszy w ziemi kostrzyńskiej w latach 1232-1261', *Studia i Materiały do Dziejów Wielkopolski i Pomorza*, xxxii (1987), 111-28; B. Zientara, *Henryk Brodaty*, 278-80; P. Stróżyk, 'Fundacja preceptorii tempariuszy w Tempelhof', *Roczniki Historyczne*, lviii (1992), 14-20; E. Rymar, 'Komandoria chwarszczańska templariuszy i joannitów (1232-1540)', *Nadwarciański Rocznik Historyczno-Archiwalny*, ix (2002), 11-35.

[34]   Starnawska, 'Crusade Orders', 119-36; id., *Między Jerozolimą*, 13-14, 183-94.

[35]   Id., 'Rola', 110-15; id., 'Krucjata i Ziemia Święta w duchowości zakonów krzyżowych w Polsce średniowiecznej', *Saeculum Christianum*, iii, 1 (1996), 167-74, 177; id., *Między Jerozolimą*, 157-74; R. Grodecki, 'Dzieje klasztoru premonstrateńskiego w Busku'. *Rozprawy Akademii Umiejętności, Wydział Historyczno-Filozoficzny*, lvii (1913), 12-13; B. Szcześniak, *The Knights Hospitallers in Poland and Lithuania* (The Hague, 1969), 36-37; Dola, 'Zakon', 51, 52, 78.

[36]   A. Czacharowski, 'Die politische Rolle der Johanniter im pommerschen Grenzgebiet im Mittelalter', in *Die Ritterorden zwischen geistlicher und weltlicher Macht im Mittelalter*, ed. Z. H. Nowak (Toruń, 1990), 143-52; Zientara, *Henryk Brodaty*, 278-80; Starnawska, 'Mnisi-rycerze-szlachta. Templariusze i joannici na pograniczu wielkopolsko-brandenbursko-pomorskim', *Kwartalnik Historyczny*, xcix (1992), 21.

[37]   Id., 'Mnisi – rycerze – szlachta', *passim.*

[38]   K. Dola, 'Szpitale średniowieczne Śląska', *Rocznik Teologiczny Śląska Opolskiego*, i (1968), 247, 269, 271, 273, 288, 291, ibid., ii (1970), 182, 195; Starnawska, *Między Jerozolimą*, 228-46, 354-58; M. Słoń, *Die Spitäler Breslaus im Mitelalter* (Warsaw, 2001), 149-202.

[39]   M. Starnawska, 'Duszpasterstwo parafialne joannitów w miastach Śląska i Wielkopolski w późnym średniowieczu' in *Klasztor w kulturze Polski średniowiecznej*, ed. A. Pobóg-Lenartowicz, M. Derwich (Opole, 1995), 115-26.

art.[40] The present author has detected similarities in the processes of adaptation of the military and hospitaller (devoid, that is, of the military aspects) orders, and has proposed a joint interpretative evaluation of the whole group on their basis.[41]

However rich and diverse the range of problems examined by the Polish historians of the military orders, further study can still provide new insights and fascinating results.

---

[40]   For example, H. Golasz, 'Joannicki kościół w Tyńcu nad Ślężą', in *Z badań architektury Śląska. Prace Naukowe Instytutu Historii Architektury, Sztuki i Techniki Politechniki Wrocławskiej*, ed. J. Rozpędowski, nr 2, *Studia i Materiały*, nr *1* (Wrocław, 1972), 3-35; T. Kołodziejska, 'Achitektura kościoła parafialnego w Choszcznie', *Materiały Zachodniopomorskie*, viii (1962), 301-33; J. Kostowski, 'Kamienna nastawa ołtarzowa w kościele Bożego Ciała we Wrocławiu', *Poznańskie Towarzystwo Przyjaciół Nauk. Wydział Nauk o Sztuce. Prace Komisji Historii Sztuki*, lii (2002), 67-80; E. Łużyniecka, *Gotyckie świątynie Wrocławia. Kościół Bożego Ciała. Kościół świętych Wacława, Stanisława i Doroty* (Wrocław, 1999), 13-72; Z. Radacki, *Średniowieczne zamki Pomorza Zachodniego* (Warszawa, 1976), 109-111, 123-54, 252-60; Z. Rawska-Kwaśnikowa, 'Próba datowania budowy joannickiego kościoła w Strzegomiu', *Biuletyn Historii Sztuki*, xxxiii (1971), 103-115; Z. Rawska-Kwaśnikowa, 'Trzy kościoły joannickie na Dolnym Śląsku', *Sprawozdania Wrocławskiego Towarzystwa Naukowego,* ix (1954), 42-45; J. Rozpędowski, 'Rozwój przestrzenny joannickiego kościoła p. w. Bożego Ciała we Wrocławiu', *Prace Naukowe Instytutu Historii Architektury, Sztuki i Techniki Politechniki Wrocławskiej*, xxii (1989), 163-74.

[41]   Starnawska, *Między Jerozolimą*, 9-14; id., 'Crusade Orders', 121-23.

Chapter 3

Historiography and History: Medieval Studies on the Military Orders in Spain since 1975

Luis García-Guijarro Ramos

In July 1999, at a meeting in Israel of the Society for the Study of the Crusades and the Latin East, the secretary Catherine Otten pointed out the very limited presence of scholars from Spain in that association.[1] A brief perusal of the list of members that each bulletin includes confirms the almost total absence of university professors and lecturers from that country, as well as of scholars of the Higher Council for Scientific Research (CSIC).[2] This indicates a certain reluctance by Spanish medievalists to get involved in international associations, an unwillingness that is also shown at home in relation to the Spanish Society for Medieval Studies, which should be the gathering point for those interested in the Middle Ages in Spain; instead, some historians regard it as the bulwark of conservatism, while most of its members do not care to turn up at the yearly meetings. This kind of behaviour, though not alien to other nations, is peculiar to a country that has not yet completely relinquished some of the traits of past decades of authoritarian rule, and one that reached modern development at all levels at a very late date in relation to other western European countries.[3] Among medievalists, there are still remnants of an intellectual autarky, one that assumes the double form of lack of research on non-Spanish topics and of insufficient involvement in societies that bring together scholars from all over the world.[4] With

---

[1]   The term Spain (or Spanish) refers both to present-day Spain and to Spain in the Middle Ages. In no way does it imply the projection of the idea of Spain into medieval times

[2]   Only five Spanish members are listed in the last issue of the *Bulletin of the Society for the Study of the Crusades and the Latin East*, xxv (2005), 43-62. In 2002 there were seven. This situation is, for instance, also reflected in the Medieval Academy of America. Its 2003 Directory shows that few Spanish medievalists living in Spain have joined the oldest association of medieval studies.

[3]   Spain had no École des Chartes, no Monumenta, and no Rolls Series, or their equivalents. These were products of a social, economic, and cultural development that Spain had not yet reached in the nineteenth century. The two CODOINs were isolated efforts: *Colección de documentos inéditos para la Historia de España*, ed. Martín Fernández Navarrete *et al.*, 112 vols (Madrid, 1842-95); *Colección de documentos inéditos del Archivo General de la Corona de Aragón*, ed. Próspero Bofarull y Mascaró *et al.*, 41 vols (Barcelona, 1847-1910).

[4]   *Autarquía* (Autarky) refers to the economic isolationism which marked Francisco Franco's policies in the 1940s and 1950s. I have transferred this concept to the intellectual world.

a few exceptions, globalization has not yet touched the field of medieval research or the socializing attitudes of historians of the Middle Ages in Spain. Dictatorships are deeply suspicious of any form of collective expression which they do not directly inspire. The most lasting and harmful effects of Franco's rule in Spain were inflicted not so much on political parties, which seemed to emerge with vigour immediately afterwards, but on all kinds of associations. Civil society became so weakened that individuals were not used to those real forms of democracy which associations represented; indeed they reacted against them. It is true that in the last decade or so many such associations have emerged, but they are directly related to political events – ETA terrorism being the most obvious example; they hardly concern the academic world. Thus a deeply ingrained uneasiness, bordering on distrust, towards academic societies, together with a view intellectually and socially restricted to Spain, are some of the reasons that explain that strange absence of Spaniards from a society devoted to the study of the crusades.

However, the most puzzling explanation relates to the very core of research. Spanish scholars have shown no interest in the crusading movement. This lack of attention affects not only the 'traditional' focus on the Near East, but also the different Spanish kingdoms, in spite of the fact that the *Reconquista* had on occasions, from the late eleventh century onward, a distinct crusading imprint – the conquest of Saragossa in 1118 or the battle of Las Navas de Tolosa of 1212 are among the hundreds of instances that we can record. No significant book on the crusades in the Iberian Peninsula has been published by Spanish medievalists since José Goñi Gaztambide wrote a thorough institutional overview in 1958.[5] This vacuum reflects the nationalist type of historiography that developed from the late nineteenth century, and was thus cherished not only by the victors after the end of the Civil War in 1939, but also by intellectuals in exile. Such was the case, for example, of Claudio Sánchez Albornoz or Américo Castro, who wrote their best known and polemical books in the 1950s. The idea that the *Reconquista* was a peculiar Spanish experience greatly stressed the differences brought about by what was then regarded as an eighth-century struggle against the Muslims to recover the territories snatched from Christian hands after AD 711. The fact that several elements of that long-term confrontation had aspects in common with principles shared by most Latin Christians, which took shape in the crusade, was not taken into account.[6] If one considers that this obvious line of

---

[5] José Goñi Gaztambide, *Historia de la Bula de la Cruzada en España* (Vitoria, 1958). Goñi's study is still the basic starting point for any research on the crusades in Spain. The fact that nearly fifty years later this book is still available in bookshops indicates the little interest that this comprehensive survey has aroused in Spain. In spite of the several works dealing with the *Reconquista* in the past decades, José Manuel Rodríguez García's bibliographical essay on the crusades provides clear evidence of this intellectual desert. 'Historiografía de las Cruzadas', *Espacio, Tiempo y Forma, Revista de la Facultad de Geografía e Historia de la UNED*, 3rd ser., *Historia Medieval*, xiii (2000), 341-95. The only two books published recently in Spain on this topic are based on the secondary literature rather than on archival sources: Francisco García Fitz, *Edad Media: Guerra e Ideología. Justificaciones religiuosas y jurídicas* (Madrid, 2003); Carlos de Ayala Martínez, *Las Cruzadas* (Madrid, 2004).

[6] The terms *Reconquista* and crusade are not exactly synonymous; they were indeed two entirely different concepts. However, the several elements that both movements had in

thought was, and to some extent still is, disregarded at home, and that most research is nationally oriented, it is no surprise that nothing relevant has been published on Outremer in Spain, despite the existing similarities on warfare, settlements, and institutions between both ends of the Mediterranean. No wonder, then, that there is hardly any inclination among Spanish medievalists to join a Society whose aim is to study a subject almost entirely foreign to their interests.

An even deeper contradiction follows the paradox of a crusader country with no crusade historians. Many European scholars marvel today at the strength of medieval studies on the military orders in Spain. The production has certainly been massive over the last three decades. Its sheer numbers can easily be appreciated by comparing two very comprehensive bibliographies that included Portugal and were published in the span of just over fifteen years. Derek Lomax's repertory, which came out in 1976, included around nine hundred titles, from the eighteenth century to its date of compilation.[7] A group of scholars, under the direction of Carlos de Ayala Martínez, brought that list up to date in 1992-93 by adding another thousand titles – five hundred for the Kingdoms of Castile and Leon, and an equal number for the Crown of Aragon, Navarre, and Portugal.[8] The numbers are really spectacular, even

---

common in the Central Middle Ages cannot be ignored. For studies in Spanish relating to both concepts, José Luis Martín Rodríguez, 'Reconquista y Cruzada', in *Il Concilio di Piacenza e le Crociate*, (Piacenza, 1996), 247-71; and in *Studia Zamorensia*, viii (1996), 215-41. For a recent view of the relationship between the *Reconquista* and the crusade, Vicente Ángel Álvarez Palenzuela, 'El componente cruzado de la Reconquista', in *Jerusalem the Golden: The Conquest of the Dream (From the West to the Holy Land)*, ed. Luis García-Guijarro Ramos (forthcoming).

[7]   Derek W. Lomax, *Las Órdenes Militares en la Península Ibérica durante la Edad Media* (Salamanca, 1976).

[8]   Carlos de Ayala Martínez *et al.*, 'Las Órdenes Militares en la Edad Media Peninsular. Historiografía 1976-1992. i: Reinos de Castilla y León', and ibid., 'ii: Corona de Aragón, Navarra y Portugal', *Medievalismo. Boletín de la Sociedad Española de Estudios Medievales*, ii (1992), 119-69; Ibid., iii (1993), 87-144. C. de Ayala has recently added some further works in *Las Órdenes Militares hispánicas en la Edad Media. Aproximación bibliográfica* (Madrid, 1999). They include works listed previously in several bibliographical essays. José Vicente Matellanes Merchán, 'Historiografía medieval de la Orden de Santiago en los últimos años (1974-1989)', *Hispania, 1* (1990), 965-85; Enrique Rodríguez-Picavea Matilla, 'Catorce años de historiografía sobre la Orden de Calatrava en la Edad Media (1976-1989), ibid., 941-64; Concepción de la Fuente 'La historiografía sobre la Orden de Alcántara en la Edad Media (siglos XII-XIV), *Hispania Sacra*, xlv (1993), 487-502; Enric Guinot Rodríguez, 'Els estudis sobre l'orde de Montesa en temps medievals i les seues bases documentals', *Saitabi. Revista de la Facultat de Geografia i Història de la Universitat de València*, xliv (1994), 23-32. In 1996 Miguel Ángel Ladero Quesada published a general survey on the bibliography of the military orders in the Kingdoms of Castile and Leon in the Middle Ages: 'La investigación sobre Órdenes Militares en la Edad Media hispánica durante los últimos decenios: Corona de Castilla y León', in *Las Órdenes Militares en la Península Ibérica*, ed. Ricardo Izquierdo Benito and Francisco Ruiz Gómez, i: *Edad Media* (Cuenca, 2000), 9-31. Carlos Barquero Goñi has recently brought up to date the state of research on the Hospitallers: 'La Orden del Hospital en España durante la Edad Media: un estado de la cuestión', *Hispania Sacra*, lii (2000), 7-20. See also Philippe Josserand, 'Les ordres militaires dans les royaumes de

after deducting the works of non-Hispanic scholars; in less than two decades, more titles came out of the press than in the previous three centuries. A bibliographical update for the period 1993-2003 included more than six hundred titles published in one single decade.[9] Another sign of this quantitative vitality is the appearance in 2001 of a review devoted specifically to the military orders.[10]

Some of the studies registered in these bibliographies were contributions to scientific meetings devoted totally or partially to the military orders. In 1971, just before our proposed starting date of 1975, a joint Spanish–Portuguese itinerant conference, with British and Italian participants, took place on a fortnight's tour through several cities in Castile and Portugal.[11] More than forty papers were read, showing the state of research at the time. The conference was organized by Emilio Sáez Sánchez; along with Eloy Benito Ruano, he was the main driving force behind this type of research in Spain in the Sixties and Seventies. From then on, there have been no less than ten general, regional, or thematic conferences, whose contributions sometimes have unfortunately taken years to reach the public, thereby giving a somewhat distorted image of the stage this research had reached at a given time.[12] The last two great events were the international conferences held in May 1996 at Ciudad Real – a most suitable place, having been a royal city in the past, lying at the very heart of the domains of the Order of Calatrava – and in July 2001 at Teruel. The

---

Castille et de León. Bilan et perspectives de la recherche en histoire médiévale', *Atalaya. Revue Française d'Études Médiévales Hispaniques*, ix (1998), 5-44.

[9]   Carlos de Ayala Martínez and Carlos Barquero Goñi, 'Historiografía hispánica y Órdenes Militares en la Edad Media, 1993-2003', *Medievalismo. Boletín de la Sociedad Española de Estudios Medievales*, xii (2002), 101-161.

[10]   *Revista de las Órdenes Militares*, i (2001), ii (2003) and iii (2005).

[11]   The papers were published ten years later in *Las Órdenes Militares en La Península durante la Edad Media. Actas del Congreso Internacional Hispano-Portugués (Madrid-Uclés-Valladolid-León-Salamanca-Cáceres-Tomar-Lisboa, 29 de marzo - 9 de abril de 1971)*, (Madrid-Barcelona, 1981): an offprint from the *Anuario de Estudios Medievales*, xi (1981).

[12]   Such conferences were held in Madrid-Ciudad Real, 1983: *Las Órdenes Militares en el Mediterráneo Occidental (siglos XII-XVIII)* (Madrid, 1989); Cáceres, 1985: *El Arte y las Órdenes Militares* (Cáceres, 1985); Montblanc, 1985: *Actes de les Primeres Jornades sobre els Ordes Religioso-Militars als Països Catalans (Segles XII-XIX)* (Tarragona, 1994); Barcelona, 1988: *Els Ordes Eqüestres, Militars i Marítims i les Marines Menors de la Mediterrània durant els Segles XIII-XVII* (Barcelona, 1989); Madrid, 1990: *Primer Simposio Histórico de la Orden de San Juan de Jerusalém* (proceedings unpublished); Ciudad Real, 1995: *Alarcos, 1995. Actas del Congreso Internacional Conmemorativo del VII Centenario de la Batalla de Alarcos*, ed. R. Izquierdo Benito and F. Ruiz Gómez (Cuenca, 1996); Aguilar de Campoo, 1995: *Los Monjes Soldados. Los Templarios y otras Órdenes Militares. Actas IX Seminario sobre Historia del Monacato* (Aguilar de Campoo, 1996); Madrid, 1997: *Jornadas sobre el Maestre Juan Fernández de Heredia. Tiempo, personalidad y proyección histórica en el sexto centenario de su muerte* (proceedings unpublished); Castellón, 1998: *Las Órdenes Militares. Realidad e Imaginario*, ed. María Dolores Burdeus, Elena Real, Joan Verdegal (Castellón, 2000); Puerto de Santa María, 2000 : 'II Semana de Estudios Alfonsíes. Alfonso X y las Órdenes Militares' in *Alcanate. Revista de Estudios Alfonsíes*, ii (2000-2001), 13-224.

proceedings of the first meeting appeared in print in 2000.[13] The Teruel papers will be published in 2007. Another sustained effort must also be highlighted. Ever since 1991, Wifredo Rincón García has been organizing a conference on the Order of the Holy Sepulchre in Saragossa every four years.[14] The meetings are supported by the Order itself and so, as often happens in such cases, some of the papers have nothing to do with historical work, but are rather based on modern misconceptions. Many Spanish members of the military orders seem nowadays more ready to reaffirm a rosy past than to work hand in hand with historians. Such conferences are to be regarded with suspicion – their titles are indeed attractive, but their historical content and approach are rather shallow. In the case of the Order of the Temple, a number of the intellectual meetings devoted to its study have been taken over by the defenders of esoteric proposals who, hailed by the media, have tended to make genuine historians the object of derision.[15]

Further evidence of such vitality is also provided by the several university research groups studying in depth regional histories of the different orders. In the late Seventies and Eighties, Miguel Ángel Ladero Quesada supervised a few doctoral theses aimed at unearthing the rich late medieval sources of the Orders of Calatrava and Santiago in the southern part of Spain.[16] Carlos de Ayala Martínez has been directing another group over the past fifteen years, focusing on the main so-called Hispanic orders, including the Hospitallers, in both Castiles from their origins in the twelfth century to the 1350s.[17] No similar research initiatives have been taken in eastern Spain, though a profound interest in the military orders lies behind certain ambitious publishing projects like the one designed by Josep Maria Sans i Travé.[18]

---

[13] *Las Órdenes Militares en la Península Ibérica.* i: *Edad Media*, ed. Ricardo Izquierdo Benito and Francisco Ruiz Gómez (Cuenca, 2000).

[14] Calatayud-Zaragoza, 1991: *La Orden del Santo Sepulcro. I Jornadas de Estudio* (Calatayud-Saragossa, 1991); Saragossa, 1994: *La Orden del Santo Sepulcro. II Jornadas de Estudio* (Saragossa, 1996); Saragossa, 1999: *La Orden del Santo Sepulcro. III Jornadas de Estudio* (Saragossa, 2000). Saragossa, 2003: *La Orden del Santo Sepulcro. IV Jornadas de Estudio* (Saragossa, 2004).

[15] A good example is the international conference held at Jérez de los Caballeros, Badajoz, Extremadura, in May 2001. Its title, *The Order of the Temple: Between History and Myth*, was misleading.

[16] The main objectives of this line of research were summed up by Miguel Angel Ladero Quesada: 'Comentario sobre los señoríos de las Órdenes Militares de Santiago y Calatrava en Castilla la Nueva y Extremadura a fines de la época medieval', in *Las Órdenes Militares en el Mediterráneo Occidental (siglos XIII-XVIII)* (Madrid, 1989), 169-80.

[17] Carlos de Ayala has supervised the doctoral theses of Enrique Rodríguez-Picavea Matilla, Carlos Barquero Goñi, José Vicente Matellanes Merchán, and Feliciano Novoa Portela. Only two have been published so far: E. Rodríguez-Picavea Matilla, *La formación del feudalismo en la meseta meridional castellana. Los señoríos de la Orden de Calatrava en los siglos XII-XIII* (Madrid, 1994); and F. Novoa Portela, *La Orden de Alcántara y Extremadura (siglos XII-XIV)* (Mérida, 2000).

[18] He is the General Editor of the series that aims at covering the whole spectrum of the military orders in Catalonia. Four titles have appeared so far, dealing with Templar history and with the history of the minor Order of San Jorge de Alfama. Josep Maria Sans i Travé is also the driving force behind a collection of Catalan medieval texts published in Barcelona under the

How can one explain the stark contrast between this sudden spiralling in research and the paucity of crusade studies?[19] This is a historiographical riddle that has obvious connections with modern history. The last quarter of the twentieth century in Spain has got itself a name within the country and abroad: *la transición* ('the transition'), a period which began on the very day General Francisco Franco had passed away, 20 November 1975. *Transición* is the term used to indicate the peaceful transition from dictatorship to democracy. That success appears to have extended to a tiny fraction of the cultural heritage: the study of the military orders. Tentative explanations of its achievements, of the lacunae that still exist, and of the many contradictions that it betrays form precisely the main focus of the present paper. It is almost a confession, not just because its time span coincides exactly with my own career as a historian, but also because it brings to light the social and individual components of any research interests.

Today historiography has become a fashionable topic; it is a time when great paradigms are finding themselves in crisis and we tend to look everywhere to inquire how fellow historians have built up their works. Some present-day scholars regard this concern as a minor task, a sort of journalistic activity that diverts attention away from the tough work on primary sources, the only respectable and acceptable approach to our profession. This attitude connects with a long-standing tradition that looks upon history as primarily made out of records of any kind, with only subsidiary intervention by those who get in touch with them, a role almost limited to testing their reliability. But, as soon as history is considered as a compound of evidence and the intellectual treatment of it, historians and consequently historiography attain paramount importance. This form of study requires a double skill: a solid grasp of the past under survey and of the present from which it is looked at. Implicit personal and social circumstances which model historians' views of their objects of study must be made explicit, and that demands a wide spectrum of knowledge and perception, rare qualities indeed when scholars today have become overspecialized both by training and profession. The difficulty of interrelating the historical past with the historian's present is great, but complexities grow when we deal with our own time and look at the works of others from the very common ground we all share. Some would claim that we lack even the minimum perspective for attempting any study above the mere level of enumeration. That is, however, no obstacle so long as we are prepared to understand our own work and that of the scientific community we belong to – both as individual enterprises and as social products of a given time. When the period we are dealing with is as dense and as rich as post-Franco Spain, the

---

auspices of the *Fundació Noguera*. The series includes the documents relating to the Templar house of Gardeny and to the Hospitaller monastery of Alguaire: Ramón Sarobe i Huesca, *Collecció diplomàtica de la Casa del Temple de Gardeny (1070-1200)*, 2 vols (Barcelona, 1998); Jesús Alturo i Perucho, *Diplomatari d'Alguaire i del seu monestir santjoanista, de 1076 a 1244* (Barcelona, 1999).

[19] The opposite in part applies to an emblematic intellectual enterprise, the so-called Wisconsin *History of the Crusades*. This massive work covers six volumes and has a total of eighty-seven chapters. None of them, however, is monographically devoted to the military orders as a whole, or to the Templars and the Hospitrallers in particular. Indrikis Sterns wrote on the Teutonic Order.

relationship of research on the military orders to its social context cannot be ignored. Those thousand titles reveal as much about the life of those institutions as about the intellectual possibilities and constraints of the Spanish *transición*.

The main historiographical essay referred to above, 'Las Órdenes Militares en la Edad Media Peninsular', written by Ayala and others in 1992-93, shares with Lomax's repertory a similar geographical heading which is historically misleading. The term 'Iberian peninsula' or 'peninsular' refers to a physical feature that relates to present political units. The use of this aseptic term became popular among some Spanish historians a few decades ago, and it still is, as a substitute for 'Spain', a name that has been and is considered too reminiscent of the form of nationalism fostered by Franco's regime. The name Spain is unsuitable for an age that lacked a single political identity in the peninsula and the other ones that are used are highly inappropriate when applied to the Middle Ages. The Crown of Aragon was not confined to the peninsular States. By applying that geographical term, Sicily, Sardinia, and Naples would thus be artificially excluded from their fourteenth- and fifteenth-century political milieu. Why do authors show partiality towards the name 'Majorca' and not towards the other islands? Why is the geographical expression used as heading bound to include Valencia but not Naples? James II or Alfonso the Magnanimous would not have understood it.[20]

Labels are not innocent terms. The word 'Hispanic' specifically applied to the military orders that originated in what is now Spain or Portugal is also misleading, because it again projects into the past the idea and borders of modern nations, and it can easily comply with the highly debatable distinction between national and international orders. A recent general survey carried out by Carlos de Ayala Martínez on these Hispanic institutions did not take into account the Hospitallers and the Templars because their orders had been founded in Outremer.[21] Is an Aragonese Hospitaller or a Valencian Templar less 'Hispanic' than a Castilian Calatravan? Ayala's book is an ambitious project intended to cover the history of the military orders in Spain in the Middle Ages, an impressive attempt to assemble information on printed sources and modern historiography. Unfortunately, however, it leaves out to all intents and purposes Aragon, Catalonia, Majorca, and thirteenth-century Valencia, because Castilian orders had not been very significant in the Crown of Aragon. The same holds true for the Kingdom of Navarre. Peripheral regionalisms might argue that this is again another proof of Castilian **or** central cultural 'imperialism'.

Ayala's and Lomax's bibliographical works also share a common plan: a short introduction where most entries are arranged according to institutions and, within them, other related themes, followed by a comprehensive list of titles in alphabetical order. Lomax has added valuable information on hitherto inedited sources, but Ayala's scheme covers published material only. Other later works by Ladero and Ayala obviously omit this list and consist only of a descriptive account of historiographical material to indicate its existence, provide an idea of its contents, and offer a few suggestions on new fields of research. These are extremely useful and

---

[20]   I owe this point to Dr Maria Eugenia Cadeddu of C.N.R., Cagliari, Sardinia.

[21]   Carlos de Ayala Martínez, *Las órdenes militares hispánicas en la Edad Media (siglos XII-XV)* (Madrid, 2003).

essential guides to the boundless horizon of literature on the military orders. *Sensu stricto*, however, these articles may well be considered as falling outside the limits of proper historiography, since they do not contain the slightest reference to the contemporary intellectual and historical background of that massive production. That notwithstanding, a special tribute must be paid to Derek Lomax. Thirty years after he first published his bibliography, it is still the basic tool for any student approaching the history of the military orders in Spain, not just because he traces back studies to the eighteenth century, but because of the richness and comprehensiveness of his comments and observations. In no way do recent works supersede his synthesis; they simply supplement it with new titles.

The basic spadework has been carried out. Thanks to that, we have today exhaustive and thorough information on the work done on the military orders over the past three decades, so there is no point in having it reproduced in an abridged version. It has been a necessary step, though certainly not a final one. Neither is the ultimate goal of historiographical deliberation on modern research simply to mark the trodden territory of present surveys and indicate potential virgin ground for the future. This approach to historical studies has been especially favoured by the French, who coined the phrase *bilan et perspectives* for it. One of the most famous 'trade marks' of post-war history-book collections, *La Nouvelle Clio*, based the structure of each volume on it, and like many other French intellectual products, it has been successfully exported. But this concept implies an extensive idea of historical research. As in medieval agriculture, growth seems to come only through the accumulation of new fields. There appears to be no place for rethinking old problems in the hope of increasing their productivity by adding new perspectives. Apart from the idea, deeply rooted in positivism, that once questions are tackled they are solved forever, such an approach offers no clues to the milieux in which studies develop; so strictly speaking, this is not historiography either.[22]

We must conclude that neither complete catalogues nor inquiries into the state of research provide satisfactory answers to the several questions posed by recent studies on the military orders in Spain; in most cases they simply ignore them. This is because publications are regarded as entities in themselves, with more or less intrinsic value, but with hardly any interrelation with one another or connection to Spanish intellectual history in the last decades. There is a wide common ground, though, that most of them share at least in part: a complete disregard for the two basic pillars of the military orders, the crusade and ecclesiastical reform; a predominance of socio-economic studies; the local or regional scope of the research; a purely descriptive approach to the sources, or, at the other extreme, employing the sources

---

[22]   The article by Philippe Josserand (*supra*, note 8) follows this line. A brief overview of the work done on the orders over eight centuries leads into the usual *bilan et perspectives*. Not a single reference is made to the historical context in which works were written. Achievements or inadequacies are thus not related to the contemporary milieu. Lack of synthesis, localism, and the neglect of religious aspects are of course mentioned, but bear no relation to the recent intellectual history of Spain. The as-yet untilled field seems to be prosopography, which will probably redress many of the flaws of present-day Spanish studies on the military orders. The obvious question that arises is: prosopography, what for?

to support preconceived theories or models; unproblematic reasoning; a lack of comparative approach to the different orders in Spain and their development outside the peninsula; studies with nationalist overtones in some regions; little concern for the understanding of such complex institutions which are regarded as instrumental to other fields of inquiry, like, for example, the phenomenon of repopulation. When so many features are found in common – the catalogue is by no means complete – and when a great part of these traits are closely related to one another, it would be reasonable to assume that the intellectual course of such studies can be comprehended not only within the social and political context of the *transición*, but also within the framework of the long-term intellectual trends prior to 1975. .

Choice is inevitable when relating the individual items of such a bulky bibliography to a wider context. It is also fruitful because it makes the selection criteria explicit. Books have been preferred to articles because they convey wider panoramic views, far more relevant to our aim than brief specialized studies, notwithstanding the latter's remarkable contributions. A short but representative group of volumes tries to combine different years of publication, various methodologies, and diverse theoretical standpoints with sufficient coverage of the orders and territories. We must bear in mind that we are dealing here with six major institutions and three distinct geopolitical areas – the Kingdoms of Castile and Leon, the Kingdom of Navarre, and the Crown of Aragon. The otherwise unmanageable quantity of 1600 publications has been reduced to a total of about 20 books. 'History,' observed Gary Dickson when touching recently on crusade historiography, 'is the art of omission.'[23]

Anyone looking for a solid introduction to the military orders in the Spanish language will be surprised to find only one small general book, together with a huge companion devoted to the Iberian Peninsula written by the same author years later. This is not just a deficiency in peninsular historiography. General views on the military orders have been rare until very recent times in practically any country. That compares unfavourably with the crusades. A reader is faced with a wide range of choices when she approaches the study of those movements for the first time.[24] In 1998 Carlos de Ayala wrote a short general survey of the military orders in the Middle Ages, covering three major locations: the Holy Land, Spain, and the Baltic.[25] Its structure is simple – concept, organization, activities, economic foundations, relationships, images, destiny – and appears to have been inspired by a previous work by Alan Forey.[26] The questions that arise after reading its seventy pages are varied. One such relates to the character of any summary – the shorter it is, the

---

[23]   The quote comes from an unpublished discussion following the reading of one of the papers at a conference on the First Crusade held in Huesca in September 1999.

[24]   Between the publication of Hans Prutz's work in 1908 and that of Alan Forey in 1992, no substantial overview of the military orders has been written, apart from the general summary by Desmond Seward. Some progress has been registered since the appearance of Forey's book, which covered the twelfth and thirteenth centuries. See for example the recent works by Alain Demurger, *Chevaliers du Christ: les Ordres religieux-militaires au Moyen Âge, XIe-XVIe siècle* (Paris, 2002), and Carlos de Ayala Martínez, *supra*, note 21.

[25]   Id., *Las Órdenes Militares en la Edad Media* (Madrid, 1998).

[26]   Alan Forey, *The Military Orders. From the Twelfth to the Early Fourteenth Century* (London, 1992).

more crucial the problem becomes. Should it be informative or interpretative? If the former option is adopted, as in the case of Ayala, two further alternatives present themselves: should the information provided lead to explanation, or should it be just descriptive?[27] The latter alternative assures that the basic facts are known, but cannot guarantee a real grasp of the topic, which cannot be obtained by simply adding material. Ayala's résumé is of this type; it provides a useful detailed background, but fails to convey a clear idea of what a military order really was. The first chapter, which should be the basis for the other six, is weak in securing firm ground on that point. The concept of military order does not automatically grow out of the conjunction of origins, typology, and geographical distribution. Nevertheless, this book deserves attention. It is the only Spanish effort at the complex task of compressing in so short a space the relevant data on this matter.

It has been convenient to start the review of books with a *Que-sais-je?* type of approach, and this for various reasons. The briefer the summary, the more clearly it shows the dominant historical tendencies. Brevity forces concentration on what a certain age considers essential. Ayala's guide is perhaps the best introduction to the strengths and weaknesses of Spanish studies on the military orders. He has been one of the main promoters of this movement in Castile and Leon. An immense and successful effort to unearth information that has touched major and minor institutions is without doubt the guide's main asset. Along with it runs the difficulty in disentangling studies from restricted views in the hope of reaching a balanced idea of what religious orders were in an age of feudal expansion, which meant settlements, but also ecclesiastical reform, new lands, but also novel forms of spirituality. The same applies too, for example, to studies on the Cistercians. This analysis is equally valid for the solid work Ayala has recently produced on the military orders in Spain. In eight hundred pages, the book offers all sorts of detail about them and the author's effort to provide the facts deserves praise. Nevertheless, he describes, but does not explain. As happened in the brief general overview he published in 1998, the introductory chapters are too feeble to sustain the massive edifice. They show the widespread tendency of Spanish medieval historiography to prescind from a firm West European and Mediterranean background on which to anchor Spanish developments. In the main sections of the book, information is provided in a neat but unhistorical way that follows no rational sequence. The arrangement of the chapters does not follow the logic of historical development, while the religious character of the orders is consigned to a marginal place.[28]

The lack of general overviews of the different orders has been a common trend often indicated in bibliographical essays. Huge domains, a long term spanning several centuries, and the overwhelming number of sources are among the reasons put forward by one scholar to justify that absence.[29] Conversely, publications on the Castilian Templars and on the short-lived Orders of San Marcos de León and Santa

---

[27]   A companion volume in the same collection, which deals with Castilian orders in the early modern period, favours a distinct interpretative approach. See José Ignacio Ruiz Rodríguez, *Las Órdenes Militares castellanas en la Edad Moderna* (Madrid, 2001).

[28]   See *supra*, note 21.

[29]   Miguel Ángel Ladero Quesada, 'La investigación sobre Órdenes Militares', 12.

María de España have been rendered possible by the fact that the time spans, the territories involved, and the relevant information available were comparatively very limited.[30] This opinion restricts the possibilities of such work to institutions that are manageable in terms of data, and conveys the idea that overviews are ultimately formed by extracts from documents. If that were so, summaries of the histories of the major military and religious orders would hardly ever be feasible, as it is almost impossible to gain complete mastery of all relevant information in its minutest detail. On the other hand, it is highly debatable whether a historical synthesis should be so construed. Rather than attaching the greatest importance to archival documentation, one should perhaps assign primacy to global interpretation. This does not lie in registers waiting to be picked up; it is born of the historian's mind in constant contact with his sources. So it is not tenable to claim that such significant a vacuum in the studies of the military orders derives from insufficient knowledge of the data. The reason goes deeper and has probably something to do with the higher analytical than synthetical skills of Spanish historians. The educational system, at its secondary and university levels, certainly does not favour the latter. The English essay or the French *composition* is unknown to the Spanish student. Intellectual parochialism, which has by no means disappeared in Spain, is another obstacle; it is not easy to take an overview when eyes and mind are permanently focused on a local or regional level. The fact that the main advance made in the study of the military orders has been confined for all intents and purposes to those born and bred on Spanish soil has been of little help too. Those studying Santiago or Calatrava, Alcántara or Montesa have failed to look beyond the Pyrenees or the Western Mediterranean shores. These orders were strictly peninsular institutions. But the Templars and the Hospitallers have hardly received any better treatment.

Carlos Barquero Goñi, a scholar who has worked extensively on the history of the Hospitallers, has devoted one of the few general surveys on the military orders in medieval Spain to the Order of St John.[31] The structure of the book follows the main lines of other studies written by members of Carlos de Ayala's team. The general descriptive approach and the considerable weight given to the analysis of the Order's landed property, constituting a third of the text, are highly representative of this type of study. The paragraph introducing the chapter on Hospitaller domains clearly depicts the theoretical basis of this approach: 'It is only reasonable to think,' he writes, 'that the foundations of the power, the influence, and the activities of the Order of St John in the Iberian Peninsula during the Middle Ages must have been its goods, properties and domains.'[32] This statement seems to be of a historical materialism type, but there are subtler forms of this theory that do not ignore the fact that the foundations lay on the religious standing of the military orders within a Latin

---

[30] Gonzalo Martínez Díez, *Los Templarios en la Corona de Castilla* (Madrid, 1993); Juan Torres Fontes, 'La Orden de Santa María de España', *Miscelánea Medieval Murciana*, iii (1977), 73-118; José Luis Martín Rodríguez, 'La Orden Militar de San Marcos de León', in *León y su Historia. Miscelánea Histórica*, iv (León, 1977), 19-100.

[31] Carlos Barquero Goñi, *Los caballeros hospitalarios durante la Edad Media en España* (Burgos, 2003).

[32] Ibid., 17.

Church that had experienced a radical change since the second half of the eleventh century. It is obvious that those institutions formed part of the manorial world – it could not be otherwise; but it was not at that level that they found their *raison d'être*. They received manors because they represented a new and popular path to salvation and certainly not the other way around. When this issue, crystal clear though it is, is disregarded, when material living is highlighted and spiritual forces are ignored, the historical meaning of the military-religious orders is bound to remain obscure and incomprehensible. Nevertheless, as with all other works of this type, Barquero's book is very useful in providing information.

As it is widely known, the orders founded in the Holy Land were predominant in the Crown of Aragon, owing to the compensations made in 1140 and 1143, when the controversies raised by Alfonso I's will had been finally settled. In 1131 Alfonso had bequeathed the kingdoms of Aragon and Navarre to the Temple, the Hospital, and the Holy Sepulchre. Calatrava and Santiago held some territories there, namely the commanderies of Alcañiz and Montalbán in southern Aragon, which have been thoroughly studied,[33] together with certain rights and rents in other places. But Templar and Hospitaller prominence has led me to restrict the focus in eastern Spain to these two orders along with the fourteenth-century offshoot of Montesa.

In the 1970s, Josep Maria Sans i Travé began to study the Catalan Templars under the direction of Emilio Sáez. More than twenty years later he produced a general survey, the first of its kind after the classic work by Joaquím Miret i Sans of 1910.[34] It may be regarded as an overall reflection after years of work on the subject, and it provides a good insight into the character of the regional histories of the orders. Three aspects (identified below) are common to similar works produced anywhere else in Spain; the fourth is peculiar to ample sectors of Catalan historiography. The first pages of *Els Templers Catalans* betray a very superficial knowledge of the crusades. Runciman is extensively quoted; a venerable figure no doubt, but he is the only authority cited, as if nothing else has been produced since 1951. Quotations lead to similar observations. It would appear that after long years of research on the subject, the author does not entertain any personal opinion on the general history of the Templars. He relies entirely on the works of Malcolm Barber and Alain Demurger. These are indeed excellent guides, of course, but one is allowed to expect some new ideas. Moreover, references to the Hospital are few and far between, and are always based on Santos García Larragueta's study of 1957.[35] The overall approach is symptomatic – anything that has no immediate relation to Catalan territory (one might as well include Castilian, Aragonese, or Valencian lands in similar studies) is of no interest beyond an introductory cliché.

---

[33] Carlos Laliena Corbera, *Sistema social, estructura agraria y organización del poder en el Bajo Aragón en la Edad Media (siglos XII-XV)* (Teruel, 1987). Regina Sáinz de la Maza Lasoli, *La Orden de Santiago en la Corona de Aragón. La Encomienda de Montalbán (1210-1327)* (Saragossa, 1980); id., *La Orden de Santiago en la Corona de Aragón. ii: La Encomienda de Montalbán bajo Vidal de Molina (1327-1357)* (Saragossa, 1988).

[34] Josep Maria Sans i Travé, *Els Templers catalans. De la rosa a la creu* (Lleida, 1996); Joaquím Miret i Sans, *Les cases de Templers i Hospitalers en Catalunya* (Barcelona, 1910).

[35] Santos García Larragueta, *El gran priorado de Navarra de la Orden de San Juan de Jerusalén (siglos XII-XIII)*, 2 vols (Pamplona, 1957).

A cursory look at the index of Sans i Travé's book brings one back to the previous question of the character of general surveys. Almost a third of the volume is devoted to a minute description of the basic facts known for each commandery, and there are twenty-five of them. That clutter of unrelated bits of information adds very little to our knowledge of the Order in Catalonia. Neither is recourse to the Rule or the *Retraits* very revealing of Templar life there when the author touches certain aspects that are not sufficiently documented. It is quite obvious that norms cannot be taken as everyday practices.

Alan Forey's masterpiece on the Templars in the Crown of Aragon offers a balanced and sober view of all aspects.[36] It also offers a sharp contrast with the pervasive tone of Catalan nationalism in Sans i Travé's book. Gross historical anachronisms apart, the latter work gives the impression that relevance lies not with the Templars themselves, but with the glorious fact of their being Catalan, whatever that may have meant in the twelfth and thirteenth centuries. No wonder that little attention is paid to the crusades or to general Templar history. The hot seasoning of Catalanism has naturally not been added to the only other regional history of the Order published in 1993 – that devoted to the Castilian Templars and written by Gonzalo Martínez Díez, emeritus professor of the History of Law in the University of Valladolid.[37] The structure of the index is almost identical to that of Sans i Travé's: origins and expansion, growth of domains in different ages, commanderies, and dissolution. The space devoted to the description of Templar convents is even greater here, though this heavy leaning is welcome because of a dearth of information on the Temple in Castile and Leon. The second longest section of the book is dedicated to the abrupt end of the Order, the obvious final part of all such treatises.[38] Martínez Díez had to squeeze the scanty Castilian information dry. Eastern Spain is fortunate in having abundant documentary material kept at the archives of the Crown of Aragon in Barcelona. Sans i Travé's treatment of this theme, based on his previous work on the dissolution of the Temple,[39] is restricted to two main sources: the royal register number 291 and Heinrich Finke's transcriptions.[40] There is ample space for a more comprehensive approach to the years 1307-19, based on a wider range of documentation, as Alan Forey has shown in a new book.[41] One of the many negative consequences of overspecialization and wild productivity and competition is insufficient and superficial contact with the basic material. Unnecessary haste forces concentration on an increasingly narrow basis of information.

María Luisa Ledesma Rubio was, until her death a few years ago, the main exponent of studies on the military orders in Aragon. Her doctoral thesis focused

---

[36]   Alan Forey, *The Templars in the Corona de Aragón* (London, 1973).

[37]   Gonzalo Martínez Díez, *Los Templarios en la Corona de Castilla* (Burgos, 1993).

[38]   In a recent general study of the Templars in the Spanish kingdoms, Gonzalo Martínez Díez repeats this pattern, underscoring the importance of the years 1307-12, which thus receive the same attention as the previous two centuries. See *Los templarios en los reinos de España* (Barcelona, 2001).

[39]   Josep María Sans i Travé, *El procés dels Templers catalans. Entre el turment i la glòria*, 2nd edn. (Lleida, 1991).

[40]   Heinrich Finke, *Papsttum und Untergang des Templerordens* (Münster, 1907).

[41]   Alan Forey, *The Fall of the Templars in the Crown of Aragon* (Aldershot, 2001).

on the Hospitaller commandery of Saragossa;[42] her supervisor was José María Lacarra de Miguel, the master of post-civil-war medieval studies at the University of Saragossa. That work and the classic monograph by García Larragueta on the Order of St John in Navarre were in the late sixties, and still are today, the main shining lights on Hospitaller activities in the higher and middle Ebro valley. In 1982 and 1994, Ledesma Rubio published two general histories of the military orders in the Kingdom of Aragon. We shall concentrate on the former, which dealt specifically with the Templars and the Hospitallers.[43] Once again, the structure of the book is similar to that of works that have already been discussed on the Temple. All of them resemble very much the basic pattern of Forey's survey of 1973, with only some minor changes, including one feature common to all the works already mentioned and to most of the ones to come: the unproblematic character of their approach. Their descriptive method allows little room for problems. Such historians appear to be sailing on a waveless sea of evidence and ignoring the undercurrents.

When discussing the Order of St John, we cannot overlook the great contribution made by Anthony Luttrell to Spanish Hospitaller studies and his influence on Spaniards working on the subject. He has undoubtedly helped to widen the horizons of many scholars by inducing them to leave the commandery temporarily and travel eastwards across the Mediterranean to Rhodes. This is a voyage that Juan Fernández de Heredia had undertaken several times. Through Luttrell's research papers on the Master and other related topics, historians of the Crown of Aragon have profitably followed that intellectual route.[44]

The world of the Catalan Hospitallers has not yet been given an overall assessment. Pierre Bonneaud has just published a book on this theme, covering the first part of the fifteenth century, but a general survey on the complete medieval period is still a desideratum.[45] This gap has been partially filled by an interesting work written from the perspective of southern Catalonia, though it is far more ambitious.[46] María Bonet Donato has studied one of the provinces of the Order in eastern Spain, the Castellany of Amposta, in the Late Middle Ages. The title suggests a wider time span, but the author has concentrated mainly on the post-1319 period, the year when Hospitaller provincial administration was rearranged in the Crown of Aragon as a result of the new developments that emerged in the wake of the dissolution of the Temple. The old single unit was now divided in two – the Priory of Catalonia and the Castellany of Amposta, which covered the Kingdom of Aragon and Catalan territories on the Lower Ebro valley. The chapters of the book, rather than simply juxtaposing information, follow a logical sequence, leading from the general organization of the

---

[42]   María Luisa Ledesma Rubio, *La encomienda de Zaragoza de la Orden de San Juan de Jersusalén en los siglos XII y XIII* (Saragossa, 1967).

[43]   María Luisa Ledesma Rubio, *Templarios y Hospitalarios en el Reino de Aragón* (Saragossa, 1982); id., *Las Órdenes Militares en Aragón* (Saragossa, 1994).

[44]   Several articles by Anthony Luttrell have been published by Ashgate in its Variorum Reprint Series.

[45]   Pierre Bonneaud, *Le prieuré de Catalogne, le couvent de Rhodes et la couronne d'Aragon, 1415-1447* (Millau, 2004).

[46]   María Bonet Donato, *La Orden del Hospital en la Corona de Aragón. Poder y gobierno en la Castellanía de Amposta (ss. XII-XV)* (Madrid, 1994).

district at different levels to the particulars of a convent, that of Ulldecona. This is one of the few works that approach the commandery within the wider perspective of the province and of the Order as a whole. Unlike most other studies, this work refrains from giving the impression that these Hospitaller units constituted a world of their own.

The minor military orders have also been taken into consideration. San Jorge de Alfama, whose small set of domains lay north of the Ebro delta, has been studied by Regina Sáinz de la Maza, another member of that group of historians introduced to the military orders by Emilio Sáez.[47] The origins of this military order, the various stages in its short history, ranging from the thirteenth century to the time it reached its highest peak between the 1360s and 1380s, followed by the crisis which led to its absorption by Montesa in 1400, the nature of its domains, its rents and finances – all these constitute the various sections of this brief work, a significant contribution to the knowledge of a second-rank institution. The book contains an appendix of about two hundred carefully transcribed documents. The inclusion of additional material, such as this appendix, was a usual feature in traditional studies. Today it is becoming increasingly rare, owing to the reaction against what was disdainfully regarded years ago as empirical historiography and to some extent it still is. Today students of medieval history are inadequately trained in basic skills, like palaeography or a decent knowledge of Latin. Young and not so young historians suffer from this. We have in fact got what we deserve. I can still recall our outcries in the early seventies against Latin, Greek, or any other similar subject, in favour of courses with more ideological content – seminars on Herbert Marcuse, for instance – when Spanish universities, in the midst of the final crisis of Francoism, had no intellectual authority that we could respect. It is true that transcriptions are no substitute for history and should in no way be used as a diversion from the historian's true commitment to explain the past; but it is equally true that the publication of a select number of documents that can help to illustrate the writer's interpretation can be of immense value.

One has simply to cross the river Cenia, south of the commandery of Ulldecona, which has been studied by María Bonet, to get into the old Kingdom of Valencia. The military orders had played a significant role in the thirteenth-century conquest of that kingdom and were awarded territories in compensation, especially in the northern regions. Later Templar landed estates there increased considerably too, either through exchange of property or through direct purchase.[48] There is no general treatment of these institutions for the pre-1319 period, apart from the information given by Alan Forey in his seminal book on the Templars in Crown of Aragón.[49] In spite of

---

[47]   Regina Sáinz de la Maza Lasoli, *La Orden de San Jorge de Alfama. Aproximación a su historia* (Barcelona, 1990).

[48]   Luis García-Guijarro, 'The Growth of the Order of the Temple in the Northern Area of the Kingdom of Valencia at the Close of the Thirteenth Century: A Puzzling Development?', in *Knighthoods of Christ: Essays on the History of the Crusades and the Knights Templar, Presented to Malcolm Barber*, ed. Norman Housley (Aldershot, 2007), 165-81.

[49]   See *supra*, note 36. See though Eugenio Díaz Manteca, 'Notas para el estudio de los antecedentes históricos de Montesa', *Estudis Castellonencs*, ii (1984-85), 235-305.

Robert Burns's enormous contribution to the study of what he calls 'The Crusader Kingdom of Valencia', his chapter on the military orders is of no great value. Owing to its many inaccuracies, it could not have been a positive starting point for research in the decades that followed.[50] In 1319, the papal bull issued two years earlier to establish a new strictly Valencian *militia* was put into effect. It marked the birth of the Order of Montesa. A complete history of this order, covering the period from its origins to 1592, the year when it was incorporated with the Crown, has not yet been written. Nor is there a general account of any aspect of its historical development, except perhaps for a few valuable short studies on very narrow themes. A book written in 1986 by Enric Guinot Rodríguez might give the wrong impression that it is a contribution to our knowledge of pre- and early Montesian times. It is not. The orders of the Temple, the Hospital, and Montesa, are simply a documentary excuse to fit into them a theoretical model, which is a restrictive interpretation of historical materialism synonymous with sheer economism. The title is not entirely misleading for it indeed refers to 'expansive feudalism' in northern Valencia, but it makes no reference to the military orders, other than in minuscule type in the subtitle, inside, but not on the cover.[51] That in itself would not create a serious problem; it would have indeed been an asset had the concept of feudalism encompassed the whole of society in its material and spiritual manifestations. Rather, feudalism in this work is restricted solely to production, an orthodox and structuralist trend of Marxist ideas imported from Louis Althusser's circle (especially Marta Harnecker's cathecism) and from French historians like Guy Bois.[52] The Templars, the Hospitallers, and the Montesians were simply forces that extorted rents and other dues from Valencian peasants. It is no surprise then that this work's documentary foundations are feeble; there are no signs of any intensive research done at the archives of Madrid or Barcelona, where most of the sources on the military orders are to be found. Evidence is used simply to confirm the main lines of a pre-established scheme, not an inch further. Guinot's book does little favour to historical materialism as it shows the least flexible and dialectical side of the theory, while at the same time it conceals the great possibilities it has for integrated studies of the military orders.

Guinot's study betrays evident reliance on some French theoretical models. That raises the question of the methodological and theoretical originality of Spanish works on the military orders, and indeed of Spanish medieval historiography in the last decades. Spanish historians tend to get rather annoyed when foreign scholars, the Americans in particular, tend to refer only to Claudio Sánchez Albornoz, Américo Castro, or Jaume Vicens-Vives, as if these were the only Spanish scholars of any

---

[50]   Robert Ignatius Burns, *The Crusader Kingdom of Valencia. Reconstruction on a Thirteenth-Century Frontier*, i (Cambridge, Mass., 1967), 173-96.

[51]   Enric Guinot Rodríguez, *Feudalismo en expansión en el norte valenciano. Antecedentes y desarrollo del señorío de la Orden de Montesa. Siglos XIII y XIV* (Castellón, 1986).

[52]   Apart from Marta Harnecker, *Los conceptos elementales del materialismo histórico*, 7th edn. (Madrid, 1976), two highly influential works were widely read by history students in the late seventies and eighties. These were Ciro Flamarion Santana Cardoso and Héctor Pérez Brignoli, *Los métodos de la historia: introducción a los problemas, métodos y técnicas de la historia demográfica, económica y social* (Barcelona, 1976); and Joseph Fontana Lázaro, *Historia: análisis del pasado y proyecto social* (Barcelona, 1982).

worth in the twentieth century. Adeline Rucquoi's remark, in a Festschrift in honour of Jacques Le Goff, that Spanish medieval historians had no intellectual personality of their own and that they were just followers of the first generation of the Annales school, caused an uproar among Spanish medievalists.[53] Apart from the fact that the three eminent Spanish historians had either lived in the United States or had had their books translated into English there, and making some allowance for Rucquoi's imperial cultural hubris, there is perhaps some truth in these statements. Creativity in method and theory has been weak in Spain since 1975. No constructs such as those of Sánchez Albornoz or Américo Castro, nor wide-range enterprising personalities like that of Vicens Vives capable of a thorough analysis and a brilliant synthesis have emerged. The reason is obvious. They were not children of an authoritarian regime: the first two lived in exile; the third belonged to the Catalan cultural élite which remained uninterruptedly wide open to European currents of thought.

The end of ideological constraints after 1975 did not unlock the door to innovation in methods and theories of research in Spain. There has been a tendency to import from the 'centres' ideas about how to treat material or interpret it. The Braudelian flavour of this intellectual flow to the Spanish 'periphery' is evident. Regional histories, socio-economic studies, frontier or colonial models, structuralism in its diverse forms – all evident in the studies of the military orders that have already been discussed – have come from abroad. Before 1975, Spain exported raw material in the form of making our archives accessible to foreign scholars; today Spanish historians tend to process much of these sources themselves, but they still rely to a great extent on foreign guidance to do it. There can be no doubt that this situation is the outcome of decades of cultural seclusion that limited views to the peninsula and cut historians away from wider intellectual horizons beyond its shores. That gap cannot be bridged over easily. Criticism of empirical approaches and theoretical poverty have driven Spanish historians to a twofold deficiency – no solid basis of original data and no interpretative threads. These conditions encouraged native scholars to seek solutions abroad and fall prey to foreign intellectual fireworks, while important contributions from beyond the Pyrenees have remained on a secondary level.

The growth of research interest in Castilian-Leonese military orders has been no less remarkable, and it has definitely been organized in a more coherent way. A significant number of studies have appeared as a result of such research. The point of departure has also had an Anglo-Spanish character. Eloy Benito Ruano had shown constant interest in the military orders since the 1950s.[54] In 1965 Derex Lomax published an overview in Spanish of the Order of Santiago up to 1275. It had an immediate influence on students and scholars.[55] Since the late 1950s Joseph

---

[53]   Adeline Rucquoi, 'Spanish Medieval History and the *Annales*: Between Franco and Marx', in *The Work of Jacques Le Goff and the Challenges of Medieval History*, ed. Miri Rubin (Woodbridge, 1997), 123-41. The title of the article is as unfortunate as its contents. Some interesting comments are just like drops of water in an ocean of serious historiographical errors, gross oversimplifications, and an intellectual arrogance which has no corresponding intellectual base.

[54]   For several of his works, Lomax, *Las Órdenes Militares*, 75.

[55]   Derek W. Lomax, *La Orden de Santiago (1170-1275)* (Madrid, 1965).

O'Callaghan had been working on Calatrava. Variorum Reprints published a selection of his papers in 1975;[56] its impact too was considerable. A year earlier, José Luis Martín Rodríguez had published a book on the origins of the Order of Santiago.[57] It was the first published research which emerged from the student groups gathered around Emilio Sáez Sánchez.

Mention has already been made of the two groups that took up research in central and southern Spain. Through the academic posts he held at the universities of La Laguna (Tenerife), Seville, and Madrid, Miguel Ángel Ladero produced researches on the military orders in the fifteenth century, the period of his special interest, and particularly on rents and finance, one of his favourite research themes. A project to unearth the wealth of one class of documentation, the Visitation Books, was developed in three doctoral theses – Emma Solano Ruiz worked on Calatrava's landed property in New Castile; Daniel Rodríguez Blanco researched the Order of Santiago in Extremadura; and Pedro Andrés Porras Arboledas studied the Order of Santiago in the province of Castile.[58] The three theses shared a distinctive pattern: a short political and institutional introduction, followed by a detailed description of socio-economic aspects of the orders under survey; in two of the books, appendices of quantitative material were added.[59] These features are common to many other studies: they provide regional narrative histories of institutions, whose religious character is almost overlooked.

Carlos de Ayala's research team has focused its attention on an earlier period, from the mid-twelfth century to mid-fourteenth, and has followed lines that complement or enrich those pursued by Lomax and O'Callaghan on Santiago and Calatrava. Carlos Barquero Goñi has also dealt with the Hospitallers in several studies.[60] Apart from Barquero's general survey on the Order of St John, two books have been produced as a result of these efforts so far. The first was by Enrique Rodríguez-Picavea Matilla on Calatrava in the region of La Mancha.[61] It is interesting to compare this work with that by Emma Solano; both works deal with the same institution and geographical area; they differ only in the period studied. They devote considerable space to the commanderies, just under a third of the whole work; they contain a detailed study of the economic structure. These and the other parts of the books are integrated

---

[56]   Joseph F. O'Callaghan, *The Spanish Military Order of Calatrava and its Affiliates* (London, 1975).

[57]   José Luis Martín Rodríguez, *Orígenes de la orden militar de Santiago (1170-1195)* (Barcelona, 1974).

[58]   Emma Solano Ruiz, *La Orden de Calatrava en el siglo XV. Los señoríos castellanos de la Orden al fin de la Edad Media* (Seville, 1978). Daniel Rodríguez Blanco, *La Orden de Santiago en Extremadura en la Baja Edad Media (Siglos XIV-XV)* (Badajoz, 1985). Pedro Andrés Porras Arboledas, *La Orden de Santiago en el siglo XV. La Provincia de Castilla* (Madrid, 1997).

[59]   For a summary, *supra*, note 16.

[60]   A list of his publications appeared in Carlos de Ayala *et al.*, *Las Órdenes Militares*, i, 147-48.

[61]   Enrique Rodríguez-Picavea Matilla, *La formación del feudalismo en la meseta meridional castellana. Los señoríos de la Orden de Calatrava en los siglos XII-XIII* (Madrid, 1994).

though within different intellectual frameworks – a purely descriptive approach in Emma Solano's, a distinctly historical materialistic outlook in Enrique Rodríguez-Picavea's. The structure of the latter's book does not challenge orthodoxy: domains and their economic use lie at the base of the social relations of production expressed in feudal rents and dues. This clear theoretical leaning appears in the title and subtitle of the book: *La formación del feudalismo en la meseta meridional castellana: Los señoríos de la Orden de Calatrava en los siglos XII-XIII* (The formation of feudalism on the southern Castilian plateau: The domains of the Order of Calatrava in the twelfth and thirteenth centuries). The great resemblance with Enrique Guinot's title is quite revealing. Once again, within the framework of the military-religious orders, feudalism has been restricted to the infrastructure and any reference to religion suppressed. A recent effort to deal with the military orders in the territories of La Mancha by a scholar native to the area but unrelated to Ayala's team has been explicitly limited to the contribution the orders of Calatrava, Santiago, and the Hospitallers made to the repopulation of those lands. The book shows no concern with other issues.[62]

The Order of Alcántara had until very recently lacked a proper study. Some years ago, Bonifacio Palacios Martín set up a research group with the aim of collecting documentary source material to publish a *diplomatarium* to make up for the destruction of the central archive at San Benito de Alcántara in the Peninsular War.[63] The collection began to appear in 2000.[64] This type of work has been supplemented by general approaches to the history of the institution. The book by Feliciano Novoa Portela was the second thesis supervised by Carlos de Ayala to reach us almost in full length.[65] The theory and methods were similar here to those prevalent in other works written by members of that research group. The author devoted two-thirds of the whole space to a detailed description of Alcántara's domains and to the rent that they produced. Origins, organization, and external relationships were all squeezed into the remaining third. It is quite relevant to this view of the military orders that Alcántara's link to the Apostolic See was considered as external to the Order, alien to its basic core. As such, it could be confined to a few descriptive pages in the last chapter of the book.[66]

One of the most significant contributions to the study of the Order of Alcántara came in 1999 with Luis Corral Val's *Los monjes soldados de la orden de Alcántara en la Edad Media*,[67] which brought a breath of fresh air to the historical approach to

---

[62]   Francisco Ruiz Gómez, *Los orígenes de las Órdenes Militares y la repoblación de los territorios de La Mancha* (Madrid, 2003).

[63]   For a description of this project, Bonifacio Palacios Martín, 'Proyecto Alcántara. Un intento de reconstrucción de la colección diplomática de la Orden de Alcántara', *Medievalismo. Boletín de la Sociedad Española de Estudios Medievales*, v (1995), 301-304.

[64]   *Colección diplomática medieval de la Orden de Alcántara (1157?-1494): De los orígenes a 1454*, ed. Bonifacio Palacios Martín (Madrid, 2000).

[65]   Feliciano Novoa Portela, *La Orden de Alcántara y Extremadura (siglos XII-XIV)* (Mérida, 2000).

[66]   Novoa, *La Orden de Alcántara*, 281-89.

[67]   Luis Corral Val, *Los monjes soldados de la orden de Alcántara en la Edad Media. Su organización institucional y vida religiosa* (Madrid, 1999).

the military orders. Rather than focusing on the economic and social aspects, Corral Val looked into the institutional organization and the spiritual life of Alcántara. Basic aspects, like the Order's relationship with the papacy and its religious practices in general, were given appropriate attention. This study has helped to usher in an intellectual process that should redress the balance, which has been so much tilted in favour of socio-economic works; it should also free feudalism from the grip of economism and extend the concept to all human activity in the Middle Ages.

To conclude, three observations are necessary. The historical materialistic trend followed by some of the works discussed above is mostly based on the debatable identification of feudal rents and dues with feudalism. That link derives from an interpretation of historical materialism that favours simple forms of economism. This view determines the character of society from the relationship between the forces of production and social relations of production, and therefore with rents and dues which are considered as the visible sign of that interaction. An approach such as this leads research into quantitative methods to estimate the amounts extracted from peasants, but it does not get us anywhere nearer to understanding better these feudal societies whose distinctive features were essentially qualitative. This explains why most of what might be considered neo-Marxist studies on the military orders have adopted a descriptive methodology in their approach to rents and dues. In the process, they have disregarded other basic non-economic aspects, which could not only bring to light the inner character of such payments made by peasants, but also help to bury forever that most futile recourse to the idea of 'non-economic constraints'.

A great number of the studies on the military orders have been confined to lands conquered from the Muslims from the twelfth century onwards. The old myth of a *Reconquista*, based on a continuous aspiration to reconstruct the broken Visigothic unity, has made way to the idea of territorial expansion and settlement. Feudal rents, non-Marxist models, like frontier or colonial schemes, and sometimes a mixture of the whole, have tried to unveil the main features of that society. The intellectual inclination towards getting to know better the organization of new or old lands perhaps explains the primacy enjoyed by socio-economic studies and the consideration of the military orders as mere agents of resettlement. The approach leads neatly to the study of rents and finances.

It is that approach which ultimately explains why in their treatment of the history of the military-religious orders, Spanish historians have almost completely disregarded the various religious roles they played. These ranged from the spiritual life of their members as individuals or as part of a community, to their function as institutions on the broader map of Latin Christendom, and to the part history assigned to them in the development of ecclesiastical reform and in the life of the Church in the fourteenth and fifteenth centuries. It is true that archival documentation that provides insights of a socio-economic nature is by far much vaster, and that scholars tend to fall into the trap of trying to reconstruct the military orders on the basis of that information only. The answer, however, is not found primarily in the archives; it lies firmly in the historian's mind. One of the most negative intellectual consequences of Francoism in Spanish medieval historiography has been the prevailing suspicion of anything related to Church history, which was deemed an unworthy and reactionary intellectual pursuit by most historians. As has already been indicated, that deep distrust still survives today, and it applies to the approach to the history of the military orders as it does to that of Benedictine or Cistercian monasteries. This reluctance to undertake any rational historical analysis of spiritual life or of its institutionalization in the Church explains the dearth of serious crusade studies. In brief, the *Transición* has been neither as promising nor as optimistic for the study of the military orders as the sheer number of publications might imply. With no place allotted anywhere for the study of the crusades or for the religious character of the military orders, with major theoretical weaknesses, and with the domineering power of localism, it can be claimed that the general context of Spain's medieval historiography over the last twenty-five years has been the loser. I would not like, however, to depict Spanish historiography on the military orders in such a disparaging manner. Useful and valuable work has indeed been done, and possible failure is common to other national historiographies. It is worth recalling at this stage the popular Spanish proverb *En todos los sitios cuecen habas* ('It is the same the whole world round'). Following the metaphors so dear to David Cannadine, there are more 'truffle hunters' everywhere than 'parachutists'.[68]

---

[68]   Cited by David Snowman, *Historians* (Basingstoke, 2007), 14 and 24.

Chapter 4

The Knights Templar between Theatre and History: Raynouard's works on the Templars (1805–1813)

Alain Demurger

Historians still find useful information about the Templars in *Les Monumens historiques relatifs à la condamnation des chevaliers du Temple et à l'abolition de leur ordre*, which Raynouard wrote and published in 1813. But they pay no attention to another work by the same author: *Les Templiers*, a tragedy performed with great success in May 1805 on the stage of the Théatre Français. This paper sets out to examine the relationship between these two works, to try to explain Raynouard's purpose in writing them, and then to turn to various aspects of the play's success. It will end by stressing the importance of the subject of the Templars in the Napoleonic period.[1]

Just-François-Marie Raynouard was born in 1761 at Brignolles in Provence. He was a barrister and followed the first steps of the Revolution as a Girondin. He came to Paris with some pieces of poetry and the ambition to succeed in a literary career. And success – nothing short of a triumph – came in 1805 with *Les Templiers*. It opened to him the doors of the Institut. He wrote another historical play, *Les Etats de Blois*, but the censor forbade its performance. It was then, with the transfer to Paris in 1810 of the Vatican's Secret Archives, that Raynouard had the opportunity to pursue new researches into the Templars and so to bring together the materials for his historical work, *Les Monumens historiques*.

As an independent spirit, Raynouard survived the various changes of regime and devoted the last twenty years of his life to the Institut and to philological researches into the Occitan language and troubadour poetry. He died in Paris in 1836.[2]

---

[1]   François Just Marie Raynouard, *Les Templiers*, *Tragédie en cinq actes* (Paris, 1805: repr. Nîmes, Lacour éditeur, 1997). *Les Templiers, tragédie, suivie de l'extrait de la tragédie espagnole des Templiers par Perez de Montalban* (rev. edn.: Paris, 1815). The 1815 revised version of *Les Templiers* and Raynouard's second tragedy, *Les Etats de Blois*, were published by Ch. Nodier, *Bibliothèque dramatique ou répertoire universel du théâtre français, 4ᵉ série. Auteurs contemporains* (Paris, 1824). *Monumens historiques relatifs à la condamnation des chevaliers de l'Ordre du Temple et à l'abolition de leur ordre* (Paris, 1813).

[2]   *Dictionnaire Napoleon*, ed. J. Tulard (Paris, 1989), 1442.

HISTORICAL TRAGEDY AND ITS HISTORICAL BACKGROUND

Let us examine the play, first performed in May 1805. Its dramatic force turns on various conflicts. One pits the Knights Templars' enemies against their friends: the king, Marigny, and Nogaret against the queen, the constable, and Marigny's son. A second features two strong-willed men: the king, Philippe IV le Bel, and Molay, the Grand Master. The former thinks the Templars are guilty but he is ready to forgive them if they, in the person of Molay, are prepared to recognize their guilt. Molay declines the offer: the Templars' honour is incompatible with an admission guilt: 'J'aime à vous pardoner. Je vous offre la vie', the King says, but Molay answers: 'Sire, offrez-nous l'honneur'.[3] Thirdly there is the conflict between love and duty with the character, created by Raynouard, of the young Marigny, the son of Philippe's first minister, who is secretly a member of the Order of the Temple. Of course he will choose duty!

Raynouard took some liberties with a history he knew well, but that is the privilege of the poet! The queen died in 1305; the character of the young Marigny is not historical; and the constable, Gaucher de Châtillon, played no part in the trial of the Templars. The character of Molay, the Grand Master, steady and determined, bears no resemblance to that of the historical figure.

The play was presented to the Théatre Français and accepted. The censor's intervention was insignificant: some verses were suppressed or altered. Censorship was exercised by the Bureau des Théatres dependant of the Police Ministry (the minister was Fouché). It should be noted that censorship was not definitely established before 8 June 1806.[4] The first performance was given on 14 May, with famous actors including Talma and Mademoiselle George. At that time the Théatre Français was under the guardianship of the Comte de Rémusat, *Intendant des Spectacles* and first chamberlain of the emperor. In this capacity he often had to be away from Paris, accompanying the emperor on his travels, and often going ahead of him. However, his wife, Elizabeth de Vergennes, comtesse de Rémusat, wrote to him every day and gave him (and us) a great deal of news and precise information about the shows and plays performed in Paris. She attended the general rehearsal of the new play, *Les Templiers*, and she paid much attention to its fortunes.[5] Public reception was enthusiastic; newspaper critics were positive. Only Julien Geoffroy, the fearsome critic of the almost official *Journal des Débats (de l'Empire)* disagreed with the general opinion.[6] Later, in 1815, Raynouard produced a new version of his play in which he introduced noticeable and interesting changes. This new version is, dramatically, far better than that of 1805.

Soon afterwards, on 26 June 1805, the play was published. As a preface to this edition, Raynouard wrote an important 'Précis historique sur les templiers'. It was

---

³   *Les Templiers* (1815 edn.), Act V, Scene v.

⁴   Henri. Welschinger, *la Censure sous le Consulat et le premier Empire* (Paris,1887)

⁵   *Lettres de Madame de Rémusat, 1804-1814, publiées par son petit-fils Paul de Rémusat*, 2 vols. (Paris, 1881), i, 122-6, 146.

⁶   *Journal des Débats (de l'Empire)*, 16 May 1805. Reproduced in J. Geoffroy, *Cours de Littérature dramatqiue*, 6 vols (Paris, 1825), iv, 334-40.

here that he revealed himself as a historian. He directed his demonstration like a historian, using a historical method. He used valuable documentation: manuscript sources, including the Trésor des Chartes, the 'Collection Gaignière', and the trial documents; printed primary materials from the publications of Martène, Henriquez, Dupuy, and Baluze; and medieval narratives, such as the works by William of Tyre, Matthew Paris, and John of Saint-Victor. Raynouard knew the Molay confessions, and he tried to explain them: in his view the Grand Master wanted to save his Order, and, when he realized he had failed, he changed his attitude and retracted.[7] As already indicated, the Molay of the tragedy was not the historical character; Raynouard was well aware of this fact.

So *Les Monumens historiques* of 1813 must be understood as a development of the 1805 'Précis'. Raynouard used new materials from the Vatican Archives, then in Paris, and he extended his inquiry to all European countries. He published a list of the original documents he was using for the first time, and he presented many tables and gave abstracts of the various trials throughout Europe. When *Les Templiers* was reprinted in 1823, *Les Monumens historiques* was added to the play, although without the annexes, as a substitute for the 'Précis'.

THE AUTHOR'S REASONS AND THE REASONS FOR SUCCESS

Raynouard's purpose is set out clearly in the short preface to *Les Monumens*. He wished to solve a historical problem – to prove the innocence of the Templars and, by so doing, contribute to the glory of his homeland. For him, of course, the Order of the Temple was French, and he considered its rehabilitation a patriotic cause. To Raynouard, theatre and history complemented each other as valuable instruments for the nation's instruction.

The success of the play can be rated by using different criteria. The number of performances is one such criterion: there were thirty-eight in 1805, despite two long interruptions caused by Talma's illness.[8] Each evening the theatre was full, and the public enthusiastic. The publication of the play as early as 26 June is another indicator. According to Julien Geoffroy, who gave a ferocious criticism of that publication in two articles in the *Journal des Débats* (13 and 14 July), three weeks later six thousand copies had been sold.[9] Translations into Italian and Dutch followed within a few months.[10] Even more interesting is the fact that, although it was then quite usual, the success of *Les Templiers* was followed by the performances of spin-offs in the form of parodies, *vaudeville*, and melodramas. As early as 5 June, the Théâtre de la Cité presented a parody, *Les pompiers de Bergame* (*The firemen of Bergamo*).[11] The governor of Bergamo was very covetous and wanted to seize the firemen's money. They were arrested and condemned to the stake. But there was a rule in

---

[7]   *Les Templiers* (1805 edn.), pp. lxii-lxvii.

[8]   Analysis of the *Courrier des Spectacles* for the year 1805: Bibliothèque de l'Arsenal (henceforth Ars.), RJ 26.

[9]   Geoffroy, iv, 357.

[10]   Ars., Rf 33018, 33019, 33021.

[11]   *Courrier des Spectacles*, 8 June 1805.

Bergamo which said that the fire engines had to be burnt first. The governor forgot about this rule, and so the firemen, though already on the stakes, were able to use the fire engines and extinguish the fire. In August, the Théatre du Vaudeville presented *Du Belloy ou les templiers*, a *vaudeville* by Chazet and Lafortelle.[12] In September a melodrama, *Odon de Saint-Amand, grand maître des templiers*, was performed, but this play is not related to Raynouard's.[13] We also find an undated fantasy, *Le caveau de la vieille rue du Temple où la réunion des bambocheurs* on the theme 'To drink like a Templar'.[14] And finally, in 1807, there was the play, *Jacques de Molay*, which was not accepted by the Théatre Saint-Martin because it was thought too serious for a *vaudeville*.[15]

The success of the play led the public to history, which had been precisely Raynouard's intention. The newspapers published articles or readers' letters to explain certain historical aspects of the Templar trial. Madame de Rémusat wrote, 'the play *Les Templiers* is much spoken of in Paris and therefore much is said about the Templars themselves'.[16] The editors of the *Almanach des Gourmands* thought they would make a good deal by publishing for public instruction an *Almanach des Templiers* dedicated to Mademoiselle George and composed of a historical abstract of the history of the Order of the Temple.[17] All this was an indictment of Julien Geoffroy, the only critic to disparage Raynouard's play. Geoffroy was laughed at by the newspapers and the public. But with Geoffroy, discussions left the field of literature and turned instead to that of history, for Geoffroy was a 'royalist' who thought the Templars guilty and he could not imagine a king of France to be wrong. Raynouard's position was the exact opposite.

So theatre and dramatic art on the one side, and history and the search of truth on the other were intricately mixed – not without some confusion. We cannot appreciate this situation without taking notice of the taste of the public at that time for national subjects, the *théâtre national*.

THE *THÉÂTRE NATIONAL*

After the first performance of *Les Templiers*, the *Courrier des Spectacles*, a daily newspaper dedicated to theatre and opera in Paris, wrote: 'For a long time the theatre has called for this national theme'.[18] A *théâtre national* was a major ambition in cultural circles in France during the eighteenth century and the first half of the nineteenth. In 1824, Charles Nodier, introducing a new edition of Raynouard's two tragedies, *Les Templiers* and *Les Etats de Blois*, said: 'Almost all the nations which

---

12   Ibid., 20 August 1805.
13   Ibid., 14 September 1805.
14   This play was printed; S. Travers, *Catalogue of Nineteenth-Century French Theatrical Parodies* (New York, 1941), 86, n° 884.
15   Ars., Rf 33022.
16   *Lettres de Madame de Rémusat*, i, 151-2.
17   Ars., Rf 33025.
18   *Courrier des Spectacles*, 15 May 1805.

have the chance to be themselves, have had a historical theatre'.[19] To him, historical, national, and popular all meant the same. England had Shakespeare and ten plays about its kings, but France had Corneille, and Racine, and a lot of Greek and Roman heroes. It should be emphasized, however, that Raynouard in his *Templiers* shows the influence of Corneille, but ironically the Corneille of *Le Cid*, the model of Spanish national theatre.

M. H. Jones has written about the question of the *théâtre national* in France at the beginning of the nineteenth century.[20] Voltaire was the first to try something of this sort, but without any success. Then, in 1765, one finds du Belloy's play *Le siège de Calais*, and, in 1789, Marie-Joseph de Chénier's *Charles IX*. Chénier 'wanted to introduce to the French stage the great moments of history where passion and tragedy are mixed and which present great political and moral teachings'. During the Consulate and the Empire, two major national tragedies were performed with great success: *Les Templiers* (as has been seen) and *La mort de Henri IV* by Legouvé the following year, in 1806. Talma appeared in both casts, and he used Napoleon's friendship to obtain authorization to perform in the second. Like Raynouard, Legouvé was criticized, or at least commented on, for having presented hypotheses about the responsibilities of the murder, and, like Raynouard, he answered by writing historical observations with a publication of historical materials.

It should be pointed out of course that the historical subjects of the *théâtre national* were primarily political subjects. It was therefore not possible to avoid censorship and the particular interest, or special attention, of the political authorities. Napoleon was greatly interested in the subject of the Templars, both on stage and in history and politics. Raynouard's path inevitably crossed Napoleon's.

RAYNOUARD AND NAPOLEON

At that time, the myth of the Templars was, to cite Peter Partner's study,[21] very popular. The new Templarism of Fabré-Palaprat arose alongside Templar Masonry. In 1804, a certain Doctor Ledru forged the Larmenius charter, the basis of the legend of the Templar Order's continuity. Raynouard would have nothing to do with such flights of fancy. He was a rationalist. For him the Templars belonged to both national history and to what one can claim as scientific history. In 1818 he reviewed and criticized the fantasies of Hammer-Purgstall about the Templars' 'Baphomet'.[22] Napoleon was of the same mind. He knew French history and the episode of the Templars well. For him this episode was not, and would never be, completely explained. So he could

---

[19]   C. Nodier, *Bibliothèque dramatique ou répertoire universel du théatre français* (Paris, 1824), 2.

[20]   M. H. Jones, *Le théâtre national en France de 1800 à 1830* (Paris, 1977), especially ch. 3 and 4, where the author analyses Raynouard's works.

[21]   P. Partner, *The Murdered Magicians. The Templars and their Myth* (Oxford, 1981): quoted from the French translation, *Templiers, Francs-maçons et sociétés secrètes* (Paris, 1992), 201-203.

[22]   *Journal des Savants* (1819), 152-61, 221-29.

not accept Raynouard's *a priori* belief in the Templars' innocence. For historians, Napoleon's questions on the matter are valid ones.

Napoleon was in Milan when he heard of the success of Raynouard's play; he was informed by newspapers and by his first chamberlain, Monsieur de Rémusat.[23] As early as 1 June he wrote to Fouché, his Minister of the Police (and also responsible for censorship), to express his satisfaction about the success of the first performance, but also his fears: historical subjects, he said, are a good thing, but they must be chosen carefully and should not belong to a past which is too close to us. He disagreed with Legouvé's project *La mort de Henri IV*. Instead, he suggested the theme of the succession from the first French royal dynasty to the second, from the degenerate Merovingians to the Carolingians, the nation's saviours. Napoleon, the new Charlemagne.[24]

Was there a meeting, or at least some form of contact, between Napoleon and Raynouard during this period? One of Madame de Rémusat's letters to her husband, which bears the date of 5 July 1805, might suggest an affirmative reply. She wrote that Raynouard had paid a visit the day before and that she was delighted with his conversation. Talking about his tragedy *Les Templiers*, Raynouard had told her how grateful he was to Napoleon for the 'happy advice' the Emperor offered while Fontanes was reading the play to him.[25] When he was at Saint-Cloud, Napoleon used to call on certain actors of the Théatre Français to enact for him privately performances of plays then just premiered in Paris. On other occasions he simply listened to the reading of a play.[26] Napoleon did not come back from Italy until 12 July, and from 18 July to 3 August he was at his favourite Saint-Cloud residence.[27] These 'pieces of advice' from Napoleon cannot possibly have been spoken to Raynouard, and Fontane's reading of the play to the Emperor cannot have taken place before 18 July. This means that Napoleon could have gained some acquaintance with the play only during his sojourn in Milan. However, there is other evidence too that a private performance had taken place at Saint-Cloud in September. We know the substance of a conversation between Napoleon, Fontanes, and Monsieur de Rémusat about Raynouard and his *Templiers* thanks to a report by Bausset, one of the Emperor's counsellors. In his *Mémoires* written in 1829, Bausset included the unofficial report of the conversation he made at the time. Fontanes and Rémusat, to whom he had read his report, had no objection to it.[28] This conversation must have dated to September: Napoleon was in the 'camp de Boulogne' during August and at Saint-Cloud from 5 to 23 September. Rémusat, who was not back from Italy before July, was also at home at the time and, unfortunately, we do not have any of his wife's precious letters during the summer of 1805. So what exactly had Napoleon said? He had

---

[23]   *Lettres de Madame de Rémusat*, i, 175-6.

[24]   *Correspondance de Napoléon Ier*, x (Paris, 1862), 466-67.

[25]   *Lettres de Madame de Rémusat*, i, 228 (5 July 1805).

[26]   *Mémoires de Madame de Rémusat*, ed. C. Kunstler (Paris, 1957), 244.

[27]   According to the indications given by *Correspondance de Napoléon Ier*, xi (Paris, 1863), 1-25.

[28]   L. F. J., Baron de Bausset, *Mémoires anecdotiques sur l'intérieur du palais et sur quelques événements de l'Empire depuis 1805 jusqu'au 1er mai 1814, pour servir à l'histoire de Napoléon*, 2 vols. (Paris, 1827), i, 44-49.

criticized Raynouard's conception of tragedy because the author had wanted to prove something that would not work in the theatre. Then he gave his views on the characters: the King, Philippe le Bel, was too weak, and Molay, the Grand Master, too perfect. In order to move the public, Napoleon said, tragic heroes had to be human and to show elements of weakness. In sum, Raynouard had great qualities, but his play was not as good as the public believed; nor was it as bad as Geoffroy claimed.

It was not the Emperor's last word on the subject. On 31 December 1806, Napoleon wrote again to Fouché, this time from Pultusk, a military camp in Poland, and spoke of Raynouard and his *Les Templiers*.[29] He set out in a few lines his idea of modern tragedy: the key phrases are 'nature des choses' and 'force des choses'. In *Les Templiers* the true hero should have been the king, who did what he did because he had no choice. It was the tragic dilemma of the statesman. The relationship between Napoleon and Raynouard was not entirely cheerful. In 1806, Raynouard became a deputy of the *Corps legislatif*; in 1807 he entered the Academy (or *Institut*). He then began a new historical tragedy, *Les Etats de Blois*, based on the murder of the Duke of Guise. Napoleon saw it at the theatre of Saint-Cloud, but he did not like it; and in 1810, no further performances of the play were allowed.[30] Then Raynouard worked on the Vatican records and wrote *Les monumens historiques*. But the publication of the book was postponed until the end of 1812, when the censors accepted the work but changed the title from the *Preuves pour servir à l'innocence des templiers* to the more impartial *Mémoire sur l'affaire des templiers*.[31] His second tragedy, *Les Etats de Blois*, was not to be performed until the first Restoration in 1814; nor would Raynouard repeat the triumph of *Les Templiers*. The relationship between Napoleon and Raynouard remained cool and detached. The former would have liked to have the second at his service, but Raynouard was very careful not to prejudice his independence. Napoleon was literally obsessed by the subject of the Templars, and certain historians have given a psychological and political explanation: in 1804 the Duke of Enghien was executed after an arbitrary and hasty trial; this crime soon came to be regarded as a grievous mistake, and it seems that, like Philippe le Bel in Raynouard's tragedy, Napoleon repented his deed. There were times when the 'nature des choses' did indeed direct kings or emperors to extremes. In a sense, therefore, it may be claimed that Raynouard's play succeeded in disclosing the truth about Napoleon's conscience.[32]

Raynouard's *Les Templiers*, an emblem of the *théatre national*, survived the Emperor. Performances continued to be given during the nineteenth century, and in the 1870s the play was published in a popular collection, *Les Bons livres* or

---

[29]   *Correspondance de Napoléon Ier*, xiv (Paris, 1863), 158.

[30]   Welschinger, 242-43.

[31]   Ibid., 318, with the publication of the document from Archives Nationales (Paris), F 18/149.

[32]   A. Aderer, 'Napoleon critique dramatique', *Le Temps*, 15 mai 1911, with an answer by Welschinger, Ars., Rf 33034.

Cent bons livres à dix centimes constituant une bibliothèque pour chaque famille.[33]
Raynouard's play was among the four titles on French historical themes – the others
were *Joan of Arc*, *Charles IX*, and *Le Siège de Calais* – apart from those by Corneille
and Racine.

---

[33]   Raynouard, *Les Templiers* (Paris, 1873). 63pp., in *Les Bons Livres*, n° 97. Repr. 1875,
1877, 1879.

PART II
Liturgy and Fiction, Heraldry and Piety

Chapter 5

Sad Stories of the Death of Kings: Last Illnesses and Funerary Rites of the Grand Masters of the Order of St John from Aubusson to the Cotoners

Ann Williams

The acquisition of Rhodes by the Order of St John gave the grand master a small state to govern as well as a religious order to administer. By the second half of the fifteenth century the elaboration of the records kept, particularly the Council proceedings, give us insights into the working of government in both its religious and secular aspects. Periods of crisis, especially, produced reactions from the record keepers that illuminated the events they described, and over a period of time, reflected the changes which the order underwent.

The deaths of grand masters were some of these periods of tension. The Council scribes frequently give accounts of last illnesses, events surrounding the last days of the Masters, and funerary ritual. They are also interesting from the point of view of *sede vacante* problems and new elections, but I have gone into this in more detail in the book on the Convent of the order which I am at long last finishing.[1] This paper will concentrate on illnesses and funerals.

The medical aspects of these death-bed scenes are valuable because although the medical work of the order was so important, the records are poor in this respect for both the Rhodes and the Malta periods. For the latter, the daybooks of the hospital were destroyed when the French invaded the islands in 1798. The information about disease and its treatment in these documents would have been invaluable, because they were kept by the infirmarian with information from the doctors and pharmacists in the hospital. The vice-chancellor and his scribes of the Council had no such knowledge; they were not qualified diagnosticians, but they were at the centre of affairs and they, on occasions, did go into detail about the course of illnesses, diets, and treatment given.

The second valuable aspect of these death-bed scenes is the increasing light they shed on the secular position both in Rhodes and Malta, as the rituals surrounding the death and burial of the head of state were worked out. The grand master held the islands as ruler in his own right. It is even possible sometimes to see what the 'popular' reaction to the grand master was. This is particularly clear in the cases

---

[1]   Ann Williams, *Servants of the Sick: The Convent of the Order of St John in Rhodes and Malta 1421-1631* (forthcoming).

of Pierre d'Aubusson and Jean de la Vallette, both of whom defended their islands against the Turks in 1480 and 1565 respectively.

The records for deaths became rich with the demise of Aubusson, so I shall begin here, although with a backward glance at his predecessor Orsini's illness, which Bosio described with such vividness that we can make a confident judgment about what happened to him.[2] Giovanni Battista Orsini's health had caused concern throughout his mastership and he had taken to his bed on several occasions, which must have been demoralizing for his companions when the threat of Turkish attack was so constant in these years. At the end of March 1475 he continued to work in spite of his indisposition, but at the beginning of the new year, April 1476, the Prior of Catalonia, as President of the Council, called the doctors of the infirmary. They said he had fever, and a certain sort of dropsy, which was dangerous because of his great age. It was in the hands of God whether he lived or died. On the following day, Holy Saturday, 13 April, a violent and terrible accident befell the grand master. In a moment he lost his speech, his sight, his hearing, and all his senses. There remained no sign of life, except for the warmth of his body and the movement of his eyelids. He did recover from what was obviously a stroke, but did not live for long afterwards.[3]

It is not easy when illnesses are described to be certain what the complaint really was. The assumptions of the Hippocratic / Galenic tradition lasted well into the seventeenth century. This tradition said that health depended on a balance of the four humours in the body, black bile, yellow or red bile, blood and phlegm. Disease was an imbalance of these humours and depended on the constitution of the patient rather than a specific complaint.[4] Therefore descriptions, such as fever and, as in this case, dropsy, were more likely to be symptoms of other problems, such as renal failure, rather than diseases in their own right. It is rare to get as detailed a description as that of Orsini's stroke.

Orsini's successor, Pierre d'Aubusson, was one of the longest serving grand masters in the order's history. He held office for twenty-seven years, during which he led the defence of Rhodes against the Turks in 1480, and in numerous other crises in the last part of the fifteenth century. Rhodes also suffered from famine and earthquakes in this period, and Aubusson made visits to the outlying islands to comfort and help the people as well as devoting time and thought to the administration of the order. Finally on 22 June 1503 he began to suffer from a flux of the stomach which no remedy alleviated. He managed to get to the celebrations for St John's Eve with its bonfires and salvos, and also to hear Mass in the Church of St John on the Feast Day.[5] However, by Tuesday, 27 June, on the advice of the doctors, he was taking his meals in his room rather than publicly as he was accustomed to do. He was put on a light diet, but by the 28th the flux had increased. The doctors despaired

---

[2]   Giacomo Bosio, *Istoria della Sacra Religione Militare di S. Giovanni Gierosolimitano*, 3 vols. (Rome, 1594-1620), ii, 357-61.

[3]   Ibid., 358.

[4]   Conrad Laurence (ed.), *The Western Medical Tradition 800 BC to 1800* (Cambridge, 1995), 23-25, 238-41.

[5]   AOM, cod. 80, *Liber Conciliorum*, fol. 27r.

of his health and consulted with his nephew, the Lieutenant and Prior of Auvergne, Guy de Blanchefort. (This consultation with members of the family if they were also members of the order and present in the Convent, is mentioned again in Antoine de Paule's last illness in Malta.) The doctors decided to dose Aubusson with rhubarb, rather a drastic decision if he had, as it seems, acute diarrhoea. At the beginning of July be seemed on the point of death and, finally, in the early hours of Monday, 3 July, he died.

The body was opened and the entrails embalmed, a practice that was always carried out in subsequent magisterial burials, and put in a casket in the Church of Our Lady of Victories.[6] His body was then dressed in his cardinal's robes, and the sword which he had carried in the 1480 siege, still stained with the blood of that combat, was placed upon his bier. He was then carried into the Palace where the doors were opened and a great multitude of people appeared. Later the reaction of the people of Rhodes was mentioned. Both sexes showed their grief, the women beating their breasts and tearing their hair, the men tearing their beards.[7]

It is not clear in Aubusson's case where this popular demonstration took place. The *collachio*, the area in which the Palace and auberges of the Knights were situated, was strictly preserved in Rhodes and enclosed from the rest of the city. Citizens did, however, own property within it and so were able to go into the public buildings.[8] The Greek Metropolitan with all his clergy kept vigil. The Prior of the Church said Mass, and on the morning of 4 July, led the procession to bury Aubusson in the Church of St John.

There are no further accounts of the burials of the Rhodes grand masters. Guy de Blanchefort, Aubusson's nephew, died on his way to Rhodes in 1513, and it is not clear whether or not he was buried at sea.[9] As for d'Amboise (1503-12), and Carretto (1513-21), the troubles of the last years and the loss of records when the order left Rhodes meant the loss of much information, so nothing is known of the manner of their departing from life.[10] Philippe de L'Isle Adam, like Aubusson before him and La Vallette after him, was a strong and able man who was well equipped to cope with the challenges of his time. He negotiated the evacuation of Rhodes, guided the order in the uncertain years of wandering, keeping it independent from pope and king. The acceptance of Malta from Charles V in 1530 gave the order a new island base. When he died in 1534, the Knights were settled in Birgu, later Vittoriosa, using the local Church of St Lawrence as their religious centre, while building their auberges in the narrow streets of the small city. The fort of St Angelo was where the grand master lived, and it was here, in the August of 1534, at the age of 75, that the heat prevented L' Isle Adam from sleeping and getting any rest, so he went down into the town.[11] It is not clear where he stayed. On the sixteenth of the month he began to suffer from a fever which rapidly overtook him. On Friday, 21 August, between three and four in

---

[6]   Ibid., fol. 27v.

[7]   Ibid. fol. 28.

[8]   I am grateful to Dr A.T. Luttrell for clarification of this point.

[9]   Bosio, ii, 609.

[10]   Ibid., 600 and 623.

[11]   AOM, cod. 85, *Liber Conciliorum*, fol. 133r.

the morning, he died. There was no mention of any medical treatment. His sudden and, it seemed, unexpected death, took the Convent by surprise, and a dispute arose between the grand master's Lieutenant and the Grand Marshal, who claimed that he should have been Lieutenant. The body of the grand master was taken to La Marsa and placed on the Great Ship to be taken to the gate of the Fort, where a procession met it and accompanied it into the building. On 23 August the body was taken to the Church of St Lawrence where a solemn Requiem Mass was said, and the body was later buried in the chapel of St Anne in Fort St Angelo with great funeral pomp.[12]

L'Isle Adam's two successors, St Jaille and del Ponte, only ruled for about a year each and their deaths passed without much comment. Homedes was much preoccupied with the North African town of Tripoli which the order had been commissioned to defend in the agreement with Charles V. He died on 1 September 1533 of a dry fever.[13] His successor, Claude de la Sengle, had a comparatively short magistracy of four years, although the order's commitment to Malta was furthered by the development of the suburb on the peninsula, named after him, in the Grand Harbour. In early August 1557, at the age of 63, he began to suffer from catarrh.[14] This was often a symptom of a pulmonary complaint, probably pneumonia. In an attempt to alleviate his suffering he went to the garden popularly known as La Marsa, but he continued to deteriorate and on 15 August he died. There was again only a brief account of his funeral, held as with the other early grand masters in Malta in the Church of St Lawrence.

It was, however, with the death of La Vallette that a more detailed account of the last illness occurred and the ceremonies surrounding the funeral became more elaborate.[15] His reputation as the defender of Malta in the Great Siege of 1565, his skill in directing the order in war and peace, and finally his commitment to the building of a new city endeared him to both his community and his subjects. At the beginning of August 1568 when the grand master was clearly ill, he ordered business in the Council to be suspended because of rumours of a Turkish fleet. The Grand Commander, Fr Claude de Glandeurs was appointed Lieutenant, although La Vallette still kept a close watch on events. On 1 August, he ordered a secret Council to meet in his chamber in the Palace where he lay in his bed, explaining his views in few words because of his illness. He spent some days in the garden at La Marsa, where the trees and the greenery delighted him, but his fever worsened and he returned to his Palace in the new city. His fever lasted for twenty days (obviously from its beginning, otherwise the dates do not fit). The doctors could find no art nor remedy to ease him. They said his fever was that popularly called St Paul's disease. Prayers were offered by the Greeks and the Latins alike, who implored God to spare the life of their ruler. At the end, Vallette himself asked the Prior of the Church to hear his confession and, as he confessed his sins, he held a black wooden cross

---

[12]   Ibid.
[13]   Ibid., cod. 88, *Liber Conciliorum*, fol. 163 v.
[14]   Ibid., cod. 89, *Liber Conciliorum*, fol. 116 r.
[15]   Ibid., cod. 92, *Liber Conciliorum*, fol. 89v.

tightly in his hands.[16] Then he received the last rites and rendered his soul to the Most High on 21 August.

For the first time, we are really conscious that the burial of a head of state as well as of a religious community is taking place. La Vallette's body was laid out in state in the *aula*, or hall of the Magisterial Palace. The great and beautiful sword, given to him by Philip II, was placed on his bier. Many secular people came to grieve, and it appeared on this occasion that women were allowed to view the body. Many Rhodian and Maltese women tore their hair and beat their breasts, saying 'Immortal God, what a Prince we have lost! What a generous and kind father we mourn who embraced us with love and piety and saw to all our needs!'[17]

There was no *collachio* in Malta, either in Birgu or in Valletta and, although the order had many debates on the necessity for such seclusion, it was never built. Therefore the order was even closer to the life of the city than it had been in Rhodes. There were precedents in Rome for the invasion of the papal Palace after the death of a pope, although in those cases it was a more aggressive and hostile mob that ransacked the papal apartments. All the bailiffs, priors, commanders, and other members of the order attended, offering prayers for the repose of La Vallette's soul. His domestic servants and the members of his household came forward to kiss the dead grand master's hand. On 22 August Vallette's body was taken to the Church of St Laurence, presumably because it was the only church in Malta which could hold the whole order and its servants. The body was accompanied by many laymen as well as religious. The church was lit with many candles and a solemn Requiem Mass was said by the Prior of the Church. The body then lay in state for three days in the Chapel of Our Lady of Philermo, after which it was taken back to the new city named Valletta after him, on the Captain's trireme which was dressed in black, as were all the ships in the harbour.[18] He was buried before the altar in the new Church of Our Lady of Victories, dedicated in gratitude for the victory over the Turks in 1565. There it would lie until a new Conventual Church was built.

The commitment to Malta with the building of Valletta, and the rapid growth of the city and the whole harbour area increased the order's secular role. They were more in the centre of the diplomatic activity of Western Europe than they had been in Rhodes and their ceremonies began to reflect, albeit in a modest way, those of the Courts of Europe. In their religious and hospitaller activities too they were affected by the continuing Catholic reforms that had begun in the fifteenth century and were consolidated in the legislation of the Council of Trent. Prayers for the sick and dying were multiplied in accordance with the belief that medical treatment would be more effective if the sick person made his will, confessed his sins, and removed his daily anxieties. This course of action was prescribed for every Christian, and in this respect grand masters were as other mortals. They too were destined for Purgatory. The doctrine put forward at the Councils of Lyons (1274) and Florence (1439) was

---

[16]   Ibid., fol. 90v.
[17]   Ibid.
[18]   Ibid.

reinforced at Trent.[19] Elaborate prayers for the dying, always a feature of the Eastern Church, were stressed more and more in the West. St Ignatius Loyola incorporated them into his *Spiritual Exercises*. After the arrival of the Jesuits in Malta in the 1570s, a number of grand masters had Jesuit confessors or confessors from the reformed Capuchin or Dominican orders.

Although there are a number of changes in the practices surrounding the burials of the late sixteenth- and early seventeenth-century grand masters, I will move on to the very full account of the ceremonies surrounding the death and burial of Antoine de Paule, after which the records tend to say that each grand master was buried 'in the manner of his predecessors'. De Paule held the highest office from 1623 to 1636, matched in Rome by the pontificate of Urban VIII. In his administration changes were made to the method of electing the grand master and the penultimate chapter general of the order was held in 1631. He had been criticized in the course of his magistracy by the Inquisitor Fabrizio Chigi for his profligacy and high living. He certainly made up for it by his long and painful last illness, which was described in great detail by the anguished onlookers. (His tomb in St John's Cathedral mentioned his suffering.) On 15 February 1636, at the age of 85, he was given an enema to relieve the constriction in his bladder.[20] He was trembling all over and had inflammation of the bladder. Then he passed blood and yellow urine copiously. At two o'clock in the afternoon his stomach was upset and he vomited blood, and two hours later it seemed that the ulcers on his body would putrefy unless the surgeons could operate and cure him. There is no record that they tried to do anything. On the eighteenth of the month he confessed his sins and took Communion from one of the chaplains in the magisterial chapel in the Palace. Next day he made his *dispropriamentum*. On the twentieth, the Council decreed that the Holy Eucharist should be exposed in the Conventual Church of St John, and all the brothers poured forth prayers for the health of His Eminence.

On the fifth day of his illness he had fever and could keep nothing down. His pulse was irregular and he was extremely weak. Death seemed to be on the doorstep. On the twenty-first, the grand master again confessed his sins and received Holy Communion at the hands of the Revd Salvatore Imbroll, the Prior of the Church. Prayers were offered for him. De Paule exhorted all the bystanders to preserve peace and unity in the order. All who watched were reduced to tears.[21] The formality and the very public nature of this death-bed conformed with contemporary ideas of the 'good death' acted out with the support of the dying person's community.

The usual provisions for the expected death of a grand master were made. The harbour was shut and no ships were allowed to leave, except, on this occasion, two that were sent to Sicily to get corn because of the threat of famine. Money was taken from the Treasury to tide the order over until the election of a new grand master. On the thirteenth day from the beginning of his illness, de Paule's stomach was distended

---

[19]   See, for example, R Chartier, 'Les arts de mourir 1450-1600', *Annales ESC*, xxxi (Paris, 1976), 51-75; Gordon Bruce and Peter Marshall (eds.), *The Place of the Dead: Death and Remembrance in late Medieval and Early Modern Europe* (Cambridge, 2000), 1-16.

[20]   AOM, cod. 111, *Liber Conciliorum*, fol. 207r.

[21]   Ibid.

and bilious.[22] His body was again hot. On the twenty-fifth a tumour appeared on his stomach; his tongue was dry and black and he had a terrible fever. The tumour on his stomach grew from day to day, and on the sixteenth day it attacked his legs, first the left one, and on the eighteenth day it could be observed on his hips and on his back. Then it appeared on his hands, first the left then the right. His breathing was difficult and he had fever in the night and could not pass water. He grew weaker and weaker with the strain of this long illness.

On 4 March at midday the grand master was administered the Holy Oil by the Prior of the Church. Two days later the Vice-Chancellor handed the magisterial seal to the Seneschal. On the eighth, a Sunday, the Holy Eucharist was exposed in the Conventual Church and the whole Convent offered prayers to the most compassionate God for the grand master who lay *in extremis*. The Revd Father Giorgio Tagliavia, the Rector of the Jesuit College, gave a homily. In the post-Tridentine years, sermons by Jesuits, Carmelites, or Dominicans became a common feature on important occasions in the order's life. Unfortunately I have not been able to trace any of these homilies, nor to find any record of the points that the preachers made. Finally, on 9 March, between the hours of nine and ten in the morning, the grand master's spirit returned peacefully to his Creator.[23]

Those standing round, including the Seneschal, his nephew, the Office bearers, and his servants wept openly. Father Sebastian Sallelles, a Jesuit, an unnamed Capuchin Father, and the magisterial chaplains offered prayers, commending De Paule's soul to God. The bell of the Conventual Church tolled out the years of the grand master's age. Other formalities were quickly observed and the executors of the dead Master's will were called in. The Council was summoned and, under the presidency of the Lieutenant, ordered de Paule's seal to be broken and arrangements for the new election to be set in motion. The Revd Father Matthew Resplus, a Dominican, preached in St John's on the forthcoming election.

The body of the grand master was embalmed and laid in state in the *aula* of the Magisterial Palace on 10 June with all the pomp and ceremonial enjoyed by his predecessor Vasconcellos. Priests, singing psalms, kept vigil until the burial took place. On 11 March de Paule's body, accompanied by many religious and lay people and members of his household, was taken from the Palace to the Conventual Church, where the Prior of the Church celebrated a solemn Pontifical Mass. A Capuchin father – a space was left for his name, but not filled in – gave the funeral oration. Alms were given to the poor as was the custom. The grand master was buried, as he had requested in his *dispropriamentum*, in a tomb in the chapel of St Michael the Archangel, the chapel of the Langue of Provence in the Conventual Church.[24]

The building of St John's with La Cassière's *spolia*, in the centre of the city of Valletta, gave the order for a ceremonial edifice and a processional route from the Palace to the Church, which was unrivalled from the religious and the secular points of view. Although we do not hear of women weeping and wailing after La Vallette's

---

[22]   Ibid., fol. 207v.

[23]   Ibid., fol. 208r.

[24]   Dominic Cutajar, *History and Works of Art – St John's Church, Valletta, Malta*, 3rd rev. edn. (Valletta, 1999), 72.

death, the presence of lay people lamenting and praying was a feature of all funeral processions. The Church became the resting place of all the grand masters in Malta. The crypt was first used as a monumental area. L'Isle Adam, who had been buried in the chapel of St Anne in Fort St Angelo, was removed to Valletta. La Vallette was brought from Our Lady of Victories, as were his predecessors di Ponte, Sengle, and Homedes. La Cassière, who died in Rome, was eventually brought back to the Church for which he had paid. Until de Paule, the grand masters continued to be buried in the crypt. The early monuments, like those of Homedes and La Sengle, continued to be marked like those in Rhodes, by the grand master's coat-of-arms and a flat tomb cover. L'Isle Adam's tomb, however, had a gisant figure. Verdale (1582-95) lay dressed in his Cardinal's robes. His successor Martin Garzes (1595-1601) had a fine Mannerist tomb, also showing a gisant figure. Alof de Wignacourt (1601-22), although still buried in the crypt, began the tradition of tombs with magisterial busts as well as the coats-of-arms. This practice was followed by his successor, Luiz Mendez Vasconcellos (1622-3).

As we have seen, de Paule requested that he should be buried in the chapel of his Langue in St John's, modestly just asking for 'an honourable place'. The tomb was, in fact, an ostentatious Late Mannerist one with a bust, an elaborate coat-of-arms, and an inscription. This tomb was matched on the same wall by a similar one made for his successor, Jean Lascaris Castellar (1636-57), carved by a Florentine sculptor who worked in Messina, Vitale Coveti.[25] With these elaborate tombs, the 'national' chapels of the *langues*, and the decoration of the ceiling of the nave from the late 1650s by Mattia Preti, with its symbolism of the religious, military, and Hospitaller roles of the order, the Church certainly rivalled the burial places of European rulers.

The death of de Paule consolidated the ritual of the burial of the grand masters. The public display of the body, the vigil, the hangings on the bier as well as the sword and purse as insignia of office, the procession from the Palace to the Church, carefully orchestrated by the Master of Ceremonies, added up to a very impressive display of power. Liturgical manuscripts laid out the order of the Mass and the robes to be worn. Later seventeenth-century Council minutes tended to be rather laconic in their descriptions of the deaths of grand masters. Rafael Cotoner was taken ill on 20 October 1663 and died suddenly on the same day, probably of a heart attack.[26] He was buried 'according to the tradition of his predecessor' and his funeral oration was given by a Father Luceti of the Society of Jesus. His brother, Nicolas Cotoner, who succeeded him, died in 1680, affected by a fever, and again was buried with the accustomed ceremonies.[27]

There was nothing understated, however, about the tombs of Rafael's predecessor, Martin de Redin (1657-60), the two Cotoners, and the later Aragonese grand master Ramon de Perellos (1697-1720). Their monuments adorned the chapel of the Langue of Aragon and proved, once and for all, that the grand masters were proclaiming themselves as rulers.

---

[25]   Ibid.
[26]   AOM, cod. 122, *Liber Conciliorum*, fol. 70v.
[27]   Ibid., cod. 126, *Liber Conciliorum*, fol. 184r.

Chapter 6

The Liturgical Policies of the Hospitallers between the Invention of Printing and the Council of Trent: The Evidence of the Early Printed Breviaries and Missals

Cristina Dondi

For the history of printing of liturgical texts the period from the invention of printing to the Council of Trent covers roughly one hundred years. It begins with the appearance of the first liturgical books – the Roman breviary printed in Venice in 1474,[1] and the first assigned Roman missal printed in Milan in 1474[2] – and ends with the edition of the first Tridentine Roman breviary printed in Rome in 1568[3] and the Roman missal printed in Rome in 1570.[4]

According to the data gathered from the *Incunabula Short-Title Catalogue*, 444 different editions of breviaries and 370 different editions of missals were produced between 1474 and 1500. The breviaries included 373 editions for diocesan use, of which 84 were Roman, and 71 belonged to religious orders. On the other hand, there were 345 editions of the missal for diocesan use – 94 were Roman, with only 25 belonging to the religious orders. The sixteenth century witnessed a general escalation of numbers.

---

[1]   *Breviarium Romanum*, Franciscan use (Venice, Jacobus Rubeus, 1474); 8vo. ISTC no. ib01117000.

[2]   *Missale Romanum* (Milan, Antonius Zarotus, 6 Dec. 1474); Folio. ISTC no. im00688450. This edition was preceded by three unassigned editions: a *Missale Fratrum Minorum* ([Central Italy?, n.pr., *c*.1472?]); Folio. ISTC no. im00643000; a *Missale speciale* ([Basel, Printer of the Missale Speciale (Johann Meister?), *c*.1473?]); Folio. ISTC no. im00732500; and a *Missale speciale abbreviatum* ([Basel, Printer of the Missale Speciale (Johann Meister?), *c*.1473?]); Folio. ISTC no. im00735500.

[3]   *Breviarium Romanum ex decreto ss. Concilii Tridentini* (Rome, Paulus Manutius, 1568).

[4]   *Missale Romanum ex decreto ss. Concilii Tridentini restitutum, Pii V Pont. Max. jussu editum* (Rome, apud heredes Bartholomei Faletti, Joannem Variscum, 1570).

It is often possible to evaluate the process which brought the text of a given religious order or diocese into print, together with its historical and religious context. The mandate for publication, generally written in the opening of a liturgical text, contained information about the person who commissioned the edition. This was generally the abbot of a religious order or the archbishop or bishop of a diocese. It also included the reasons, with sometimes more detailed information for the editorial process – such as the person in charge of the revision of the text, or the manuscript exemplar used to prepare the edition. From among the most enthusiastic supporters and users of the new printing invention, the abbot of Citeaux, Jean de Cirey (d. 1503), stands out. It was he who had commissioned the abbot of Baumgarten, Nicolas de Saliceto, to edit the Cistercian breviary printed in Basel in 1484[5] and in Strasburg c.1487,[6] and the Cistercian missal printed in Strasbourg in 1487.[7] He had also personally edited a collection of privileges of his order, appearing in Dijon in 1491.[8]

Much more should be said on the early involvement of religious institutions with printing. From the very beginning, the vast potential printing enjoyed was clear to most of them. It unified communities separated by great physical distance by producing books which ultimately unified liturgy. Rudolph Hirsch identified at least seven monastic presses in Germany by the 1470s.[9] Lotte Hellinga showed that the establishment of a printing press in Subiaco, in central Italy, may have been linked more closely to plans for monastic reform than is evident from what it produced, or from what has survived of its production. In 1471. Benedict Zwink of Ettal, a Benedictine monk residing in the abbey of St Specus which adjoined Sta Scolastica, wrote to the abbot of Gottweig, near Melk, in connection with plans to extend the Benedictine congregations of Bursfeld and Melk to include those who observed the rules of Subiaco and Montecassino:

> Since it might be difficult for all monasteries to compare and edit breviaries, it will be easy to produce 100 or 200 copies on the presses, just as we have also produced 200 copies of St Augustine's *De Civitate Dei* in the form of type as enclosed. In the monastery of St Specus we can make use of this technique to the full, for we have the equipment and the people [who know how to use it]. If we could form part of this religious union [the extended congregation], all books, whatever the number required, could be printed and distributed to all monasteries which in their turn would have joined the congregation, with

---

[5]   *Breviarium Cisterciense* (Basel, Peter Kollicker and Johann Meister, 4 Nov. 1484); 8vo. ISTC no. ib01135000.

[6]   *Breviarium Cisterciense* (Strasburg, Johann (Reinhard) Grüninger, [not before 1487]); 8vo. ISTC no. ib0113600.

[7]   *Missale Cisterciense* ([Strasburg: Johann (Reinhard) Grüninger], 4 Sept. 1487); Folio. ISTC no. im00635000.

[8]   *Privilegia ordinis Cisterciensis* (Dijon, Petrus Metlinger, 4 July 1491); 4to. ISTC no. ip00976000. A book of hours for the Cistercian use was also printed in Paris by Philippe Pigouchet for Simon Vostre in c.1500 (8vo. ISTC no. ih00343500), a very rare example of hours for the use of a religious order.

[9]   Rudolph Hirsch, *Printing, Selling and Reading 1450-1550* (2nd edn.: Wiesbaden, 1974), 54.

the equipment which is available on the spot, and with the help of five brethren who could be instructed in this technique.[10]

Before examining how the Hospitallers responded to the opportunities offered by the printing press, one observation should be made on the use of printing in the fifteenth century. As with editions of other texts (classical, literary, etc.), the fifteenth-century liturgical editions do not necessarily always represent the beginning of a homogeneous tradition; sometimes they simply represent the tail-end of an individual one. This is very clearly illustrated by the differences between the fifteenth- and sixteenth-century editions of the Hospitaller breviaries and missals.

The Hospitaller breviary was first printed at Mainz in 1480,[11] then at Speier in 1495.[12] In the sixteenth century, a third edition was printed at Lyons in 1517,[13] a fourth appeared in Saragossa in 1547,[14] and finally a fifth at Lyons in 1551.[15] As far as the missals are concerned, no editions were printed in the fifteenth century, but four were in the sixteenth: the first at Strasburg in 1505,[16] the second at Saragossa in 1528,[17] the third at Lyons in 1551,[18] and the last at Lyons in 1553.[19]

---

[10]   Abbey of Melk, MS 91; see Lotte Hellinga, 'The Codex in the Fifteenth Century: Manuscript and Print', in *A Potencie of Life: Books in Society, The Clark Lectures 1986-1987*, ed. N. Barker (London, 1993), 63-88, at 73-4 this English paraphrase from the Latin text published in Barbara Frank, 'Tipografia monastica sublacense: per una confederazione benedettina', *Il Sacro Speco*, lxxiv (1971), 69-72.

[11]   [*Breviarium Hierosolymitanum* (Mainz, Printer of the 'Darmstadt' Prognostication, c.1480]); 8vo. ISTC no. ib01143300; C. Dondi, 'Hospitaller Liturgical Manuscripts and Early Printed Books', *Revue Mabillon*, n.s. 14 = t. 75 (2003), 225-56, at 248 no. B.81.

[12]   *Breviarium secundum consuetudinem domus hospitalis Hierosolymitani s. Johannis* (Speier, Peter Drach, 1495); 8vo. ISTC no. ib01143310; Dondi, as note 11, 248-50, no. B.82, with a transcription of the mandate for publication.

[13]   *Breviarium secundum consuetudinem domus hospitalis Hierosolymitani s. Johannis* (Lyons, Cyriacus Hochperg, 1517); 8vo. Dondi, as note 11, 250-51, no. B.83, with a transcription of the mandate for publication.

[14]   *Breviarium secundum ritum Sixene monasterij: Ordinis sancti Joannis Hierosolymitani sub regula beati Augustini* (Saragossa, George Coci [industria vero Petri Bernuz], 4 Nov. 1547); 8vo. Dondi, as note 11, 251-2, no. B.84.

[15]   *Breviarium secundum usum ordinis s. Joannis Hierosolymitani* (Lyons, Cornelius a Septemgrangiis expensis Haeredum Jacobi Junctae, 1551); 8vo. Dondi, as note 11, 252-3, no. B.85.

[16]   *Missale secundum institutionem ordinis hospitalis s. Johannis Ierosolymitani* (Strasburg, Johannes Prüss zum Thiergarten, 1505); Folio. Dondi, as note 11, 253-4, no. B.86, with a transcription of the mandate for publication.

[17]   *Missale secundum ritum Sixene monasterij: Ordinis sancti Joannis Hierosolymitani sub regula beati Augustini* (Saragossa, George Coci, 1528); Folio. Dondi, as note 11, 254, no. B.87.

[18]   *Missale sacri ordinis s. Joannis Hierosolymitani* (Lyons, Cornelius a Septemgrangiis, 1551); Folio. Dondi, as note 11, 254, no. B.88.

[19]   *Missale sacri ordinis s. Joannis Hierosolymitani* (Lyons, Sumptibus haeredum Jacobi Juntae speciosis characteribus apud Cornelium a Septemgrangiis excusum, 1553); Folio. Dondi, as note 11, 254-5, no. B.89.

The two Spanish editions were printed specifically for the house of the Hospitaller nuns of Sigena, in the province of Huesca, and they are representative of a different tradition. As far as I am aware, the case of the nuns of Sigena is the only one, within the Hospitaller tradition, where the typical liturgical use of the Holy Sepulchre of Jerusalem, adopted by the Hospitallers,[20] was modified, adjusting to a local tradition. Variation is noted in the calendar, containing only a few saints of the Holy Sepulchre, mainly local Spanish ones – in the short office of the Virgin, the dedication of the church, and above all in the office of All Saints (for which similarities are found with Valencia and Tudela). In the office of All Souls, the Sigena breviary presents a Spanish series, found in Oloron, Huesca, Saragossa, and Valencia. This series, a derivation from Toulouse, was probably introduced to Spain from Oloron. Whatever the origin, it clearly shows how the Hospitaller nuns of Sigena had, by the sixteenth century, adapted the original Hospitaller use to a local Spanish one.[21]

The only existing copy of the first edition of the Hospitaller breviary, printed at Mainz in *c*.1480, is not complete. The copy, now in the British Library, contains only the summer part.[22] We do not know who had commissioned the work, a detail which, if present, would have been presumably contained in the opening of the winter section, as can be seen in the 1495 edition. Its contents, however, show that the breviary was certainly printed from a manuscript exemplar coming from a German Hospitaller house. In addition to the traditional feasts of the Holy Sepulchre, a number of saints venerated in the German area are listed in the calendar, the sanctorale, and the litanies. We thus find Lubentius (13 October) and Maximin (29 May) of Trier; Boniface (5 June) and Alban (21 June) of Mainz; Gereon and companions (10 October) and the 11,000 Virgins (21 October) of Cologne; Gingulfus (13 May) venerated in Bonn; Lambert (17 September) of Liege; Servatius (13 May) of Maastricht; Arbogastus (21 July) and Florence (7 November) of Strasburg; Ulrich (4 July) and Afra (7 August), patron saints of Augsburg; and Kilian (8 July) of Wurzburg.

The second edition of the Hospitaller breviary is the result of the provincial chapter of the order held in Strasburg in 1495 under Pierre d'Aubusson. It was commissioned by Rudolf Graf von Werdenberg (d.1505), Prior of Germany (1481-1505) and *Commendator* of Heitersheim.[23] The mandate for publication at the beginning of the winter section states that it was edited by the Strasburg *Commendatores* of the Order of St John. This suggests that at the Council the *Commendatores* of Strasburg were working on the basis of the previous 1480 edition, and their emendments consisted in the new insertion of antiphons between the Psalter and the Gradual Psalms, some further prayers for the suffrages, and a proper office for St Arbogastus, bishop of Strasburg – clearly a reflection of the importance of the Strasburg house.

---

[20]   C. Dondi, *The Liturgy of the Canons Regular of the Holy Sepulchre of Jerusalem: A Study and a Catalogue of the Manuscript Sources,* Bibliotheca Victorina, xvi (Turnhout, 2004), 40-44.

[21]   See notes 14 and 17 *supra*. Also K. Ottosen, *The Responsories and Versicles of the Latin Office of the Dead* (Aarhus, 1993), 169, 320. In the prologue at the opening of the Breviary the prioress of the community, "Elisabeth de Alagon", states the purpose of the publication and fixes the price at 32 *solidi*.

[22]   BL, IA.322; also note 11 *supra*.

[23]   See note 12 *supra*.

Of the seven extant copies of this breviary, there is evidence that three were being used within the Hospitaller environment. One copy was kept in the Strasburg house, where it was still found in the library in 1749, when Johann Nicholas Weislinger drew up the library catalogue. It is now preserved in the National and University Library of Strasburg.[24] A second copy was used by the Hospitallers of Heitersheim and is today kept in the University Library of Freiburg, which acquired the Hospitaller library in 1802.[25] A third copy was probably used within the Hospitaller house of Cologne, SS. Johannes et Cordula.[26]

To this period of German influence on the early printed editions can be ascribed also the publication of the first missal, printed at Strasburg in 1505 by Johannes Prüss zum Thiergarten.[27] The mandate for its publication states that a member of the Hospitaller house of Strasburg, whose name is not identified, moved both by the exiguous number of missals conforming to the Hospitaller use and by the necessity for a religious order to follow the same liturgy, prepared a text which conformed to the ordinal of the order and handed it to the printer. This editor was aware of the inclusion of some typically German feasts, which he justified by the *devotio terre* and *provincie observantia*. The edition appeared under the patronage of Grand Master Emery d'Amboise (1503-12), Rudolf Graf von Werdenberg, Prior of Germany, Johann Heggenzer, Grand Bailiff of Rhodes and later Prior of Germany (1505-12), and Erhardus Kienig from Ettlingen, *Commendator* of Strasburg. The mandate closes with an appeal to the *preceptores* and *locatenentes* of the order to buy this missal and to use it as an exemplar to correct and emend the books they had hitherto been using.

A copy of this missal was kept in the Strasburg house; it is now held by the Library of the Seminary of Strasburg.[28] Another copy was used by the Hospitallers of Haarlem; in 1625 it was transferred to the Haarlem City Library, where it is still found today.[29]

The most substantial innovation in the calendar and sanctorale was the addition of the feast of St Panthaleon (27 July), celebrated to commemorate the victory over the Turks in Rhodes in 1480. From the sanctorale rubric we read that 27 July was celebrated to commemorate the great victory over the Turks in 1480 achieved by Cardinal Pierre d'Aubusson, Grand Master of the people of Rhodes (1479-1503). Five years later Innocent VIII, by the bull *Redemptor noster* dated 31 May 1485,

---

[24]   *Armamentarium Catholicum perantiquae rarissimae ac pretiosissimae Bibliothecae quae asservatur Argentorati in celeberrima commenda eminentissimi ordinis Melitensis Sancti Johannis Hierosolymitani*, ed. J. N. Weislinger (Strasburg, 1749), 640-41 (pars hiemalis et aestivalis). Weislinger (1691-1755) was also the owner of a manuscript Hospitaller Breviary, datable to 1450-1500, now in Munich, Bayerische Sataatsbibliothek, Clm. 10111; see Dondi, as note 11, 232-3, no. A.12.

[25]   Freiburg i. B.,Universitätsbibliothek, Ink. O 9535, d.

[26]   San Juan, Puerto Rico, La Casa del Libro, no pressmark.

[27]   See note 16 *supra*.

[28]   Strasburg, Bibliothèque du Grand Séminaire, A 599; Weislinger, 251.

[29]   Haarlem, Stadsbibliotheek, 165 A 9; A. de Vries, *Catalogus Bibliothecae publicae Harlemensis* (Haarlem, 1848), 179, no. 28.

proclaimed St Panthaleon's day a solemn feast in perpetuity,[30] and offered an indulgence of 50 years attached to the office of the saint. The 1505 edition does not contain the full text of the Mass; it can, however, be found in the 1551 edition of the Hospitaller missal.[31]

A substantial shift in liturgical policies took place at the turn of the century, particularly during the magistracy of Emery d'Amboise. At the General Council of the order, held in Rhodes on 1 February 1510, the need was stressed to reinstate uniformity in liturgical observance within Hospitaller houses celebrating their offices according to different uses – literally *sub vario stilo*. With the death in 1505 of Rudolf Graf von Werdenberg, Prior of Germany, the man who had realized the relevance of printing to the unity of the order, but who had focused solely on the continental, and mostly German, component of it, the concern for a truly international uniformity struck the headquarters of the order.

It should be observed at this stage that the liturgy of the church of the Holy Sepulchre of Jerusalem, adopted by the Hospitallers and identified in the chant repertory of the major feasts, had never been changed. The evidence collected from eighty liturgical manuscripts used by the Hospitallers in various parts of Europe from the thirteenth to the sixteenth century, together with the early printed editions, shows that they all shared the same chant repertory. There were just a few local variations, identifiable in the calendars, sanctorales, and litanies, within those parts of the text where it was easier to adjust to local influence. This, in practice, resulted in the celebration of the office for different saints on certain days of the liturgical year. It was precisely this element of discrepancy that the order's general council wished to eliminate in the hope of conforming to early Hospitaller practice.

The mandate for the publication of the 1517 edition of the Hospitaller breviary[32] claims that Grand Master d'Amboise, together with the other members of the chapter general held on Rhodes on 1 February 1510, pointed out that in various Hospitaller churches the office of the canonical hours was being celebrated under different styles. This generated confusion when members from these houses attended the service at the order's conventual church on Rhodes. For this reason, the chapter general set up a commission to investigate the matter. The commission was composed by Leonardo Balestrieri OFM Obs., Latin archbishop of Rhodes (1506-39), the Spanish Ramon Riolx, Prior of the Conventual church on Rhodes (1507- *c.*1519), and Guillaume Quignon, *helemosinarius* of Emery d'Amboise,[33] Preceptor of Arnhem in the

---

[30]   K. M. Setton, *The Papacy and the Levant 1204-1571*, 4 vols (Philadelphia, Pa., 1976-1984), ii, 357 n. 37.

[31]   Dondi, as note 11, 228 n. 12 for the text of the indulgence, n. 13 for the text of the office.

[32]   See note 13, *supra*.

[33]   J. M. Van Winter, *Sources concerning the Hospitallers of St John in the Netherlands 14th-18th centuries*, Studies in the History of Christian Thought, lxxx (Leiden, Boston, and Cologne, 1998), 77.

Netherlands (1510-27),[34] and *Stamparum generalis Hospitalis Militiae per Galliam Procurator*.[35]

In its report to the chapter general, the commission claimed that the order's breviary was in several points confusing and defective. In the text the breviary is referred to as 'antiquum breviarium ecclesie sancti Iohannis', and I believe it has to be taken as the fifteenth-century printed edition of the breviary. On the advice of the commission and at the request of the chapter, Antonius Beriat was assigned the task of transcribing a good exemplar of a breviary extracted from the ordinal of the Conventual church of Rhodes. This would then be passed on to the printer, Cyriacus Hocperg of Lyons. Finally, the chapter decreed that this breviary must be adopted by all Hospitaller houses. As a result, the breviary was cleared of almost all German feasts. Instead, it now included a few Carmelite feasts, like Cirillus (6 March), the prophet Helysaeus (14 June), Focas (14 July) bishop of Sinope, whose relics were venerated at Constantinople and Antioch, and Elijah (1 December). It would appear that the exemplar used to prepare this edition was a breviary of the Holy Sepulchre previously used by the Carmelites. There is nothing surprising in that. The Carmelites, like the Hospitallers, had adopted the liturgy of the Holy Sepulchre of Jerusalem, and more than one liturgical manuscript of the Holy Sepulchre, written in Jerusalem, Acre, or Cyprus in the twelfth or thirteenth century, had ended up being used by Carmelite communities after the loss of the Holy Land. The only liturgical variant introduced at this stage, probably through the Carmelite exemplar, occurred in the short office of the Virgin, where the *Capitulum* at None now presented a form common to the Roman use. This variant, not present in the previous editions of the Hospitaller breviary based on German exemplars, can also be found in a few Hospitaller manuscripts, hitherto of unknown origin, and which may now be ascribed to Rhodes or descending from a Rhodian exemplar.[36] The Hospitaller Mathias Molitor is known to have owned a copy of this breviary in 1586.[37]

---

[34] Ibid., 77-80.

[35] As well as preceptor of Saint-Jean-du-Lateran at Paris and Prior of the order's convent of Corbeil, according to the preface addressed to him by Jean Quintin, opening the work of Antoine Geoffroi, *Estat de la court du Grant Turc, l'ordre de sa gendarmerie, et de ses finances* (Antwerp, 1542); see Anthony Luttrell, 'The Hospitallers' Historical Activities: 1530-1630', *Annales de l'Ordre Souverain Militaire de Malte*, xxvi (1968), 57-69; repr. in id., *Latin Greece, the Hospitallers and the Crusades 1291-1440* (London, 1982), III, 58.

[36] *Liber horarum* (after 1309), BL, Additional MS 41061. Probably written in Rhodes for an English Hospitaller: see Dondi, as note 11, 237-38, no. A.57.

Psalterium-Liber horarum, 1455-88, Oxford, St John's College, MS 131. Probably written for John Weston (d. 1489), Castellan of Rhodes 1470-71, Turcopolier 1471-76, Prior of England 1477-89: see Dondi, as note 11, 247-48, no. A.80.

Liber horarum, c.1460, Paris, BnF, MS lat 1400. With an early unidentified coat of arms of f. 29r: azure, in chief a cross couped gules between letters BC and CB, argent; in base a double-headed eagle, or; crest, a helmet in profile with mantling surmounted by three plumes, gules, or, and argent: see Dondi, as note 11, 239, no. A.62.

[37] London, Library of the Venerable Order of St John, A. 3. 7.

In 1551 Cornelius, a Septemgrangiis, prepared a new edition both of the Hospitaller breviary, textually similar to the one of 1517, and of the Hospitaller missal.[38] Both editions presented the same calendar, identical to the one in the 1517 breviary which had been revised by the General Council of Rhodes in 1510. Compared to the first 1505 edition, this missal no longer contained the German entries.

In 1553, a final edition of the Hospitaller missal appeared; it was a reprint of the 1551 edition.[39] While hardly any information surrounds the early use of the only surviving copy of the 1551 missal, we know that a copy of that of 1553 was used by the Hospitallers of Siracusa, in Sicily; then, after having been used also by the Capuchins of the same town, it moved to the Municipal Library in 1886, at the time of the suppression of the monasteries.[40] Another copy was used by the Hospitallers of Arles, and is now preserved in the city's Municipal Library.[41]

While the first fifteenth-century editions of Hospitaller liturgical texts represent the tail-end of the manuscript tradition of the order's large and influential German houses, it is with the beginning of the sixteenth century, and in particular with the new liturgical policies defined by the General Council in 1510, that the Hospitallers produced a standard breviary and missal to be used by all its houses. The new editions explicitly underscored their traditionally close ties with the Holy Land.

At the Council of Trent, the Grand Master of the order, engaged in the military defence of Malta, was represented by Martin Rojas Portalrubei. Summoned by Pope Pius IV on 7 November 1561, Martin Rojas was officially received on 7 September 1563, when he delivered his address, later published in Brescia by Ludovicus Sabiensis. At Trent, none of the order's privileges and immunities were revoked, though certain decree necessitated some modification to their religious activities, especially with regard to the administration of the sacraments and pastoral care.[42]

As far as liturgy was concerned, the 25th session of the Council of Trent decreed the reform of the breviary and of the missal.[43] In 1564, Pius IV set up a commission for this purpose and in 1568 both the new *Breviarium Romanum ex decreto ss. Concilii Tridentini* and the new *Missale Romanum ex decreto ss. Concilii Tridentini restitutum, Pii V Pont. Max. jussu editum* were published. Pius V's bull of 14 July 1570 decreed their use throughout the Church. No modifications to them were

---

[38]   See notes 15 and 18, *supra*; 240 copies of this edition appear in the inventory of a Lyonnaise bookseller in the late sixteenth century; see Ian Maclean, 'Murder, Debt and Retribution in the Italico-Franco-Spanish Book Trade: the Beraud-Michel-Ruiz affair, 1586-91', in *Fairs, Markets & the Itinerant Book Trade*, ed. R. Myers, M. Harris, and G. Mandelbrote (London, 2007), 96 item 79: 'douze b. Missale S Iohan. Hyerosolo. fol. a vingt la b dix rames chasq. balle r120'.

[39]   See note 19 *supra*.

[40]   Siracusa, Biblioteca Comunale, α 2 7; G. Agnello, 'I cavalieri di Malta a Siracusa: Convento e chiesa di S. Francesco. La chiesa di S. Leonardo. Il Messale dell'Ordine', *Per l'Arte Sacra* (May-August 1936), 27-33.

[41]   Arles, Bibliothèque Municipale, RB 40.

[42]   A. C. Breycha-Vauthier de Baillamont, 'L'Ordre au Concile de Trente', *Annales de l'Ordre Souverain Militaire de Malte*, xx (1962), 82-84.

[43]   E. Weber, 'Le Concile de Trente et la musique de la réforme a la contre-réforme', *Musique-Musicologie*, xii (Paris, 1982), 103.

permitted. That notwithstanding, a new edition of the breviary appeared in 1602. It was drawn up by a commission set up to correct any mistakes found in the previous edition. The year 1604 saw the publication of Clement VIII's missal; that of Urban VIII appeared in 1634.

The use of these texts was imposed on all dioceses, churches, and religious orders which could not claim a liturgical tradition older than two hundred years. However, the longevity of most institutions was such that space had had to be made for a special *proprium*, in order to retain the most significant local feasts.[44] This applied too to the Hospitallers, whose proper of saints was eventually published in 1659,[45] 1739,[46] and 1759.[47]

---

[44]   Ibid., 117-22.

[45]   *Officia propria sanctorum ordinis S. Joannis Hierosolymitani Melitensis in usum domus Coloniensis SS. Joannis et Cordulae seorsim edita* (Coloniae Agrippinae, Antonius Metternich, 1659); R. Amiet, *Missels et bréviaires imprimés (supplément aux catalogues de Weale et Bohatta), Propres des saints (édition princeps)* (Paris, 1990), 473, P 3014, a copy in Strasburg, Bibliothèque du Grand Séminaire, GS. 1 Ddi 55. Franz Paul von Smitmer, *Catalogo della Biblioteca del Sagro Militar Ordine di S. Giovanni Gerosolimitano* ([Valletta?], 1781), 173-78 (on liturgy): 175.

[46]   *Officia propria sanctorum recitanda a religiosis utriusque sexus Ordinis S. Johannis Hierosolymitani* (Strasburg, Melchior Pauschinger, 1739); see F. H. de Hellwald, *Bibliographie méthodique de l'Ordre Souverain de St. Jean de Jerusalem* (Rome, 1885), 266; Smitmer, as note 45, 175.

[47]   *Officia propria sanctorum recitanda a religiosis utriusque sexus Ordinis Militaris Sancti Joannis Jerosolymitani* (Malta, Nicola Capaci, 1759); repr. by Johannes Mallia in 1785: see Hellwald, as note 46, 266.

Chapter 7

Hospitallers, Mysticism, and Reform in Late-Medieval Strasburg

Karl Borchardt

The Hospitaller commandery of Strasburg was founded in 1371,[1] although the fourteenth century is generally said to have been a time of crisis for the Order of St John. After the fall of Acre in 1291, the Hospitallers had lost their traditional task of defending the Holy Land. Throughout the following decades they were faced with unprecedented shortages of money, despite the fact that the Templars' possessions were given to them in 1312. The causes for the financial problems included taxation by ecclesiastical and secular authorities. To raise money, the Hospitallers adopted several strategies. The conquest of Rhodes in the early-fourteenth century was one of them, because from their bases on Rhodes, the Hospitallers continued the prestigious fight against the infidel. A second strategy might have been the taking over and running of hospitals, a task for which the Hospitallers had long been famous. Strangely enough, with a few exceptions such as Breslau or Troppau where hospitals were given to them by the lay authorities, the Hospitallers did not revive their management of hospitals. Instead, the purchase of castles and landed estates was one of their favourite strategies for survival, especially in Central Europe – in places such as Biberstein, Gartow, or Sonnenburg. Around their commanderies the Hospitallers tried to build small territories and to consolidate their local or regional standing among nobles, citizens, and peasants.[2]

---

[1]   An expanded version of this paper has been printed, in German, 'Wirtschaft und Ordensreform im späten Mittelalter: Das Beispiel der Johanniter in Strasburg (mit Ausblick auf Breslau)', *Die Ritterorden in der europäischen Wirtschaft des Mittelalters,* eds. R. Czaja and J. Sarnowsky, Ordines militares: Colloquia Torunensia Historica, xii (2003), 35-53. For Strasburg, W. G. Rödel, *Das Großpriorat Deutschland des Johanniter-Ordens im Übergang vom Mittelalter zur Reformation,* 2nd ed. (Cologne, 1972), 181-99; M. Jouanny, 'Les Hospitaliers en Basse-Alsace de 1217 à 1529' (unpublished Ph.D. dissertation, cited in *École nationale des chartes: Positions des thèses,* 1931, 126); G. Trendel, 'Les commanderies des chevaliers de St-Jean de Jérusalem en Alsace', in *Recherches médiévales* ii/iii (Reichstett, 1983), 31-40.

[2]   A. Luttrell, 'The Hospitaller Province of Alamania to 1428', in *The Hospitaller State on Rhodes and its Western Provinces, 1306-1462,* Variorum Collected Studies (Aldershot, 1999), XII, 21-41. This was first published in Ordines militares: Colloquia Torunensia Historica, viii (Toruń, 1995); L. Jan and V. Jesenský, 'Hospitaller and Templar Commanderies in Bohemia and Moravia: their Structure and Architectural Form', *MO,* ii, 235-49; K. Borchardt, 'The Hospitallers, Bohemia, and the Empire, 1250-1330', in *Mendicants, Military Orders, and Regionalism in Medieval Europe,* ed. J. Sarnowsky (Aldershot, 1999), 201-231;

A fourth strategy was used at Strasburg, but this was more or less unique in the two Central European priories of *Alamania* and Bohemia. In 1371 the prior of *Alamania*, Fr. Konrad von Braunsberg, was given a flourishing religious community in the outskirts of Strasburg on Grünenwörth, the Green Island, and he organized this as a Hospitaller commandery. The community on the Grünenwörth had been founded four years earlier, in 1367, by a rich and pious banker named Rulman Merswin,[3] who was born at Strasburg in 1307. His family did not belong to the urban establishment. Rulman Merswin secured social advancement through his successful business career. His friends, partners, and rivals among great merchants and prosperous craftsmen strove hard to expel the traditional urban elite from Strasburg. During this struggle, the old urban establishment was supported by the Bishop of Strasburg. Eventually the new people took over the city, thanks, among other factors, to the help of Emperor Louis of Bavaria, who had been excommunicated by the pope. The sudden death of Louis in 1347 could be regarded as divine punishment, and pricks of conscience about usury, unjust prices, or his opposition to bishop and pope may have induced Rulman Merswin to renounce his wordly life. Influenced by the Dominican preacher at Strasburg, Johannes Tauler, a famous mystic, Rulman Merswin intensified his contacts with mystics throughout Southern Germany and travelled widely, no longer for business reasons but in a quest for spiritual experience. As he grew older, he wanted to settle down in his native city. In 1367, he paid the immense sum of 500 marks of silver to the Benedictine monastery of Altdorf, and received as a surety the area of Grünenwörth for at least one hundred years.[4]

On that area Rulman Merswin built a church, houses, and gardens; there he instituted a religious community for lay men and women to be governed by three proctors. The founder himself lived in his community and was one of the proctors. When one of the three proctors died or resigned, the other two were to choose his successor. Although the social and religious prestige of the proctors was certainly helpful, it was not easy for Rulman Merswin to obtain the licence of the bishop and his local ecclesiastical superiors. The bishop gave him permission to appoint a priest for the new community, but this permit was limited to twelve years.[5] The mendicant orders, whose brethren sometimes preached, heard confession, and said mass in the new community, did not have the personnel to man a permanent convent on Grünenwörth. Furthermore, Andreas Rüther has shown recently that the mendicant

---

M. Starnawska, Między Jerozolimą a Łukowem: Zakony krzyżowe na ziemiach polskich w średniowieczu (Warsaw, 1999).

[3]   *Merswin*, in modern German *Meerschwein*, means seahog or porpoise, *phocaena*, since the guinea-pig was not known in Europe before its discovery in Peru and Brazil in the sixteenth century. See M. Lexer, *Mittelhochdeutsches Handwörterbuch*, i (Leipzig, 1872; repr. Stuttgart, 1979), col. 2118; J. and W. Grimm, *Deutsches Wörterbuch*, xii [originally vi, ed. M. Heyne] (Leipzig, 1885; repr. Munich, 1984), col. 1859.

[4]   2 January 1367. *Urkundenbuch der Stadt Strasburg, v: Politische Urkunden von 1332 bis 1380*, eds. H. Witte and G. Wolfram (Strasburg, 1896), 580-83, nos. 744 and 745.

[5]   17 August 1366. *UB Strasburg* , v, 563-65, no. 726.

houses at Strasburg were too closely related with the exiled old urban elite to be welcome partners for upstarts like Rulman Merswin and his friends.[6]

Finally Rulman Merswin approached the Hospitallers. On 5 January 1371, after three years of negotiations, he reached an agreement with Fr. Konrad von Braunsberg, the prior of *Alamania*, who accepted Grünenwörth as a Hospitaller commandery.[7] As far as can be seen, there was nothing in the piety of Rulman Merswin and his community that showed any affinity to the Order of St John. The community on Grünenwörth did not want to fight the infidel; it did give alms to the poor and did care for the sick, but only as a part of its general concern for Christian charity; it did not run a hospital. Moral and liturgical rigour apart, the community on Grünenwörth was mainly characterized by its mystical aspirations. Rulman Merswin and other members were interested in pious contemplation and speculation, as evidenced by extant manuscripts from Grünenwörth. At that time it was the mendicant orders, rather than the Hospitallers, who were famous for mysticism in Germany. Nor, apparently, did the Hospitallers outside Germany have any interest in mysticism, in, for example, fourteenth-century Greek hesychasm.[8] Why then did they take over Grünenwörth?

The traditional answer is that the Hospitallers had simply been bribed, especially since they had debts of more than 10,000 florins in Strasburg.[9] Rulman Merswin promised to give 50 lb. from Grünenwörth to the order each year. In return, the new commandery was to pay enough priests to maintain the *servicium divinum* and the *cura animarum* of Rulman Merswin's community. The rights of the commander and of his superiors were severely restricted. According to the agreement of 5 January 1371, no property of the commandery could be bought, pawned, or sold without the consent of the three proctors. The three proctors were to decide on the reception of new brethren into the commandery. Brethren could not be moved to other houses without the consent of the three proctors. The commandery of Grünenwörth was to pay an annual response of only six florins, and was to be exempt from all other taxes imposed by the order, the pope, or the emperor. Each year the commander had to present the accounts of his commandery to the three proctors. No privileges would protect the order if it violated any one of these clauses. The only concession made by Rulman Merswin was that the Hospitaller commander was to have a deciding vote in the election of a new proctor if the other two proctors failed to agree on a candidate.

In the constitutional framework of the order, the status of the new commandery was so unusual that quarrels were inevitable. In the end, however, Master Philibert

---

[6]   A. Rüther, 'Bettelorden in Stadt und Land: Die Strasburger Mendikantenkonvente und das Elsaß im Spätmittelalter', *Berliner Historische Studien* xxvi, *Ordensstudien* xi (Berlin, 1997), especially 205.

[7]   5 January 1371. *UB Strasburg*, vi, 719-22, no. 934.

[8]   J. Meyendorff, *Byzantine Hesychasm: Historical, Theological and Social Problems* (London, 1974).

[9]   *Cartulaire de l'Église de Haguenau*, ed. C. A. Hanauer, Quellenschriften der elsässischen Kirchengeschichte, v (Strasburg, 1898), 158-65, no. 374; *Urkundenbuch der Stadt Strasburg*, vii: *Privatrechtliche Urkunden und Ratslisten von 1332 bis 1400*, ed. H. Witte (Strasburg, 1900), 302, no. 1027; ibid., 686-87, no. 2376.

de Naillac in 1417 and the chapter general in 1420 confirmed the special status of the new commandery of Grünenwörth. When Philibert de Naillac attended the Council at Constance, he used the opportunity to travel to Strasburg, attend a provincial chapter, and inspect the house of Grünenwörth in person.[10] Between 1371 and 1417 the Hospitallers had begun to show an increasing interest in the new house. The first commander was Heinrich von Wolfach, from the house of Freiburg im Breisgau. In 1386, however, he did not leave his books to the latter, as the statutes required – instead he obtained permission from the provincial chapter to leave them to Grünenwörth, more than a dozen volumes, including the Bible, the *Legenda aurea*, and St Thomas Aquinas.[11] His express purpose was to improve preaching and religious instruction at that house. Other similar donations followed. Gradually the house of Grünenwörth built up a very remarkable library. It would appear that the Hospitallers wished to profit from the intellectual and spiritual life in the community founded by Rulman Merswin. Their aim was to improve the educational level of their priests and other brethren.

This notwithstanding, the catalogues of the Grünenwörth library fail to reveal any leanings towards mysticism among the Hospitallers. Rulman Merswin died in 1382: by then he had not been able to form a community which continued his mystical activities. Only one Hospitaller priest, Nikolaus von Löwen, wrote mystical treatises and exchanged letters with other mystics. Twenty-two shorter and longer books written by Löwen are extant. Many of these claim to be composed by a certain *Gottesfreund*, an anonymous Friend of God. The first modern scholar to study these texts, Carl Schmidt, identified the *Gottesfreund* with a Nikolaus von Basel, a layman who was burned as a heretic. Later, Heinrich Denifle proved this wrong, suggesting that the *Gottesfreund* had been none other than Rulman Merswin himself. In 1905 Karl Rieder, in his basic study *Der Gottesfreund vom Oberland*, claimed that the *Gottesfreund* had been invented not by Rulman Merswin, but by Nikolaus von Löwen in the hope of exhorting the community of Grünenwörth to mystical contemplation.[12] The texts written by Löwen do provide allegedly historical information about the *Gottesfreund*, his family, his conversion to mysticism, his activities to take back

---

[10]   Basel, 13 October 1417; and Rhodes, 4 October 1420. Malta, Cod. 340, fol. 139; ibid., Cod. 345, fols. 141v-142r. Convocation at Strasburg confirmed by the master, Constance, 10 May 1417. Malta, Cod. 340, fols. 130v-131r; presence of the master at Strasburg, from 16 September to 2 October 1417. Ibid., fols. 134v-138v.

[11]   Heimbach, 27 May 1386. *UB Strasburg*, vii, 647, no. 2247. In general, J. J. Witler, *Catalogus codicum manuscriptorum in bibliotheca Sacri Ordinis Hierosolymitani Argentorati asservatorum* (Strasburg, 1746); J. N. Weislinger, *Catalogus librorum impressorum in bibliotheca eminentissimi ordinis Sancti Johannis Hierosolymitani asservatorum Argentorati* (Strasburg, 1749).

[12]   K. Rieder, *Der Gottesfreund vom Oberland: Eine Erfindung des Strasburger Johanniterbruders Nikolaus von Löwen* (Innsbruck, 1905); H. Denifle, 'Der Gottesfreund im Oberlande und Nikolaus von Basel', in *Historisch-politische Blätter*, lxxv (1875), 17-38, 93-122, 245-66, 340-54; C. Schmidt, *Nikolaus von Basel: Leben und ausgewählte Schriften* (Vienna, 1866). Fr. Nikolaus was one of the executors of the last will at Strasburg in 1371 for the citizen Heinrich Blankhart from Löwen [Leuven, Louvain] and his wife. *UB Strasburg*, vii, 431, 449, 679-80, nos. 1478, 1544, 2353.

the papal curia to Rome under Gregory XI, his attempts to heal the schism between Urban VI and Clement VII, and his miraculous meetings with other mystics from Germany, Italy, and Hungary in the Swiss mountains on 17 March 1379 and 22 March 1380. There is no reliable evidence in support of any of these details. It is not unlikely, therefore, that Löwen had indeed invented the *Gottesfreund*, whom he modelled on Rulman Merswin and who frequently alluded to contemporary events.

As a mystical writer Nikolaus von Löwen remained an exception among the German Hospitallers. His efforts to rekindle the mysticism of the late Rulman Merswin were to no avail. On the contrary, the spiritual life of Grünenwörth was increasingly influenced by traditional Hospitaller practices. As early as 1381, a hospital had been founded and lavishly endowed by Konrad zu der Megede, one of the lay proctors.[13] The original mysticism died out, but the fervour, self-discipline, and self-control achieved by new religious exercises were important assets for the Hospitallers. They used the commandery of Grünenwörth, its library, and its hospital for the instruction of their brethren. This concerned the care of spiritual and material needs, including the more mundane task of business administration. There is a trend in modern research to put spirituality and economy into two distinct categories, and to treat both separately. But all late-medieval religious reforms aimed at better standards of both morals and management. The same virtues, incessant activity, strict discipline, and rigorous control, turned the brethren into better *religiosi* and better administrators. The commandery of Grünenwörth was a shining example of economic success. Its religious prestige attracted many donations. The adroit administration of its possessions and resources rendered possible the incorporation into Grünenwörth of the two commanderies near Strasburg – the house of Schlettstadt, because of its debts in 1399,[14] and the house of Rheinau in 1406, because of the costly repairs it needed after having been destroyed by floods of the Rhine. This incorporation meant that Grünenwörth took over the estate management and paid pensions to the brethren of both houses. Moreover, Grünenwörth offered loans to other houses. And Grünenwörth guarded the records of many important decisions in the priory, as the prior had no permanent residence.

These facts challenge the traditional view that the Hospitallers had been bribed by Rulman Merswin to take over a new religious foundation completely alien to their own spirituality and hardly compatible with their long-established constitution. A detailed history of the Grünenwörth commandery has still to be written. It is true that most brethren in Strasburg did not become mystics like Rulman Merswin or Nikolaus von Löwen, but the Hospitallers at Strasburg grasped at other opportunities offered them by the new spiritual life of Rulman Merswin and his friends, the new religious fervour and rigour, and the improved morals and methods of administration. In the fifteenth century, the Order of St John continued to be proud of its commandery in Strasburg. Not only were the privileges enjoyed by the house of Grünenwörth not eroded; they were enhanced. For example, its prior and brethren were given the right

---

[13]   22 May 1381. *UB Strasburg*, vii, 570-71, no. 1978.

[14]   Confirmation by the master: Constance, 17 November 1417. Malta, Cod. 340, fol. 140r. Confirmation by the Chapter General: Rhodes, 4 October 1420. Ibid., Cod. 345, fols. 141v-142r.

to elect their commander;[15] when the commander died, the house was to pay only 100 florins of the Rhine as *mortuarium* and *vacantia* to the treasury on Rhodes.[16] Moreover, there was at least one instance where the house of Grünenwörth served as a model for other commanderies. In 1448 the hospital at Breslau in Silesia was reformed by a legate from the order's headquarters on Rhodes, and at the citizens' instigation it received the *consuetudines* and the *privilegia* of Grünenwörth.[17] And there may indeed have been some influence from Strasburg on the fifteenth-century reforms in Cologne and Utrecht.[18]

If Grünenwörth was such a success, why did the Hospitallers not copy the model more often in order to overcome their fourteenth-century crises? The main reason appears to have been the fact that the new late-medieval spirituality had not grown from within the order. The new spirituality had emerged from among the new elites in Central Europe, mostly bourgeois elites. Rulman Merswin was a classic example. Only a few relatively rare and unknown traditional or new orders, like the Carthusians, the Hermits of St Paul, the Brigetines, the Hieronymites, or the Celestinians,[19] were regarded as sufficiently strict to profit from this new spirituality. But the Hospitallers were too well established throughout Western Europe by the fourteenth century. They could profit from the new spirituality only in urban centres such as Strasburg or Breslau, where they did not have old commanderies associated with other social strata and dedicated to older religious traditions. Rulman Merswin's friend, Prior Konrad von Braunsberg, was closely connected with Cologne, but he did not endeavour to win the old commandery of St Johann and Cordula in Cologne over to the new reform. This may explain why the Hospitallers' piety at Strasburg remained an almost unique experience during the later Middle Ages. Although an exception, Strasburg highlights some of the problems with which the Hospitallers had to cope during their fourteenth-century crises and illustrates their position with regard to the late-medieval movement for religious and other reforms.

---

[15]   Confirmation by the master: Basel, 13 October 1417. Malta, Cod. 340, fol. 139v. Confirmation by the Chapter General: Rhodes, 4 October 1420. Ibid., Cod. 345, fol. 142r.

[16]   Basel, 13 October 1417. Malta, Cod. 340, fol. 139r; and Rhodes, 4 October 1420 . Ibid., Cod. 345, fols. 141v-142r.

[17]   M. Starnawska, 'Die mittelalterliche Bibliothek der Johanniter in Breslau', in *Die Spiritualität der Ritterorden im Mittelalter,* ed. Z. H. Nowak, Ordines Militares: Colloquia Torunensia Historica, vii (Toruń, 1993), 241-52; K. Borchardt, 'Die Johanniter in Schlesien (12. bis 18. Jahrhundert)', in *Jahrbuch der Schlesischen Friedrich-Wilhelms-Universität zu Breslau* xxxviii-xxxix (1997-98), 173-74.

[18]   For Cologne, Sang-Joon Ahn, *Die Johanniterkommende „St Johann und Cordula" in Köln: Geschichte, Besitz, Wirtschaft und Sozialstruktur der Kölner Johanniterkommende im Spätmittelalter* (Köln, 2006). For a very sceptical judgement on Hospitaller reforms, W. G. Rödel, 'Reformbestrebungen im Johanniterorden in der Zeit zwischen dem Fall Akkons und dem Verlust von Rhodos (1291-1522),' in *Reformbemühungen und Observanzbestrebungen im spätmittelalterlichen Ordenswesen,* ed. K. Elm, Berliner Historische Studien, xiv (Berlin, 1989), 109-129.

[19]   K. Borchardt, *Die Cölestiner: Eine Mönchsgemeinschaft des späten Mittelalters,* Historische Studien Ebering lxxxviii (Husum, 2006), 352 *et seq.* with further references.

Chapter 8

Heraldry in Medieval Rhodes: Hospitallers and Others

Anna-Maria Kasdagli

Hospitaller heraldry has been indispensable for the identification and precise dating of medieval buildings on Rhodes. Nineteenth-century western travellers[1] and early twentieth-century scholars[2] used their knowledge of heraldry to lay the foundations on which modern archaeologists and other experts have since built upon considerably.

At the latest count, the heraldic shields surviving on Rhodes number 861. Of these, 807 are found in the old town of Rhodes, 220 represent the Order of the Hospital itself, and 352 are shared between sixteen grand masters (Table 8.1). Again 178 of the grand masters' shields come from the fortifications or are still in place there. The figures are influenced by the increased popularity of heraldry and a mounting desire for self-advertisement, possibly a localized spirit of competition (Table 8.2).

Table 8.1 Arms of the Grand Masters in Rhodes, 1319–1522.

Grand Master	Reign	Number of Shields	Average per Year of Reign
Villeneuve	1319–1346	10	0.37
Gozon	1346–1353	6	0.85
Corneillan	1353–1355	3	1.5
Pins	1355–1365	6	0.6
Berenger	1365–1373	[2]	0.25
Heredia	1377–1396	10	0.5
Naillac	1396–1421	7	0.3
Fluvian	1421–1437	29	1.8
Lastic	1437–1454	29	1.7
Milly	1454–1461	10	1.4
Zacosta	1461–1467	10	1.6

---

[1]   B.E.A. Rottiers, *Description des monuments de Rhodes* (Brussels, 1830). E. Flandin, *L'Orient* (Paris, 1853). A. Berg, *Die Insel Rhodus* (Braunschweig, 1862).

[2]   A. Gabriel, *La cité de Rhodes*, 2 vols. (Paris 1921-23). G. Gerola, *I monumenti medioevali delle Tredici Sporadi*, in *ASAtene*, i (1914), 169-356.

Orsini	1467–1476	19	2.1
Aubusson	1476–1503	113	4.1
Amboise'	1503–1512	35	3.9
Caretto	1513–1521	53	6.6
V. de l'Isle-Adam	1521–1522	10	6.6
Total		**352**	

Table 8.2   Heraldry on the Fortifications of Rhodes, 1377–1522.

Grand Master	Reign	Shields on the Fortifications	Average per Year of Reign
Heredia	1377–1396	9	0.5
Naillac	1396–1421	5	0.2
Fluvian	1421–1437	13	0.8
Lastic	1437–1454	20	1.2
Milly	1454–1461	7	1.0
Zacosta	1461–1467	9	1.5
Orsini	1467–1476	17	1.8
Aubusson	1476–1503	54	2.0
Amboise'	1503–1512	9	1.0
Caretto	1513–1521	32	4.0
V. de l'Isle-Adam	1521–1522	3	2.0
Total		**178**	

Whatever the cause, this trend somehow conceals the extent of the building activity of earlier grand masters, like Naillac, Fluvian, Lastic, and Zacosta. The defences of Rhodes resemble a heraldic palimpsest; more recent additions and modifications mask earlier works whose heraldry is no longer in evidence. The extant Hospitaller defences on the landward side were begun by Grand Master Anton Fluvian (1421-37) and, for most of their length, completed by his successor, Jean de Lastic (1437-54). The new wall had become necessary as a result of the town's expansion and the increasing threat from the East.

On the new fortification every tower, segment of curtain, and fausse-braye carried a pair of shields: the order's to the left, the grand master's to the right.

Fluvian and Lastic bore arms (*a fess*) which, without tinctures, are virtually indistinguishable. On the curtain wall, all the shields are in white and red marble, rendering the proper tincture of Lastic's arms: argent on gules. The only instance where his arms show no attempt at rendering the colours is found on the tower of England, where a dated inscription obviates the need. There was a need for this differentiation because Fluvian had also left his mark on the new wall. Other shields, carved on local grey marble, are mounted on the square towers and on some sections of fausse-braye. These heraldic slabs are standardized in size, form, and relief. It would appear reasonable to assume that they are the work of Fluvian, who had had plainly carved shields mounted on his constructions, not foreseeing the need for differentiation. From heraldic evidence alone, it can be concluded that the new fortification began as a series of towers linked by the fausse-braye, and that the curtain wall proper was erected later by de Lastic for a practical reason: once the advance defences were in place, obsolete structures at the rear could be dismantled and quarried for the needs of the new curtain wall.

Surviving evidence for the use of heraldry on Rhodes antedates the establishment of the Hospitallers: on a slab of local marble[3] a Greek inscription in Byzantine capitals reads 'John Pitzos, servant of the Lord, went to his rest in the month of J[une] in the year 1306'. The lower part of the slab is missing. The shallow carving at the bottom of the surviving part may be reconstructed without much difficulty as the top of a shield *parted per pale*, with a single charge in the sinister part: either a lily or, perhaps, a star (Figure 8.1). The design cannot be otherwise interpreted on stylistic grounds, and Pitzos is clearly the Hellenized version of an Italian name. Italian adventurers active in the Aegean Sea in the thirteenth century were apparently responsible for the introduction of heraldry to Rhodes; by the time of the Hospitaller invasion, these same Italians were probably in the process of being assimilated into the local element; our inscription would have otherwise been in Latin. The slab is the earliest in a long series of tombstones, most of which have come to us in a fragmentary form. They are likely to have belonged to people of a certain standing, both laymen and clerics. Most of the latter were Hospitallers. On several such slabs the inscription is completed by the arms of the deceased. Though the quality of the work varies, this is an important category of heraldic material, and it keeps growing as new finds are brought to light.

It is usually fairly easy to distinguish Hospitaller funerary monuments from those of lay persons. Although the thorny subject of donats of the order has recently been raised, and evidence for it sought in tombstones, my feeling is that the vow of poverty never forced a dignitary of the order to repose in a pauper's grave: their colleagues and relatives saw to this.[4] In any case, when legible inscriptions accompany Hospitaller heraldry, they generally include the rank the deceased had held within the order. Similarities between Hospitaller and lay tombstones are evident, with the latter imitating the former without attempting to confuse the issue of status.

---

[3]   Unpublished. 4th Ephorate of Byzantine Antiquities Internal Inventory No. F 101.

[4]   G. Konstantinopoulos, *Rhodes Museum I, Archaeological Museum* (Athens, 1977), 30.

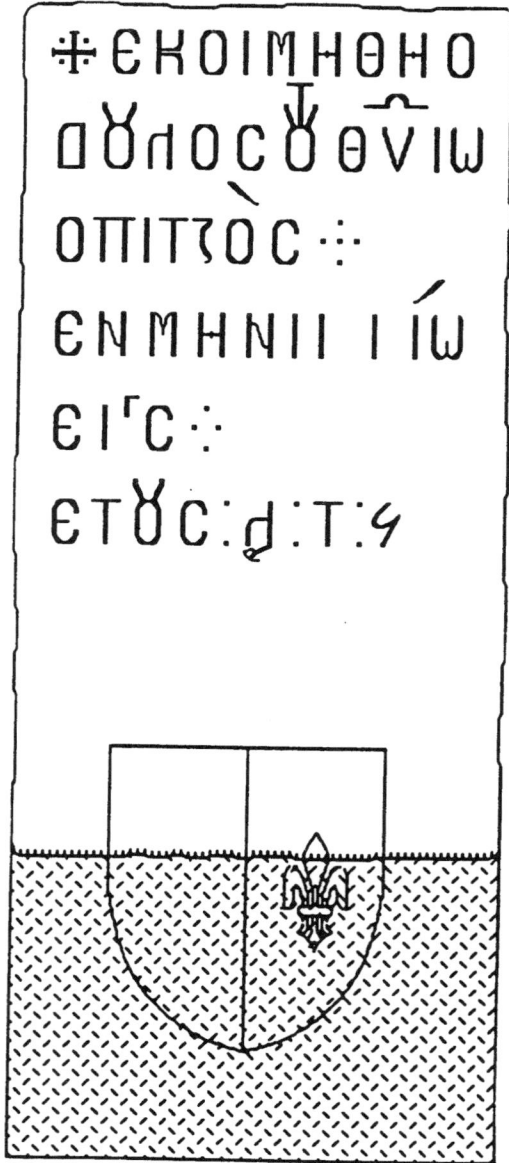

Fig. 8.1   Tomb slab of Ioannes Pitzos, d.1306

Most Hospitaller tombstones were of better workmanship than all but the very best lay slabs; the tombs of grand masters were in a class of their own.[5] The increasing importance of heraldry on the slabs is plain to see. The simpler form of heraldic tombstone bears an inscription and the arms of the deceased. Hospitallers placed their personal arms next to those of the order. Laymen who imitated this layout placed the arms of both sides of the family next to each other or repeated their arms twice.[6] In later slabs, Hospitallers had the option of placing *a chief of the order* above their arms, thus obviating the need for a second shield; from then on a feeling seems to have grown that only the highest officials of the order should place their personal arms next to the cross of the order.

In a more ornate form of tombstone, where an effigy was included, two shields added to the symmetry of the composition. In the early years of the fifteenth century, a variant placed both shields above the head of the effigy. But the most successful type, the one more widely imitated in lay tombstones, displays the arms on the spandrels of the arch framing the head. On these, family arms were usually repeated. The dominance of the coat of arms on late tombstones, lay or Hospitaller, is evident. The arms are usually set within a laurel wreath decorated with flowing ribands and form the centrepiece of the composition.

Coats of arms on (or from) buildings belong to both Hospitallers and laymen. The former are mostly found within the upper town, the *collachium*, where the Knights were expected to reside.[7] They often mark the association of Hospitaller dignitaries with public functions, and thus with the buildings where these functions were exercised. Secular shields are not totally absent from the upper town; but in the lower town they appear to outnumber Hospitaller arms by far.

Many of the *c.*220 shields belonging to some 170 different individuals are still unidentified. Normally the location, context, craftsmanship, or other details on the arms themselves are of assistance: they can indicate whether one is dealing with a Hospitaller or a layman, with a nobleman or a pretentious burgher. Such distinctions are significant because they offer insights into social complexities.[8]

Heraldry really caught on among the Greeks during the fifteenth century, though their choices sometimes overlooked basic heraldic rules. Heraldic 'errors' need not however be a sign of 'Greekness'. The degree of acculturation varied so much according to period and status that it is difficult to draw firm conclusions about not only heraldry but also religious practice, language, and dress. Latinized Greek names figure on heraldic tombstones and Greek inscriptions accompany urban heraldry. The sadly damaged murals in a house of the lower town bear a row of shields,[9] some

---

[5]   J.-B. de Vaivre, *Les tombeaux des grands maîtres des Hospitaliers de Saint-Jean de Jérusalem a Rhodes*, in *Monuments et Mémoires*, lxxvi (Vendôme, 1998), 35-88.

[6]   Konstantinopoulos, 25, ill. no. 19. and unpublished find No. F 122.

[7]   E. Kollias, *The Medieval City of Rhodes and the Palace of the Grand Master* (Athens, 1998), 90.

[8]   A. M. Kasdagli, 'Ta Rhoditika Oikosema. Merikes paratereseis gia te semasia tous', in *Istoria kai Provlemata Syntereses tes Mesaionikes Poles tes Rodou* (Athens, 1992),118-19.

[9]   Id., 'Katalogos ton Thyreon tes Rodou', in AD, xlviii-xlix (1994-95), *Meletes* (Athens, 1998), nos. 35, 51, 82, 118, 182.

of which are probably of western provenance while others are more 'eastern' in style (Figure 8.2). But the fact that they are found together suggests a remarkable degree of integration, also attested from other evidence.[10]

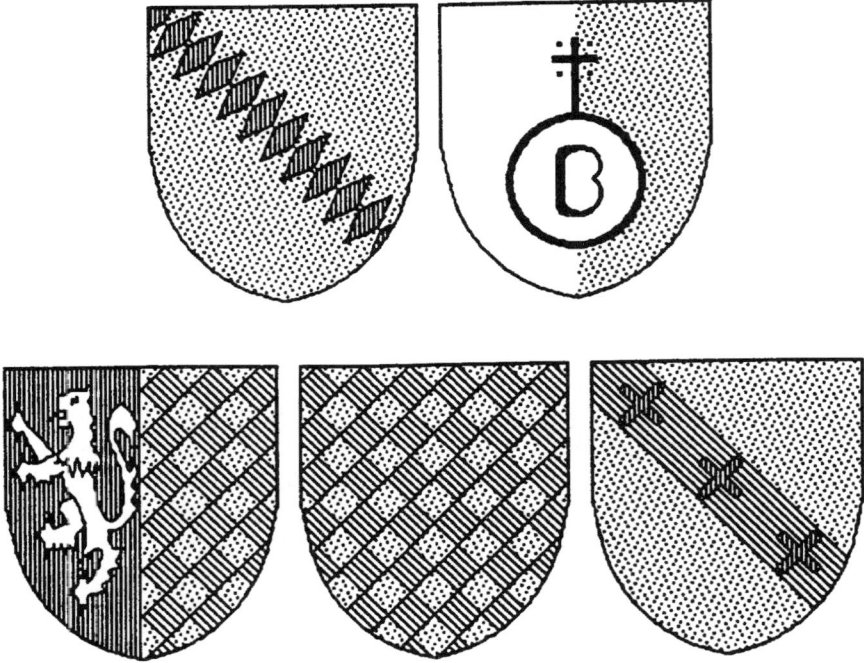

Fig. 8.2   Civic heraldry from the house at 2, Gavalas Street, Old Town of Rhodes

Secular shields dominate the category of moveable artifacts like pottery,[11] whereas surviving cannon of the period bear the arms of known Hospitallers. Two shields on small pieces probably cast in Italy are something of a puzzle, perhaps a caster's attempt to mark his clients' orders. The breech-loaded guns bearing them are thought to post-date the fall of Rhodes to the Ottomans.[12] One of the shields, however, may provide evidence of an earlier date, as it bears what appears to be *a chief of the*

---

[10]   Kollias, 56-58, 123. Also Z. Tsirpanlis, *Anekdota Eggrafa gia te Rodo kai tis Noties Sporades apo to archeio ton Ioanniton Ippoton 1421-1453* (Rhodes, 1995).

[11]   See M. Michaelidou, 'Schediasma tes eisegmenes ephyalomenes keramikes ste Rodo kata ten epoche ton Ippoton (1309-1522)': Unpublished Ph.D. thesis, University of Thessaloniki, 1994.

[12]   R. Bishop-Smith, *Sixteenth-Century Swivel Guns in Greece and Turkey, including a piece in private collection* (Lisbon, 1999), 5-6.

order. The introduction of this very useful attribute can be securely dated from the Rhodian evidence. It makes its appearance on the arms of Guy de Melay (1469), and its inception cannot be pushed much earlier than that. A Rhodian funerary slab dated 1374, now in Istanbul,[13] has created some confusion: the arms, as the inscription clearly states, are those of a layman; the *chief* is most likely explained by the man's Genoese origin since *a chief of Genoa* is attested quite early in Italy.

The knights were reluctant to place any but the grand master's arms on the fortifications. There are none such that could be dated later than the reign of Grand Master Heredia (d.1396). Even before that they must have been exceptional. A single group of arms, contemporary with Heredia, was mounted on the north tower of the arsenal and was probably associated with it because they included those of Admiral Domenico d'Allemagna. These shields are now dispersed. The only other examples are furnished by the chapel of St George, sheltering within the southeast corner tower of the upper town. This is a structure of Byzantine date whose interior was converted into a chapel in the late fourteenth century and is accessible only from the wall-walk. The carved lintel bears the arms of Heredia, of his lieutenant Pierre Culant, and of a knight who may have possibly been the Spaniard Inigo d'Alfaro.

The whole interior of the chapel is covered in murals. The apse is crowned by the English royal arms; the opposite wall is fully covered by a painting of exceptional quality representing St George on his white charger, clad in chainmail and flanked by the arms of Grand Master Philibert de Naillac (1396-1421); another shield (*barry of six argent and azure*) in the lower left-hand corner of the composition has not been identified. A similar shield is also found on the south wall in a row with three others; two have been identified as those of the FitzAlan and Holt families (Figure 8.3). We may, I think, reasonably infer that the other unidentified shields also belong to Englishmen. An earlier mural layer, best preserved on the east side of the same wall, displays another shield with a red cross on a white field, perhaps St George's cross. Whether the Englishmen who apparently paid for the decoration of the chapel were Hospitallers or laymen on crusade is unclear. As to the date, the arms of late fifteenth- and early sixteenth-century grand masters in the apse are a century later than the rest of the heraldry within the chapel. The arms of Grand Master de Naillac may easily be accounted for. They belong to the ruler who probably participated in the enterprise of embellishing the chapel; they also place the heraldic frescoes in his reign – at least the second layer, if not the first, which may be slightly earlier.

It is interesting that a group of foreigners had decided to commemorate their presence on Rhodes in such a manner. The practice recalls the quantity of arms on the English Tower at the Hospitaller fortress at Bodrum. Progress with the identification of arms in this and several other contexts will make heraldry an increasingly efficient tool in the solution of a wide range of archaeological and topographical problems.

---

[13]   Siegrid Düll, 'Drei Johanniter in Istanbul: Neue Unterschungen zu den rhodischen Grabsteinen im Archäologischen Museum', in *Istanbuler Mitteilungen*, xxxix (1989), 109.

Fig. 8.3   Heraldry from the east wall, Chapel of St George on the Collachio
           Wall

Chapter 9

The Fictional Hospitaller: Images and Stories of the Knights of Malta in Count Jan Potocki's *Manuscript Found in Saragossa*

Yuri Stoyanov

Alongside the unfolding of the Enlightenment, the course of the eighteenth century also witnessed a major revival of interest in the imagery and themes of knighthood and chivalry. On several occasions, this revival did not usually have much to do with the actual history and heritage of the military-religious and chivalric orders or the medieval ideal of chivalric quest. Rather, it represented attempts to re-interpret the notion and thereby the reality of the military orders in novel symbolic and initiatory frameworks, often in opposition to the rising rationalism of the age.

This symbolic and mythical resurrection of the knight followed different but frequently interrelated patterns in contemporary literary works, in neo-Hermetic and alchemical thought, and in the proliferation of 'chivalric' degrees in the newly introduced higher grades of speculative Freemasonry.[1] These were charged with eclectic and often abstruse symbolism intended to endow them with a mystique and a romantic attraction.[2] This symbolic and initiatory vision of chivalry represented a new stage in the development of the attitudes to the Middle Ages in early modern Europe, inspired by the continuing fascination with medieval chivalric romances and some contemporary apologias for knighthood. Among the major and symptomatic developments of this new quest for mythical knighthood were the alchemical re-interpretation of the ritual and symbolism of the Order of the Golden Fleece in

---

[1]   On this process as a whole, A. Faivre, 'Miles Redivivus (Aspects de l'Imaginaire chevaleresque au XVIIIe siècle: Alchimie, Franc-Maçonnerie, Littèrature)', in *Accès de l'Ésotérisme occidental* (Paris, 1986), 209-34.

[2]   On the process of the emergence of 'chivalric' degrees in speculative Freemasonry, see, for example, G. A. Schiffmann, *Die Enstehung der Rittergrade in Frankreich in der ersten Hälfte der 18. Jahrhunderts* (Leizpig, 1882); R. Le Forestier, *La Franc-Maçonnerie templière et occultiste aux XVIIIe et XIXe siècles* (Paris, 1970), *passim*; K. R. H. Frick, *Die Erleuchteten. Gnostisch-theosophische und alchemistisch-rosenkreuzerische Geheimgesellschaften bis zum Ende des 18 Jahrhunderts - ein Beitrag zur Geistesgeschichte der Neuzeit* (Graz, 1973), 500-609, *passim*; Faivre, 218-26; G. Galtier, *Franc-maçonnerie Egyptienne, Rose-Croix et Néo-Chevalerie* (Paris, 1989); P. Girard-Augry, *Hauts-grades chevaleresques de la stricte observance templière du XVIIIe siècle* (Paris, 1995); id., *Rituels secrets de la franc-maçonnerie templière et chevaleresque* (Paris, 1996), *passim*.

Hermann Fictuld's *Aureum Vellus oder Goldenes Vlies*[3] and the introduction of the Templar Legend into the Masonic Rite of Strict Obedience founded by Baron von Hund in 1764.[4] It also included the publication, particularly in German, of a number of literary works focused on medieval chivalry. The latter's preoccupations varied from romantic recreations of actual historical events involving the medieval knighthood and/or the military orders to, as in the case of Zacharias Werner's *Die Söhne des Thales* (1804), fictional elaborations on the new Templar legend of the Rite of Strict Observance. The aim was to establish a direct link between a medieval military order and a contemporary Masonic rite.[5]

This fluctuating eighteenth-century framework, within which the medieval knight and military orders were revived in an unfamiliar disguise to be charged with even more unfamiliar symbolic acts, has not received the attention it certainly deserves. The same can be said of its underlying social and cultural mechanisms. A very important test case for its further investigation is the widely acclaimed novel of Count Jan Potocki (1761-1815), *Manuscrit trouvé à Saragosse*. Most of the book appears to have been written in several stages, between 1797 and 1807. It boasts a highly complex publication and textual history. It was originally written in French, with various sections published during Potocki's own lifetime. However, a part of it was preserved only in a Polish text deriving from a lost French original. The process of comparing the variant readings and preparing an integral edition of the text took nearly two centuries; such an edition finally appeared in 1989[6] and was followed by the first English translation of the whole text.[7]

The book has long been recognized as one of the masterpieces of world literature, experimenting with literary genres in vogue in eighteenth-century European literature, but also anticipating later developments in Romanticism and even modern literature.[8]

---

3   Hermann Fictuld, *Aureum Vellus oder Goldenes Vlies* (Leipzig, 1749). On Fictuld's re-interpretation of the symbolism and ritual of the Order of the Golden Fleece, see, for example, Faivre, 'Miles Redivivus', 209-18; *Toison d'Or et Alchimie* (Milan, 1990), 73-85, 132-37.

4   On the introduction and the provenance of the Templar legend in von Hund's Rite of Strict Observance, see, for example, Schiffmann, *Die Enstehung,* 178 ff.; Le Forestier, *La Franc-Maçonnerie templière*, 64-83, 87 ff; Faivre, 'Miles Redivivus', 219 ff.

5   Zacharias Werner, *Die Söhne des Thales* (Berlin, 1803-4, 2 vols.). On Werner's use of the Templar legend, L. Guinet, *Zacharias Werner et l'ésoterisme maçonnique* (The Hague, 1962), *passim*.

6   Jean Potocki, *Manuscrit trouvé à Saragosse*, ed. René Radrizzani (Paris, 1990); on the publication and textual history of the novel, ibid. vii-xxii; M.-E. Żółtowska, 'La genèse du *Manuscrit trouvé à Saragosse* de Jan Potocki', in *Les Cahiers de Varsovie*, iii, 'Jean Potocki et le *Manuscrit trouvé à Saragosse*', 85-100; Z. Markiewicz, 'Quelques énigmes de la vie de Jean Potocki et du *Manuscrit trouvé à Saragosse*', in *Les Cahiers de Varsovie*, iii, 171-82.

7   Jan Potocki, *The manuscript found in Saragossa*, trans. Ian Maclean (London, 1996).

8   There is a considerable number of studies dealing with the genre and the narrative peculiarities of the novel as well as its place in world literature; see, for example, the relevant contributions in *Les Cahiers de Varsovie*, **iii**; M.-E. Żółtowska, 'Un pércurseur de la littérature fantastique: Jean Potocki et son *Manuscrit trouvé à Saragosse*', Ph.D. dissertation, Yale

The core narrative presents a kind of a rites-of-passage story. In the early 1700s, a young Walloon officer is subjected to a succession of ordeals by a noble Moorish family (leading an underground existence in Sierra Morena), intended to test if he is worthy to continue their lineage. During these ordeals, the officer encounters a diverse company of cabbalists, aristocrats, gypsies, and bandits, all of whom venture to tell him their stories over a period of sixty-six days. The themes of these stories range from ancient Egypt and the Wandering Jew to contemporary Spain and the Order of Malta, and the novel branches out into multiple stories-within-stories featuring narratives belonging to a variety of genres – the philosophical novel, the picaresque, the adventure story, the Gothic novel, etc. The subjects treated and fictionalized within the eighteenth-century time-frame of the novel range from contemporary European history and dynastic intrigues to ancient and medieval Egyptian and Jewish history and religion, from the medieval and contemporary history of Islam and trends, such as the Isma'ili and the related Druze traditions, to contemporary developments in science, rationalism and materialism, and so on. The variety of subjects covered with ease and often in some depth betrays the polymath inclinations of the author, who was one of the intriguing figures on the European political and cultural scene during the late eighteenth and early nineteenth centuries.

A scion of a very prominent noble family, Potocki received his education in Switzerland, and after becoming a novice Knight of Malta, in 1779-82 he travelled to Spain and Tunis and took part in an anti-Berber expedition. These early Mediterranean journeys foreshadowed a life of wide-ranging travel and hectic political, literary, and scholarly activities in a period that was particularly dramatic both for Poland and for the Order of Malta. The events that occurred during Potocki's lifetime included the establishment of the Grand Priory of the Order of Malta in Poland in 1776 (after intense diplomatic negotiations between Catherine the Great and Grand Master Pinto, motivated by the complex political relations between Poland and Russia); the three partitions of Poland, the last of which brought the new priory within the realm of the Russian empire and led to its conversion into a Russian priory by Tsar Paul I in 1797; Napoleon's conquest of Malta, and the election of Paul as Grand Master by the Russian priory; Paul's controversial establishment of a second Russian priory for the Orthodox nobility and the abolition of both priories by Paul's successor, Alexander I, in 1810. During this period, apart from travelling all over Europe, Potocki made voyages to the Middle and Far East. He witnessed some of the stages of the French Revolution and changed his attitudes to it. He associated himself with the cause of Polish patriots and at the same time mixed within Russian courtly circles, where he took part in the coronation of Paul I. In 1802 he was appointed a personal counsellor to Alexander I. His wide-ranging scholarly explorations led to the publication of often pioneering studies, with subjects ranging from Egyptology, ancient chronology, and travelogues to the history of the Scythian, Sarmatian, and Slavonic people. In 1805 he was appointed scientific director of Count Golovkin's important diplomatic-scientific mission to China and the imperial Manchurian house.

University, 1973; F. Rosset, *Le Théâtre du romanesque. 'Manuscrit trouvé à Saragosse' entre contsruction et maçonnerie* (Paris, 1995).

The politics surrounding the establishment of the Grand Priory of Poland, the posited Russian intentions to use it to facilitate the gradual incorporation of Polish lands into the Russian empire, and the reactions of Polish knights, like Potocki, to these developments – these are all subjects worthy of a more detailed investigation. The purpose of this essay, however, is to explore the way that Potocki, himself a Knight of Malta, created and elaborated the image of the fictional Hospitaller against the background of the contemporary symbolist and initiatory re-interpretations of the notion of the knight and the military orders. As a rites-of-passage novel, *Manuscrit trouvé à Saragosse* possesses all the necessary ingredients for such a re-interpretation, and Hospitallers do indeed appear in some of its central narratives. Moreover, the novel offers a number of cryptic and obvious allusions to Masonic themes and symbolism. This is not very surprising, as both in Paris and Warsaw Potocki associated himself with Masonic circles, some of which were involved in the creation or practice of the rites of the new, higher 'chivalric' grades.[9] In his novel Potocki demonstrates encyclopaedic knowledge of ancient and contemporary hermetic thought,[10] cabbala, and esoteric trends in Islam as well as an awareness of some very recent discoveries of ancient texts, such as the Ethiopic version of the Book of Enoch, which led to the resurrection of the influence of the Enochic tradition on European religiosity and spirituality. Furthermore, the concluding exposé of the pedigree and fortunes of the Gomelez, the underground Moorish dynasty of Sierra Morena, reveals them as an Alid family, dedicated to the cause of the return of the caliphate to the Alid descendants. It shows them also as related to the medieval Isma'ili Fatimid rulers in Egypt. Hence the contemporary Gomelez dynast has to embark on an initiatory pilgrimage to the Isma'ili and Druze sites in Egypt and the Middle East. Potocki's account of the pilgrimage of the Great Sheikh of the Gomelez in Egypt and the Middle East also betrays some echoes of the medieval European 'Assassin Legends' surrounding the Nizari Isma'ilis of Persia and Syria. As convincingly demonstrated by Farhad Daftary, these legends inherited some of the themes of the anti-Isma'ili polemics in Muslim society itself, and thus were the outcome of 'an extraordinary type of a tacit co-operation between the Christians and Muslims during Crusader times'.[11] On the other hand, European knowledge of the actual beliefs and practices of the Nizairi Isma'ili did not benefit from their actual historical contacts or indeed from their co-operation with the Hospitallers and the Templars in the 1230s.[12] With its reiteration of some of the themes of the

---

[9]   On Potocki's Masonic associations and use of Masonic themes in the novel, C. Nicolas, 'Du bon usage de la Franc-MaHonnerie dans le *Manuscrit trouvé à Saragosse*', in *Les Cahiers de Varsovie*, iii, 271-86; Rosset, *Le Théâtre du romanesque*, 189-98; I. F. Belza, 'Rukopis', naidennaia v Saragose', (Afterword), in Jan Potocki, *Rukopis', naidennaia v Saragose*, trans. A. S. Golemby (Moscow, 1968), 575, 586.

[10]   On Potocki's use of ancient Hermetic and philosophic texts in the novel, see, for example, T. Sinko *Historja religji i filozofja w romansie Jana Potockiego* (Cracow, 1920), 1-38.

[11]   F. Daftary, *The Assassin Legends. Myths of the Isma'ilis* (London / New York, 1995), 125.

[12]   For the evidence of such co-operation and contacts, see, for example, Daftari, *The Assassin Legends*, 73-77.

medieval 'Assassin Legends', Potocki's account of the initiatory journeys of the Great Sheikh of the Gomelez can be seen in some respects as a new, 'enlightened' version of the 'Assassin Legends', applied to contemporary Isma'ili (and to what he saw as related) communities and traditions, drawing both on the medieval narratives and contemporary orientalist research and discourse.[13] In Potocki's version of the 'Assassin Legends', the theme of the initiatory quest and its symbolism takes centre stage as he fictionalizes and mythicizes both medieval and modern Isma'ilis. This is precisely where his novelty lies.

It is obvious, therefore, that in harmony with eighteenth-century cultural and mytho-hermetic fashions and trends in literary, esoteric, and ritualist settings, the notions of the initiatory quest, its symbolism and personal transformation form one of the main fabrics of Potocki's novel. The question that inevitably arises is: did Potocki integrate the figures of the Knights of Malta, and indeed the Order of Malta, into this symbolic and initiatory framework, which is so crucial for his novel? An analysis of the presence and roles of the Knights of Malta in the multiple narratives of the novel shows that he chose not to do so. Potocki used his personal knowledge of the Order of Malta and of Malta to add further depth and reality to some of the stories in which Knights of Malta appear as main or secondary figures. These stories, moreover, are of a decidedly non-initiatory character and do not resort to any sets of cryptic symbols or allusions. While two of the stories involving Hospitallers (those recounted during the thirty-first day and the fifty-third) do include supernatural proceedings, they serve a very straightforward didactic purpose, such as illustrating the existence of purgatory or the need to attain absolution after unlawful duels in Malta. While the novel abounds in villains and tricksters, the fictional Hospitallers are generally on the side of ethical good and are frequently associated with one of the principal themes of the novel – that of honour.[14] The emphasis on honour could underlie the tensions between the French and Spanish Knights of Malta, as recounted in the novel. But at the same time a Spanish Knight of Malta, Toledo, could become a spokesman for Potocki's more liberal and pragmatic attitudes.

Thus, while serving a variety of literary purposes, including acting as spokesmen for Potocki's ethical ideas, the fictional Hospitallers do not play any discernible role in the stories describing the initiatory quest in the novel. In fact, the whole contemporary notion of symbolic and mythical knighthood or military order is entirely absent from those stories involving Hospitallers. This puts Potocki's novel in sharp contrast to contemporary neo-chivalric romances like Zacharias Werner's *Die Söhne des Thales* (with its elaboration of the Templar legend), the Cagliostro stories, in which the Order of Malta and Grand Master Pinto do feature in an initiatory and

---

[13]   On the reflections of the Enlightenment orientalist research and discourse in *Manuscrit trouvé à Saragosse*, see, for example, J. Reichmann, 'Jean Potocki et l'orientalisme des Lumières', in *Les Cahiers de Varsovie*, iii, 31-35; also R. W. Wołoszyński, 'Jean Potocki et son essai de synthèse des civilisations occidentale et orientale', in *Les Cahiers de Varsovie*, iii, 291-98.

[14]   On the theme of honour in the novel, Ian Maclean, 'Introduction', in id. (tr.), Jan Potocki, *The manuscript found in Saragossa*, **xvi**.

esoteric framework,[15] or the *Oration* of Andrew Michael Ramsey, which ventures to link Freemasonry with the military orders of the Crusades and specifically with the Knights of Malta (or the Knights of St John of Jerusalem).[16]

Potocki, therefore, refused to mythicize and romanticize the image of the fictional Hospitaller in his novel at a time when a preoccupation with a symbolic and initiatory knighthood was in vogue in the circles he moved in. On the other hand, he could, whenever he willed, boldly mythicize other elements and characters, like the stories of the Wandering Jew, the Isma'ili, and other Islamic initiatory societies. The reasons for the author's refusal to mythicize the image of the Knight of Malta need to be considered in the light of the very different attitudes adopted by Potocki and his contemporary mythographers of new initiatory knighthood towards the notion of chivalry and the military orders. As argued by Antoine Faivre, with the decline of the political, economic, and military importance of a number of military and chivalric orders in the early modern era, their heritage was transformed into a 'storehouse of symbols' and a 'repertory of generative images'.[17] The eighteenth-century mythographers of chivalry could freely draw on this storehouse of imagery and symbolism to construct neo-chivalric rituals and fictions. Conversely, as a knight of an old surviving military order, Potocki had been involved when his institution still had a political and military role to play in Europe, and indeed in the relations between Russia and Poland. For him, the military order was not, as it was for the mythographers of the new, initiatory chivalry, a distant and exotic relic of the past, a treasure-house of impressive and fascinating symbols and images. For Potocki, it was a living and manifestly existentially important reality. Consequently, he used his immediate knowledge of the Order of Malta for his literary and philosophical purposes – to associate his fictional Hospitallers with the moral and ethical messages and ideas of the novel, which appear to have constituted at least partially the personal legacy his days as a novice Knight of Malta had bequeathed to him.

---

[15] See the text of the Cagliostro story reproduced in W. R. H. Trwobridge, *Cagliostro* (New York, 1926), 239-42. For a contemporary reaction to Cagliostro's story involving the Order of Malta and Grand Master Pinto, L. E. Borowsky, 'Cagliostro, einer der merkwürdigsten Abenteurer unsres Jahrhunderts', in *Cagliostro: Dokumente zu Aufkärung und Okkultismus*, ed. K. H. Kiefer (Munich, 1991), 353 ff.

[16] Text in G. A. Schiffmann, *Andreas Michael Ramsay, eine Studie zur Geschichte der Freimauererei* (Leipzig, 1878).

[17] Faivre, 'Miles Redivivus', 233.

PART III
Templars, Teutonic Knights, and Other Military Orders

Chapter 10

The Templar Order in North-Western Italy: A General Picture (1142–1312)

Elena Bellomo

The history of the Order of the Temple in north-western Italy (corresponding approximately to the modern regions of Piedmont, Lombardy, Liguria, and parts of Emilia) remains of marginal interest to Italian researchers. The resultant bibliographical gap is evident at several levels. There is no general study of the Templar presence in these regions; only in the case of Piedmont can one come across isolated works of synthesis, largely incomplete and often superficial. A similar disparity marks the research on Templar foundations in this territory – the subject is rarely studied by local historians with any scientific precision.[1] The purpose of the present paper is to provide a general overview of the Templar presence in north-western Italy; this is based on an investigation into the Order's connection with local society and its links with ecclesiastical and secular institutions. The analysis rests on the most significant elements that have emerged from the study of the Templar houses found in this area.[2]

In Italy, the lack of a historiographical school for this field of study may also be attributed to the scarcity of primary sources and the difficulty in locating them. An analysis of the Temple's development in this region must necessarily begin with an examination of the documents originating from the order's foundations. After the suppression of the Temple, most of these charters were kept in the archives of Hospitaller houses which had inherited the Templar patrimony. Later the medieval part of this documentary material began progressively to disperse, rendering the study of the Temple in the region increasingly difficult.[3]

---

[1]   General works are L. Avonto, *I Templari in Piemonte. Ricerche e studi per una storia dell'ordine del Tempio in Italia* (Vercelli, 1982) and A. di Ricaldone, *Templari e Giovanniti in Piemonte tra XII e XIX secolo*, 2 vols (Madrid, 1980). On the researches of Italian *templaristi*, A. Luttrell, 'Templari e Ospitalieri in Italia', in *Templari e Ospitalieri in Italia. La chiesa di San Bevignate a Perugia*, ed. M. Roncetti, P. Scarpellini, and F. Tommasi (Milan, 1987), 19; id., 'The Hospitaller Priory of Venice in 1331', in *Militia Sacra. Gli ordini militari tra Europa e Terrasanta*, ed. E. Coli, M. De Marco, and F. Tommasi (Perugia, 1994), 102. Also F. Bramato, *Storia dei Templari in Italia*, 2 vols (Rome, 1990-94) reflects the lack of local scholarship and is often inaccurate.

[2]   This is a summary of my Ph.D. thesis 'La milizia del Tempio in Italia nord-occidentale (XII-metà XIV secolo)', Università Cattolica del Sacro Cuore, Milan, 2001. An English translation of this work is forthcoming.

[3]   For an example of this fragmentation, E. Bellomo, 'Da mansione templare a casa gerosolimitana: S. Maria del Tempio di Brescia nel XIV secolo', in *Riviera di Levante tra*

After wide archival and bibliographical research, the discovery of several edited and inedited charters has made it possible to draw up the first census of the Templar foundations in north-western Italy. The first Templar houses and other estates are identified as having been in Milan,[4] Albenga,[5] Bergamo,[6] and Vercelli in the 1140s.[7] In 1142, we also find the first document concerning the church of Santa Fede in Genoa, whose Templar ownership is definitely documented in 1161.[8] For the next ten years, there is no mention of new houses, except for the presence of some Templar properties near Chieri. This appears to indicate a further expansion of the order in Piedmont,[9] where, in 1164, the Temple also received a sizeable donation from the Earls of Biandrate.[10] New foundations are then referred to in Emilia, Piedmont, and Lombardy.[11]

This list shows that the first Templar houses lay both near the most important Ligurian ports and in centres close to the most travelled roads of northern Italy. The presence of the order in maritime cities like Genoa and Albenga reflected its need to have efficient links with the Latin East, exploiting the relations established between these ports and the crusader states of Syria and Palestine. Genoa had been the first Italian maritime city to extend its support to a crusader army in exchange

---

Emilia e Toscana: un crocevia per l'ordine di S. Giovanni. Atti del Convegno (Genova-Rapallo-Chiavari, 9-12 settembre 1999), ed. J. Costa Restagno (Genoa, 2001), 357-76.

⁴ A. Colombo, 'I Gerosolimitani e i Templari a Milano e la Via Commenda', *Archivio Storico Lombardo*, liii (1926), 213-5: docs 1-2.

⁵ P. Accame, *Notizie e documenti inediti sui Templari e Gerosolimitani in Liguria* (Finalborgo, 1902), 36-44: docs 1-5.

⁶ E. Bellomo, 'Una mansione templare dell'Italia settentrionale: S. Maria del Tempio di Bergamo', *Militia Sacra*, ii (2001), 193-94: doc. 1.

⁷ *Le carte dell'archivio capitolare di Vercelli*, ed. D. Arnoldi, G. C. Faccio, F. Gabotto, and C. Fasola, BSSS 70-71 (Pinerolo, 1912), i, 153: doc. 126; 158: doc. 128.

⁸ *Le carte del monastero di S. Siro di Genova*, ed. M. Calleri, S. Machiavello, and M. Traino, Fonti per la Storia della Liguria, v-viii (Genoa, 1997-98), i (952-1124), 162-63: doc. 104; *Il Cartulare di Giovanni Scriba*, ed. M. Chiaudiano and M. Moresco, *Regesta Chartarum Italiae*, ix-xx (Rome, 1935), 427: doc. 795.

⁹ *Cartario dell'abazia di Casanova fino all'anno 1313*, ed. A. Tallone, Biblioteca della Società Storica Subalpina, xiv (Pinerolo, 1903), 16-17: doc. 10.

¹⁰ A. Ponziglione, 'Saggio storico intorno ai Templari del Piemonte e degli altri Stati del Re', *Ozi Letterarii*, iii (1791), 151: doc. 1. The date of the document is incorrect.

¹¹ *Le carte cremonesi dei secoli VIII-XII*, ed. E. Falconi, Fonti e Sussidi. Documenti dei fondi cremonesi, 4 vols (Cremona, 1979-88), iii, 23: doc. 415; *Le carte degli Archivi parmensi del sec. XII*, ed. G. Drei, 3 vols (Parma, 1950), iii, 338-39: doc. 419; *Monumenta Aquensia*, ed. G. B. Moriondo, 3 vols (Turin, 1789; repr. 1967, ed. C. F. Savio), i, col. 84: doc. 66; Ponziglione, 139-40; Ricaldone, i, 239-40; *Le carte dell'Archivio arcivescovile di Torino fino al 1310*, ed. F. Gabotto and G. B. Barberis, Biblioteca della Società Storica Subalpina, xxxvi (Pinerolo, 1906), 96: doc. 94.

for commercial privileges.[12] The citizens of other Ligurian ports, like Albenga,[13] are also cited in these privileges; and in Albenga several documents specifically attest to the determined policy carried out by the Temple in the 1140s in the hope of strengthening its local foundation.[14]

The other houses in the Po valley, already mentioned, lay near cities with close relations with the East, often established by their citizens' participation in the early crusades.[15] The location of these Templar houses, always positioned outside the city walls, shows that the order preferred sites along the most frequented roads or near bridges and ferries. Several *domus* and *mansiones* were on the *via Francigena*, the *Postumia*, and the *Regina*[*i*].[16] Others lay on secondary roads, as in the case of some minor *domus* of Monferrat, situated on local, but very busy, itineraries.[17] Logistical needs determined the settlement strategy of the order, which was careful to place its houses on the principal routes connecting East and West. This trend is particularly evident in medieval Lombardy, which formed a natural passage between central Europe and the Mediterranean region.

The successful establishment of the Temple in north-western Italy is confirmed by the mention of several *donati* or *oblati* in twelfth-century documents. In Milan, Bergamo, Genoa, and near Pavia, reference to them is made in the first charters concerning the local Templar foundations, indicating a prompt collaboration between local societies and the Order.[18] Particularly significant is the fact that these people were members of the leading families of these cities, who had at times joined the

---

[12]   G. Pistarino, 'Genova ed il Vicino Oriente nell'epoca del Regno Latino di Gerusalemme', in *I Comuni italiani nel regno crociato di Gerusalemme. Atti del Colloquio 'The Italian Communes in the Crusading Kingdom of Jerusalem' (Jerusalem, May, 24th-28th)*, ed. G. Airaldi and B.Z. Kedar, Collana storica di Fonti e Studi, xlviii (Genoa, 1986), 59-139.

[13]   *I Libri iurium della Repubblica di Genova*, 8 vols, ed. D. Puncuh, *et al.*, Fonti per la Storia della Liguria, 1, 2, 4, 10, 11, 12, 13, 15, 17- Pubblicazioni degli Archivi di Stato. Fonti, 12, 13, 23, 27, 28, 29, 32, 35, 39 (Genoa-Rome, 1992-2002), i, 1, 102: doc. 61; 183: doc. 119. Also *Porti antichi. Archeologia del commercio*, ed. F. Varaldo Grottin (Genoa, 1996), 83-86.

[14]   Accame, 37-57: docs 1-13.

[15]   See, for instance, W. Haberstumpf, *Dinastie europee nel Mediterraneo Orientale. I Monferrato e i Savoia nei secoli XII-XV* (Turin, 1995); *Piacenza e la prima crociata*, ed. P. Racine (Piacenza, 1995); *Deus non voluit. I Lombardi alla prima crociata. 1100-1101*, ed. G. Andenna and R. Salvarani (Milan, 2003), 233-62.

[16]   See E. Bellomo, 'Templari, itinerari di pellegrinaggio e attività ospedaliera in Lombardia', in *Lungo le strade della fede. Pellegrini e pellegrinaggio nel Bresciano. Atti della Giornata di Studio. Brescia, 16 dicembre 2000*, ed. G. Archetti = *Brixia Sacra*, 3rd ser., vi, 3-4 (2001), 215-28.

[17]   This is the case of the houses of Casale Monferrato, *Crixanus*, and Paciliano. A. A. Settia, 'Strade romane e antiche pievi fra Tanaro e Po', *Bollettino Storico Bibliografico Subalpino*, lxviii (1970), 21, 25, 38-9, 51.

[18]   Colombo, 214: doc. 2; Bellomo, 'Una mansione', 193-94: doc. 12; *Il Cartulare di Giovanni Scriba*, 427: doc. 795; *Le carte di S. Pietro in Ciel d'Oro di Pavia*, ed. E. Barbieri, M. A. Casagrande Mazzoli, and E. Cau, 2 vols (Pavia-Milan, 1984-88), ii: *(1165-1190)*, 226: doc. 137.

crusades.[19] In Albenga, for example, some of these affiliates played an active role in representing the houses with which they were associated, conducting their business, and defending their interests.[20]

Owing to their location in a region profoundly touched by the dispute between the papacy and the empire, the Templar foundations in north-western Italy were inevitably involved in this conflict. At the beginning of the strife between Frederick Barbarossa and Alexander III, Lombard Templars appear to have been decidedly inclined towards the faction of the antipope Victor IV, who was supported by Frederick I. In 1158, while besieging Milan, the emperor was billeted in the local Templar house.[21] In 1160 the master of the Templar foundation in Rome confirmed the election of the antipope Victor IV.[22] Afterwards, Boniface, the first Templar master of Lombardy identified in the sources, was in Jerusalem in concomitance with a pilgrimage of several German nobles, among whom was Welf VI of Bavaria, a relative of Frederick I.[23] The master of the order had previuolsly entrusted Boniface with carrying out the sale of some Templar estates, lying in German territory, to Otto of Wittelsbach, another follower of Barbarossa.[24] It is possible that Boniface was charged with this task on account of the relations he had with the imperial court. In this context it is also easy to understand why the Earls of Biandrate, who had significant connections with the emperor, granted the Temple a large donation in 1164.[25] A document of 1169 attests to a positive contact between the Lombard Templars and Alexander III. That year the pope confirmed the Templar possession of

---

[19] 'I necrologi eusebiani', ed. G. Colombo, *Bollettino Storico Bibliografico Subalpino*, ii (1897), 383: no 172; R. Pastè, 'Per la storia dei Vercellesi Crociati in Terra Santa', *Archivio della Società Vercellese di Storia e Arte*, iv (1915), 262.

[20] Accame, 36-41: docs 1-3; 45-50: docs 6-8.

[21] *Narratio de Lombardie obpressione et subiectione*, ed. F.-J. Schmale, in id., *Italische Quellen über die Taten Kaiser Friedrichs I. in Italien und der Brief über den Kreuzzug Kaiser Friedrichs I.* (Darmstadt, 1986), 258; Otto Morena *et al.*, *Libellus de rebus a Frederico imperatore gestis*, ed. F.-J. Schmale, in *ibid.*, 84.

[22] Otto of Frising and Rahewin, *Gesta Frederici seu rectius Cronica*, ed. F.-J. Schmale (Darmstadt, 1974), 674.

[23] On this pilgrimage, see also Otto of Frising and Rahewin, *Gesta Friderici I. Imperatoris*, *appendix annorum 1160-70*, ed. R. Wilmans, *MGH SS*, xx (Hanover, 1868), 492.

[24] H. Grauert, 'Eine Tempelherrenurkunde von 1167', *Archivalische Zeitschrift*, iii (1878), 294-309; RRH, 116: no 446; K. Feldmann, *Herzog Welf VI. und sein Sohn. Das Ende des süddeutschen Welfenhauses (mit Regesten)* (Tübingen, 1971), no 125; M. Schüpferling, *Der Tempelherren-Orden in Deutschland* (Bamberg, 1915), 69-70; *Wittelsbach und Bayern*, ed. H. Glaser, 2 vols., I/1: *Die Zeit der frühen Herzöge. Von Otto I. zu Ludwig dem Bayern. Beïtrage zur Bayerischen Geschichte und Kunst. 1180-1350* (Munich-Zürich, 1980), 165.

[25] At the same time they were also connected to the commune of Milan. R. Manselli, 'La grande feudalità italiana tra Federico Barbarossa e i Comuni', in *Popolo e Stato in Italia nell'Età di Federico Barbarossa. Alessandria e la Lega Lombarda. Relazioni e comunicazioni al XXXIII Congresso Storico Subalpino per la celebrazione dell'VIII centenario della fondazione di Alessandria, Alessandria, 6-9 ottobre 1968* (Turin, 1970), 345-61; P. Brezzi, 'Gli alleati italiani di Federico Barbarossa (feudatari e città)' in *Friederich Barbarossa*, ed. G. Wolf, Wege der Forschung, cccxc (Darmstadt, 1975), 157 *et seq.*; P. Brezzi, 'I maggiori feudatari piemontesi fautori di Federico Barbarossa', in *Il Barbarossa e i suoi alleati liguri-*

the hospital of Santo Stefano in Reggio to the *magister* Boniface himself.[26] A possible change in the Templar attitude towards the pope in this period could be attributed to the insufficient legitimacy of Victor's successors. It should also be noted that in 1167 the Lombard league was founded, and Barbarossa's power in northern Italy found itself in crisis. In the end, the new alignment of the Lombard Templars might also reflect the evolution of local political situations. Between 1167 and 1170 numerous bishops in this area in fact began to intensify their relations with Pope Alexander III at the expense of their ties with Barbarossa. At the same time, a number of important episcopal sees were occupied by prelates faithful to the pope.[27]

At a considerably narrower level, the Templars had an important influence on the balance of local powers. Of particular significance is the case of the foundations in the hills surrounding Turin. They controlled stretches of the *via Francigena* and the local rivers. In 1196, the bishop of Turin, Arduin of Valperga, entrusted the Templars with the running of St Egidius Hospital in Testona, a travellers' shelter that lay near one of the most important bridges over the river Po. This decision showed the bishop's esteem for the Temple and at the same time protected his interests by keeping an important transit point under the control of an ecclesiastical institution of his choice. Arduin also ordered the Templars to rebuild the bridge, which still belonged to the church of Turin. The favourable location of this place and probably the efficient Templar administration made this hospice a catalyst in the development of this area. Near the Templar foundation, a new village, Moncalieri, began to take shape. It was primarily inhabited by merchants and artisans attracted by the good location of the site. Probably between 1204 and 1227, during the war against Chieri, the nearby commune of Testona placed its new see precisely here.[28]

---

piemontesi. Atti del Convegno Storico Internazionale, Gavi, 8 dicembre 1985, ed. G. C. Bergaglio (Gavi, 1987), 18-26.

[26]   G. Tiraboschi, *Memorie storiche modenesi col Codice diplomatico*, 5 vols (Modena, 1793-95), iii, 54: doc. 446; PL, CC, col. 613; *Regesta pontificum romanorum ab condita Ecclesia ad annum post Christum natum MCXCVIII*, ed. P. Jaffé, *et al.*, 2 vols (Lipsia, 1885-1888), no. 11659.

[27]   O. Capitani, 'Alessandro III, lo Scisma e le Diocesi dell'Italia settentrionale', in *Popolo e Stato in Italia*, 236; A. Ambrosioni, 'Alessandro III e la Chiesa ambrosiana', in *Miscellanea Rolando Bandinelli, Papa Alessandro III*, ed. F. Liotta (Siena, 1986), 30-1; F. Oppl, *Federico Barbarossa* (Genoa, 1994; orig. edn.: *Friederich Barbarossa*, 1990), 113-25; J. Laudage, *Alexander III. und Friedrich Barbarossa, Forschungen zur Kaiser und Papstgeschichte des Mittelalters*, xvi (Cologne, 1997), 183-85.

[28]   *Le carte dell'Archivio arcivescovile di Torino*, 96-7: doc. 94; *Appendice al Libro Rosso del comune di Chieri*, ed. F. Gabotto, Biblioteca della Società Storica Subalpina, lxxvi (Pinerolo-Turin, 1913-24), pp. xxix-xxxii: doc. 39; C. La Rocca, *Da Testona a Moncalieri. Vicende del popolamento sulla collina torinese nel medioevo*, Biblioteca della Società Storica Subalpina, cxcii (Turin, 1986), 153-92; M. Montanari Pesando, *Villaggi nuovi nel Piemonte medievale. Due fondazioni chieresi del secolo XIII: Villastellone e Pecetto*, Biblioteca della Società Storica Subalpina, ccviii (Turin, 1991), 11-48; E. Meyer, *Die Function von Hospitälern in städtischen Kommunen Piemonts (11.-13. Jahrhundert)*, Europäische Hoschschulschriften, Reihe III, Geschichte und ihre Hilfswissenschaften, 492 (Frankfurt-am-Main, 1992), 270-80; G. Casiraghi, 'I cavalieri del Tempio e le vicende dei loro insediamenti sulla collina torinese', *Bollettino Storico Bibliografico Subalpino*, xci (1993), 233-45; id., 'Fondazioni templari

Moreover, the Order of the Temple tried to exploit fully the potential for development of its house in Gorra (Turin), situated in an area of increasing value. Part of this estate was sold to the commune of Chieri, which concurred with Testona to build a new village here in order to control the rivers Po and Stellone. Both waterways were vital to the needs of the town and for the treatment of grain. The Temple, too, hoped to make substantial profits from the creation of a new settlement in the area. The project failed, however, and a long quarrel ensued between Chieri and the Temple.[29]

In both cases, the Templar territories, not yet improved, were economically and politically gaining in importance and the order tried to exploit them as best it could, taking advantage of the expansion of other local institutions.

The Temple was thus deeply rooted in north-western Italy. At the same time, the Lombard Templars, because of the very nature of their institution, had strong links with the East, where the order was fighting for the faith. Lombard brethren were probably engaged in the preparation for crusading expeditions. Unfortunately, this is evident only during the Fourth Crusade, in which Venice and several crusaders from Lombardy were involved. Noteworthy is the fact that the new Latin emperor of Constantinople, Baldwin I, chose Barochius, the Templar *magister* of Lombardy, to communicate the news of the foundation of the Latin Empire to Pope Innocent III.[30] While Barochius was on his way to the papal court, some Genoese pirates assaulted his ship and stole the relics and the precious items he was carrying as gifts for the pope and *ad opus Templi*.[31]

During the thirteenth century the increasing influence of the order and its patrimonial power provoked several disputes with communes and ecclesiastical institutions. However, the fact that several hospitals were entrusted to the Temple demonstrates once more a positive attitude towards the order at the local level.[32]

---

lungo la via Francigena: da Torino a Chieri e da Testona-Moncalieri a S. Martino di Gorra', in *Luoghi di strada nel Medioevo. Fra il Po, il mare e le Api occidentali*, ed. G. Sergi (Turin, 1996), 125-45; id., 'Da Torino a Chieri: insediamenti templari lungo la via Francigena', in *I Templari in Piemonte. Dalla storia al mito* (Turin, 1994), 11-29.

[29]   *Il 'Libro Rosso' del comune di Chieri*, ed. F. Gabotto and F. Guasco di Bisio, Biblioteca della Società Storica Subalpina, lxxv (Pinerolo, 1918), 80-93: docs 45-48.

[30]   *Die register Innocenz'III.*, ed. O. Hageneder, A. Haidacher *et al.*, 9 vols (Graz-Cologne-Rome-Vienna, 1964-2004), vii, 262: doc. 152.

[31]   Ibid., vii, 235: doc. 147; V. Polonio, 'Devozioni di lungo corso: lo scalo genovese', in *Genova, Venezia, il Levante nei secoli XII-XIV. Atti del Convegno Internazionale di Studi, Genova-Venezia, 10-14 marzo 2000*, ed. G. Ortalli and D. Puncuh = *Atti della Società Ligure di Storia Patria*, n.s., xli (2001), 365-66; P. Lock, *The Franks in the Aegean 1204-1500* (London, 1995), 57-60, 234-35; H. Nicholson, 'The Motivations of the Hospitallers and Templars in their Involvement in the Fourth Crusade and its Aftermath', *passim*, available on http://www.hmml.org/centers/malta/publications/lecture3.html.

[32]   On this topic, A.J. Forey, 'The Charitable Activities of the Templars', *Viator*, xxxiv (2003), 107-41.

Besides the one of Testona, the Temple had hospitals in Pavia,[33] Tortona,[34] and Piacenza.[35] Through these foundations, the order could strengthen its settlement in these cities, taking advantage of donations, which were usually offered to charitable institutions. The Templars' assumption of these responsibilities also played a significant role in the complex dynamic of local powers: thanks to these assignations, a military order exempt from diocesan control was somehow tied to the bishopric; at the same time, the bishop prevented communal interference in the administration of these hospitals.[36] Moreover, at least in one case, the Templars' charitable acts seem to have brought them even closer to lay people. In Milan there is documentary evidence that in 1226, a *scola mansionis Templi*[37] had a layman and the master of the local Templar foundation as its *decani*. The institution was probably similar to other contemporary confraternities formed at the time by clerics and laymen and engaged in charitable activities.[38]

The favours granted to the Temple by laymen and other exponents of the ecclesiastical hierarchy is mirrored at a much higher level in the continuous presence of Templars among the pope's followers. During the twelfth and thirteenth centuries, several members of the order were appointed *camerarii, cubicularii, marescalci,* and *hostiarii pontificii.* They were entrusted with important diplomatic and administrative missions, especially in the papal dominions, and were then rewarded with revenues and the grant of fiefs.[39] Some of these Templars were Italian, and

---

[33] C. F. Savio, *Gli antichi vescovi d'Italia dalle origini al 1300 decritti per regioni. La Lombardia*, 2 vols (Florence-Bergamo, 1913-32), ii (2), 468.

[34] *Le carte dell'Archivio capitolare di Tortona (sec. IX-1220)*, ed. F. Gabotto and V. Legé, Biblioteca della Società Storica Subalpina, xxix-xxx (Pinerolo, 1902), ii, 209: doc. 532.

[35] Piacenza, Archivio del Capitolo Cattedrale, Convenzioni 33, Cassetta 3, Notary Ruffino Arlotti, copy of the original charter issued in 1318; Giovanni Musso, *Cronaca*, RIS xvi (Milan, 1730), col. 481; *Chronicon Placentinum*, in *Chronica tria Placentina a Johanne Codagnello, ab anonymo et a Guerino conscripta* (Parma, 1859), 332; P.M. Campi, *Dell'Historia ecclesiastica di Piacenza*, 3 vols (Piacenza, 1651, repr. 1995), ii, 52, 78; E. Nasalli Rocca, 'Della introduzione dei Templari a Piacenza', *Bollettino storico piacentino*, xxxvi (1941), 16-8.

[36] G. Albini, *Città e ospedali nella Lombardia medievale* (Bologna, 1993), 20-83. Unfortunately, no data are available on the charitable activities of these Templar hospitals.

[37] The document is edited in L. Tacchella, *Gli insediamenti dei Templari a Nice e Grasse, in Lombardia e Veneto* (Milan, 1999), 69-70.

[38] *Antichi diplomi degli arcivescovi di Milano e note di diplomatica episcopale*, ed. G. C. Bascapè (Firenze, 1937), 79-81: doc. 10; Albini, 37-38.

[39] U. Nicolini, 'Bonvicino', in *Dizionario Biografico degli Italiani*, xii (Rome, 1970), 471-72; E. Göller, 'Die Kubikuläre im Diensten der päpstlichen Hofverwaltung vom 12. bis 15. Jahrhundert', in *Papstum und Kaisertum. Forschungen zur politischen Geschichte und Geisteskultur des Mittelalters: Paul Kehr zum 65. Geburtstag dargebracht* (München, 1926), 622-47; G. Gerola, 'La iconografia di Innocenzo IV e lo stemma pontificio', *Archivio della Reale Società Romana di Storia Patria*, lii (1929), 471-84; B. Rusch, *Die Behörden und Hofbeamten der päpstlichen Kurie des 13. Jahrhunderts* (Königsberg, 1936), 92-99, 122-28; A. Paravicini Bagliani, *La vita quotidiana alla corte dei papi nel Duecento* (Bari, 1996; 1st edn.: *La cour des papes au XIIIᵉ siècle*, 1995), 62, 101-102; *Documenti sulle relazioni tra la*

particularly from Lombardy. Morever, the *cubicularii* of Vercelli (1278-*c*.1303) and James of Moncucco (1303-1308), were masters of the Templar province of Lombardy simultaneously.[40] Among such dignitaries, one can also find members of the Canelli family, relatives of Manfred, son of Bianca Lancia d'Agliano and Frederick II. Though connected through this relationship to the Ghibelline faction, the family was still able to maintain good relations with the papal court, where the Templar Albertinus de Canelli was *hostiarius pontificius*.[41]

---

casa di Savoia e la Santa Sede nel Medioevo (1066-1268), ed. P. Fontana, Biblioteca della Società Storica Subalpina, cxlii (Turin, 1939), 310: doc. 212; *Les registres d'Urbain IV*, ed. J. Guiraud: *Bibliothèque des Écoles françaises d'Athènes et de Rome, II série. Registres et lettres des papes du 13. siècle*, 4 vols (Paris, 1896-1906), i, 14: doc. 59; 33: docs 126-27; 152: doc. 329; ibid., ii, 427: doc. 880; ibid., iii, 154: doc. 1244; 216-17: doc. 1504; 280: doc. 1786; 419: doc. 2487; iv, 57 doc. 2948; *Les registres de Clément IV*, ed. E. Jordan, in ibid. (Paris, 1893-1945), 9: doc. 24; *Les registres de Nicolas IV*, ed. M. E. Langlois, in ibid., 3 vols (Paris, 1886-93), ii, 945: doc. 7001-7002; 995: doc. 7288; 997: docs. 7304-7305; 1047: docs. 7653-54; *Les registre de Boniface VIII*, ed. G. Digard *et al.*, in ibid., 4 vols (Paris, 1884-1939), i, cols. 917-18: docs. 2331-2332; cols. 547-48: doc. 1508; ibid., iv, cols. 40-: docs. 5503-5505; T. Bini, 'Dei Tempieri e del loro processo in Toscana', *Atti della Reale Accademia Lucchese di Scienze, Lettere ed Arti*, xv (1845), 485: doc. 9; Bramato, *Storia*, i, 164-65; M.-L. Bulst-Thiele, 'Templer in königlichen und päpstlichen Diesten', in *Festschrift Percy Ernst Schramm*, eds. Classen and P. Scheibert, 2 vols (Wiesbaden, 1964), i, 302-308; id., 'Warum wollte Philipp IV. den Templerorden vernichten? Ein neuer aspekt', in *I Templari. Mito e storia. Atti del Convegno internazionale di studi alla Magione di Poggibonsi, Siena 29-31 maggio 1987*, ed. G. Minucci and F. Sardi (Siena, 1989), 29-35.

[40]　On Uguccio, F. Baethgen, 'Quellen und Unterschungen zur Geschichte der Päpstlichen Hof-und Finanzverwaltung unter Bonifaz VIII', *Quellen und Forschungen aus italienischen Archiven und Bibliotheken*, xx (1928-29), 196-9, 201, 204; A. Luttrell, 'Two Templar-Hospitaller preceptories north of Tuscania', *Papers of the British School at Rome*, xxxix (1971), 105, also in id., *The Hospitallers in Cyprus, Rhodes, Greece and the West* (London, 1978), article X; *Les registres de Nicolas IV*, ii, 966-67: docs. 7144-47; 1047: docs. 7653-54; Paravicini Bagliani, 62; G. Silvestrelli, 'Le chiese e i feudi dell'Ordine dei Templari e dell'Ordine di San Giovanni di Gerusalemme nella regione romana', *Rendiconti della Reale Accademia dei Lincei: classe di scienze morali, storiche e filologiche*, 5th ser., xxvi (1917), 494, note 1; Milan, Archivio di Stato, Fondo Religione, Miscellanea Materiale Restaurato, cart. 5, 16 October 1304; *The Trial of the Templars of the Papal State and Abruzzi*, 132, 173, 189, 201, 214-15, 222, 250-51; *Les registres de Boniface VIII*, iii, col. 664: doc. 5032. On James of Montecucco, Bini, 464-66, 478, 479 486: doc. 9; F. Tommasi, 'Interrogatorio dei Templari a Cesena (1310)', in *Acri 1291. La fine della presenza degli ordini militari in Terra Santa e i nuovi orientamenti del XIV secolo*, ed. F. Tommasi (Perugia, 1996), 288, 293; N. Pezzella, 'Santa Maria *de Cunio*: chiesa templare di Padova', in *Atti del XV Convegno di Ricerche Templari* (Latina, 1998), 51-2; *The Trial of the Templars in the Papal State and Abruzzi*, 132, 252; Tommasi, 'L'ordine dei Templari a Perugia', 60: doc. 17; Silvestrelli, 528; Parma, Archivio di Stato, Conventi e Confraternite, Archivio di S. Giovanni in Canale, lxxxvi, *busta* 2, *fascicolo* A3, 8 July 1304; Vatican City, Archivio Segreto Vaticano, Obligat. et solut. ii, fol. 114v (document kindly pointed out by Barbara Bombi); *Regestum Clementis papae V*, 9 vols and Appendix (Vatican City, 1885-92), vii, doc. 7183.

[41]　Tommasi, 'L'ordine dei Templari a Perugia', 60: doc. 17; Silvestrelli, 528.

The relations between the Temple and the Hospital, the other military order present in north-western Italy, are equally interesting. In Acqui[42]in 1186 and in Alba[43]in 1217, the Templars and Hospitallers were both admonished for trying to extend their pastoral care to people under the jurisdiction of the local cathedrals. These episodes may possibly indicate that the two orders were acting in similar ways at the local level. There is also evidence that relations between the two were good even during the trial of the Templars. However, the dearth of information makes the shape and quality of these relations difficult to reconstruct accurately. Both military orders had been setting up houses in this area since the 1150s,[44] and in the following century each developed a capillary network of foundations throughout the region.[45] The settling of both orders in this area was influenced by the identical need of a solid link with the Latin East and the production of surplus goods to finance the struggle against Islam. The houses of the Order of St. John combined these functions with their work in hospitals for pilgrims and the poor. As a result, the houses of both orders were often situated near each other, on the same routes.[46] The fragmentary quality of our documentary sources and the lack of adequate studies of the Hospital make it difficult to define an accurate chronology of its establishment in the area. However, in several places the times between the earliest references to the houses of both orders are often very short, suggesting by and large a simultaneous expansion.[47]

The presence in the same region of two similar orders, which had assumed different political positions on the Holy Land,[48] could have created strong elements of animosity, even in the North of Italy. This does not appear to have been the case, however. The absence of such a spirit of antagonism between them may possibly

---

[42] *Monumenta Aquensia*, i, col. 84; *Italia pontificia sive repertorium privilegiorum et litterarum a Romanis Pontificibus ante annum MCLXXXXVIII Italiae ecclesiis, monasteriis, civitatibus singulisque personis concessorum*, ed. F. Kehr, 10 vols (Berlin, 1906-1975), iv, 195.

[43] *Monumenta Aquensia*, i, col. 84; Ricaldone, i, 239-40.

[44] R. Caravita, *Rinaldo da Concorezzo, arcivescovo di Ravenna (1303-1321) al tempo di Dante* (Florence, 1964), Appendix, 307; doc. 49; R. Bordone, 'I Cavalieri di San Giovanni ad Asti e nel Monferrato durante il Medioevo', in *Cavalieri di S. Giovanni e territorio. La Liguria tra Provenza e Lombardia nei secoli XIII-XVII. Atti del Convegno, Genova-Imperia-Cervo, 11-14 settembre 1997*, ed. J. Costa Restagno (Genoa, 1999), 339.

[45] *'Gentilhuomini Christiani e Religiosi Cavalieri'. Nove secoli dell'Ordine di Malta in Piemonte*, ed. T. Ricardi di Netro and L.C. Gentile (Milan, 2000), 186-87.

[46] E. Nasalli Rocca, 'Lineamenti di organizzazione regionale e della funzione assistenziale dell'Ordine gerosolimitano degli 'Ospedalieri' nel Medioevo italiano', in *Studi in onore di C. Calisse*, 3 vols (Milan, 1939), iii, 297-328; Bordone, 338-39; R. Greci, 'Prime presenze gerosolimitane nell'Emilia Occidentale e nella Bassa Lombardia', in *Riviera di Levante*, 405-6, 411-13.

[47] R. Bordone and D. Gnetti, 'Distribuzione geografica delle 'domus' gerosolimitane in Piemonte e situazione patrimoniale del gran priorato di Lombardia (commenda di Asti)', in *'Gentilhoumini Christiani'*, 142-45.

[48] J.C.S. Riley-Smith, *The Knights of Saint John in Jerusalem and Cyprus. c.1050-1310* (London, 1967), pp. 117, 132, 161, 443-50, 460, 467; A. Demurger, *Vie et mort de l'ordre du Temple* (Paris, 1985), pp. 196-98; H. Nicholson, *Templars, Hospitallers and Teutonic Knights. Images of the Military Orders. 1128-1291* (Leicester-London-New York, 1993), pp. 122-23.

be attributed to the fact that both orders recruited their members from the same sphere. A clear example is that of the aforementioned Canelli family.[49] Between 1287 and the beginning of the fourteenth century, Albert,[50] William,[51] and Albertinus of Canelli[52] were employed as Templar officers in southern and northern Italy. Obertus of Calamandrana, a close relative of the Canelli, was master of the Temple in Lombardy in 1271,[53] and Ivanus of Canelli was probably a local preceptor in 1268 and 1271.[54] The adhesion of the Canelli to the Hospital was no less significant. Otto Grecus of Canelli is mentioned in 1251 and 1277 as provincial prior of the Hospital in Lombardy.[55] Within the Hospitaller institution, Boniface of Calamandrana was invested with the high dignity of general preceptor *in partibus cismarinis*.[56] Other high-ranking members are identified in the list of the Hospitaller preceptors present in 1302 at a provincial chapter at Asti.[57] These included James of Canelli, responsible for the house of Castellazzo Bormida and a future prior of Lombardy.[58] In the same period his relatives, Conrad and Perceval, are known to have administrated the Hospitaller foundation of Milan.[59] The enrolment in military orders was also determined by a crisis of a political and patrimonial nature. The Canelli were involved in the struggle between the communes of Asti, Alessandria, and the Marquises of

---

[49] A. Barbero, 'I signori di Canelli fra la corte di re Manfredi e gli ordini monastico-cavallereschi', in *Bianca Lancia d'Agliano. Fra il Piemonte e il regno di Sicilia. Atti del Convegno, Asti-Agliano 1990*, ed. R. Bordone (Alessandria, 1992), 219-33.

[50] E. Trota, 'L'Ordine dei cavalieri templari a Modena e l'ospitale del ponte di S. Ambrogio', *Atti e Memorie della Deputazione di Storia Patria per le Province Modenesi*, ser. xvi, 6 (1984), 48, 52; M.-L. Bulst-Thiele, '*Sacrae Domus Militiae Templi Hierosolimitani Magistri'. Untersuchungen zur Geschichte des Templerordens 1118/9-1314*, Abhandlungen der Akademie der Wissenschaften in Göttingen. Philologisch-Historische Klasse, Dritte Folge, lxxxvi (Göttingen, 1974), 278.

[51] D. Wilkins, *Concilia Magnae Britanniae et Hiberniae ad MCCLXVIII-MCCCXLIX*, 2 vols. (London, 1737), ii, 372; Bust-Thiele, *Magistri*, 279-80; *Acta Aragonensia. Quellen zur deutschen, italienischen, französischen, spanischen Kirchen und Kulturgeschichte aus der diplomatistischen Korrespondenz Jaymes II. (1291-1327)*, ed. H. Finke, 3 vols (Berlin-Leipzig, 1908-22), iii, 10: doc. 5; 36: doc. 18; K. Schottmüller, *Der Untergang des Templer-Ordens*, 2 vols (Berlin, 1887), ii, 174-75; *The Trial of the Templars in Cyprus. A complete English Edition*, ed. A. Gilmour-Bryson, The Medieval Mediterranean, xvii (Leiden, 1998), 90; Bini, 465, 474: doc. 9; *The Trial of the Templars in the Papal State and Abruzzi*, 189, 201; *Le procès des Templiers*, ed. J. Michelet, 2 vols, Collection de documents inédits sur l'histoire de France (Paris, 1841, repr. 1987), ii, 425.

[52] Tommasi, 'L'ordine dei Templari a Perugia', 60: doc. 17; Silvestrelli, 528; *The Trial of the Templars in the Papal State and Abruzzi*, 216; *Le procès*, ii, 424-27. he may also be identified with the Templar Ubertinus de Cavelle, mentioned in the Trial. Bini, 474: doc. 9.

[53] *I registri della cancelleria*, vii, 171: doc. 218.

[54] Trota, 48, 52.

[55] Bordone, 354-56.

[56] Barbero, 232-33.

[57] *Documenti sulle relazioni tra Voghera e Genova (960-1325)*, ed. G. Gorrini, Biblioteca della Società Storica Subalpina, xlviii (Pinerolo, 1908), 318-22: doc. 485.

[58] Bordone, 369-70.

[59] Colombo, 238: doc. 36; Bordone, 369.

Monferrat,[60] and found themselves victims of an extreme patrimonial division. In 1217 the members of this family gave up their rights and belongings to the consuls of Asti. On that occasion, notaries had to draw up more than twenty separate deeds, one for each of the heirs approving the concession.[61] The political eclipse of the Canelli was abated by their adhesion to the military orders, helped by the fortunate ascension of their relative, Manfred Lancia, to the throne of Sicily. The concern of the most important figures of the Ghibelline party (Manfred himself, then Peter III of Aragon and his wife Constance, Manfred's daughter) had probably helped the Canelli to attain the leadership of certain Templar and Hospitaller provinces in Italy. It can also be noted that this development later caused the transfer of these Templar dignitaries [supporting the Angevin faction to] from Angevin South to North Italy.[62]

This example shows that that admission into the Temple or the Hospital in north-western Italy could have been a suitable choice for the cadets of lineages in crisis. They were often employed as administrators of houses lying within their family dominions, and in this way they could retain some authority over their native territories at a time when their political and patrimonial status was in decline.

This is a picture of the development of the Temple in north-western Italy before the beginning of their trial. In this region, the inquest was directed by a commission, supervised by Rainald of Concorezzo, archbishop of Ravenna, that included the bishops of Cremona and Florence. Rainald's role was decisive in the development of the trial, asserting the invalidity of confessions made under torture, and thus advocating the innocence of the Templars.[63] Before the beginning of the trial in north-western Italy with the issue of the papal bull *Faciens misericordiam* in 1308, evidence keeps emerging of continuing economic activity under Templar management.[64] In 1311, probably after being acquitted by provincial councils, several brothers of the Order regained their freedom.[65] In some places, both bishops and communes tried to defend the Temple, while the inquisitors were even threatened with death.[66] At the end of the inquest, in Emilia, all the prisoners were released after an individual *purgatio*.[67] Further proof of a local positive attitude toward the Templars is provided

---

[60] Barbero, 219 *et seq.*

[61] Ibid., 219-25.

[62] Barbero, 229 *et seq*; E. Bellomo, 'Mobility of Templar Brothers and Dignitaries: The Case of North-Western Italy', in *International Mobility in the Military Orders (Twelfth to Fifteenth Centuries). Travelling on Christ's Business*, eds J. Burgtorf and H. Nicholson (Cardiff, 2005), 102-13.

[63] Caravita, *Rinaldo da Concorezzo*, 97-116.

[64] Milan, Archivio di Stato, Fondo Religione, Miscellanea Materiale Restaurato, cart. 5, 6 April 1308; Turin, Archivio di Stato, Materie politiche per rapporto all'interno, Ordini Cavallereschi, Ordine dei Templari, *mazzo* 1, no. 5.

[65] For instance, in 1311 a Templar master is mentioned in two charters written on behalf of the bishop of Ivrea. Ivrea, Archivio Storico della Diocesi di Ivrea, VIII.3.310/320, fols. 6v, 10r-v.

[66] *Carte in appendice ai Monumenti ravennati del conte M. Fantuzzi*, ed. A. Tarlazzi, 2 vols. (Ravenna, 1872-79), i (2), 550-51: doc. 340; 577, 583: doc. 350.

[67] R. Caravita, 'La *purgazione* nel processo inquisitorio. Il caso dei Templari processati a Ravenna', in *Atti del XV Convegno di Ricerche Templari. Castrocaro Terme, 6-7 settembre*

by the fact that the master of Lombardy, James of Moncucco, who had been arrested in France, was able to escape from his prison and may have later served the Church in Piedmont.[68]

In north-western Italy, therefore, the Temple played a relevant role at two different levels. As in other regions, the Temple tried to adapt itself to local conditions, using them to its own advantage. In addition, owing to the particular political situation of medieval Lombardy, the Templar foundations in this region came into direct contact with the two greatest powers of the period, the papacy and the empire. Both tried to make an ally out of the Temple and use it as an instrument of their political power. As a consequence of these multiple relations, north-western Italy provides further proof of the importance of this order even on the western coasts of the Mediterranean.

1997 (Latina, 1998), 7-32.

[68]   H. Finke, *Papsttum und Untergang des Templerordens*, 2 vols (Munster, 1907), ii, 59, note 5: doc. 39; 114, note 2: doc. 74; 165: doc. 164. Finke wrongly identified the *comandator Lombardie* arrested in France with *Oliverius de Penne*, a *cubicularius pontificius*, who had never been *magister Lombardie*. After *comandator Lombardie*'s escape, Oliverius was still in prison. For the reference to James of Moncucco after his flight, Milan, Archivio di Stato, Fondo Religione, Miscellanea Materiale Restaurato, cart. 5, 6 April 1308. One Brother James of Moncucco was in Ivrea in 1314 and 1316. Ivrea, Archivio Storico della Diocesi di Ivrea, XII.5.AM.313/317/1, fol. 31; ibid., VIII.3.310/320/1, fol. 23v.

Chapter 11

The Templar James of Garrigans:
Illuminator and Deserter

Alan Forey

James of Garrigans was received into the Temple in the early 1290s in the chapel of the convent of Mas-Déu in Roussillon.[1] He later claimed to have been an acolyte and to have received the tonsure before becoming a Templar, but he remained a brother sergeant throughout his career in the order.[2] He was therefore, like most recruits, presumably of free status, but not of knightly descent. He resided at Mas-Déu for several years, for another Templar reported that James had been present at his admission ceremony there about the year 1295.[3] Roussillon then formed part of the kingdom of Mallorca, but the Templars in the county belonged to the order's province of Aragon and Catalonia, and James was soon transferred south of the Pyrenees. He administered Chivert in northern Valencia in 1297, when the castle there no longer housed a convent but was subordinate to the recently established house at Peñíscola, and he was present at an admission ceremony that took place at Peñíscola apparently in the spring of 1298.[4] From the later part of that year until early 1301, he was a member of the Catalan convent of Gardeny near Lérida.[5] In 1303 he was back in Roussillon and in charge of Saint Hippolyte, a dependency of Mas-Déu.[6] Three years later, however, he was in the entourage of the provincial master, acting as his sergeant, and when proceedings began against the Temple he was commander of Gebut, which was subject to the convent of Miravet on the lower Ebro.[7] By 1307 James of Garrigans had served, as many did, in various places within

---

[1]   *Procès des Templiers*, ed. J. Michelet, 2 vols (Paris, 1841–51): ii, 462. Raymond of Guardia, who admitted him, is known to have been commander there in 1292 and 1294: E. G. Léonard, *Introduction au cartulaire manuscrit du Temple du Marquis d'Albon* (Paris, 1930), 90; L. Verdon, *La terre et les hommes en Roussillon aux XIIe et XIIIe siècles. Structures seigneuriales, rente et société d'après les sources templières* (Aix-en-Provence, 2001), 218.

[2]   H. Finke, *Papsttum und Untergang des Templerordens*, 2 vols (Münster, 1907): ii, 167, doc. 94; Barcelona, Archivo Capitular (henceforth ACB), codex 149A, fols. 48v–49v; A. J. Forey, *The Templars in the Corona de Aragón* (London, 1973), 415, doc. 44.

[3]   ACB, codex 149A, fols. 37v–38.

[4]   Barcelona, Archivo de la Corona de Aragón (henceforth ACA), Cancillería real, pergaminos, Jaime II 914; ACB, codex 149A, fols. 48v–49v.

[5]   ACA, Ordenes religiosas y militares, San Juan de Jerusalén, pergaminos, Gardeny 377–80, 825, 1667, 1876.

[6]   Léonard, 92. On the dependencies of Mas-Déu, see Verdon, 24–6, 218–19.

[7]   Forey, *Templars in Aragon*, 415, doc. 44; Finke, *Papsttum*, ii, 168, doc. 94; ACA, Canc. real, Registro (henceforth R.) 291, fol. 131–131v.

his province, but had achieved only minor office; and like most sergeants recruited in western Europe, he did not serve in the East. Had Philip IV not initiated action against the Temple, his career would probably not have been worthy of note, except to illustrate patterns of service.

It is for his activities during the proceedings against the Temple that he is mainly of interest. When James II of Aragon, after hearing of Templar confessions in France. moved against the members of the order in his own realms at the beginning of December 1307, many Templars in these lands converged on a group of castles which the order sought to defend, the largest numbers gathering in Miravet and the stronghold of Monzón, on the river Cinca.[8] It was natural that James of Garrigans, as commander of Gebut, should be among those assisting at Miravet. The Templars there held out for a year, while Monzón resisted for six months longer. The defence of Miravet was led by brother Raymond of Guardia, who in 1307 was commander of Mas-Déu and who also took the place of the provincial master after the latter's arrest by royal officials in Valencia early in December. James of Garrigans was already well known to Raymond, for the latter had not only received his profession but had also been commander of Peñíscola when James belonged to that convent.[9]

James II sought to overcome Templar resistance mainly by a blockade of the defended castles, but he also sought to use persuasion,[10] while the Templars, among whom Raymond of Guardia was the most vociferous, were anxious first to assert their innocence in order to win royal support and later to seek a compromise which would not leave them completely at the mercy of king or pope. During the siege there were therefore numerous contacts between the Aragonese king and the brethren defending Miravet. Raymond of Guardia wanted to be allowed to see James II in order to make his views more fully known, and in order to secure a safe-conduct he dispatched James of Garrigans to the king at Valencia in the earlier part of April 1308.[11] Yet, although the king was willing to grant a safe-conduct, Raymond wanted it to mention the pope's order for the Templars' arrest: he was seeking to ensure that this would not be used to override assurances given in the king's name. James II was, however, unwilling to accede to Raymond's wishes about the wording, although James of Garrigans was allowed to return to Miravet.[12] A similar difficulty was encountered in July: the king again offered a safe-conduct to Raymond of Guardia, but the latter refused to accept it unless it was worded in a certain way. It was therefore agreed that James of Garrigans should again visit the king in Raymond's place, taking proposals submitted by the commander of Mas-Déu. This substitution was apparently made at the suggestion of James of Garrigans, who had already expressed to local royal

---

[8]   A. J. Forey, *The Fall of the Templars in the Crown of Aragon* (Aldershot, 2001), 15.

[9]   He was commander of Peñíscola from at least 1295 until 1298: Forey, *Templars in Aragon,* 439.

[10]   For James II's measures against Templar castles, Forey, *Fall of the Templars*, chap. 2.

[11]   Later in the year it was stated that James had seen the king on Palm Sunday (7 April 1308): ACA, Canc. real, Cartas reales diplomáticas (henceforth CRD), Templarios 157.

[12]   ACA, CRD, Templarios 75; R. 291, fol. 349v.

officials a desire to visit the king on his own behalf.[13] James of Garrigans was of some education, and was obviously expected to speak to the proposals. These apparently included the suggestion that the Templars would remain in their castles, either giving guarantees or with the king's men on guard outside; the king would, however, take no further offensive action, and would supply the Templars with food and clothing.[14] Raymond's intention was that the brethren should be in a position to continue resistance if an unfavourable verdict was given by the pope. James saw the king in the later part of July, but James II, who was insisting on surrender, rejected the proposals.[15]

James of Garrigans again returned to Miravet, but his position there had become increasingly difficult, and in September, nine months into the siege, he deserted his colleagues.[16] He claimed that after his first visit to the king the brothers in the castle of Miravet had become suspicious of him, because the king had agreed to return to him clothing and equipment which he had entrusted to the Catalan noble Oto of Moncada: in the autumn of 1307, when the Templars were anticipating royal action against them, they had disposed of a considerable amount of movable goods in this way. The restoration of James of Garrigans's belongings made his colleagues wonder what had passed between the Templar and the king, and they made their hostility apparent. He further asserted that when he was deputed to see the king a second time, most of the Templars in Miravet expected him to seek favours for himself. When he returned without obtaining any concessions on the proposals, his colleagues (except Raymond of Guardia, who alone was still well-inclined towards James II) accused him of seeking to harm them, although – given the king's stance – James of Garrigans can scarcely be blamed for the failure of his mission. He said that after he had returned to Miravet he felt as if he were 'in the midst of the devils of hell'.[17]

This description of James's situation in the late summer of 1308 is based on his own account, but as conditions in the castles became more difficult disagreements among the besieged were to be expected, and there is evidence of other tensions within Miravet in the later stages of the siege.[18] Support for his account is furthermore to be

---

[13] ACA, CRD, Templarios 157. This is reported in a letter which was written, apparently by a royal official involved in the siege of Miravet, between 26 June, when Raymond of Canet wrote to the king about a safe-conduct for Raymond of Guardia, and 18 July, when the king stated his readiness to offer a safe-conduct for James of Garrigans: Finke, *Papsttum*, ii, 151–2, doc. 89; ACA, R. 291, fols. 120v–121.

[14] The proposals were probably those contained in a letter by Raymond of Guardia which has usually been ascribed to a later date: Finke, *Papsttum*, ii, 173–6, doc. 97; J. M. Sans i Travé, 'Recull de cartes de fra Ramon de Saguàrdia durant el setge de Miravet (Novembre 1307–Desembre 1308)', in *Miscel.lània en honor del Doctor Casimir Martí* (Barcelona, 1994), 445–7, doc. 11; cf. Forey, *Fall of the Templars*, 62, n. 45.

[15] ACA, CRD, Templarios 141; R. 291, fol. 121.

[16] He had apparently already alluded to the possibility of abandoning his colleagues two months earlier: ACA, CRD, Templarios 157.

[17] Finke, *Papsttum*, ii, 164–71, doc. 94. Finke omits several brief passages. For the full texts, ACA, CRD, Templarios 38, 74.

[18] Forey, *Fall of the Templars*, 43–4.

found in an anonymous letter written to James of Garrigans after he had deserted: it was in fact sent by Raymond of Guardia. The latter stated that he had been criticized by brothers in Miravet for placing too much trust in James of Garrigans and for relying on his counsel to the exclusion of that of others: they were glad to be rid of James.[19]

James had planned his escape from Miravet with care. At the time of his desertion, the Templars there, despairing of support from James II, had been composing appeals to the pope, the king of Mallorca, and several others. These letters were written by James of Garrigans.[20] On the night when a messenger, obtained by the *cambrer* of Miravet, was expected to smuggle this correspondence out of the castle, James asked to be allowed to accompany the *cambrer* and to be on guard outside the walls of the castle in the *porqueria*.[21] Raymond of Guardia assented and handed over the letters to James, who took these on guard with him. When the coast was clear, he abandoned his equipment and made for the nearest house in the town, which lay below the castle. His success in effecting his escape illustrates the difficulty of maintaining a total blockade: there was in fact some movement in and out of all castles that the Templars defended.[22] The first dwelling he reached belonged to a Muslim — Muslims comprised the bulk of the population of Miravet — and James stated that he was going to the royal vicar of Tortosa, who had charge of the siege, and then asked him to accompany him to the house of Peter Martínez, who had apparently travelled with James on his first visit to the king. When he arrived there, he sent a message to the vicar at the *bastidas*, which were the towers constructed outside the castle to protect the besiegers. When the vicar arrived, James explained his situation. He also asked the individual in charge of the part of the town just below the castle to sound a horn, since he had told a servant that when he was in the town a signal would be made in that way: the servant was then to lower his equipment down by rope. By this time, however, his flight had been discovered and a fruitless search was made for him outside the castle by the Templars; James did not recover his equipment at this stage.[23]

The brothers in Miravet were right in thinking that James of Garrigans was likely to seek his own advantage. Not only had he tried to obtain an audience with the king on his own behalf in the early summer of 1308: after deserting, he dispatched the correspondence he was carrying – this contained criticisms of the king – to James II, together with a letter of his own written from the town of Miravet on 10 September. In this he not only asserted that he had deserted the Templars for good and that if he returned to Miravet he would be killed, but also asked to be assigned revenues in Catalonia or Valencia which would provide a livelihood, and to be allowed to live freely. If the king was unwilling to allow this, James wanted to reside at Alcarrás or at Gebut in the power of Nicholas of San Clemente, who then held Gebut for the

---

[19]   ACA, CRD, Templarios 194.

[20]   ACA, CRD, Templarios 74. The relevant section is not included in the version published in Finke, *Papsttum,* ii, 164–8, doc. 94.

[21]   This probably refers to a rubbish tip rather than a pigsty.

[22]   Forey, *Fall of the Templars*, 33–4, 40–2.

[23]   Finke, *Papsttum*, ii, 164–71, doc. 94.

king; he sought alternatively to stay at Avellanes under the authority of Gombaldo of Monlor, *portero* of one of James II's sons. But he expected not to be held in prison or under guard. He seems naïvely to have hoped that his desertion and renunciation of the Temple would alone be sufficient to free him from further proceedings.[24]

The king was unimpressed by this approach. On 15 September, after receiving the letters dispatched by James, he instructed the vicar of Tortosa to keep the Templar in irons in the castle of Tortosa, ensuring that he could not escape or speak to anybody. He thought that the whole enterprise had been engineered by the Templars in authority in Miravet and viewed it with suspicion. He did not explain his reasons, but he possibly thought that supposed appeals to the pope were intended as a means of putting pressure on himself.[25] James of Garrigans thus became the first Aragonese Templar in custody to be placed in irons. Unlike their colleagues in France, other Aragonese brethren who had been detained by this time were being treated with more consideration.[26]

After his flight, James also wrote to Raymond of Guardia, who was still in the castle of Miravet, seeking the return of some of his possessions, including books. He received a friendly response, although Raymond refrained from sending his belongings; in his letter Raymond did, however, take the opportunity to stress his own loyalty towards James II: he presumably expected his views to be transmitted to the king.[27] James of Garrigans did in fact send this reply to the king in the second half of September, together with another letter of his own. In this, he rather tactlessly displayed the breadth of his knowledge by commenting that he had discovered the truth of Psalm cxviii, 9: 'it is better to trust in the Lord than to put confidence in princes'. He nevertheless sought the king's mercy, and asserted that if the king treated him well, many brothers defending Miravet and Monzón would soon surrender.[28] James II did not deign to reply, and on 30 September ordered that James of Garrigans should remain in irons.[29] The latter was still at Tortosa when the Templars in Miravet surrendered early in December 1308 and were brought to the castle of Tortosa.[30] If he encountered his former colleagues again, it could scarcely have been a pleasant reunion.

James's predicament was, however, apparently eased by his calligraphic skills, and during his captivity he, unlike his fellow Templars, was given a function to fulfil. In possessing this skill, James of Garrigans was exceptional: brother chaplains sometimes wrote letters, but most sergeants were illiterate.[31] When James of Garrigans had himself sought an audience with the king, it had been mentioned that 'he knows how to write with a skilled hand and to illuminate in gold with brush

---

[24]   Ibid.

[25]   ACA, R. 291, fol. 131–131v.

[26]   On the treatment of Aragonese Templars in custody, Forey, *Fall of the Templars*, chap. 3.

[27]   ACA, CRD, Templarios 194.

[28]   Finke, *Papsttum*, ii, 164–71, doc. 94.

[29]   ACA, R. 291, fol. 145.

[30]   ACA, CRD, Templarios 453.

[31]   A. J. Forey, 'Literacy and Learning in the Military Orders during the Twelfth and Thirteenth Centuries', *MO*, ii, 185–97.

and quill', and – as one means of securing his objective – James of Garrigans had suggested that the king or queen should say that they had a book to illuminate and should summon him for this purpose.[32] Although in July 1308 James of Garrigans had journeyed to the king as Raymond of Guardia's envoy, letters written by the royal bailiff of Tortosa in November, apparently in the year 1308, reveal that the king later asked this official to arrange for James, while in custody, to compile a book of the hours of the Virgin Mary, following the Dominican usage. The bailiff in reply sent the king a prayer book of his own, at the back of which James of Garrigans had provided samples of three forms of script, so that the king could select which he preferred.[33] It was perhaps in connection with work of this kind that in 1309 the king ordered that the Templar should be sent from Tortosa to the bishop of Valencia, who was the royal chancellor.[34]

James of Garrigans's responses to the charges against the Temple have apparently been lost. Records exist of only about seventy Templar testimonies given in Aragon and Catalonia in 1309–10.[35] Yet none of the testimonies which do survive from James II's realms, including those of Templars questioned under torture in 1311,[36] contains any confession to the more serious accusations. After the dissolution of the Temple, all brothers were absolved at a provincial council at Tarragona in November 1312, which also decreed that they should be pensioned off and live in former houses of the order.[37] All these buildings remained under royal authority until the end of 1317, when those in Aragon and Catalonia passed to the Hospital. The Aragonese Templars were therefore able to enjoy much more freedom than their English colleagues, who were sent to religious houses belonging to other orders.[38] In the years after 1312, many Aragonese brethren engaged in activities with which they were already familiar, such as warfare (against both Muslims and Christians) and administration, which often took them away from their places of residence. James of Garrigans was

---

[32] ACA, CRD, Templarios 157.

[33] ACA, CRD, Jaime II 13029; H. Finke, *Acta Aragonensia*, 3 vols (Berlin, 1908–22): ii, 924–5, doc. 596. Finke suggests that the letter he published was written after 1308, but he provides no evidence. The bailiff, who could not obtain a suitable book of hours in Tortosa to serve as an exemplar and who therefore sought to secure one from the prior of the Dominicans in Tarragona, was happy for the king to keep his prayer book.

[34] ACA, R. 291, fol. 256v. At the same time the king ordered that Templar books which had been found at Miravet and neighbouring places should be sent to the bishop. The bishop of Valencia was involved in the questioning of Templars in Aragonese lands, but this did not start until the later part of 1309, and the interrogations were normally conducted locally by the diocesan — in this case the bishop of Tortosa — with the assistance of some of those named by the pope.

[35] ACB, codices 124, 149; Forey, *Fall of the Templars*, 76.

[36] A. Mercati, 'Interrogatorio di Templari a Barcellona (1311)', *Spanische Forschungen der Görresgesellschaft: Gesammelte Aufsätze zur Kulturgeschichte Spaniens*, vi (1937), 240–51.

[37] On the Aragonese Templars after the trial, Forey, *Fall of the Templars*, chap. 6.

[38] A. J. Forey, 'Ex-Templars in England', *Journal of Ecclesiastical History*, liii (2002), 20–22.

apparently sent to Gardeny, but it is not known what pension he received.[39] In 1315, however, he was collecting Templar revenues in and around Lérida on behalf of the king, and James II ordered that he should be given a suitable salary for this work: in the following year he was in fact being paid 500s. annually.[40] In April 1317 he made payments in the king's name to several non-Templars employed at the convent of Gardeny.[41] This is, however, apparently the last surviving reference to the Templar James of Garrigans.

There was admittedly a Hospitaller of the same name in Aragon in the 1320s and early 1330s. In 1325 he had charge of the former Templar castle of Chalamera and was later acting as the proctor of the Hospitaller commander of Monzón.[42] Yet it is questionable whether this Hospitaller is to be identified with the Templar of that name. In 1318 John XXII had certainly ordered surviving Templars to enter houses of other religious orders,[43] and this decree was belatedly implemented in Aragonese lands. But James of Garrigans is not mentioned in lists of pensions paid to former Templars drawn up in 1319[44] or in documents relating to efforts to enforce John XXII's ruling in the 1320s.[45] Moreover, very few Templars in Aragon and Catalonia obeyed the pope's instructions: most preferred to live in the world and be deprived of their pensions. It seems likely therefore that James of Garrigans had died by 1319.

He was obviously a self-seeking Templar, who thought first of his own interests when the order was in danger. It is, of course, easy for those who have not been in such a situation to criticize: but the only other Templars known to have deserted their colleagues during the sieges were three who abandoned Monzón shortly before it surrendered.[46] His skill as an illuminator also set him apart from his colleagues. Yet his career throws light on various aspects of the last stages of the history of the Temple in the Aragonese province, most notably: the patterns of service among

---

[39]   ACA, R. 278, fol. 158v. In the summer of 1313 he was seeking to ensure that pension arrears were paid to the executors of a Templar who had died in Roussillon, but James was presumably resident at that time in James II's realms: ACA, R. 274, fol. 51. Templar sergeants were usually given 500s.B. a year.

[40]   ACA, R. 251, fol. 118v; R. 277, fol. 1.

[41]   ACA, R. 278, fol. 158v.

[42]   ACA, R. 185, fol. 135; R. 436, fol. 73; R. 438, fol. 97–97v; R. 442, fol. 184v. Finke, *Papsttum*, i, 300, n. 1, and *Acta Aragonensia*, ii, 925, is incorrect in stating that the Templar became a Dominican.

[43]   H. Prutz, *Entwicklung und Untergang des Tempelherrenordens* (Berlin, 1888), 293-94.

[44]   J. Villanueva, *Viage literario a las iglesias de España*, 22 vols (Madrid, 1803–52): v, 226–32, doc. 9; J. Miret y Sans, *Les cases de Templers y Hospitalers en Catalunya* (Barcelona, 1910), 390–95. Admittedly, several names are known to have been omitted from these.

[45]   Documents relating to the dioceses of Lérida and Tortosa include ACA, R. 178, fols. 94v, 281–281v; R. 179, fols. 273v–274; R. 183, fols. 145v–146, 146v–147.

[46]   ACA, R. 291, fols. 201v–2, 227; A. Masiá de Ros, *La Corona de Aragón y los estados del Norte de Africa* (Barcelona, 1951), 490–92, doc. 186; Forey, *Fall of the Templars*, 28.

sergeants in the years before 1307; the increasingly difficult conditions within Templar castles under siege, when no help could be expected from a relieving force; and the comparative freedom enjoyed by Aragonese Templars after the end of the trial.

Chapter 12

The University of Paris and the Trial of the Templars

Paul F. Crawford

Most historians concur today that the Poor Knights of the Temple of Solomon were generally innocent of the charges lodged against them by Philip the Fair of France in 1307. Yet the affair contains so many mysteries, so many contradictions, so many complexities, that we can still say, with contemporaries like the inquisitor Bernard Gui and the chronicler John of St. Victor, that it is an 'astonishing matter.'[1]

It might be helpful to review the course of the trial briefly. In the early morning hours of 13 October 1307, virtually all the Templars in the kingdom of France were suddenly arrested, in a carefully pre-planned operation ordered by King Philip the Fair. The brethren and other personnel of the order were charged with a long, and by now famous, list of offences, and confessions to these offences were soon extracted from the prisoners. Philip turned immediately to Pope Clement V (claiming, almost certainly falsely, to have been acting in concert with the pontiff), and demanded that the order be condemned and dissolved promptly.

Philip was frustrated in this attempt, for a variety of reasons, and a long and messy trial began and dragged out until March 1312, when Clement, against the advice of the majority of church fathers attending the Council of Vienne, unilaterally suppressed the Order of the Temple without actually condemning it.

Even at this late date, some of the complexities of the trial remain at least partially unexplored. One such area is the interaction during the trial between some of the masters of theology at the University of Paris and Philip the Fair's government. It is that interaction which this essay addresses. Some of the ground here has already been gone over (notably by Malcolm Barber in his 1978 *Trial of the Templars*), but it bears re-examining, partly because of the odd composition of the respondents to a government questionnaire in 1308, and partly because of some interesting differences between the behaviour of the university masters in 1303 and 1308.

The role of the university of Paris in the trial was not insignificant. Philip and his officials seem to have been almost as concerned about the opinion of the masters of the university as they were about the opinion of the pope himself. In fact, the masters were virtually the first authorities to whom the government turned. On Saturday, 14 October 1307, the day after the arrests, the royal officer William of Nogaret assembled

---

[1]   Bernard Gui, *RHGF* 21, 719; Jean of St. Victor, *RHGF* 21, 649.

the masters of the university along with the canons of the cathedral of Notre Dame and presented the government's case to them.[2] The government exhibited the high officials of the order, properly subdued, to almost all the bachelors and the masters (regent and non-regent alike) of the faculty of the university a week and a half later, on 25 and 26 October, and forced the Templars to repeat their confessions for the benefit of the university men. Names of many of the attendees were taken down at both convocations.[3]

None of this was particularly unusual. Five years earlier, in 1303, when Philip had been deep in his controversy with Boniface VIII, the masters of the university of Paris, along with practically everyone else of consequence in France, had been required to sign statements aligning themselves with the king and against the pope. In 1303, the masters of the university of Paris acquiesced to the king's demands, or at least the majority signed, or otherwise adhered to, documents to that effect.[4] The penalties for not doing so were severe; clerics who refused to go along had their clerical privileges revoked in France, lost the support of their French benefices,[5] and were exiled (though in the end only temporarily) from the kingdom.[6] As William Courtenay noted in a 1996 *Speculum* article, the support of the university in 1303 was very important to Philip's government. The university, especially its faculties of theology and canon law, was an internationally prestigious institution, and its members were drawn both from within and without France and so might help spread support for Philip's position.[7]

And yet there is, again as Courtenay has demonstrated, considerable reason to think that in 1303 the university of Paris lacked enthusiasm, at best, for Philip's project against Boniface. The documents to which the university was required to assent were not copied into the university's own register, and no attempt was made to do anything other than acquiesce to the government's form statement. Still, dissenting voices within the university, which Courtenay shows were almost certainly there, were generally ignored and do not usually show up in the records.[8] Swiftly and ruthlessly, Philip's government extorted consent and suppressed the dissent that did exist in 1303.

The same process, which had been relatively successful from the government's point of view, seemed about to be repeated four years later, in 1307. But this time events proceeded somewhat differently.

Some months after the arrests and initial exhibitions of Templar officers to the masters of the university, probably in early February 1308, and probably before the government officially requested an opinion from the masters, an anonymous

---

[2]   Ibid., 649.

[3]   Finke, *Papsttum und Untergang des Templerordens*, ii (Münster, 1907), 48–49 (#32); ibid., 307–313 (#149–150).

[4]   William J. Courtenay, 'Between Pope and King: the Parisian Letters of Adhesion of 1303,' *Speculum* lxxi (1996), 580–84; *Chartularium Universitatis Parisiensis*, ed. Heinrich Denifle, ii (Paris, 1891; repr. Brussels, 1964), 101, #634.

[5]   Courtenay, 585.

[6]   Ibid., 589.

[7]   Ibid., 587.

[8]   Ibid., 587–9, 604.

author wrote a passionate open letter to the university, denouncing the government and pleading on behalf of the Templars.[9] The Templars were innocent, the writer said, and the process manifestly unjust. The Templars had been tortured hideously during the three months that had elapsed since their arrest, and they were dying as martyrs to the truth. It was incredible that so many good men seeking their souls' salvation would have entered the order over 200 years, encountered the evil that Philip claimed was in the order, and promptly and silently submitted to that evil. Someone would have betrayed the awful secrets. Furthermore, if the order was so evil, why were there still a hundred Templars in prison in Egypt, when by converting to Islam they could gain wives, horses, arms, and a place amongst the honoured nobility of Egypt?

The author ended his letter with a plea and an implicit warning. Think before you render your verdict, he said. Keep your eyes on God alone, and give the kind of counsel that will bring you reward from God and praise from men.

Whoever the author may have been, he seems to have known both the events in the case and the intentions of the government well. At about the time the anonymous defence of the Templars was written, the king's officials were accusing Clement V of nepotism in his appointments and threatening to see that the men he had appointed to high church offices were replaced after his death by persons drawn from the 'great masters of theology' of the university of Paris.[10] In 1303 the government had apparently relied more heavily on threats to motivate the university. Now they were adding a carrot of reward to the stick of exile which, having been imposed only four years earlier, hardly needed to be repeated explicitly now. 'Take our line, and be rewarded with lucrative appointments later on.' The anonymous defender of the Templars either knew this or anticipated it, and was evidently trying to even the pressures on the masters.

Probably in late February 1308, the government's inquiry arrived at the university. There were questions that had arisen regarding the disposition of the goods and persons of the Templars, the document said, and it proceeded to list seven of them.

1. Can a prince take action independently of the Church against a blatant heresy that he perceives in his jurisdiction, or does the New Testament restrain this exercise of princely power and require that a prince may not act except at the express request of the Church?
2. Since the crime of the Templars was so horrible and abominable (no challenges to this particular issue were to be accommodated!), and posed such imminent danger to the community, could the prince at least in this case act to forestall that danger to the community, or was the fact that the Templars were 'said to constitute a religious order' prevent this? Did not the plain confessions of the Templars nullify their supposed exemption from outside interference, especially (and here is a fascinating claim) since they were after all, said the government, merely a college of knights and not primarily

---

9   C. R. Cheney, 'The Downfall of the Templars and a Letter in Their Defence,' in *Medieval Texts and Studies*, ed. C. R. Cheney (Oxford, 1973), 314–27. The letter is reproduced in ibid., 322–27.

10   Georges Lizerand, *Le Dossier de l'affaire des Templiers* (Paris, 1923), 90–91.

a clerical order at all?

3. Since over fifty French Templars had confessed the evils of their 'sect' (the master and other officers of the order among them), was this sufficient to condemn the order as a whole, or must one wait until similar confessions were extracted in other kingdoms before taking this so obviously necessary step?

4. Since all the brothers were required to apostasize upon entering the order (again, no discussion of the veracity of this claim was provided for), how should one handle those few brothers who refused to admit apostasy, and whose receptors were dead or otherwise unavailable? Did one have to treat them as good Catholics merely because they could not be forced to acquiesce to the charges?

5. If there were, say, ten, twenty, even thirty Templars who refused to confess and against whom nothing could be proven, did this prevent the order as a whole from being suppressed? Or did the fact that so many members had given depositions against the order allow for the suppression of the order?

6. Assuming that the order could be suppressed (and the government fairly obviously intended for the answer to be 'yes, it could'), then who got the goods of the suppressed order: the prince who carried out the suppression, the Church, or the needs of the Holy Land (for which, the government admitted, the goods had been earmarked in the first place)?

7. Last of all, if the law required the goods to be reserved for the needs of the Holy Land, or if the 'devotion of the prince' set them aside for this purpose freely, who should have control over the disposition of the goods: the Church or princes, most of all the kingdom of France, which as everyone knew had had a special interest in the Holy Land from 'antiquity'?

These were, to say the least, leading questions. Combined with the hints we find of current blandishments, and the past threat provided by Philip's treatment of those who dissented from the letters of adhesion in 1303, it is perfectly plain that the government had specific answers it wanted from the Parisian masters of theology, answers which it intended to extract. But this time the government was considerably less successful than it had been in 1303. After a delay of several weeks, fourteen university masters returned a verdict to the government.[11]

They began with an appropriately submissive introduction and then rather pointedly noted that regent and non-regent masters alike were agreed on the counsel that followed. They begged pardon for their delay in answering him, attributing it to the fact that the questions were weighty and also that some of the more important of their number had been away.

In answer to the first question, they said that a secular prince had no authority to take action against heretics unless expressly requested to do so by the Church. The only exception to this would be if the danger from the heresy were great and imminent, and the Church's approval entirely sure. In that case the prince might proceed, but must turn the arrested persons over to the custody of the Church at the first possible opportunity (which the government had certainly not done in 1307). The masters were also of the opinion that any statutes or laws founded solely on Old Testament practice and not explicitly renewed by the New Testament were revoked from New Testament times on; that is, the New Testament did not grant the prince

---

[11]   Ibid., 62–71.

as wide a scope of action as did the Old, and hence he was not entitled to exercise that wider scope.

On the second question the masters were even more firm. The fact that the Templars were knights did *not* in any way preclude them from being part of an order of exempt religious, and since they had made their professions to the Church, it was for the Church alone to determine whether those professions had been properly implemented. Philip's government could scarcely have received a sharper rebuff on this point, which seems to have been something of a concern of more than one of the participants and especially of the regent master Jacques of Thérines, as may be seen below.

Having flatly opposed the government on the first two points, the masters then proceeded to give rather more equivocal answers to the rest of the questions. On the third question (whether the confessions tainted the whole order), the masters agreed that widespread confessions of serious heresy by some members of the order cast 'vehement suspicion' on the entire order, in and out of France. Here as elsewhere they expressed no opinion whatsoever about the veracity of those confessions, and as we shall see, at least one of them would later express doubts about the confessions in writing (again, Jacques of Thérines). They had not, of course, been asked their opinion on that subject, so there was no need for them to offer such a dangerous thing.

On the fourth question (whether those who would not confess and who could not be proved to have done anything wrong should be considered good Catholics), the masters believed that since the whole order was, again, under 'vehement suspicion,' even those who had not confessed or been convicted of anything might be quarantined to keep the 'infection' from spreading elsewhere. Again, they expressed no opinion whatsoever on how the confessions had been obtained or whether they were in fact accurate.

On the fifth question (whether a handful of innocent Templars would be enough to allow the order to go on functioning), the masters believed they had answered adequately in their replies to the third and fourth questions.

On the sixth and seventh questions (dealing with possible disposition of the goods of the Templars), the masters were of the opinion that since the goods were not given to the Templars as lords, but rather given to them for the needs of the Holy Land, and that since the Holy Land still needed them, they should be reserved for that use. As for who should have custody of them, the masters thought (perhaps evading the issue) that they should go to whoever could best ensure that they were used for the Holy Land.

This, said the masters, was the best advice they could manage, and they were all agreed on it. Above all, they added somewhat anxiously, they wished to serve both the king and truth. They had no desire to offend him, and they hoped that he would be successful in quickly suppressing such a great scandal.

They might well end on an anxious note: they had not provided the government with the cover it had wanted to obtain, and what they had given had been rather grudging. And given that the government had been quick to suppress most evidence of dissenting opinions in the affair of 1303,[12] it seems likely that this record was the furthest the masters of the university of Paris were willing to go in publicly supporting the government's position – this was the best the government could get.

There seems to have been yet another reason for the understandable anxiety of the masters over this affair. We find a clue to that anxiety in the composition of the group of fourteen masters who actually signed the university's 1308 response to the government's questionnaire.

As mentioned earlier, there were fourteen masters who responded. About half of the fourteen were regent masters, and, as they themselves had said, the group represented the opinions of both regents and non-regents. More significantly, the respondents were comprised primarily of members of the religious orders, and exempt orders at that; few secular masters, regent or non-regent, are represented in the list, nor did the most important of the secular masters respond.[13] Of the masters who did respond, at least eight were definitely members of exempt religious orders; only three were clearly secular clergy.

The exempt orders included the Dominicans, Franciscans, Carmelites, Augustinian Hermits, Cistercians – and the military orders. An attack on one of their number might well be seen as an attack on all, and might provoke them to defend each other. The composition of the university respondents alone might lead one to draw the conclusion that that was in fact what was happening.

There is more evidence to support this conclusion. At least one of the masters, the Cistercian prior Jacques of Thérines, wrote an extensive tract on the issue of the exempt orders later on, *Contra impugnatores exemptionum et privilegiorum,* at about the time of the Council of Vienne in 1312. Several pages of this work are devoted to the issue of the Templars.[14]

Jacques of Thérines apparently found the case against the Templars shaky – repeatedly, he referred to the charges and then appended 'if what they say is true' or similar disclaimers. But he was plainly concerned that the attack on the Templars would spill over onto other exempt orders. So he was left with a balancing act, trying to point out that the Templars may not have been guilty, while at the same time arguing that even if they were guilty, they were structured differently from other non-military exempt orders, in that they were a lay-run order, and that even if problems had arisen within the Templars, this was no reason to condemn the whole idea of exempt clergy.

The impression that the exempt clergy felt themselves threatened by the government's attack is further strengthened if one considers the work of an Augustinian Hermit, a master who did not sign the university's response to the government's questions, but who nevertheless produced his own, independent commentary on the affair in 1308. This is Augustine Trionfo, or Augustinus Triumphus. In his *De facto*

---

[12]   Courtenay, esp. 583.

[13]   I am grateful to William Courtenay for having pointed this out to me in a private communication.

[14]   See *Bibliothecae patrum Cisterciensium,* ed. Bertrand Tissier, iv (Bonnefontaine, 1662), 261–315 (and note that the pagination in that edition is defective); and Noël Valois, 'Jacques de Thérines, Cistercien,' *Histoire littéraire de la France,* xxxiv (1914), 179–219.

Templariorum,[15] he lays out the case in favour of the government's position and then proceeds to demolish it, point by point, with considerable force and even humour. Although there are reasons for thinking that a secular prince might intervene on his own initiative in a case involving idolatry or sodomy, he said, in fact it was only permissible if the prince saw a clear and imminent danger, and then only if he handed them over promptly to the Church for adjudication. The Old Testament forbade any other course, he said, as did the New Testament and even reason itself. Furthermore, he said pointedly, the Templars possessed exempt status, and so no secular power might exercise authority over them.

Augustine went even further. Some sixty-five years old, born in Italy, he perhaps cared little for the opinion of the French government. 'Modern princes,' he said, making an unveiled reference to Philip the Fair, 'resemble a physician who gives his patient a laxative, and only then goes away to consult his books to see if he has done the right thing. When he returns, he finds that the patient has died!'

As noted above, three secular masters did join the religious masters in signing the university's response to the government. At least one secular master who did not join the fourteen respondents also wrote independently on the matter, at about the time Jacques of Thérines was writing favourably of the Templars (*c*.1312). This was the regent master John of Pouilly. But John of Pouilly did not support the Templars or the exempt orders. On the contrary, he wrote against both the Templars and the exempt mendicant orders in rather forceful terms.[16] The Templars were obviously guilty, he said. The fact that many of them retracted their confessions and died professing their innocence only sealed their fates, as far as he was concerned. Such courage only proved, perversely, that they were capable of gross heresy. They were plainly relapsed heretics. He was all for handing them over to the secular authorities for punishment. In this position John of Pouilly was in harmony with many of the French prelates, such as the archbishop of Sens, which is hardly surprising since he seems to have had connections with the royal court as well.

But John of Pouilly seems to have represented a minority opinion on the Templar question, both in the university and at the Council of Vienne. At any rate, few other secular masters even bothered to declare themselves on the issue.[17] The composition of the respondents to the questions put by the French government to the university of Paris in 1308, therefore, leads one to suspect that the other exempt orders – the Dominicans, Franciscans, Augustinian Hermits, Carmelites, and others – felt their positions to be directly threatened by the government's actions against the legally-exempt Templars. As a consequence, the masters who belonged to those orders put

---

[15]   In *Die Publizistik zur Zeit Philipps des Schönen und Bonifaz' VII*, ed. Richard Scholz (Stuttgart, 1903), 508–16.

[16]   Noël Valois, 'Deux nouveaux témoignages sur le procès des Templiers,' in *Comptes rendus des séances de l'année 1910 [Académie des inscriptions & belles-lettres]* (Paris, 1910), 229–41; and id., 'Jean de Pouilli, Théologien,' in *Histoire littéraire de la France*, xxxiv (1914), 220–81.

[17]   It should be noted here that John of Pouilly later found himself in serious trouble with John XXII, and was forced to recant some of his own works as heretical.

up considerably more resistance to the government's policies in 1308 than they had done five years earlier, in 1303, in the matter of Boniface VIII.

More research on the subject remains to be done. And all this is not to imply that the masters who rejected the government's claims were not also genuinely concerned about the illegality and injustice of the proceedings. But this much, at least, seems clear: that the members of the exempt orders were themselves frightened by the government's actions.

Chapter 13

A Look through the Keyhole: Templars in Italy from the Trial Testimony

Anne Gilmour-Bryson

We have only limited testimony from the hearings or trials of the Order of the Temple and its members in Italy.[1] A trial is thought to have occurred in Naples, but the documents have been lost.[2] The history of the Templars in Italy has been the subject of several fairly recent books and pamphlets, including Bianca Capone, *I templari in Italia*, and *Vestigia Templari in Italia;* Litterio Villari, *I templari in Sicilia*; Enzo Valentini, *I templari a Civitavecchia* and *Santa Maria in Carbonara, chiesa templare a Viterbo.* None of us who has seen it can forget Gaetano Lamattina's *I templari nella storia.* Maria lo Mastro who ruled the *Casa templari* in Rome authored *Dossier Templari.* Something useful may be found in each of these, but errors or omissions abound. For a much better look at the Italian Templars, see with precaution Fulvio Bramato, *Storia dell'ordine dei Templari in Italia*, and the old but reliable Telesforo Bini, 'Dei Templari in Lucca'; Luigi Avonto, *I Templari in Piemonte;* Francesco Tommasi, *L'ordine dei Templari in Perugia,* and his other works.[3] The trouble with

---

[1]   Hearings also occurred in Ravenna and Brindisi. For the Papal State and the Abruzzi, including the regions of Campania and Marittima, and the duchy of Spoleto, see my Latin edition, *The Trial of the Templars in the Papal State and the Abruzzi* (Città del Vaticano, 1982), (henceforth *TTPSA*).. Ravenna data comes from Rossi (Rubeus), *Historiarum Ravennatum, liber* vi (Venice, 1590); and R. Caravita, *Rinaldo da Concorrezo arcivescovo di Ravenna 1303-1321 al tempo di Dante* (Florence, 1964), 97-166, 265-1307. For Tuscany itself, Vatican Library, MS Vat. Lat. 4011, transcribed in T. Bini, 'Dei Tempieri e del loro processo in Toscana', *Atti della reale Accademia Lucchese*, xiii (1845), 460-501. Brindisi depositions are in Konrad Schottmüller, *Der Untergang des Templer-Ordens* (Berlin, 1887: repr. New York, 1970), ii, 105-40.

[2]   On Italian Templar hearings including Naples, Malcolm Barber, *The Trial of the Templars* (Cambridge, 1978), 213-15.

[3]   Bianca Capone, *I templari in Italia* (Milan, 1977), and id., *Vestigia Templari in Italia* (Rome, 1979); Litterio Villari, *I templari in Sicilia* (Latina, 1993); Enzo Valentini, *I templari a Civitavecchia* (Latina, 1992); id., *Santa Maria in Carbonara, chiesa templare a Viterbo* (Latina, 1993); Gaetano Lamattina, *I templari nella storia* (Rome, 1981); Fulvio Bramato, *Storia dell'ordine dei Templari in Italia* (Rome, 1991); Telesforo Bini, 'Dei Templari in Lucca', Reale Accademia Lucchese, 27 August, 1838 (repr. Latina, 1992); Luigo Avonto, *I Templari in Piemonte* (Vercelli, 1982); and Francesco Tommasi, 'L'ordine dei Templari in

research on Italian Templars is that enthusiastic amateurs have flooded the market with insufficiently researched and inaccurate articles and monographs.

Given the impossibility of discussing the situation of Italian Templars for the entire period of their existence in Italy,[4] focus will be laid here entirely on what can be gleaned from testimony given between 1309 and 1311 in two hearings, Tuscany, and the Papal State and the Abruzzi.[5] The hearing in Brindisi heard only two witnesses, who added little to the testimony discussed below.[6] Routine evidence regarding illicit acts will not be discussed.

The hearing in the Papal State and the Abruzzi, conducted by Pandulfus Savelli, a papal official, and James, bishop of Sutri, lasted from September 1309 until July 1310.[7] The inquisitors heard seven witnesses. In April 1310 an apostate, brother Cecchus from Chieti, testified first in the episcopal palace in Penna.[8] Like all but one of the witnesses interrogated in these proceedings, the articles of interrogation had to be translated into Italian. One of the most valuable pieces of information to be found in this and similar testimony concerns the names and functions of senior Templar officials. When asked the names of regional grand preceptors, he answered that there was only one, Peter Ultramontanus, who used to govern Apulia and the Abruzzi. He had heard that he was dead and that now Odo of Valdris was the grand preceptor.[9] He explained that the other regions in the area included Rome, Marittima, Campania, the Papal State, Lombardy,[10] the March of Ancona, and the Duchy of Spoleto, though he was not very sure. The grand preceptor Hugh of Vercellis received him.[11] James

---

Perugia', in *Bollettino della Deputazione di Storia Patria per l'Umbria,* lxxviii (1981), and printed as an offprint in the same year.

⁴   The order was established in Rome in 1138. See Malcolm Barber, *The New Knighthood. A History of the Order of the Temple* (Cambridge, 1994), 19. On the basis of G. Guerrieri, *I cavalieri templari nel regno di Sicilia* (Trani, 1909), 6-7, Lamattina, 60-61, suggests that they may have had a preceptory in Sicily as early as 1131. Bramato, 46-7, suggests that the earliest Roman Templar house may predate 1148.

⁵   Bini's transcription of BAV MS Vat. Lat. 4011 uses the date 1312. The manuscript itself gives Monday 20 September, indiction 9 which, according to A. Cappelli, *Cronografia* (Milan, 1930), 76-77, can only refer to 1311.

⁶   See *supra,* note 1, for publication details.

⁷   See Secret Vatican Archives, Fondo di Castel Sant'Angelo, MS Armadio D-207 for the only manuscript.

⁸   *TTPSA,* 130-44. All references to Cecchus come from these pages.

⁹   Odo of Valdris, Valdareto, and variants testified at the trial of the Templars in Cyprus. See *The Trial of the Templars in Cyprus,* ed. and trans. Anne Gilmour-Bryson (Leiden, 1998), 80, 163-67. He confirmed there that he had been preceptor of Apulia. He denied completely any wrongdoing whatsoever.

¹⁰   Lombardy is sometimes included in the list of regions under the same preceptor, but in the scribes' listing of areas to inquire about, it is not mentioned. Presumably these inquisitors were not ordered to enquire in the area of Lombardy, where the only remaining information concerns one Templar in Ancona. Barber, *Trial of the Templars,* 214. See also the testimony of the preceptor Egidius, *infra.*

¹¹   Hugh was a well-known Templar and papal chamberlain. *TTPSA,* 133, n.24.

of Montecucco[12] later took over and Cecchus had seen him in Perugia at the time of Pope Benedict XI (1303-1304). Cecchus's own licit reception had occurred in Rome, in a room which Hugh had in the Lateran Palace near the *sancta sanctorum*.[13] This information on reception indicates that in Rome receptions were not only held in Santa Maria sull'Aventino but also in the Lateran itself.

Three or four years later Hugh sent Cecchus off with sealed letters to be delivered to the preceptor of the provinces of Apulia and Abruzzi, indicating that simple serving brothers were used for such tasks. Cecchus attended another Templar reception in Barletta at which French Templars were present, attesting to Templar mobility.

In spite of considerable testimony regarding idolatry and other nefarious deeds, he himself insisted that he believed in all the sacraments of the church. He was, nevertheless, not sufficiently knowledgeable to know whether priests of the order omitted words during the consecration. He admitted that he and others were told that if they sinned, the Templar preceptor could absolve them, a clear misunderstanding of canon law, but not surprising in an unlettered brother. He confirmed the fact that when received Templars promised obedience, chastity, and to live without property, and that they were immediately professed without a novitiate. He mentioned the astonishment and curiosity shown by others regarding secret reception. Neither he, nor the others whose receptions he saw, were received at night but at Tierce.

Like Templars in Cyprus and elsewhere, he insisted that while hospitality was not a common practice within the order, he saw charity being distributed in Santa Maria sull'Aventino and in Barletta.[14] He knew that it was wrong to acquire goods dishonestly. He had never been told same-sex acts were licit. It was just two months after the illicit acts he described took place that he quit the order, presumably without permission, casting serious doubt on his testimony since he could have been prosecuted for so-doing.

The second witness Andrew, apostate and serving brother, testified in the episcopal palace in Chieti.[15] He had previously been married and obtained permission from his wife to become a Templar. He had remained in the order for only eight or nine months. He insisted that it was common knowledge that grand preceptors, and others, had boys with whom they united carnally.[16]

Concerning charity, Andrew added that in Barletta, alms were distributed on Sunday, Tuesday, and Thursday, consisting of bread and leftover food from the

---

[12]   A number of variants of this name exist, including Monte Cuccho and Monteacuto.

[13]   Peter of Bologna attended this reception. He was one of seven Templars undertaking to defend the order in Paris in 1310. See Jules Michelet, *Le procès des Templiers* (Paris, 1841-51), i, 164-69.

[14]   On the impressive church of Santa Maria sull'Aventino, a very important Templar church in the thirteenth century, *TTPSA*, 32, n.21.

[15]   His testimony is found in *TTPSA*, 145-57 from which the above description of his testimony is taken.

[16]   Ibid., 149: 'audivit dici communiter a fratribus dicti ordinis . . . quod dictus magnus preceptor qui eum recipit, et alii preceptors et magni fraters in dicto ordine, habebant pueros quibus se carnaliter commiscebant.'

community table. He stated that the preceptory there had no infirmary so that sick brethren had to be sent outside to a hospital.

On 7 June, in the episcopal palace in Viterbo, the hearing began against William, a Templar priest who, unlike the others, heard the questions in Latin.[17] Hugh of Vercellis had received him in Santa Maria sull'Aventino. He insisted that he had always had, and still had, faith in redemption by Jesus Christ. His belief in the sacraments had never varied since he reached the age of discretion. He affirmed that although he had been told to omit the words of consecration of the host when saying mass, he had never done so. He stated that on one occasion, the doors of the room were not closed when a new brother was received. He seems to have attended very few reception ceremonies, and not to have travelled much whilst in the order. In Rome he had seen three paupers fed by the Templars every day, as well as the thrice-weekly distribution of alms. He insisted that Templars could confess to priests who were not members of the order when required, indicating that, as we know, the order was short of chaplains.

The fourth witness, Gerard, another serving brother, testified in the same place.[18] He had been incarcerated in a papal prison prior to testifying. He was received in Piacenza twenty-four years earlier when Blancus was grand preceptor, followed after his death by William Provintialis who died overseas, and then by Artusius of Pocapalgia who, he believed, died in Viterbo and was buried in the Templar church of Santa Maria in Carbonara. William of Cannellis, the next local grand preceptor, was sent off to the Templar province of Hungary, dying in Rieti on his return.[19] Hugh of Vercellis succeeded him and he was buried in Santa Maria in Capita in the diocese of Bagnoregio; the grand preceptor was now James of Montecucco.[20] What is surprising about this answer is the amount of data possessed by this simple serving brother, information going back almost a quarter of a century.

At his reception, Gerard not only made the usual three vows but also promised not to leave the order, a promise often mentioned elsewhere and part of the Templar Statutes.[21] He asserted that James of Bologna, vicar of James of Montecucco, committed carnal acts with brother Manfred of Bagnoregio. Gerard asserted that Templars could confess to Carmelite priests if their own chaplains were not available, adding that he had confessed his illicit acts to a priest and been absolved.

Blancus had received the next witness, Peter, a serving brother, between 1277 and 1280 in Rome.[22] Peter provided a list of grand preceptors similar to that of Gerard, adding the information that Hugh of Vercellis died in Iterapano, a town I have not

---

[17]   For the testimony of William of Verduno, *TTPSA*, 172-86.

[18]   For his testimony, ibid., 187-99.

[19]   On Hungary, *infra*, n. 20.

[20]   For information on all these Templar notables, *TTPSA*, 188, nn. 4-7. Hospitaller and Templar documents usually add 'Hungary', probably Dalmatia, to the province of Rome. See *TTPSA*, 189, n.8.

[21]   See *inter alia*, *The Rule of the Templars*, ed. and trans. J. Upton-Ward (Woodbridge, U.K, 1992), nos. 238-39, and more explicitly, no. 474, stipulating that a man may not leave the order to enter any other without permission from the master and the convent.

[22]   For his testimony, *TTPSA*, 200-12.

been able to locate.[23] He added that William Cernerius was grand preceptor only of the *Patrimonium beati Petri in Tuscia*, while brother Morus occupied the same post in Sardinia, Rome, and the Roman territories. In spite of his humble status, he had attended various receptions in the area of Viterbo, Rome, close to St Mary Major, in a house where the grand preceptor lived, Bagnoregio, Santa Maria sull'Aventino, and Castell'araldo. Peter named the persons who had ordered the commission of illicit acts: Blancus in his own case, George, vicar of Hugh of Vercellis in another case, and William Cernerius in yet another. Like many others in Cyprus, he insisted that chapter meetings took place after Matins, not ever in the late evening or night hours. Like most others he stated that chapter meetings were held without any outsiders present.

The penultimate witness in Viterbo was Vivolus, a serving brother received in Castell'Araldo.[24] Most unusually for this hearing, he insisted that he made no denials of Christ, God, or the saints at his reception and had not heard that any others did so. He denied that he had ever been threatened with serious punishment or imprisonment if he discussed his reception with outsiders. He claimed that brothers might confess to priests of any order when necessary. He had been fairly mobile, serving in Santa Maria in Capita in the diocese of Bagnoregio, St Sabine in Tuscanella, Santo Iulio in Civitavecchia, Burleo in the diocese of Viterbo, St Heramus, Rome, and finally in Pingioctus, a Templar possession dependent on Santa Maria sull'Aventino.[25] He also served in the retinue of the preceptor of San Bevengiate in Perugia, accompanying him to Santa Maria in Carbonara.[26] None of the Templars in this inquiry appears to have ever left Italy, unlike the second Brindisi witness who had served in Cyprus.[27]

The last witness, an apostate serving brother named Walter, testified in the *palatium Rocche*.[28] Hugh of Vercellis had received him in Castell'Araldo in 1300 in the presence of more than seven brethren. He mistakenly believed that the dignitary presiding (not usually a priest) could absolve the neophyte from all previously committed confessed sins. He did receive a penance: to fast on bread and water every Saturday of his life. He insisted that he had been told to believe in the same god worshipped by the Saracens and not in the Christian God.[29]

---

[23] An electronic communication from the American medieval history list suggested that the text may have read 'iter a Pano'. I have re-checked the manuscript, which does appear to give 'Iterapano' in one word.

[24] For his testimony, *TTPSA*, 213-27.

[25] See notes on these places in *TTPSA*, 90, n.12, n.17; ibid., 221, nn. 8-9, and the index to that work.

[26] On San Bevignate in Perugia, *TTPSA*, 105, n. 9.

[27] Schottmüller, ii, 132.

[28] Probably a property of the Savelli family near Palombara Sabina. The family had acquired the castle of Castiglione near there. See *Les Registres d'Honorius IV*, ed. M. Prou (Paris, 1886), i, p. xvi. The testimony appears in *TTPSA*, 248-60.

[29] This statement is almost certainly an invention, in that the overwhelming majority of Templars everywhere denied that such an order had ever been given.

The hearing in Tuscany[30] began in the church of St Egidius in Florence on 20 September 1311 before Antony, bishop of Florence, and Peter, *Judicis de Urbe*, a canon from Verona.[31] The preceptor Egidius, a Templar for at least thirty years, was the first of the six to testify.[32] The witness affirmed that Lombardy had its own grand preceptor, William of Nove, who also conducted a reception in Bologna. Egidius had attended a reception in Piacenza, and a chapter meeting in Rome. He mentioned information concerning members serving in Apulia, Sicily, and Crete. He asserted that at least two hundred brothers believed that the master or the visitor could absolve them of all their sins. He declared that James of Montecucco conducted a reception ceremony in Bologna. He insisted that errant Templars were sent to jail in Rome or elsewhere. He concurred with his colleagues that confessions could be made to Carmelites if necessary, or to Augustinians, or to any other nearby clerics. He insisted that chapter meetings took place during the early part of the night or at dawn.

A serving brother, Bernard of Parma, received thirty years earlier when Blancus of Pighazzano was grand preceptor of Lombardy and Tuscany, followed him.[33] He stated that a certain Gandulfus was preceptor of Florence. Bernard concurred in the misunderstanding shared by many that non-priestly members of the order had powers of ecclesiastical absolution. He considered it a public scandal that brothers believed the commission of carnal acts with one another was not a sin. Like others in this hearing, he had attended provincial chapter meetings in Bologna, but had not served overseas himself although he knew others who had.

The third witness, Guido of Cietica, preceptor of Caporsoli in the diocese of Fiesole, testified next.[34] He had belonged to the order since about 1301. He said that James of Montecucco was grand preceptor of Lombardy and Tuscany in 1302. Illicit acts took place in Bologna and in Piacenza, ordered by Montecucco's vicar Raymond. According to Guido, about twenty brothers participated in chapter meetings in those places, giving us some idea of the size of the cohort in Italian preceptories at the time. He mentions chapter meetings held at several Templar houses by senior members of the order in the late evening, and later at dawn when the whole group of eligible Templars met together. This practice is not mentioned elsewhere. He named several Tuscan Templars: Arrigus of Panzano; William of Nove; Martin, preceptor of Pisa; Gandulfus, preceptor of Florence; and Villanus, preceptor of Montelopio,[35]

---

[30]   On Tuscan houses of the order from the beginning of the thirteenth century, Bramato, 105-108.

[31]   I am using the Bini transcription referred to in *supra*, n. 1.

[32]   See Bini, 460-70, for his testimony.

[33]   For his testimony, ibid., 472-78. This statement appears to imply that at times Lombardy and Tuscany formed one unit, while at other times Lombardy seems to have been attached to the Roman province.

[34]   For his testimony, ibid., 478-85. The diocese is transcribed as 'Flesulanensis' by Bini, but an electronic message from Lynn Nelson on 27 July 2000 suggested that it should have read 'Fesulanensis' for Fiesole. According to Bramato, 111, Caporsoli is ten kilometers from Florence.

[35]   On this place, Bramato, 111 and n. 262.

as '*maxime subdomite*'.[36] According to him, Gandulfus actually kept a boy as his 'wife', who later became a member of the order.

He is more than usually informative about chapter meetings. He made the novel statement that if a chapter meeting was composed of twelve or more brothers, it was held in secret, but if there were only six, such precautions were not taken. In Tuscany, a provincial chapter meeting was held every year in the month of May. Concerning Templars who left the order because of the improper acts required of them, he insisted that he had heard that many brothers had left for this reason. He knew only one of them, James, marshal of the lord pope.[37]

The next witness, Nicholas Reginus, a member since 1299, was preceptor of St Saviour in Grosseto. Wicked acts not described here occurred at his reception in Bologna before forty or fifty Templars, and in Campania. He also implicated James of Montecucco, William of Nove, and others in Ancona in illicit behaviour. Unlike almost all others questioned anywhere, he affirmed that the sashes or cords were wrapped around an idol and worn to venerate it; brothers refusing to conform were either killed or sent to distant places such as Sardinia. Unlike almost every other Templar (more than 900) who testified in other trials, this man insisted that charity was not undertaken.[38]

Lanfranc of Florenzuola appeared next; he had been a Templar for more than fifty years.[39] He names William of Bobbio as grand preceptor of Lombardy and Tuscany at the time, with a certain Isuardi (or Isnardi) as his lieutenant. He was also familiar with the diocese of Parma. Regarding chapter size, he said that thirty-six years ago in Bologna fifty brothers attended. Like other witnesses, he suggested that permission to leave the Templar order would only be granted in order to join one that was even stricter. He affirmed that unless a reception was taking place, outsiders could attend chapter meetings, something denied by almost all other witnesses.

The sixth and last Templar, James of Pighazzano of the diocese of Piacenza, testified on 22 October.[40] He had seen numerous receptions and attended several provincial chapter meetings. He understood the knotty problem of absolution by non-priests, stating that Templars could only absolve the brethren of faults against the Rule: '*quod posset absolvere solomodo a disciplinis*'. He, like Gerard above, implicated James of Bologna and Manfred as sodomites.[41] In his opinion, while some receptions contained the illicit practices he described, others took place just as St Bernard had ordered in the Templar Rule. Most unusually, this hearing ended

---

[36]   On the Templars and sodomy, A. Gilmour-Bryson, 'Sodomy and the Knights Templar', *Journal of the History of Sexuality*, vii, 2 (October, 1996), 151-83.

[37]   'Malescalcum' in the text, a variant of 'mariscalcus', one occupying the function of marshal.

[38]   Given the detailed evidence from others in France and Cyprus about precisely what alms and food were given out, when, and where, this answer must have been invented to please the inquisitors.

[39]   See his testimony in Bini, 491-95.

[40]   Ibid., 495-501.

[41]   Other testimony on commission of same-sex acts can be found in the Brindisi hearing in Schottmüller, ii, 128.

with the notary's statement that seven other Templars had been interrogated whose depositions were not retained in spite of their denials of guilt, because they had no power or status in the order, because they simply carried out rustic tasks, or because they had not been in the order long enough to know the secrets. These men had been tortured, but apparently without result.[42]

What conclusions can be drawn from a look at the testimony of these thirteen men regarding Templar practices in Italy? These men appear to be well informed about their own areas and about other parts of Italy. They appear cognizant of major provisions of the Rule. None of them was noble or held a senior rank. Probably only the priest was literate. Their confessions regarding idolatry, sacrilege, and blasphemy are similar to confessions by Templars at Poitiers, another hearing which heard many apostates. While I do not find their confessions credible with regard to major illicit acts, the information they provide on Templar practices of holding receptions and chapter meetings, confessions to other priests, mobility in the order, names of properties and dignitaries, and other information related to central Italian Templars in the early fourteenth century, is crucial to any understanding of the order in its last years.

---

[42]   Bini, 501.

Chapter 14

Teutonic Castles in Cilician Armenia: A Reappraisal

Kristian Molin

This paper will focus on castles held by the Teutonic Knights in Cilician Armenia during the thirteenth century. Some scholars have suggested that these formed part of an elaborate system of intervisible castles covering all of Cilicia, but in this paper it will be argued that the archaeological and written evidence does not bear this out. To understand this topic fully, it is important to begin with a brief description of the military situation in this region. Cilician Armenia had originally belonged to the Byzantine empire, but between the late twelfth century and its conquest by the Egyptians in 1375, it became an independent Christian kingdom controlled by local Armenian dynasties. During this period the Armenians, like their Latin neighbours in the Holy Land, often found themselves outnumbered by numerically superior Muslim opponents. In the first half of the thirteenth century they were frequently attacked by Seljuk Turks from the Anatolian interior, and after 1260 they were subjected to a series of devastating Mamluk incursions from the south which culminated in the Egyptian conquest of 1375. Although the mountainous terrain of Cilicia made it difficult for attackers to penetrate the area, Muslim pressure eventually forced Armenian rulers to adopt the same policy as their Latin neighbours and to grant castles to the military orders in exchange for military assistance.[1]

The first castle acquired by the Teutonic Knights in Cilicia was Amouda, granted to them by the Armenian King Leon II by 1212.[2] This fortress was situated on a rocky outcrop at the centre of the Cilician plain, and consisted of a relatively simple fortified enclosure. After 1212 the Teutonic Knights strengthened Amouda by building a square three-storey keep at the highest point of the castle. Clearly, the order spent a lot of time and money on this stronghold, and intended it to act as their

---

[1]   For a history of Cilician Armenia during this period, T.S.R. Boase, 'The History of the Kingdom', in *The Cilician Kingdom of Armenia*, ed. T.S.R. Boase (Edinburgh, 1978), 1-33; S. der Nersessian, *The Armenians* (London, 1969); S. der Nersessian, 'The Kingdom of Cilician Armenia', in *A History of the Crusades*, ed. K.M. Setton, 6 vols. (Madison, 1955-89), ii (1962), 630-59. For details on warfare and troop numbers, K. Molin, *Unknown Crusader Castles* (London, 2001), ch. 13.

[2]   *Le trésor des chartes d'Arménie, ou cartulaire de la chancellerie royale des Roupéniens*, ed. V. Langlois (Venice, 1863), no. 6, 117-20; *Tabulae ordinis Theutonici*, ed. E. Strehlke (Berlin, 1869), no. 46, 37-9.

local headquarters.[3] To the east of Amouda, the Teutonic Knights were also given the fortress of Harunia by King Hethoum I and Queen Isabelle in 1236.[4] Harunia was smaller than Amouda and consisted of an elongated shell keep with a cramped central courtyard, two floors of shooting galleries and a rounded tower in the north-west corner. This tower seems to have been repaired by the Teutonic Knights and may have been used by them as a chapel.[5] Apart from these two principal castles, the Teutonic Knights possessed a number of smaller fortified structures on their estates, such as the Black Tower, an isolated toll station referred to in a document from 1271.[6] The ultimate fate of these properties remains unclear, although it seems that Amouda was abandoned after the Muslims sacked it in 1266 and that Harunia had also been lost by the end of the thirteenth century.[7]

In return for their generosity toward the Teutonic Knights, Armenian rulers expected to gain military aid against the Muslims. This was most apparent in the case of Harunia, for in his donation charter Hethoum I referred to the order's constant struggle with 'the enemies of Christ'.[8] Furthermore, Harunia was situated relatively close to the Amanus Gates, which were strategically important because they constituted one of the few mountain passes Muslim armies could use to penetrate the Cilician interior. The Seljuk Turks had used this route in 1187 and did so again during the 1220s and 1230s.[9] Later this was also a point of attack for Mamluk armies from Syria, who passed through the Amanus Gates and ravaged the Cilician plain in 1266, 1275, and 1298.[10] Presumably Hethoum I hoped that the Teutonic Knights

---

[3]   R.W. Edwards, *The Fortifications of Armenian Cilicia*, Dumbarton Oaks Studies, xxiii (Washington, DC, 1987), 59-61; H. Hellenkemper, *Burgen der Kreuzritterzeit in der Grafschaft Edessa und im Königreich Kleinarmenien* (Bonn, 1976), 123-31; K. Forstreuter, *Der deutsche Orden am Mittelmeer* (Bonn, 1967), 61.

[4]   *Le trésor des chartes d'Arménie*, no. 18, 141-3; *Tabulae ordinis Theutonici*, no. 83, 65-6.

[5]   Edwards, *Fortifications*, 143-6; Hellenkemper, 116-9; T.A.. Sinclair, *Eastern Turkey: An Architectural and Archaeological Survey*, 4 vols. (London, 1990), iv, 328.

[6]   Document translated in L.M. Alishan, *Sissouan ou l'Arméno-Cilicie* (Venice, 1899), 239.

[7]   1266: Ibn al-Furat, 'Selections from the Tarikh al-Duwal wa'l-Muluk', in *Ayyubids, Mameluks and Crusaders*, ed. and trans. U. and M.C. Lyons, with an introduction by J.S.C. Riley-Smith, 2 vols. (Cambridge, 1971), ii, 99; al-Makrizi, *Histoire des sultans mamlouks de l'Egypte*, trans. M.E. Quatremère, 2 vols. in 4 parts (Paris, 1845), i (b), 33-34. See also J.S.C. Riley-Smith, 'The Templars and the Teutonic Knights in Cilician Armenia', in Boase, *The Cilician Kingdom of Armenia*, 92-117, at 115.

[8]   *Le trésor des chartes d'Arménie*, no. 18, 142.

[9]   1187: Constable Sempad, *La chronique attribuée au connétable Smbat*, ed. and trans. G. Dédéyan (Paris, 1980), 63-64. 1220s and 1230s: Constable Sempad, 'Chronique du royaume de la Petite Arménie', in *RHC DArm*, i, 648-49; C. Cahen, *La Syrie du Nord à l'époque des croisades et la principauté franque d'Antioche* (Paris, 1940), 651; der Nersessian, 'The Kingdom of Cilician Armenia', 652.

[10]   'Les Gestes des Chiprois', in *RHC DArm*, ii, 780 (1275), 839-40 (1298); Constable Sempad, *Chronique*, ed. Dédéyan, 117-18 (1266); Constable Sempad, 'Chronique', *RHC DArm*, i, 653 (1275); Hethoum the Historian, 'Table chronologique de Héthoum, comte de Gorigos', in *RHC DArm*, i, 487 (1266 and 1275); Vahram of Edessa, 'Chronique rimée des

would help him to halt incursions of this kind, either by sending troops to blockade the Amanus Gates, or by luring the Muslims into a siege of Harunia itself.

It is now important to consider the observations made at the beginning of this paper. Some scholars have suggested that both Harunia and Amouda also had a wider defensive role to play because they supposedly belonged to a nationwide system of intervisible castles. According to the archaeologists Robert Edwards and Hansgerd Hellenkemper, this system incorporated virtually all major Armenian fortresses, and was based around a complex system of beacons. Whenever the garrison of a particular castle spotted an approaching Muslim army, it could supposedly use a heliograph or a beacon to send a warning signal to other strongholds in the region. According to Edwards this system allowed for 'rapid communication and the efficient mustering of troops', making it possible to confront Muslim invaders as quickly as possible. The existence of such a network would have required a strong central ruler to manage it. Hellenkemper suggests that this was King Leon II, whose reign from 1198 until 1219 marked a high point in Armenian fortunes. Hellenkemper claims that Leon deliberately constructed a large number of strongpoints to fit into a vast network, which eventually included Ayas, Misis, Yilan, Gökvelioglu, Tumlu, Anavarza, Ak Kale, Toprak, Bodrum, Amouda, and Harunia (Figure 14.1). The overall conclusion drawn by both Edwards and Hellenkemper is that this early warning system helped the Armenians to withstand their Muslim opponents until as late as 1375 despite being so heavily outnumbered.[11]

But let us consider the possibility that no such warning system ever existed. A number of reasons can be given for this, starting with the archaeological evidence. If a castle network had been created over a relatively short space of time by Leon II, one would expect to find a large group of fortifications built to a standard pattern. But this is not the case, for although many of the strongholds just mentioned share certain architectural characteristics, most of them contain a wide range of Roman, Byzantine, Arabic, Armenian, Crusader, Mamluk, or Ottoman remains. A good example is the castle of Anavarza, situated on a steep outcrop on the Cilician Plain. According to Hellenkemper, this fortress was vital to the Armenian network because the defenders of its citadel could see Yilan, Tumlu, and other surrounding castles. However, Anavarza was actually a Roman-Byzantine acropolis which was occupied by the Armenians at a much later date. Furthermore, the highest point of this fortress was defended by an early twelfth-century keep constructed by Frankish crusaders rather than Armenians. In other words, the defences which made intervisibility with surrounding castles possible pre-dated the reign of Leon II by many years. Anavarza's original defences had been built long before the thirteenth-century frontiers of the Cilician kingdom were known, and had not been intended to form

rois de la Petite Arménie', in *RHC DArm*, i, 521-22 (1266); Samuel of Ani, 'Extrait de la chronographie de Samuel', in *RHC DArm*, i, 461 (1266), 463 (1298); Bar Hebraeus, *The Chronography of Gregory Abu'l Faraj, the Son of Aaron, the Hebrew Physician Commonly Known as Bar Hebraeus*, trans. E.A. Wallis Budge (Oxford, 1932), 446 (1266), 452-54 (1275); Ibn al-Furat, 'Selections', 99 (1266); al-Makrizi, *Histoire des sultans*, i (b), 31, 33-34 (1266), 123-25 (1275); ibid., ii (b), 60-65 (1298).

[11]   Edwards, *Fortifications*, 38 (quote), 41-42; Hellenkemper, 262-63.

part of an Armenian defence network.[12] Indeed, Edwards himself has pointed out that this was one of several local fortresses which were merely repaired by Leon II and not built from scratch by him.[13]

The acropolis of Anavarza can also be used to highlight some of the practical difficulties that rule out the existence of an intervisible network. Such a network would have required part of Anavarza's garrison to maintain a large beacon on top of the castle keep which could be lit at short notice and in all weather conditions. Not only would this have been extremely expensive and time consuming, it would have been hampered further by the fact that the roof of the keep can only be reached via three partially blocked storeys.[14] The usefulness of an early warning system relying on simple beacons is also limited because it cannot describe the nature of an invading army or the direction in which it is travelling. The cost of maintaining such an unwieldy system at many different castles across several hundred square miles would surely have been prohibitive. Indeed, several centuries earlier the Byzantine authorities had abandoned a similar string of beacons which connected Cilicia with Constantinople. This was done because the system proved far too expensive and inefficient.[15]

Having looked at the archaeological evidence, let us turn to the written sources. The first thing to note is that Armenian chroniclers do not mention an intervisible castle network at any point in the thirteenth or fourteenth centuries. On the other hand, they describe a number of internal feuds which would have made the operation of such a system virtually impossible. Some of the castles which Hellenkemper includes in his proposed network, such as Anavarza, belonged to the Armenian kings. Others were held by baronial families. Indeed, a list of Armenian nobles who attended Leon II's coronation in 1198 indicates that Cilicia as a whole contained more than forty strongholds held by different baronial families.[16] Therefore a nationwide system of fire signals would rely on the ability of Armenian kings to keep all these vassals in check and to work in close harmony with many different baronial garrisons. But the written sources tell us that this was not the case, for Armenian history was marked by a series of violent internal disputes. In 1201 and 1207 respectively, the lords of Lampron and Silifke had their castles confiscated by Leon II for treason.[17] After Leon's death in 1219 there followed a long period of instability until Leon's

---

[12]   Hellenkemper, 191-201, 262-23; M. Gough, 'Anazarbus (Anavarza)', *Anatolian Studies*, ii (1952), 85-150, at 122-23. See also R.W. Edwards, 'The Crusader Donjon at Anavarza in Cilicia', *Abstracts of the Tenth Annual Byzantine Studies Conference* (Cincinnati, 1984), 53-55; Edwards, *Fortifications*, 65-70.

[13]   Edwards, 'The Crusader Donjon at Anavarza', 53-55; Edwards, *Fortifications*, 33-37, 41-42.

[14]   Gough, 122-23; Edwards, 'The Crusader Donjon at Anavarza', 53-55.

[15]   P. Pattenden, 'The Byzantine Early Warning System', *Byzantion*, liii (1983), 258-99.

[16]   Constable Sempad, *Chronique*, ed. Dédéyan, 73-81; Constable Sempad, 'Chronique', *RHC DArm*, i, 634-40; T.S.R. Boase, 'Gazetteer', in Boase, *The Cilician Kingdom of Armenia*, 145-85, at 146-48.

[17]   Constable Sempad, *Chronique*, ed. Dédéyan, 81-82 (1201), 85 (1207); Hethoum the Historian, 'Table chronologique', 481 (1207); Boase, 'The History of the Kingdom', 21, 23-25 (1207).

successor Philip was murdered and a rival dynasty seized the throne in 1225.[18] In 1271 a major baronial uprising, centred around the fortress of Anavarza, had to be suppressed.[19] Until his death in 1307 King Hethoum II (1289-1307) was involved in a bloody dispute with his own brothers: the first of several fourteenth-century power struggles which severely weakened the Armenian throne.[20] Episodes of this kind indicate that the strong central authority and amicable baronial relations needed to run a nationwide early warning system were often missing, even during the reign of Leon II.

If we now apply these observations to the Teutonic Knights' castles, it is clear that these strongholds did not belong to an intervisible network either. It has already been mentioned, for example, that after they obtained Amouda, the Teutonic Knights constructed a new keep there. This structure was similar in appearance to the central towers built at the order's Galilean strongholds of Montfort and Judin, and can even be compared with thirteenth-century fortifications in Germany.[21] This implies that the German occupants of Amouda were free to do as they pleased with their new acquisition, and that far from incorporating Amouda into a local defence network monitored by Leon II, they tried to adapt it so that it would resemble their other strongholds in the Holy Land. In other words, the fact that some neighbouring fortresses can be seen from Amouda's keep is not the result of deliberate Armenian policy, but is simply a coincidence. Indeed, bearing in mind that virtually all local fortifications were constructed on isolated hill tops, it would be surprising if castles like Amouda did not enjoy good views of surrounding strongholds.

It is also important to note that both Amouda and Harunia, like the acropolis of Anavarza, had already been fortified in some way long before the Cilician kingdom of Armenia came into existence.[22] Far from being picked by the Armenians because they could be fitted into an elaborate chain of castles, these sites had originally been chosen for more mundane economic reasons. Amouda, for example, was situated next to the Ceyhan River, one of the key waterways of the Cilician Plain. According to the German traveller Willbrand of Oldenburg, who visited Amouda in 1212, this

---

[18]   Constable Sempad, *Chronique*, ed. Dédéyan, 93-94, 95-96; Constable Sempad, 'Chronique', *RHC DArm*, i, 647-48; Hethoum the Historian, 'Table chronologique', 485; Samuel of Ani, 'Chronographie', 460; Bar Hebraeus, *Chronography*, 375, 379-81, 389-90; Boase, 'the History of the Kingdom', 23-25; Cahen, 631-32.

[19]   Bar Hebraeus, *Chronography*, 449-50; Vahram of Edessa, 'Chronique rimée', 527; Constable Sempad, *Chronique*, ed. Dédéyan, 125.

[20]   Samuel of Ani, 'Chronographie', 464-65; Hethoum the Historian, 'Table chronologique', 489-90. For an outline of this and subsequent fourteenth-century power struggles, see also Boase, 'The History of the Kingdom', 29-33.

[21]   Amouda: Edwards, *Fortifications*, 59-61; Hellenkemper, 123-31. Montfort: D. Pringle, 'A Thirteenth-Century Hall at Montfort Castle in Western Galilee', *Antiquaries Journal*, lxvi (1986), 52-81, at 54-56. Judin: D. Pringle, A. Petersen, M. Dow and C. Singer, "Qal'at Jiddin: A Castle of the Crusader and Ottoman Periods in Galilee', *Levant*, xxvi (1994), 135-66, particularly at 159-62.

[22]   Edwards, *Fortifications*, 59 (Amouda), 143 (Harunia).

river provided the castle with a plentiful supply of fish.[23] More than fifty years later, in 1266, Muslim chroniclers reported that 2,200 people sheltered inside Amouda during a Mamluk raid.[24] These accounts indicate that Amouda was primarily built to defend an important river crossing and lay at the heart of an extremely fertile and well-populated area. The castle's real purpose, therefore, was to protect and exploit the local economy, not to form part of an intervisible network.

Let us now turn to the political role of the Teutonic Knights. When Leon II became the first Armenian king in 1198, he received his crown from the German emperor Henry VI. Although Henry had died the previous year, Leon's subsequent coronation was attended by members of the imperial court.[25] Leon therefore owed his new royal title to a carefully fostered friendship with the German empire, indicating that his decision to grant the Teutonic Knights land in Cilicia had a political as well as a military dimension to it. Indeed, when the Knights' possession of Amouda was confirmed in 1212, the order was still relatively new and could probably not contribute many troops to the struggle with the Seljuks.[26] Amouda itself was situated far from any exposed frontier regions, and was not threatened by an imminent Seljuk attack. By contrast, we have seen that Harunia was located much closer to the vulnerable Amanus Gates and was granted to the Teutonic Knights in 1236, by which time their wealth and military power had increased considerably. Thus Harunia had more strategic importance in its own right, whereas Amouda was handed over by Leon II in exchange for much broader political support from the German empire. In short, these strongholds were granted to the Teutonic Knights at different times by different rulers and for different reasons, undermining the suggestion that they formed part of a carefully coordinated castle network supervised by the Armenian kings.

Finally, it is important to remember that after the Teutonic Knights arrived in Cilician Armenia, they became involved in the political upheavals which affected the region. It has already been mentioned that after Leon II died in 1219, there followed a long period of political instability. Leon was eventually succeeded by his daughter Isabelle and her Frankish husband Philip, but in 1225 Philip was assassinated by Constantine of Lampron, the leader of a baronial faction opposed to Leon's family. Constantine then placed his own son, Hethoum I, on the throne and forced Isabelle to marry him.[27] During these events the Teutonic Knights supported Constantine and Hethoum rather than Philip, who was allegedly imprisoned and murdered at

---

[23]   Willbrand of Oldenburg, 'Itinerarium Terrae Sanctae', ed. S. de Sandoli, in *Itinera Hierosolymitana Crucesignatorum*, 4 vols. (Jerusalem, 1978-84), iii, 224; Edwards, *Fortifications*, 59.

[24]   Ibn al-Furat, 'Selections', 99; al-Makrizi, *Histoire des sultans*, i (b), 34.

[25]   Constable Sempad, *Chronique*, ed. Dédéyan, 73; Constable Sempad, 'Chronique', *RHC DArm*, i, 634; Cahen, 588-90; Forstreuter, 59; Riley-Smith, 'The Templars and the Teutonic Knights', 111.

[26]   The confirmation of Amouda coincided with the visit of Willbrand of Oldenburg, who had been sent by the German Emperor Otto IV with a new crown for Leon II. See Willbrand of Oldenburg, 'Itinerarium', 222-24; Riley-Smith, 'The Templars and the Teutonic Knights', 111-13.

[27]   For references, *supra*, note 18.

Amouda.[28] This alliance bore fruit for the order in 1236, when Hethoum I granted it Harunia. Thus the Teutonic Knights had no qualms about turning against the family of Leon II, the man who gave them Amouda, and involving themselves in the murder of Philip, a fellow westerner who was married to Leon's daughter. The conclusion we can draw from this is that the Teutonic Knights were just as likely to become embroiled in factional struggles as local Armenian barons. It seems unthinkable that during this period of in-fighting the German garrisons of Amouda and Harunia (or anyone else, for that matter) participated in a system of intervisible fire signals which relied on the close cooperation of royal and baronial castles throughout Cilician Armenia.

To sum up, it can be said that the Teutonic Knights played an important role in the political life of Cilician Armenia during the opening years of the thirteenth century. Their military presence, particularly that at the fortress of Harunia, also helped the Armenians in their struggle with the Seljuk Turks. The evidence of medieval chroniclers shows that Amouda and Harunia also played an important role in exploiting and protecting the local economy. However, I would argue that there is no firm written or archaeological evidence to indicate that these or any other local castles ever belonged to a nationwide network of intervisible strongholds.

---

[28]   Bar Hebraeus, *Chronography*, 380-81; Cahen, 635; Riley-Smith, 'The Templars and the Teutonic Knights', 113.

Chapter 15

The Use of Indulgences by the Teutonic Order in the Middle Ages

Axel Ehlers

In April 1362, the Teutonic Knights in Prussia launched a campaign against the Lithuanian stronghold of Kaunas. They were accompanied by many Western European knights who wished to participate in the war against the heathen that the Teutonic Order was waging continuously against pagan Lithuania.[1] Kaunas was besieged and finally taken shortly before Easter. On Easter Sunday that year, Bishop Bartholomew of Sambia (*Samland*), a member of the Teutonic Order, said mass for his brethren and their noble guests.[2] After the sermon, the 'indulgences of the order' were proclaimed (*indulgentie quoque ordinis sunt pronunciate*), and at the end of the mass the congregation received the blessing.[3] The rhymed chronicle written by the herald Wigand von Marburg in the last decade of the fourteenth century is the source for this information. As Wigand's German chronicle is not preserved in its entirety, it is only a fifteenth-century translation into Latin that reports the event. This does not, however, diminish the value of the passage. What is striking here is the mention of the order's indulgences and their proclamation. These indulgences appear also in other sources.

In 1402, for instance, the grand master sent Andreas Slommow, a brother and parish priest of Danzig, to Prague, where he was to negotiate something that can no longer be identified. Because this was official duty, he travelled on the expenses of the grand master, and his costs were entered up by the Order's treasurer at Marienburg. The account book for that year has survived. For the feast of Saint Elizabeth, 19 November, it lists the expense of nineteen *groschen* for beer and wine offered to those *herren*, probably noblemen, who had gone to the Order's church at Prague to win 'the Order's indulgence' (*des ordens aplas*).[4]

---

[1]   On this war and those who participated in it, W. Paravicini, *Die Preußenreisen des europäischen Adels*, 2 vols., Beihefte der Francia, xvii/1-2 (Sigmaringen, 1989-94).

[2]   Wigand von Marburg, *Die Chronik Wigands von Marburg*, ed. Th. Hirsch, in *SRP*, ii (Leipzig, 1863, repr. Frankfurt am Main, 1965), 427-662: 531-37; on Bartholomew, [Chr.] Krollmann, *sv* 'Bartholomäus', in *Altpreußische Biographie*, i, ed. Chr. Krollmann (Königsberg, 1941), 31.

[3]   Wigand von Marburg, 537.

[4]   *Das Marienburger Tresslerbuch der Jahre 1399-1409*, ed. [E.] Joachim (Königsberg, 1896), 242; on Slommow, H. Koeppen, *sv* 'Slommow, Andreas', in *Altpreußische Biographie*, ii, ed. Chr. Krollmann *et al.* (Marburg, 1967), 681 (with additional literature).

Thirty years later, in 1431, the Teutonic Order's house and chapel at Halle were devastated by a flood of the river Saale.[5] Shortly afterwards, the commander of the house, Erhard Schütze, issued a letter for the collection of alms. The letter explained that alms-giving was a highly significant act of charity, one that promised the remission of sin. Thus, whoever offered something for the restoration of the order's house and chapel at Halle was promised 'grace and great indulgence, namely 40,820 years and 3,921 *quadragenae*'. Several popes, claimed the letter, had confirmed this generous indulgence granted to benefactors of the Teutonic Order. The respective charters were to be found at Halle and other houses of the order. They were valid for all the order's houses, churches, and hospitals.[6] In the case of Halle, the order's indulgences were intended to attract alms for the rebuilding of the commandery's houses.

The three particular episodes illustrate the way the Teutonic Order used and advertised indulgences. What was the substance of these advertisements? Who were the popes who had granted these indulgences and what was the purpose of the privileges? Was it correct for the Order to use them? Do these three episodes reflect a common practice, or were they simply exceptions? There are several questions one could ask on the 'indulgences of the Order'. Historical research has hitherto succeeded in answering only a few of them, if any at all. In the 1920s, Nikolaus Paulus published his magisterial study of the history of indulgences in the Middle Ages. The recently reprinted three-volume work is still an indispensable source for any study on medieval indulgences.[7] Paulus examined both the pardons granted to individual orders and those that the orders claimed had been granted to them. His four pages on the Teutonic Order have been the best account on the subject for almost a century.[8] However, he makes no reference to any of the three episodes just mentioned. Apart from an essay by Maria Starnawska on the churches of the military orders in Silesia as centres of indulgence,[9] the subject has failed to attract any further scholarly attention, notwithstanding the fact that, through their intimate relationship with the crusades, the military orders, according to the late Hartmut Boockmann, were predestined for the reception and use of special indulgences.[10] Indulgences are, of course, mentioned in several publications on the military orders, but there is

---

[5]   R. Wolf, *Das Deutsch-Ordenshaus St. Kunigunde bei Halle a.d.S. von seiner Entstehung bis zu seiner Aufhebung (1200-1511) unter besonderer Berücksichtigung seiner rechtlichen und wirtschaftlichen Verhältnisse*, Forschungen zur thüringisch-sächsischen Geschichte, vii (Halle/Saale, 1915), 43.

[6]   MS Magdeburg, Landesarchiv -Landeshauptarchiv-, Rep. Cop. 398, fol. 41v; printed in *Reliquiae manuscriptorum omnis aevi diplomatum ac monumentorum ineditorum adhuc*, 12 vols., ed. J. P. von Ludewig (Frankfurt, 1720-41): v (1723), 131-34, no. 108.

[7]   N. Paulus, *Geschichte des Ablasses im Mittelalter*, 3 vols. (Paderborn, 1922-3; 2nd edn.: Darmstadt, 2000).

[8]   Paulus, 1st edn., iii, 234-38.

[9]   M. Starnawska, 'Kościoły zakonów krzyżowych na Śląsku jako ośrodki odpustowe', in *Peregrinationes: Pielgrzymki w kulturze dawnej Europy*, ed. H. Manikowska and H. Zaremska, Colloquia Mediaevalia Varsoviensia, ii (Warsaw, 1995), 313-18.

[10]   H. Boockmann, 'Über Ablaß-"Medien"', *Geschichte in Wissenschaft und Unterricht*, xxxiv (1983), 709-21: 717.

no systematic account that analyses the worries of any particular order concerning its indulgences.[11] Were indulgences an important part of the propaganda, say, of the Teutonic Knights? Did the Knights value their indulgences? What exactly did they do to obtain them? What did they gain through them in the end? In my doctoral dissertation on the use of indulgences by the Teutonic Order, these questions have been discussed in considerable detail.[12] The commentary the present paper offers on the three episodes referred to above will highlight some results of my research.

What exactly did Bishop Bartholomew proclaim when, in 1362, he announced 'the indulgences of the Order'? The bishop was addressing his brethren and their 'guests', noblemen whom modern historiography often calls crusaders. This poses the question whether he was possibly announcing a crusade indulgence. According to Norman Housley, there were 'no discernible spiritual rewards attached' to the *Reisen*, as the Order's campaigns were known.[13] As a result, he doubted the crusading character of the war against Lithuania.[14] Lately, however, he has adopted an argument put forward by Jonathan Riley-Smith who, in a papal charter of 13 August 1245, identifies the basis for a 'perpetual crusade' the Teutonic Knights could conduct.[15] This mandate (*De negotio Pruscie*) by Innocent IV, however, was limited in its effects. Innocent had written to the archbishop of Mainz about an earlier concession to the Teutonic Knights (*Considerata magnitudine negotii*, 7 May 1245),[16] granting them the right to recruit German crusaders for the war against the Prussians without public preaching. These crusaders would be granted the same indulgence as those who proceeded to Jerusalem. In the *De negotio Pruscie*, the archbishop was instructed to supervise the grant of the indulgence.[17] This was not a proclamation of a 'perpetual' crusade; nor did it entitle the Teutonic Knights to the unlimited recruitment of crusaders. In his *Considerata magnitudine negotii* of May 1245, Innocent had granted the right to recruit one hundred German knights and their entourage for the crusade against the Prussians under specified conditions. It is possible that there had been conflicts between the recruiting Order and the archbishop over this rather unusual concession, making it necessary to appeal to the pope once more. *De negotio Pruscie* did indeed preserve the spiritual rights of the archbishop;

---

[11] See, for example, H. Prutz, *Die geistlichen Ritterorden: Ihre Stellung zur kirchlichen, politischen, gesellschaftlichen und wirtschaftlichen Entwicklung des Mittelalters* (Berlin, 1908, repr. 1977), 156-57; A. Forey, *The Military Orders: From the Twelfth to the Early Fourteenth Centuries,* New Studies in Medieval History (Basingstoke, 1992), 113; H. Boockmann, *Der Deutsche Orden: Zwölf Kapitel aus seiner Geschichte*, 4th edn. (München, 1994), 35-37.

[12] A. Ehlers, *Die Ablaßpraxis des Deutschen Ordens im Mittelalter*, QuStDO, lxiv (Marburg, 2007) This has been my Ph.D. thesis, University of Göttingen, 2002.

[13] N. Housley, *The Avignon Papacy and the Crusades, 1305-1378* (Oxford, 1986), 101; on the term *Reise* and its meaning, Paravicini, *Preußenreisen*, ii, 13.

[14] Housley, *Avignon Papacy*, 101, 272, 298.

[15] J. Riley-Smith, *The Crusades: A Short History* (London, 1987), 163, 213; N. Housley, *The Later Crusades: From Lyons to Alcazar, 1274-1580* (Oxford, 1992), 340-41.

[16] *Preußisches Urkundenbuch*, 6 vols., ed. [R.] Philippi *et al.* (Königsberg/Marburg, 1882-2000): i, 1 (Königsberg, 1882), 124, no. 167.

[17] *Preußisches Urkundenbuch* i, 1, 124-5, no. 168.

it also protected the order's recruitment of crusaders. But there is no evidence that these two papal letters had had any long-term effects. The Teutonic Knights are not known to have ever quoted them; nor did they ever copy them into their collections of papal privileges. Moreover, the traditional method of recruitment for the crusade by way of public preaching did not cease or change during the next twenty years or so.[18] For the fourteenth-century war against Lithuania, it was much more significant that, between 1257 and 1260, Pope Alexander IV allowed the clerical brethren of the Order the right to grant the crusading indulgence to those who had completed their task (1257), to preach the cross as the mendicants did, to absolve crusaders from excommunication, and to redeem their crusading vows (1260).[19] It would appear that these privileges enabled Bishop Bartholomew to do precisely what he did.

Several manuscripts at Berlin, Vienna, and Philadelphia, most of them dating from the fifteenth century, contain a list of 'the Order's indulgences' which include numerous pardons, mostly granted by thirteenth-century popes. One such manuscript, now at the University of Philadelphia, contains a section bearing the title: 'This is the indulgence of the *Reise*. Whosoever hears this letter being read out loud is granted an indulgence of twenty days' (*Das ist der aplas von der Rayse. Wer disen brive hort lesen der hat XX tag aplas*).[20] The following text is also found in four other manuscripts. It reads:

> all the grace that used to be given to those who travelled overseas (*obir mer*) to the Holy Land, which is the remission of all sin [...], this [...] indulgence can now be found in Prussia and Livonia for all those who, making true repentance and confess, come at their own expense to fight against the heathen.[21]

Alexander IV, Gregory IX, and Innocent IV had granted this grace, the manuscripts claimed. And there was more to it. This indulgence was valid not only for those who fought the pagans, but also for those who fought the supporters of the heathen – Christians, for example, who had allied themselves with the Lithuanians. The Order's priests were given the right to absolve those who had been excommunicated.

---

[18]   See, for example, Peter von Dusburg, *Chronicon terrae Prussiae*, ed. M. Toeppen, in *SRP*, i (Leipzig, 1861, repr. Frankfurt am Main, 1965), 3-219: 85, 100, 124; *Preußisches Urkundenbuch* i, 2, ed. A. Seraphim (Königsberg, 1909), 7, 15-6, 74-6, no. 11, 21, 83; for a more detailed discussion, A. Ehlers, 'The Crusade of the Teutonic Knights against Lithuania Reconsidered', in *Crusade and Conversion on the Baltic Frontier, 1140-1500*, ed. A. V. Murray (Aldershot, 2001), 21-44: 24-30.

[19]   *Preußisches Urkundenbuch* i, 2: 18-19, 46, 72-73, 82-83, no. 24, 49, 81, 94-95; see M. Purcell, *Papal Crusading Policy, 1244-1291: The Chief Instruments of Papal Crusading Policy and Crusade to the Holy Land from the Final Loss of Jerusalem to the Fall of Acre*, Studies in the History of Christian Thought, xi (Leiden, 1975), 90-91.

[20]   MS Philadelphia, University of Pennsylvania, Annenberg Rare Book and Manuscript Library, German 10, fol. 22r.

[21]   Berlin, Geheimes Staatsarchiv Preußischer Kulturbesitz, XX. Hauptabteilung (Historisches Staatsarchiv Königsberg) [hereafter quoted as GStA PK, XX. HA], Schieblade 17 Nr. 29; print from a later copy in *Liv-, est- und kurländisches Urkundenbuch*, 2nd Abteilung, ed. L. Arbusow, 3 vols. (Riga/Moscow, 1900-1914), iii, 668, no. 913; for additional proofs, Ehlers, *Ablaßpraxis*, 63-70.

Those crusaders who could not fulfil their vow themselves but sent instead someone else on their behalf would also enjoy the indulgence, as would the substitutes. The 'indulgences of the *Reise*' were also briefly referred to in other texts.[22] It is likely that this list had originally been drawn up in Prussia, and it was probably this same set of privileges that Bishop Bartholomew had in mind when he proclaimed 'the Order's indulgences' to the 'guests'. The pardons can be traced back to the thirteenth century when the popes were eager to support the Order's wars. Between 1230 and 1267 more than 120 papal charters related to the crusade can be made out. These included the privileges identified in the list, and the twenty-day indulgence granted for listening to the preaching of the cross.[23] It was not Innocent's mandate *De negotio Pruscie* that the knights were quoting, but more general and wider privileges. Many of them had originally been directed to the mendicants, who were preaching the cross for the Baltic region in the thirteenth century.[24] But since the Order's clerics had obtained the right to join them, they could actively use these privileges themselves. This was the decisive factor for the Order's independence in creating a 'private' crusade without the need of any additional papal privileges.[25] Bishop Bartholomew's proclamation is but one reflection of this. The Order's marshal, who usually organized the *Reisen*, sold certificates of the 'indulgence of the Prussian *Reise*' to the 'guests'. Werner Paravicini has discovered a travel account of one such guest, providing tangible evidence of this fact.[26]

There were also lists of more general indulgences, not specifically connected to the war against the heathen. These indulgences could be won not only in any church of the Teutonic Order, but indeed anywhere by simply fulfilling the charitable and pious work demanded in return. Lists containing indulgences of this kind were produced in great numbers by the second half of the fourteenth century at the latest. Four major traditions can be identified. By far the most successful and detailed version was composed at Trier in 1371 or 1372 by the lector of the local Dominicans, who probably acted on the Knights' request. In April 1372, the Order's priest Hermann von Amelburg had this list transcribed by two Notaries Public. The charter is now lost, but three years later another transcription was commissioned, one that quotes the text of 1372. At least four different copies were made, two of which have

---

[22]   MSS Wien, Zentralarchiv des Deutschen Ordens (DOZA), Abteilung Handschriften, 100, fols. 119r-120r: 120r; Berlin, GStA PK, XX. HA, Ordensfoliant 68, fol. 97r.

[23]   See, for instance, *Preußisches Urkundenbuch* i, 1: 68, 111-2, no. 89, 146; *Vetera monumenta Poloniae et Lithuaniae gentiumque finitimarum historiam illustrantia*, 4 vols, ed. A. Theiner (Romae, 1860-64), i, 69-70, no. 137 (indulgence of twenty days, indulgence for substitutes and their clients); *Preußisches Urkundenbuch* i, 2: 18-19, 72-73, 82-83, no. 24, 49, 81, 94-95.

[24]   Chr. Maier, *Preaching the Crusades: Mendicant Friars and the Cross in the Thirteenth Century*, Cambridge Studies in Medieval Life and Thought, 4th ser., xxviii (Cambridge, 1994), 46-52, 77-78, 87-92.

[25]   See C. Tyerman, *The Invention of the Crusades* (Basingstoke, 1998), 41; Maier, 92-93.

[26]   W. Paravicini, 'Die Preußenreisen des europäischen Adels', *Historische Zeitschrift*, ccxxxii (1981), 25–38: 30.

survived.[27] From Trier the list began to spread. It was known in the bailiwicks of Lorraine, Franconia, Thuringia, Austria, Lombardy, and perhaps Westphalia or what was then Saxony.[28] Then, in 1513, an abbreviated version of the text was painted on a triptych for the Order's church at Graz.[29] There were probably several other places were the text was known. Prague is one example where people sought 'the Order's indulgence' in 1402. In Eger (Cheb) the text was received as early as 1382.[30] Because Eger served as a connecting point between the bailiwicks of Franconia, Thuringia, and Bohemia, it would be no surprise if Prague also had had a copy. In addition to the thirty or so, partly lost, Latin copies that can be made out, there were German, Italian, and French translations, summaries of the list, and different adaptations. The triptych of 1513 offered both a Latin and a German version.[31]

The composition and tradition of this particular list did not rely on the grand master in Prussia. It was achieved independently by the Order's commanderies in the empire. The 'indulgences of the *Reise*' were missing because they were of no particular interest to the Order's establishments outside the Baltic region. What they aimed at was support for their own needs, such as in Halle. The astonishing figures of tens of thousands of years of indulgence most likely originated from a summary like the ones just mentioned, although it remains uncertain which tradition was used in Halle. In Prussia, lists of that kind were as familiar, evidenced by a letter of 1449 in which the grand master sent such a text to the bailiwick of Thuringia.[32] It was different, however, from the lists already circulating in the empire.

Two years later, the papal legate Nicolaus Cusanus prohibited the preaching of obscure indulgences by the Teutonic Order – as well as by the Hospitallers and the Templars – in Thuringia until the brethren had shown the original papal letters granting the unusual pardons.[33] The German master was upset and informed the grand master in Prussia that the legate had stopped the brethren in Thuringia from announcing their indulgences as they had done before.[34] A brisk correspondence developed between Germany, Prussia, and the Order's procurator-general in Rome.[35] As soon as Cusanus had ended his mission, however, the resultant tension

---

[27]   Wien, DOZA, Abteilung Urkunden, 1 July 1375 (Trier); Stuttgart, Württembergisches Hauptstaatsarchiv, B 343 U 431 (1 July 1375, Trier).

[28]   *800 Jahre Deutscher Orden*, ed. G. Bott and U. Arnold (Gütersloh/München, 1990), 419-20 (no. VI.5.25); Ehlers, *Ablaßpraxis*, 185-189, 201-204.

[29]   *800 Jahre Deutscher Orden*, 420-21 (no. VI.5.26); Boockmann, 'Ablaß-"Medien"', 716-17; for proof of origin (Graz), Ehlers, *Ablaßpraxis*, 264-66.

[30]   MS Weimar, Thüringisches Hauptstaatsarchiv, F 570a, fols. 89r-95r: 89v.

[31]   See Ehlers, *Ablaßpraxis*, 176-208, 264-71.

[32]   Berlin, GStA PK, XX. HA, Ordensbriefarchiv 9953 (8 June 1449, Marienburg): *Regesta historico-diplomatica Ordinis S. Mariae Theutonicorum 1198-1525*, ed. E. Joachim and W. Hubatsch, pt. 1 (3 vols.) and pt. 2 (Göttingen, 1948-73), i, 1: 649, no. 9953.

[33]   *Acta Cusana. Quellen zur Lebensgeschichte des Nikolaus von Kues*, ed. E. Meuthen and H. Hallauer, (Hamburg, 1976-2000), i, 960-1, no. 1423 (26 June 1451, Magdeburg).

[34]   Ibid., i, 1135, 1209-10, no. 1740, 1876.

[35]   Ibid., i, 1361-3, no. 2102-4; Berlin, GStA PK, XX. HA, Ordensbriefarchiv 11010 (28 Dec. 1451), 11140 (11 Apr. 1452).

disappeared. The Order seems to have gotten away with just a rebuke, without serious consequences.[36]

The event indicates that the Order had indeed made full use of the indulgences set up in the lengthy summaries. The reaction to the legate's criticism shows how valuable these graces must have been to the Order. There is definitely no doubt that the use of indulgences by the Teutonic Order deserves a more detailed study. It helps to place these single events firmly within their proper context, and to highlight the role which military orders as indulgence brokers played for late medieval piety.

---

[36] See E. Maschke, 'Nikolaus von Cusa und der Deutsche Orden', *Zeitschrift für Kirchengeschichte*, xlix (1930), 413-442: 428-31; E. Maschke, 'Nikolaus von Kues und der Deutsche Orden', in id., *Domus hospitalis Theutonicorum: Europäische Verbindungslinien der Deutschordensgeschichte: Gesammelte Aufsätze aus den Jahren 1931-1963*, QuStDO, x (Bonn-Godesberg, 1970), 117-49: 133-35, first printed in *Cusanus-Texte IV: Briefwechsel des Nikolaus Cusanus, vierte Sammlung*, Sitzungsberichte der Heidelberger Akademie der Wissenschaften, Philosophisch-historische Klasse, 1956, i (Heidelberg, 1956), 26-64: 45-47; Ehlers, *Ablaßpraxis*, 345-49.

Chapter 16

Innocent III and the Origins of the Order of Sword Brothers

Barbara Bombi

At the beginning of the thirteenth century a new military order, later called the Order of the Sword Brothers, was created in Livonia to support the mission and crusade in that region. In *c*.1185, Maynard, a canon regular from Segeberg in Mecklenburg, began to preach the Gospel to the heathens in Livonia, present-day Latvia. Maynard's preaching was by no means an isolated activity, but it must be set in the context of the *Drang nach Osten*, pursued by Henry the Lion as well as the archbishops of Hamburg-Bremen in the second half of the twelfth century in north-central Germany. It also involved the German traders of Mecklenburg's harbour towns, who were interested in gaining renewed access to the Baltic Sea in order to facilitate trade with Russian merchants. In the second half of the twelfth century, as a result of Henry the Lion's expansionist policy and the interests of German traders, Livonia was chosen as fertile territory for a mission to be undertaken by some Cistercians and by several canonical foundations in central Germany. Their aim was to preach the Gospel to the heathens *verbo vel exemplo*.

In 1190, in support of the mission to the heathen, Clement III granted an indulgence concerning their observance over food and drink.[1] In 1193, Celestine III declared that the *proposita*, or way of life of monks and canons regular who were going to Livonia to preach the Gospel *ex diversis ordinibus*, should be of equal value.[2] Subsequently, several pagan attacks took place against the preachers in Livonia, while news of the active preaching of a crusade to the Holy Land in 1195 by Archbishop Conrad of Mainz encouraged a similar movement against the heathen of Livonia between 1196 and 1197. Clerics, soldiers, traders, and laymen, drawn widely from the whole of Saxony, Westphalia, and Friesland, all participated in this crusade.[3]

---

[1] W. Holtzmann, 'La *Collectio Seguntina* et les décrétales de Clément et de Cèlestin III', *Revue d'histoire ecclésiastique*, i (1955), 425-26; P. Jaffé, *Regesta Pontificum Romanorum : ab condita ecclesia ad annum post Christum natum 1198*, ii (Leipzig, 1888), 16587. This letter was later incorporated into the *Liber Extra* 5. 6. 10.

[2] Coelestini III 'Epistolae', *Patrologia Latina*, 206, col. 996.

[3] Arnoldi Lubicensis, *Chronica Slavorum*, ed. J. M. Lappenberg (Hanover, 1868: MGH *in usum scholarum*, 14), bk. 5, ch. 30, 214-15. See also M. Maccarrone, 'I papi e la cristianizzazione della Livonia', in *Gli inizi del cristianesimo in Livonia-Lettonia: Atti del colloquio internazionale di storia ecclesiastica in occasione dell'VIII centenario della Chiesa in Livonia (1186-1986) Roma, 24-25 giugno 1986* (Vatican City, 1989), 40-51; repr. in *Nuovi Studi su Innocenzo III*, ed. R. Lambertini: (*Nuovi Studi Storici*, xxv: Rome, 1995), 369-420;

Thus, by the end of the twelfth century, the Livonian mission had been transformed into a crusade. The Saxon nobility and Berthold, the new bishop of Livonia, together with the preachers, associated this movement with pilgrimage (*peregrinatio*) and the crusade against Muslims in the Holy Land. *Milites* and laymen, interested in gaining remission of sins through their pilgrimage to Livonia, joined those traders and clerics who had preached to the heathen in the early days of the mission. Furthermore, on 5 October 1199, Pope Innocent III once again sought the support of laymen and *milites* from Westphalia, Saxony, and the lands beyond the Elbe, who were already settled in Mecklenburg and the Baltic region from the second half of the twelfth century. He granted remission of penance to anyone joining the crusading army or *exercitus*, gathered together in God's name (*in nomine Domini*) for the purpose of defending *potenter et viriliter* not only converts, but also Christians living in Livonia.[4] As a result of Innocent's decision, a group of pilgrims (*peregrini*) began to form a fighting force in order to create a lasting organization to defend preachers in Livonia under the leadership of Albert, their new bishop. At Albert's request, Innocent III addressed all the faithful residing in Westphalia, Saxony, and the lands beyond the Elbe, where in 1199 the bishop had initiated his preaching mission to Livonia.[5]

Both the Scandinavian Church and the Danish monarchy had become involved in this mission, following King Valdemar I's attempt from the 1170s onwards to convert Estonia to Christianity. However, no evidence exists to show that any Templar or Hospitaller brother from houses in north-central Germany or in Scandinavia participated in the Livonia crusades in 1196/1197 and 1200. All that can be said is that in the last quarter of the twelfth century, the Templars and the Hospitallers were indeed present in Scandinavia and in Germany. In Scandinavia, Tore Nyberg has demonstrated the influence of the Hospitaller houses in Antvorskov in Denmark (1167), in Lücke, in Verne or Vara, close to Oslo in Norway (1177), and in Eskilstuna in the bishopric of Strängnäs in Sweden (before 1185).[6] The Templars and the Hospitallers were also thriving in northern Germany, and were considerably involved in preaching the Livonian crusade. As Schüpferling pointed out, Templar houses were established in Lippsringe in the bishopric of Paderborn in

---

B. Bombi, *Innocenzo III e la «praedicatio» ai pagani del Nord Europa. Crociata e Missione (1198-1216)*, (Milan, 2000), 2.2.

[4]   *Die Register Innocenz' III., 2. Pontifikatsjahr, 1199/1200, Texte*, ed. O. Hageneder-W. Maleczek-A. A. Strnad (Graz-Cologne, 1979) (Publikationen des Österreichischen Kulturinstituts in Rom, II/I), no. 182, 349. Maccarrone, 'I papi', 52, suggests that Innocent III intended to follow the example of Eugenius III and Alexander III.

[5]   Heinrici *Chronicon Livoniae*, ed. L. Arbusow and A. Bauer (Hanover, 1955: MGH *in usum scholarum*, xxxi), bk. 3, ch. 2, 12.

[6]   T. Nyberg, 'Deutsche, dänische und schwedische Christianizerungsversuche östlich der Ostsee im Geiste des 2. und 3. Kreuzzuges', in *Die Rolle der Ritterorden in der Christianizerung und Kolonizerung des Ostseegebiets*: Universitas Nicolai Copernici. Ordines militares. Colloquia Turnensia Historica, 1 (Thorn, 1983), 110. Id., *Monasticism in North-Western Europe (800–1200)* (Aldershot, 2000), 227-31; Z. H. Nowak, 'Milites Christi de Prussia. Der Orden von Dobrin und seine Stellung in der preussischen Mission', in *Die geistlichen Ritterorden Europas*, ed. J. Fleckenstein and M. Hellmann (Sigmaringen, 1980: Vorträge und Forschungen, xxvi), 339–52.

Westphalia, related to the family of the Count of Lippe, which had been involved in crusading in Livonia from the beginning of the thirteenth century.[7] Templar houses also existed in Saxony, linked to Henry the Lion and to Cistercian foundations in Riddagshausen and Loccum, which were supported by the same Duke of Saxony and which had sent preachers to Livonia from the end of the twelfth century. The Templar house at Brunswick in Ostphalia could also be cited, founded as it was by Henry the Lion following his pilgrimage to the Holy Land and by the Cistercian Abbot, Sigebodus of Riddagshausen. Henry the Lion also established the Templar house in Supplingenburg, and it is likely that there was another house of the Temple in Loccum, close to the eponymous Cistercian abbey, even if some scholars claim that it had never been a Templar possession.[8]

Furthermore, in 1200 a hospital, established in the bishopric of Schwerin in Mecklenburg, received some donations from counts Guzelinus and Henry of Schwerin. The Hospitallers were equally well established at Eichsen in the bishopric of Ratzeburg (1200).[9] According to Nowak and Borchardt, there were also three Hospitaller houses in Pommern – Stargard on the Ferse, Stargard on the Ihna, and Schlawe, settled in the 1180s; all three participated in the conversion of Prussia at the beginning of the thirteenth century.[10] Finally, at the beginning of the thirteenth century, the Templars too set up two houses in Schlesien – Klein-Oels and Liegnitz.[11]

All these records indicate that there was a massive Templar and Hospitaller presence within those same areas where the Livonian crusade was preached in the early thirteenth century. The first reliable evidence that a group of *peregrini*, following a different *propositum* of regular life, was indeed active in Livonia, together with monks and canons regular, consists of a letter sent by Innocent III on 19 April 1201. In it, the pope responded to questions addressed to him by the Livonian Bishop Albert, who had sent the Cistercian monk Theodoric to Rome

---

[7]   M. Schüpferling, *Der Tempelherren-Orden in Deutschland* (Bamberg, 1915), 83–84; M. Ledebur, 'Die Tempelherren und ihre Besizungen im preussischen Staate, ein Beitrag zur Geschichte und Statistik des Ordens', *Allgemaines Archiv für Geschichtskunde des preussischen Staates*, xvi (1835), 117-18. See also K. Militzer, 'The Recruitment of Brethren for the Teutonic Order in Livonia, 1237–1562', in *MO*, i, 271.

[8]   Schüpferling, 86–91; F. Benninghoven, *Der Orden der Schwesterbrüder. Fratres Milicie Christi de Livonia* (Cologne-Graz, 1965: Ostmitteleuropa in Vergangenheit und Gegenwart, ix), 30–34. A. Transehe-Roseneck, *Die ritterlichen Livlandfahrer des 13. Jahrhunderts. Eine genealogische Unterschung*, ed. von W. Lentz (Magdeburg, 1960: Marburger Ostforschungen, xii), points out that crusaders going to Livonia in the thirteenth century came mainly from central Germany.

[9]   On the house of the Hospitallers in Schwerin, *Mecklenburgisches Urkundenbuch*, i: *786-1250* (Schwerin, 1863), no. 163, 161-62. See also J. Traegger, *Die Bischöfe des mittealterlichen Bistums Schwerin* (Leipzig, 1984), 272-73.

[10]   Z. H. Nowak, 'Der Anteil der Ritterorden an der preußischen Mission (mit Ausnahme des Deutschen Orderns)', in *Die Rolle der Ritterorden in der Christianisierung und Kolonisierung des Ostseegebietes*, ed. Z.H. Nowak (Torun, 1983: Universitas Nicolai Copernici. Ordines Militares, Colloquia Torunensia Historica, i), 82-84; K. Borchardt, 'The Hospitallers in Pomerania: Between the Priories of Bohemia and *Alamania*', in MO, 2, 296-99.

[11]   Nowak, 84.

to ask for a proclamation of a new crusade against the heathens. Taking up papal provisions over compliance with drinking and eating regulations, given to preachers in Livonia by Clement III and extended to clothing by Celestine III in 1193, Innocent III now stated that the *propositum* of the monks leading a regular life and wearing the monastic habit should be united with that of the canons regular *vel alii etiam regularem vitam sub alia districtione professi.*[12] Accordingly, it might be suggested that among the *alii regularem vitam sub alia districtione professi*, there were also some brethren from the foundations of the military orders in north-central Germany working on behalf of the German preaching mission of Bishop Albert. They probably represent the original group of the *Militia Christi de Livonia* created between 1202 and 1203.[13] At that time, according to Henry of Livonia's *Chronicon*, Theodoric, Cistercian abbot of Dünamünde, close to Riga, established the *Militia Christi*. Preoccupied with pagan attacks and their numerical superiority, Theodoric organized a group of the faithful in accordance with Bishop Albert's aim to carry out Innocent III's stated aim of 1199, when he had asked the bishop to assemble an army.[14] As Arnold of Lubeck also points out in his *Chronica*, Theodoric gathered round him those *milites* who came to Livonia and decided to stay, 'voventes continentias et soli Deo militare cupientes'.[15] From the beginning, the Sword Brothers adopted their *propositum* of regular life, taking the vows of chastity and poverty, and following the existing Templar Rule, which was closely related to the Cistercian tradition as represented by Theodoric himself. Both he and Albert gave shape to the new military order, organized *sub obedientia episcopi* with the duty of converting the heathen and defending the Church in Livonia.

In the summer of 1203, Theodoric went to Rome to give Innocent III notice of the achievements gained by Albert's preaching and by the hard work of the many pilgrims in Livonia. It was probably at this time that the pope made the acquaintance of the new military order. On 12 October 1204, soon after Theodoric's visit to Rome,

---

[12]   Maccarrone, 78. The idea of a connection between the German *milites* and the Sword Brothers in Livonia was first suggested by F. Bosquet, *In epistolas Innocentii III pontificis maximi notae* (Toulouse, 1635), 86: 'Fallitur quisquis contra credit et multum deflectit si non errat, dum Christi fidem in Livonia primum a militibus Teutonicis, satam, cultam, propagatam refert. Nam vel hoc ex uno loco patet, Christi milites sub fratrum Templi regula primos religiosa stipendia eo in orbis tractu meruisse'. On the other hand, Benninghoven suggests that the origins of the Sword Brothers could be connected with the pilgrimage of Henry the Lion to Spain. Benninghoven, 11-12.

[13]   Heinrici, bk. 6, ch. 4, 18. See also 'Narratio de fatis Livoniae, exhibita a legatis Svecicis in tractatu Oliviensi anno 1660', in *Scriptores rerum Livonicarum. Sammlung der wichtigsten Chroniken und Geschichtsdenkmale von Liv-, Esth- und Kurland*, i (Riga-Lipsia, 1853), 330: '... Subegit autem eam gentem Albertus ope Ensiferorum, sive ordinis fratrum militiae Christi, et Mariani Cruciferorum, in quem magister Livoniae paulo post cooptatus, certis autem legibus magistro Prussico subiectus fuit...'. Benninghoven points out that the Sword Brothers were not yet founded by 1200. Benninghoven, 39-40.

[14]   Heinrici, bk 6, ch. 4, 18; Arnoldi, bk. 5, ch. 30, 216.

[15]   'Multi etiam continentiam voventes et soli deo militare cupientes, forma quadam Templariorum omnibus renunciantes, Christi militiae se reddiderunt et professionis sue signum in forma gladii, quo pro Deo certabant, in suis vestibus preferebant'. Ibid.

Innocent III addressed a letter to Archbishop Hartwig II of Hamburg-Bremen. He highlighted the fact that Albert's division of the preachers had resulted in three religious orders (*tres religiosorum ordines*) – the orders of monks and canons regular, 'who were fighting the heathen with the spiritual weapons of discipline and doctrine', and that of the laymen (*fideles laici*), who adopted the habit of the Templars and defended the mission *viriliter et potenter* against the heathen.[16] The *fideles laici*, brought together by Albert and Theodoric into the *Militia Christi* and clothed in the Templar *habitus*, were indeed concerned to defend the mission (*novella plantatio fidei*) against pagan attacks *viriliter et potenter*, employing the material sword. Once more, Innocent III cast his mind back to the letter of 5 October 1199, by which he had left the defence of preachers and faithful in Livonia to the army gathered in God's name (*in nomine Domini*) using the same expression *potenter et viriliter* with relation to the army (*exercitus*).

Shortly after 1204, as Henry of Livonia points out, the *Militia Christi* joined up with crusaders from Germany and, since 1206, those from Denmark.[17] They vowed to take part in the Livonian crusade, which was once more being preached by Albert in Germany. By 1207, the whole of Livonia had almost been converted to Christianity as a result of the work of the missionaries and the brothers of the *Militia Christi*. Subsequently, the bishop divided the converted lands on the east bank of the Düna River into three ecclesiastical districts. Treiden was given to Caupo, one of the first heathens converted to Christianity; Riga was placed under the care of the bishop; and Methsepole, the easternmost region exposed to pagan attacks, was granted to the *Militia Christi*. Nevertheless, the Sword Brothers asked Albert for one third of the bishop's tithes, collected from the lands of converts and pagans, in order to support themselves and in return for their duties.[18] Albert agreed to leave to the *milites* just one third of the bishop's tithes accrued from the converts' lands, but denied them dues on those of the pagans'.[19] His only partial consent to the Brothers' request to receive one third of the bishop's tithes brought about a serious dispute between the same bishop and the *milites Christi*.[20]

Between 1208 and 1209, the mission to Livonia had been extended to include the northern coast of the Baltic Sea, inhabited by Estonians. The Sword Brothers of

---

[16]   'Verum quia ex parte compluit Dominus terram illam et ex parte ipsam reliquit hactenus incomplutam, venerabilis frater noster Albertus, eorundem episcopus, ad conversionem illorum operam tribuens efficacem, tres religiosorum ordines, Cisterciensium videlicet monachorum et canonicorum regularium, qui discipline insistentes pariter et doctrine spiritualibus armis contra bestias terre pugnent, et fidelium laicorum, qui sub Templariorum habitu barbaris infestantibus ibi novellam plantationem fidei Christiane resistant *viriliter et potenter*, studuit ordinare ...'. *Die Register Innocenz'III, 7. Pontifikatsjahr, 1204/1205, Texte und Indices*, eds. O. Hagenender-A., Sommerlechner-H. Weigl (Graz-Cologne, 1997: Publikationen des Österreichischen Kulturinstituts in Rom, II/I), no. 139, 225-27.

[17]   Heinrici, x, 32-47.

[18]   Heinrici, xi (3), 48-49. Between 1204 and 1206 Sword Brothers were about 50 or, at least, 100 people. Benninghoven, 63-64. Also J. Morgan, 'The Rise and Fall of the Sword Brothers of Riga', *St. John Historical Society Proceedings*, vii (1995), 55-68.

[19]   Heinrici, xi (3), 49; Arnoldi, v (30), 217.

[20]   Heinrici, xi (3), 49.

the *Militia Christi* were first and foremost involved in this, since Bishop Albert had given them the lands of Methsepole and Wenden, bordering on Estonia. The earliest Livonian document was thus drawn up, providing evidence of the presence of the Sword Brothers in that area – a *donatio iure feudi* of some lands close to Ydowen, in the Methsepole's area, which Wenno, the first master of the *Militia Christi*, granted to the Livonian Manegintes and his brethern between 1207 and 1209.[21]

The dispute between Bishop Albert and the *Militia Christi* grew worse as a result of further military conquests undertaken by Christians against the heathen and, in October 1210, the situation was brought to the attention of Innocent III. Bishop Albert and Volquinus, the new master of the *Militia Christi*, went to Rome to seek papal intervention in the sharing out of the lands of converts and pagans in Livonia. Innocent III mediated, giving the Sword Brothers one third of the lands of the converts in *Lectia seu Livonia*. The *milites* were to offer no temporal service, other than their defence of the Church in Livonia, but the master of the *Militia Christi* was to render obedience (*obedientia*) to his bishop. The Pope also exempted clerics, engaged in the cure of souls of the brothers, from paying the bishop's tithes and oblations. Furthermore, the *coloni* of the *Militia Christi* had to pay tithes to their parish churches, one-fourth of which would go to the bishop. Finally, the Sword Brothers were given the right to nominate to their bishop suitable persons, *personae idoneae*, to perform the cure of souls. On his part, the bishop was awarded the right to visitation, while the Brothers would be entitled to one-third of those lands settled and converted outside Livonia. Innocent III also allowed the Sword Brothers to follow the Rule of the Temple, even though they were distinguished by the sign (*signum*) on their habit. This meant that the *Militia Christi de Livonia* was an exempt order of the Church. The *Milites* were also granted burial rights.[22]

In the second of his letters addressed to Master Volquinus, Innocent III granted the requests submitted to him by both parties – the *Militia Christi* and the bishop.[23] Actually, the Pope seemed anxious to grant the Brothers' requests to have their rights recognized to converted lands as well as over lands which would be settled in the future. Moreover, Innocent III confirmed the rights of Bishop Albert concerning obedience and stressed that the *Militia Christi* had been set up to defend the Church against pagan attacks and to assist Livonia's conversion to Christianity. Additionally, the Pope stressed the right of the Sword Brothers to choose the clerics performing the cure of their souls. In the end, according to the situation in Livonia, Innocent III confirmed that the *Militia Christi de Livonia* had adopted the Rule of the Temple, but declared that they should henceforth be distinguished from the Templars by the sign (*signum*) on their clothing, just as the Brothers had requested.

In 1210, the new military order was officially established and recognized by the Apostolic See on the basis of agreements reached in Livonia since 1203. In spite of the above-mentioned papal arbitration, conflicts between the bishop and the Sword Brothers in Livonia continued throughout the thirteenth century. Then, between 1316

---

[21]   *Livländische Güterurkunden (aus den Jahren 1207 bis 1500)*, i, ed. H. von Bruningk and N. Busch (Riga, 1908), 1. On Wenno, Benninghoven, 420-21.

[22]   *Die Register*, xiii, 141-42, col. 326-27. Also Heinrici, xv (2), 82.

[23]   *Die Register*, xiii, 142, col. 327.

and 1318 a new controversy broke out, involving Frederick, archbishop of Riga, and the Teutonic Knights, whose order had joined with the Sword Brothers in 1236. The new allegations were discussed at the Papal Curia in Avignon. To defend their rights against the archbishop, the Teutonic Knights turned to the two letters Innocent III had issued in 1210. Their report, however, omitted the three clauses which had ensured the Sword Brothers' *servitium temporale* to their bishop. Instead they sustained an account which completely favoured their order, enabling it to prove its case against that of the archbishop's.[24]

When in the first half of 1211 the papal judgment over the dispute between the bishop and the master of the *Militia Christi* was known in Livonia, John, the Provost of Riga's cathedral chapter, and the Brothers of the *Militia* reached a new agreement.[25] As a result of this, Livonia was indeed divided into three ecclesiastical districts: two, the southern and western lands, were given as part of the bishop's revenue; the third, consisting of the north-eastern region, was allotted to the *Militia Christi*.

Innocent III concurred with this new state of affairs that the mission and the crusade had brought to Livonia. The Christian mission to Livonia had originally aimed at preaching the Gospel to the heathen and converting them to Christianity by means of the 'spiritual sword'. For this purpose, in 1199 and 1204 the Pope allowed Bishop Albert of Livonia to preach the crusade against the Livonians. Nevertheless the pilgrimage had become an instrument of defence for preachers and converts alike, in accordance with the handling of the 'material sword'. It was under these circumstances that a completely new military order was established, symbolically and in name identified by the sign (*signum*) of the Sword.

---

[24]   B. Bombi, 'I procuratori dell'Ordine Teutonico tra il XIII e XIV secolo. Studi sopra un inedito rotolo pergamenaceo del Geheimes Staatsarchiv PK di Berlino', *Römische Historische Mitteilungen*, xliv (2002), 197-98, 208-13; ibid., xxxvii-xxxviii, 264-65.

[25]   *Scriptores rerum Livonicarum*, i (63), 410-11. In early 1213 this agreement was confirmed by Albert, bishop of Livonia. *Scriptores rerum Livonicarum*, i (64), 411.

Chapter 17

The Military Orders and Papal Crusading Propaganda

Rudolf Hiestand

The crusade and the military orders of the twelfth century were both products of the papacy. So in discussing the role played by the military orders in papal crusading propaganda, their interdependence will feature prominently. The main argument in the present paper will focus strictly on papal crusading propaganda rather than on the much wider field of papal crusading policy or indeed the relationship between the papacy and the military orders in general. Geographically and chronologically, attention will be cast exclusively on the crusades, the East, and the period before the mid-thirteenth century, for it was precisely then, as Ursula Schwerin convincingly demonstrated some sixty-five years ago, that a definite change can be discerned in the papal crusading encyclicals.[1] The Baltic Crusades and the Teutonic Order in north-eastern Europe, as well as the *Reconquista* and the Iberian military orders such as Santiago and Calatrava, will not be considered here.

Papal crusading propaganda includes two different categories of documents. There are, first, the well-known appeals, such as (to mention a few of the most outstanding) Eugenius III's *Quantum praedecessores*, Gregory VIII's *Audita tremendi*, Innocent III's *Post miserabile*, and Innocent IV's *Terra Sancta Christi*. These were issued by popes determined to launch the massive expeditions known as the 'crusades'. But there exist a somewhat greater number of other, though similar, appeals. Written in between those associated with the traditionally numbered crusading expeditions, these appeals called with equal vigour on western Christians to help their Latin brethren in the East, but did not result in equally large armies setting out by land or by sea.[2] In a historical sense, we are faced with the problem of having to distinguish between intention and effect. In most cases, the papacy could not foretell what response its letters would have. It was not possible to predict whether an appeal would be followed by a major crusade involving huge numbers, or by the departure of a larger or smaller group of individual knights, or indeed whether it would attract any response at all. On a formal level, however, our first group of documents from the papal chancery is quite homogenous in its internal structure. From *Quantum praedecessores* and the other papal letters of 1146/1147 onwards, it invariably follows the pattern *narratio – exhortatio – privilegia*. It is the first two of these elements that are of direct interest to us here. The *narratio* usually

---

[1]   U. Schwerin, *Die Kreuzzugsaufrufe der Päpste zur Befreiung des Heiligen Landes bis zum Ausgang Innozenz IV*, Eberings Historische Studien, ccci (Berlin, 1937).

[2]   Ibid., Appendix.

provided a picture of the actual military situation in the East in the light of recent events that would explain the necessity of a new enterprise from the West. On the other hand, the *exhortatio* announced the pope's particular goals.[3] In the *narratio* one would therefore expect to find praise of Templar and Hospitaller activities as an incentive for western knights, followed, in the *exhortatio,* by, for example, a call for their imitation. Our second category of letters either accompanied those of the first group or were issued separately in varying circumstances and with slightly different intentions. They resemble the first group only partially or not at all. Normally, they did not follow any fixed formulary, but were just 'letters' in the strict sense as opposed to the public demonstrations to the whole of Christendom or to particular kingdoms and principalities that characterized the first group.

For the twelfth century, as far as the documentary basis is concerned, one can add four or five letters of Alexander III, Lucius III, Urban III, and Clement III that have come to light since 1937, when Ursula Schwerin was carrying out her research on the subject.[4] The dozens of solemn papal privileges and the hundreds of *litterae de gratia* addressed to the Hospital and the Temple and granting them protection, tithes, burial rights, exemptions, and so on, including, of course, the well known but often misinterpreted privilege which Pascal II had granted to Giraldus, *institutor et praepositus*, in February 1113, will not be considered here. They did not concern the crusade as a military, political, or religious phenomenon, but rather the juridical status of the two orders as ecclesiastical institutions.[5]

In recent years much research has been carried out in the field of papal crusading propaganda – its language and ideas, for example, and the role the Cistercians and Mendicants played as crusading preachers.[6] Within this context, however, the military orders have never received much attention. Penny Cole's recent study does not mention Templars and Hospitallers, except in a few footnotes.[7] At first glance

---

[3]   Cf. Schwerin, *Aufrufe*, 38-67.

[4]   See R. Hiestand, *Papsturkunden für Templer und Johanniter.* Vorarbeiten zum Oriens Pontificius I, Abhandl. der Akad. der Wiss. zu Göttingen. Phil.-hist. Kl. Dritte Folge, 77 (Göttingen, 1972), no. 53 (p. 251), no. 175 (p. 363); id., Papsturkunden für Kirchen im Heiligen Lande, Vorarbeiten zum Oriens Pontificius III, Abhandl., cxxxvi (Göttingen, 1985), no. 2 (p. 88), no. 148 (p. 322), no. 157 (p. 335). Another appeal attributed to Clement III was mentioned by P. Sinopoli, 'Tabulario di S. Maria Latina di Agira', *Archivio storico per la Sicilia orientale*, xxii (1926), 168, as conserved in the archives of Agira (Sicily), but the text cannot be traced.

[5]   Marquis d'Albon, *Cartulaire général de l'Ordre du Temple 1119?-1150* (Paris, 1913); J. Delaville le Roulx, *Cartulaire général de l'Ordre des Hospitaliers de St-Jean de Jérusalem 1100-1310*, 4 vols (Paris, 1894-1906); for the additions to these works, Hiestand, *Papsturkunden für Templer*; and id., *Papsturkunden für Templer und Johanniter. Neue Folge*, Abhandl., 135 (Göttingen, 1984).

[6]   Cf. V. Cramer, 'Die Kreuzzugspredigt von Bernhard von Clairvaux bis Humbert de Romanis', *Das Heilige Land in Vergangenheit und Gegenwart*, i (1939), 43-204; also C.T. Maier, *Preaching the Crusades. Mendicant Friars and the Cross in the Thirteenth Century* (Cambridge, 1994).

[7]   P. J. Cole, *The Preaching of the Crusade in the Holy Land 1095-1270* (Cambridge, Mass., 1991).

this looks quite bizarre. Founded to provide military help for the Crusader States, as in the case of the Templars, or to provide assistance to *pauperes, peregrini*, and *infirmi* on their way to, or after they had arrived in, the Holy Land, as in the case of the Hospitallers, who later engaged in military activities as well, one would expect to find them in the forefront whenever the popes decided to launch a new crusade.[8]

However, the result of examining closely papal crusading propaganda is unequivocal: the military orders had never been at the centre of papal appeals; no pope had ever ordered the Templars or the Hospitallers to join a crusading expedition, or to assist the crusaders financially, or indeed to preach the crusade. A similar conclusion would be reached if one considered the addressees or recipients of such appeals. Of *c.*110 papal crusading appeals and crusading letters, written between Clermont in 1095 and the mid-thirteenth century, only one was addressed to the Templars and none at all to the Hospitallers.[9] In view of the interdependence between papal crusading propaganda and the military orders, it appears as if we are trying to address a non-existent historical issue. But the problem is this: why did not the military orders play a leading part in papal crusading propaganda? Put differently, if indeed they did have a role to play in it, what exactly was the nature of this role? This question definitely demands a more thorough examination. The military orders were always involved in military activities whenever crusader armies were present in the East. They participated in the attack on Damascus in 1148 and were accused of having betrayed the Christian cause. They were present at the siege of Acre in 1189-91, and it was there that the master of the Templars died on 4 October 1189. They took part in the expedition to Egypt of 1218-21, where one of his successors died on 16 August 1219. They were again in Egypt in 1249-50, accompanying St Louis. Significantly, on these occasions they did not fight as part of the western crusading armies, but alongside the troops recruited in Latin Syria, as happened too when no crusaders were present in the East.[10]

In seeking to answer the first question, it would be necessary to take a closer look at the papal crusading letters and the various problems that were related to them. There is ample convincing evidence, of course, in support of the military orders' prominent contribution to the military strength of the Crusader States from the second half of the twelfth century and particularly after *c.*1180. So, to begin with the Second Crusade, it is quite surprising to find that in their respective correspondences, Eugenius III and St Bernard made no mention either of the Templars or the Hospitallers. Even the *nova militia*, highly praised by the abbot of Clairvaux, appears to have been non-existent in this context. Neither in the *narratio*, nor in the *exhortatio* of the three papal crusading encyclicals is there any allusion to their activities. This was no exception. True, forty years later, in his brief account of the disaster at Hattin incorporated in his bull *Audita tremendi*, Gregory VIII included the news that, after the battle, the Templars and Hospitallers captured by Saladin were beheaded in the

---

[8]   Cf. A. Forey, *The Military Orders from the twelfth to the early fourteenth centuries* (Basingstoke, 1992), with an extensive bibliography.

[9]   See *infra*, note 12 (no. 78).

[10]   For this aspect, R. C. Smail, *Crusading Warfare 1097-1187* (Cambridge, 1956); C. Marshall, *Warfare in the Latin East 1192-1291* (Cambridge, 1992).

presence of King Guy, himself among the prisoners.[11] But this mention of them is unique in general crusading appeals from the years before 1245. Indeed, if one were to reconstruct the history of the Crusades on the basis of these appeals, the military orders would be assigned only marginal significance.

A little more information about the role of the military orders emerges from the second group of letters, which could be classified as less formal and which did not follow the classic pattern established above. From the Second Crusade, the first of these papal crusading letters was written by Hadrian IV at the end of 1157. With the *Incipit quantum strenui*, it has a rather detailed account of King Baldwin III's expedition to succour Banyas in the Golan region, mentioning that the Templar Master Bertrand de Blanchefort had been taken prisoner by the Muslims.[12] This is the first occasion when a military action of any military order found its way into a papal crusading appeal or into a papal letter on crusading affairs. Considering that the Templars were *the* military order, it might appear quite natural that they should feature in a document from the papal chancery earlier than the Hospitallers. However, as we learn from the chronicle of William of Tyre, the lordship of Banyas had been divided between the baronial family of the Honfrois and the Hospitallers, who had had a decisive role in the fighting.[13] Thus, it would have to remain open to question whether *Quantum strenui* was the Templar version of a more general papal intervention in favour of the Latin East with a non-extant parallel text written for the Hospitallers or for others, or indeed whether this letter ought to be considered as evidence of the Templars' superior efficiency in obtaining papal support for their institution owing to the fame their military activity enjoyed in the Latin East.

The next papal appeal, dated 15 July 1165, repeats the phrasing of Eugenius III's *Quantum praedecessores*. Here again, as in 1145 and 1146, there is no mention of the military orders.[14] A year later, however, a letter by Alexander III of 29 June 1166, *In quantis pressuris*, recently discovered in a Spanish archive, recommends the Hospitaller Master, Gilbert d'Assailly, to all Christians. It deplores the fact that Bohemund III of Antioch and Raymond III of Tripoli had been defeated, adding especially that the clash had occurred while they were fighting *simul cum magna multitudine fratrum Hospitalis et milicie Templi*.[15] Thus in 1166, nine years after the first mention of the Templars, the Hospitallers too emerge in a document emanating from the papal chancery as a fully militarized institution. A sharp break then occurred in what may appear to have been the beginning of a continuous evolution. Perhaps as a consequence of their internal crisis after the failure of King Amalric's Egyptian expeditions of 1167-69, a crisis still not definitively explored, but one which is strongly associated with their master, Gilbert d'Assailly, the Hospitallers vanish

---

[11]   *Gesta Henrici regis*, ed. W. Stubbs, Rolls Series, xlix (London, 1866): i, 15.

[12]   Ed. Migne, *PL* 188, *c*. 1537 and the parallel letters sent to the count of Barcelona, P. Kehr (ed.), *Papsturkunden in Spanien I*, Abhandl. d. Akad. der Wiss. Göttingen. Neue Folge, xviii/2 (Berlin, 1926), no. 77 (p. 358) to a Spanish bishop, and no. 78 (p. 360) to the master of the Temple in Aragón Peter de Roveira.

[13]   William of Tyre, *Chronica* XVIII 11-15, ed. R. B. C. Huygens, Corpus Christianorum. Continuatio mediaevalis, 63/63 A, 2 vols (Turnholt, 1985), 825-32.

[14]   Ed. *PL* 200, c. 384, dated 14 July.

[15]   *Papsturkunden für Templer*, no. 53 (p. 251).

from papal crusading correspondence as a military force in the Latin East for more than twenty years. The only exception is a passing mention by Alexander III in two letters of 26 February and 12 April 1180 announcing the captivity and subsequent death of the Templar master, Odo de Saint-Amand, in the battle at Jacob's Ford in 1179. In the first of these, which was addressed to all Christian prelates, the pope emphasized the services provided for the Holy Land *per ipsos* (i.e. *fratres militie Templi*) *et fratres Hospitalis*.[16] Strictly speaking, this was not a papal crusading appeal but rather a letter calling for aid for the Templars, together with a report of the master's death.

Matters changed again in 1187 as the fate of the Crusader States took a turn for the worse. In a letter dated 3 September, Urban III had already announced to all Christians the death of the Hospitaller master, Roger des Moulins, at Cresson on 1 May.[17] Then, in October and November, with his *Audita tremendi severitate*, Gregory VIII launched the Third Crusade. In the following years, between 1188 and 1192, a series of papal mandates, *Non absque dolore*, essentially intended to protect the Templars against the violent assaults of the laity, provided news of events in the East, clumsily inserted into the middle of the text.[18] It seems as if the pope could not see any other possible way of informing the wider public of these developments, except through the award of special grants to the Templars. Of course, as in 1180, these papal letters were not actually calling for a general expedition – this had already been underway since the end of 1187 with the calling of the Third Crusade. They were asking for specific and substantial aid for the Templars. Parallel papal letters in favour of the Hospital, with similar references to their military engagements in the East, are not known before or after 1187. The popes, it would appear, still kept away from highlighting too openly the military character of the Hospital. It was an issue that could have come to a head in the decades that followed, but instead it ceased to be of any consequence, because at the end of the twelfth century, for reasons still unknown, in both the general crusading appeals as well as in the other papal crusading correspondence, direct reference to actual events involving the military orders ground to an abrupt halt, both in the *narratio* and the *exhortatio* parts of papal crusading letters.

A third point in the present enquiry concerns references to Templars and Hospitallers carrying news from the Holy Land to the papacy, or to brethren of the two orders bringing news of the Latin East from the Roman Curia to western princes and prelates. Again the findings remain scanty, but there are a number of such instances that point to a more promising field of research. In 1157, for example, it was a Templar brother who had come to seek help at Pope Hadrian IV's Curia and was afterwards recommended to France and Spain. In 1166 the master of the Hospital, Gilbert d'Assailly, stayed in Rome where he received a letter of recommendation for the continuation of his journey to France. A new level in such relationships appears to

---

[16]   D'Albon, 'La mort d'Odon de Saint-Amand, grand-maître du Temple (1179)', *Revue de l'Orient latin,* xii (1908-11), 279-82. For the date, Marie Luise Bulst-Thiele, *Sacrae domus militiae Templi Hierosolymitani magistri*, Abhandl. ..., 86 (Göttingen, 1974), 94-95.

[17]   Hiestand, *Papsturkunden für Kirchen im Heiligen Lande*, no. 148, 322.

[18]   See id, *Papsturkunden für Templer,* no. 222, 396; no. 225-57, 401-2.

have been reached in 1169, when the king and the barons of the Holy Land included the Hospitaller preceptor G[uy de Mahón] in their embassy to Pope Alexander III.[19] The envoys had to report on the Egyptian affairs, and once again they persuaded the pope to appeal to the princes and prelates for help. It is not known how far the preceptor Guy accompanied them on their way through Western Europe. He is found in autumn 1169 at the Duke of Burgundy's court and afterwards in Spain.[20]

With this official embassy, the military orders were now undoubtedly recognized and integrated into the political and ecclesiastical structure of the Crusader States and were entrusted, together with members of the episcopate, with representing the Latin settlers in the West and especially at the Roman Curia. Some fourteen years earlier a large embassy from the same episcopate, with the patriarch as its leader, had proceeded to the Curia to protest violently against the arrogance of the Hospitallers.[21] It is uncertain whether the masters of both orders were present at the Third Lateran Council in 1179, but in 1184 both Roger des Moulins, head of the Hospitallers, and Arnold of Torroga, Odo of Saint-Amand's successor as Templar master, remained with the Patriarch Heraclius at the Curia in Verona.[22] It was here that Arnold passed away,[23] but Roger des Moulins and the patriarch proceeded to France and England with the papal crusading letter *Cum cuncti praedecessores*.[24]

So far, all these contacts and the ensuing papal crusading correspondence were initiated in the East. It was either the Church of Latin Syria and the barons of Jerusalem or the Hospital and the Temple that had initially decided to go to the Curia with news of the fall of Edessa or the loss of Banyas, the capture of the princes of Antioch and Tripoli or the clash at Cresson, the battle of Hattin or the capture of Jerusalem: it was these contacts that precipitated the papal crusading appeals.

What is rather surprising, however, is that throughout the twelfth century, the Roman Curia (as far as we know) had never asked for a full report on the state of affairs in the East. All it knew depended on reports that could not be verified, and so its activities retained the appearance of a haphazard reaction. Then, on the eve of the thirteenth century, it was Pope Innocent III who, for the first time, asked for reports from the patriarch of Jerusalem and the military orders on the political and military situation. He requested information not only about conditions on the Christian side; he was particularly interested in the state of affairs on the Muslim side too, because the military orders had earlier established contacts with the Muslims, utilizing brethren with a knowledge of Turkish and/or Arabic.[25] The *aide-mémoires* that were sent back

---

[19]   In his Ph.D. thesis (University of Düsseldorf), Jochen Burgtorf. (Göttingen/Düsseldorf) has argued for 1170 as the beginning of the crisis.

[20]   For this crisis, J. Riley-Smith, *The Knights of St John in Jerusalem and Cyprus, c.1050-1310* (London, 1967), 399-400.

[21]   Ibid., 60-64.

[22]   1157: see *supra*, note 12; 1165: Hiestand (ed.), *Papsturkunden für Templer,* no. 53 (p. 251); 1169: *PL*. 200, *c*. 599; see Riley-Smith, 64.

[23]   Bulst-Thiele, *Magistri*, 102-3.

[24]   JL. 15151, ed. *PL*. 201, col. 1312-13; cf. H. E.Mayer, 'Henry II of England and the Holy Land', *English Historical Review,* xcvii (1982), 721-39.

[25]   Potth. 851, 935; the patriarch's answer, cf. RRH. no. 762. For a letter of the Templar master to Honorius III, Potth. 5622.

to Rome provided essential intelligence for planning the Fifth Crusade. However, not until shortly before the fall of Acre in 1291 did the Hospitallers ever submit a detailed crusading plan of their own to a pope. They now presented Nicholas IV with the text called *La devise des chemins de Babiloine*, again proposing a crusade directed, as in 1217 and 1248, against Egypt.[26]

A further issue remains to be considered, one that emerged at the very moment when Innocent III had begun to rationalize crusading propaganda and planning. On 15 August 1198, in his appeal *Post miserabile*, the pope commissioned the archbishop of Narbonne to preach the crusade in his province. He did the same with other prelates in southern France, Vienne, Lyon, England, and Hungary. For the first time the Curia resolved to organize a large-scale crusading appeal and assume the initiative for recruitment. (Here it should be pointed out that this conclusion has been drawn on the evidence found in the papal registers, and that no such records have survived for the preceding period.) What is of direct relevance to the present argument is that towards the end of his letter, the pope prescribed that each bishop should be accompanied by a Templar and a Hospitaller.[27] This innovation was obviously the result of the revolutionary change announced earlier in the letter – that everybody could take the cross, not only persons fit for military action. In case of inability owing to age, sex, health, etc., the vow could be commuted into a financial contribution.[28] Appropriate men were needed to collect the money, and evidently the pope regarded members of the military orders, with their long experience in financial transactions concerning crusading matters, as the right men for the job. The brethren of both military orders might have perhaps appeared to him more reliable and trustworthy, and indeed less likely to employ such funds for their own ends than the *curiales* sent from Rome or the episcopal officials and princes.[29] A few years later Honorius III was explicit in this regard, with reference to both the Templars and the

---

[26]   *Itinéraires à Jérusalem et descriptions de la Terre Sainte*, ed. H. Michelant-G. Raynaud (Paris, 1882), 239-52; C. Schefer, 'Etude sur la *Devise de Babiloine*', *Archives de l'Orient Latin,* ii (1884), 89-101; V. Laurent, 'La croisade et la question d'Orient sous le pontificat de Grégoire X (1272-1276)', *Revue historique du Sud-est européen,* xi (1945), 105-37 (at 136-7); also S. Schein, *Fideles Crucis. The Papacy, the West and the Recovery of the Holy Land 1274-1314* (Oxford, 1991), 50.

[27]   Potth. 347; *Die Register Innozenz'III.,* i, ed. O. Hageneder and A. Haidacher (Rome, 1962), no. 336 (p. 498): 'ad quod etiam laudabilius exsequendum vobis unum de fratribus militie Templi, alterum de fratribus Ierosolimitani Hospitalis, viros honestos et providos, assumatis'.

[28]   See H. Roscher, *Innozenz III. und die Kreuzzüge* (Göttingen, 1969), 75-84 and *passim*; G. Martini, 'Innocenzo III e il finanziamento delle crociate', *Archivio della Società Romana di Storia Patria,* lxvii (1944), 309-35; M. Menzel, *Historisches Jahrbuch,* cxx (2000), 39-79 (at 65-68).

[29]   This began to change with the papal crusading taxes. A. Gottlob, *Die päpstlichen Kreuzzugssteuern des 13. Jahrhunderts* (Heiligenstadt, 1892). When the clerics had to pay a tenth or a twentieth, it would seem logical that the military orders should have been exempt. But in the second half of the thirteenth century, firm opposition emerged against this privilege until Gregory X declared that there would be no more exceptions. However, after a short time he had to rescind this order See Schein, *Fideles Crucis,* 47.

Hospitallers – *alios, de quibus videamur melius posse confidere, non habemus.*[30] In the eyes of the pope, the Templars and the Hospitallers had become the ideal financial officials for the crusade.

With Templars and Hospitallers featuring so rarely in papal crusading propaganda, one might easily overlook a most important aspect. It was not enough to compose crusading appeals; they had to be publicized, to be made known throughout Christendom. For the Second Crusade, besides Eugenius III's famous *Quantum praedecessores*, addressed to the French King Louis VII and to all Christians – was spread throughout the West by Suger of Saint-Denis and Bernard of Clairvaux[31] – and besides the *Divini dispensatione* for an expedition against the Wends, circulated by Bishop Henry of Olomuce,[32] there was a third appeal, one directed to the Italians. This appeared in print for the first time at the end of the nineteenth century, when Paul Kehr and Luigi Schiaparelli discovered it in the archives of the Order of St John in Malta on the basis of two manuscripts concerning the Hospitaller preceptory at Rome or another central Italian house – in any case, not from the East.[33] Obviously, some Hospitallers must have been present and were charged with its dissemination, when on 5 October 1146 at Viterbo the pope proclaimed his appeal to the Italians.[34] It is not yet known whether they themselves had offered their services to the pope, or whether they had received papal instructions. There is no evidence either as to what extent they executed it; but at least they succeeded in preserving the text by having it transcribed on two of their cartularies.

Though at first glance the military orders in 1145-47 may very well appear to have been confined to only marginal significance, it is now clear that the Hospitallers had in fact played a decisive role in the Second Crusade as the real agents of papal crusading propaganda, at least in Italy. In modern terms, they served as the pope's messengers or postmen. Even more important, perhaps, in a methodological sense, is the need, when examining papal appeals, to study carefully not only the wording of the text and its historical context, but also the nature of the manuscript or archival tradition. This may well provide clues to hitherto unknown or obscure insights.

What happened in 1146 was not unique. Ten years later Hadrian IV's *Quantum strenui*, containing news about Banyas that a French knight, Arnulf de Landast, had brought from the Latin East together with a call for help,[35] was then diffused in at least three copies, one to the archbishop of Rheims, another to a Spanish prelate, and

[30]   Potth. 6310; Pressutti no. 2574; cf. Gottlob, *Kreuzzugssteuern*, 182-84.

[31]   P. Rassow, 'Die Kanzlei St Bernhards von Clairvaux'; *Studien und Mitteilungen aus dem Benedictinerorden*, xxxiv (1913), 63-103, 243-93; E. Caspar, 'Die Kreuzzugsbullen Eugens III.', *Neues Archiv der Gesellschaft für ältere deutsche Geschichtskunde*, xlv (1924), 285-305; for the part of Suger of Saint-Denis, R. Große, 'Einige Überlegungen zu den Kreuzzugsaufrufen Eugens III. in den Jahren 1145/46 – mit einer Neuedition von JL. 8784', *Francia*, xviii (1991), 85-92.

[32]   Migne, *PL.* 188, col. 1293; cf. J. Bistricky, 'Studien zum Urkunden-, Brief- und Handschriftenwesen des Bischofs Heinrich von Olmütz', *Archiv für Diplomatik*, xxvi (1980), 135-258.

[33]   Hiestand, *Papsturkunden für Kirchen im Heiligen Lande*, no. 93 (p. 193).

[34]   See *supra*, n. 33.

[35]   *PL.* 188, col. 1537.

a third to Petrus de Roveira, master of the Temple in Aragón.[36] The latter two are preserved as originals in the former Templar archives of San Gervasio de Cassoles, which are now in the Crown Archives at Barcelona. The copy addressed to the Spanish prelate is in a fragmentary state. In 1157, therefore, it was the Templars who served as intermediaries.[37] There is no surprise here at all, since the letter itself refers, as already indicated, to the heavy losses the Templars had suffered in the East.

Cor nostrum was Alexander III's last appeal, dated 16 January 1181. It was later inserted into the *Gesta Henrici regis*[38] and other English chronicles, and again it fails to mention the military orders in its *narratio*. However, *Cum orientalis terra*, a second letter issued the following day, recommended some Templars coming from the East to the addressees.[39] Together with the Aragonese cartularies that have preserved the text, too, it becomes clear that both letters were widely circulated through Western Europe, from the British Isles to the Iberian Peninsula, and that it was again the Templars who brought them over from the Roman Curia to the different countries.[40]

When *Cor nostrum*, which in 1181 appeared to have been a 'Templar' text, was repeated with minor modifications by Lucius III in 1184 and 1185, a first copy, issued in November or December 1184, went to the Hospitaller priory at Messina.[41] A second, with a few stylistic changes, which was dispatched on 23 January 1185, has survived in the Hospitaller houses at Strasburg and Frauenfeld.[42] The Curia had substituted the Hospitallers for the Templars.

If we assume that Alexander III's *Quantum praedecessores* of 1165 had reached England with Templar brethren,[43] then almost the entire papal crusading propaganda between 1148 and 1187 must have passed through the hands of the military orders. The only exceptions are four letters preserved in a famous manuscript of Arras, but we do not know how they arrived at Rheims.[44] They could have been brought over either by one of the easterners mentioned in the letters, or indeed by Hospitallers or Templars.

---

[36]   See supra, note 12.

[37]   See Kehr, *Spanien*, nos. 77-8 (pp. 359-62).

[38]   *Gesta Henrici regis* (*supra*, note 11), 272.

[39]   Ibid., 275.

[40]   Cf. Kehr, *Papsturkunden in Spanien*, 57 ex reg. 309 fol. 7, no. 19. Schwerin has overlooked this copy. A third copy, now lost, could have been at Messina, from where Antonino Amico took the text for his collections of Sicilian documents. Kehr, 'Papsturkunden in Sizilien', *Nachrichten der K. Gesellschaft der Wissenschaften zu Göttingen* (1899), 300, no. 26.

[41]   Amico (*infra*, note 42) gives explicitly 'ex autographo'.

[42]   Kehr, 'Papsturkunden in Sizilien', (Messina edn.), 329, no. 26; Hiestand, *Papsturkunden für Templer,* no. 165 (p. 352) from Antonino Amico's seventeenth-century manuscripts, *historiographus* of the king; for the German archives, ibid., no. 175 (p. 363).

[43]   It may have been among the Templar material confiscated after 1308. See W. Holtzmann, *Papsturkunden in England* I, Abhandl. ... Neue Folge, 25/1 (Berlin, 1940),112.

[44]   See J. Ramackers, *Papsturkunden in Frankreich* 3, Abhandl. ... Göttingen 3. Folge, 23, (Göttingen, 1940), 16-22, for JL. 11105 (1164-65) January 20, 11637-38 (both 29 July 1169), 12247 (23 December 1173).

This important role assumed by the military orders in the dissemination of papal appeals and letters was not accidental. Since the middle of the twelfth century, the two orders, driven by financial, material, and personal motives, had built up a network of communications between their central houses in Jerusalem and their commanderies in the West. The papal Curia in Rome often served as a point of reference along these lines of communication. It was here that the orders received the confirmation or extension of their rights; it was here that they had had to defend their interests. This effective network became known to the papacy, and the papacy did not hesitate to make use of it for its crusading appeals and propaganda until, as already indicated, a complete change occurred shortly after Hattin. Indeed, it should be stressed that after 1200, no papal crusading appeal for large expeditions or letters of secondary importance appear to have been carried to their destinations by either a Templar or a Hospitaller. Nor could they have been preserved in a Hospitaller or Templar archive. The papal chancery had now itself become a most efficient instrument, and could reach all parts of western Christendom through its own intermediaries without relying any further on the military orders.

However, the crucial question still persists: why were Templars and Hospitallers virtually absent from papal crusading propaganda except for their employment for the latter's physical transmission? A closer look at canon law might provide the answer. A crusading appeal exhorted its listeners to take the cross, offering indulgences in return. Quite unlike missions that were merely intended to raise funds, the crusaders' vows, the proclamation of an indulgence, the future crusaders' confession of sins, the imposition of penance, and occasionally the absolution from a vow – all these required priestly involvement and liturgical functions. Indeed, the very expression 'to preach a crusade' is itself quite revealing. In the medieval tripartite social *schema* of *oratores – milites – laboratores*, both the Templars and the Hospitallers were *milites, not oratores*: they could not preach because of their legal and social status.

It may be argued, of course, that from the beginning both orders had priests in their ranks. A study of the solemn papal privilege *Omne datum optimum* of 29 March 1139, however, shows that at least in the Temple, such brethren were rather servants *in spiritualibus*, who could be received or dismissed more or less according to the master's arbitrary will. They were not fully professed members.[45] The true Templars and the true Hospitallers were not priests, but armed knights, and with regard to the latter institution, male nurses.

The papacy was, of course, aware of this legal problem. In his letter of 1157, following the *narratio* about the events at Banyas, Pope Hadrian IV asked his addressee, as he normally did, to circulate his letter and to preach in support of the Holy Land.[46] As already shown, one of the three surviving copies had been addressed to the master of the Temple in Aragón, Peter de Roveira, and this is the only known papal crusading letter ever addressed to a military order. From a close study of the text, it becomes evident that the final clause about preaching was missing.[47] As this is an original copy, the omission could not have been an unintended error of the

---

[45]   Hiestand (ed.), *Papsturkunden für Templer*, no. 3 (p. 204).
[46]   'quatinus commissum vobis populos studeatis diligentissime commonere', ibid.
[47]   See *supra*, note 12.

copyist; it must have been the work of the chancery itself. Templars and Hospitallers simply could not preach the crusade. What they did in a most impressive way, with their castles and in battle against the Muslims, was to set an example for others of what daily fighting against the infidels really meant. They thereby sometimes provided the factual material for the *narratio* of papal crusading appeals – exhorting others to set out for the East.

There was a fundamental difference between the crusaders and the military orders. Members of a military order could not take the cross and become crusaders, because a crusader enjoyed only a temporary legal status. Once a crusader returned home, he was no longer a crusader, unless of course he took a new vow. On the other hand, a Templar or a Hospitaller took vows that bound him for life. There were, of course, exceptions to this rule. The case of the master Philip of Nablus in 1170[48] is one classic example. But such cases were just that, rare exceptions. A member of a military order could not even go to the East on the strength of his own decision: it was always the master and the chapter who decided who should go and when.

It was only logical that crusading preachers refrained from exhorting their listeners to join the military orders. Such action would not only be rash. Being or becoming a Templar or a Hospitaller could in no way guarantee the journey to the East. Allowing Hospitallers and Templars to preach the crusade would have created a dilemma – that of being disloyal either to one's order by exhorting listeners to go on the crusade or offer alms for it, or to the crusade by exhorting them to give money (and goods) to one's order instead of setting out for the East.

To sum up, the military orders played a crucial role in the Latin East, over and above their role as its *milites perpetui*. Through their very efficient network of communications, they served the popes from the Second to the Third Crusade as messengers for crusading appeals. Later they provided the Curia with first-hand information on the prevailing political, military, and psychological conditions in the East, in both the Christian and Muslim world. They thus prompted papal appeals for help in various forms – men, money, and other material. It should be born in mind, however, that institutionally, legally, and politically the crusade and the military orders were two completely distinct institutions.

---

[48]   See Bulst-Thiele, *Magistri*, 75-86.

Chapter 18

The Hospitaller and Templar Houses of Périgord: Some Observations

David Bryson

This paper will first look at the separate Templar and Hospitaller establishments in Périgord as they were before 1313 – that is, before the acquisition of the Templar properties by the Hospital. It will then present the subsequent record of errors made by nineteenth- and twentieth-century historians in assigning Templar origins to Hospitaller houses which were always Hospitaller, and, in at least one case, Hospitaller origins to what had been a Templar house. It will conclude by speculating on how and why such errors occurred, have been perpetuated, and will continue to be repeated, unless a new project is undertaken.

The old county of Périgord, now the department of the Dordogne, corresponded to the diocese of Périgueux, which was part of the archbishopric of Bordeaux. The following survey of its Templar and Hospitaller houses is not intended to be comprehensive.

The Templar houses are marked on the map (Figure 18.1) by the lightly shaded circles. These are:

1. Andrivaux (commune of Chancelade);
2. Lagut (Saint Front de Pradoux);
3. Pontarnaud (Monsec);
4. Allemans;
5. Puylautier (Pélautier, Saint Pierre d'Eyraud);
6. Saint Paul la Roche;
7. Sergeac;
8. Saint Michel de Rivière;
9. Bonnefare (Bonneville et Saint Avit de Fumadières).

The Templar house of Puymartin (Chappelle-Faucher) does not appear on this map, because its precise location could not be confirmed. These Templar houses were under the jurisdiction of the master of Aquitaine and were, as can be seen here, grouped in western Périgord north of the river Dordogne, around their principal house of Andrivaux (circle A on the map), west of Périgueux. Andrivaux, formerly a Benedictine abbey, was granted to the Templars in 1139. Its last preceptor was Gerald of Lavergne, who served in this position for the final 32 years from 1275 until 1307.[1]

---

[1] *Gallia Christiana* (Paris, 1739-1880) 2, 1467.

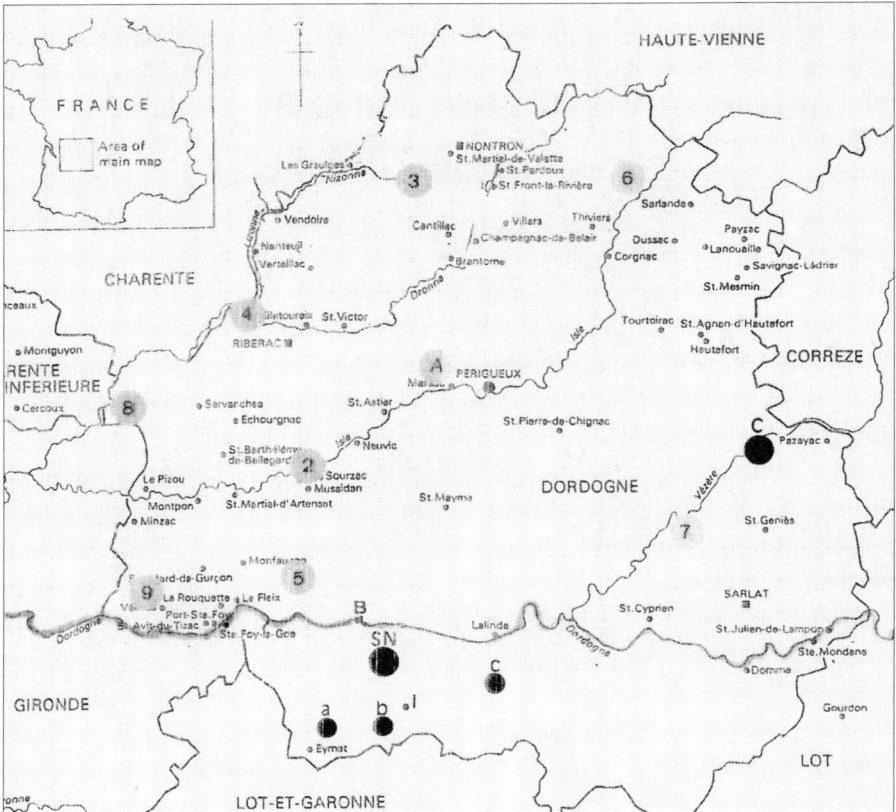

Fig. 18.1   Hospitaller and Templar Houses of Périgord

The Hospitaller houses, marked with black circles on the map (Figure 18.1), were under the jurisdiction of the Grand Priory of Saint Gilles in the southern Rhone, and grouped around two principal houses: Saint Naixent in the Bergeracois south of the Dordogne (SN on the map), and Condat (commune of Condat-sur-Vézère) north of the river (C on the map). The houses of Montguyard (Serres-et-Montguyard, black circle a on the map), Falgueyrat (b), and Naussannes (c) were annexed to Saint Naixent.

In 1254, Hélie Rudel, lord of Bergerac, made a last will and testament, in which he left his seigneury to his daughter Margaret, and requested burial, as its benefactor, at the Hospital of Saint Naixent. This will is witnessed by Roland Prévost, then preceptor of the Hospital. The original manuscript is held in the archives of the Pyrénées-Atlantiques at Pau.[2]

In 1277, Peter of Valbéon became preceptor of Saint Naixent and of all of the Hospitaller priories and houses of the diocese of Périgueux, and remained in that

---

[2]   ADPA, E.17 (1254).

position until 1304.[3] Peter increased the Hospital's property holdings on both sides of the river, most importantly in the suburb of La Madelaine at the south end of the bridge across the Dordogne at Bergerac (map, B).[4] Thus the Hospital could control the bridge, and the bridge controlled the traffic, not only of armies, but also of pilgrims to Compostela, and of wine to Bordeaux. By 1378, the Hospitaller preceptor of Saint Naixent was sending eighteen to twenty *tonneaux* (some 16,000 to 18,000 litres) of wine in a single shipment.[5]

These acquisitions by the Hospital soon attracted the wrath of the lords of Bergerac, within whose seigneury the properties were situated. One way in which the seigneurs could seek to limit the power of the two orders in Périgord was to play one off against the other. That may have motivated the sale of the properties and rights of the lord of Bergerac at Sergeac to the Temple (circle 7), because Sergeac stood between the principal Hospitaller houses of Condat and Saint Naixent.[6] But in 1300, the reckless and covetous young lord Renaud of Bergerac - whose ancestor had been the benefactor of the Hospital of Saint Naixent - turned to more violent methods. First, he attacked and burned the deanery of Issigeac, just south of Saint Naixent (black dot I on the map). The dean, Amblard, was assassinated. Renaud then set about the recovery for himself of the properties newly-acquired by the Hospital of Saint Naixent. The preceptor Peter of Valbéon appealed for a royal safeguard, but by 1304 Peter was missing, presumed dead.[7] The order sent Dragonet of Mondragon, grand prior of Saint Gilles, to confront the lord of Bergerac. At the same time, Bertrand of Got, then archbishop of Bordeaux, began his archiepiscopal visit to the diocese, recorded in a manuscript held in the archives of the Gironde in Bordeaux, starting out from the Templar house of Bonnefare (map circle 9) on September second, arriving and taking up residence at the deanery of Issigeac on the eighteenth and nineteenth of September, 1304.[8] Two days later, as a manuscript of the Pau archive shows, the contested properties were restored to the Hospital of Saint Naixent.[9] At Poitiers on 31 August 1307, in the presence of Bertrand of Got, then Pope Clement V, Fulk of Villaret, grand master of the Hospital, finally appointed Clement's own chamberlain, Raymond Bernard of Fumel, as the new preceptor of Saint Naixent.[10] This appointment was, therefore, made by Clement just six weeks before the seizure of the Templars and their properties, and was confirmed by Clement a year later, in November 1308.[11]

But that was not the end. During Christmas of 1316 the bailiff and sergeants of the lord of Bergerac again led an attack on the Hospital of Saint Naixent. This

---

[3]   *CH*, iii, nos. 4034-35 (1289), 533-34.

[4]   ADPA, E.125 (21 September 1304).

[5]   L. de la Roque, *Annales historiques de la ville de Bergerac* (Bergerac, 1891; repr. Marseilles, 1976), 40.

[6]   ADPA, E.611, fols. 65-67.

[7]   J. Charet, *Le Bergeracois des origines à 1340* (Bergerac, 1950), 295-97.

[8]   Archives départementales de la Gironde, Bordeaux, G264.

[9]   ADPA, E.125, 21 September 1304.

[10]   *Regestum Clementis Papae V (1305-1314), 10 vols. (Rome, 1886)*, iii, no. 3389, 275, and *CH*, iv, no. 4749, Poitiers, 31 August 1307, 143.

[11]   Ibid., no. 3393, 277; *CH*, iv, no. 4826.

time, the preceptor and the royal prosecutor successfully brought charges against the lord of Bergerac, and two plaques proclaiming the royal protection of the Hospital's property were affixed, one to the residence and one to the church of Saint Naixent on Wednesday, 16 February 1317.[12]

This plaque remains on the south wall of the church. Its fourteenth-century provenance has been confirmed to me by Robert Favreau of the Centre d'Etudes Supérieures de Civilisation Médievale of the University of Poitiers, but I owe its precise identification to the Condat Inventory of the archive of Malta held by the archives of the department of the Haut-Garonne at Toulouse, to which I will return.[13]

The order ceding the possessions of the Temple in Périgord to the Hospital was given at Cahors on 30 April 1313. Western Périgord then having been under English rule, Edward II ordered the transfer of the Templar properties in Aquitaine to the Hospital seven months later, on 28 November 1313.[14] The takeover of the Templar properties led – in a way not unfamiliar to us now – to a more efficient restructuring of the Hospitaller organization in France. For Périgord, the administration was transferred from Saint Gilles in the south, to Toulouse. Not long after that, no doubt to accommodate the new reality of the combined Templar and Hospitaller possessions, Condat became the principal Hospitaller house of Périgord, and Saint Naixent was annexed to it.[15]

But now, turning to the historiography of the question, what do we find?

The opening of the Vatican Archives to scholars in 1879 unleashed a flood of published works on the Templars and Hospitallers that was to continue unabated for more than twenty years. These are the monumental works we continue to use, whether in their original editions or in the modern facsimile reprints that have made them so accessible. But, while one can only admire the amazing dedication and application of these scholars, their works have preserved many errors that, like nineteenth-century Trojan Horse viruses, lie in wait for their next repetition. I will give some examples for Périgord.

In 1883, Antoine du Bourg published his massive *Histoire du Grand-Prieuré de Toulouse*, in which he dedicates an entire chapter to the 'Commandery of Condat,' five pages of which are devoted to Saint Naixent. He begins this chapter by stating that

The suppression of the Order of the Temple added numerous and important possessions to those which formed the original domain (of the Hospitallers) . . . the previous Temples of

---

[12]   Archives Saint-Nexans, L. I, cited in M.A. Du Bourg, *Histoire du Grand-Prieuré de Toulouse* (Toulouse, 1883; repr. Marseilles, 1978), 517.

[13]   Archives départementales de la Haute Garonne, Toulouse, H. Malte, Inventaire Condat.

[14]   M.A. Du Bourg, *Prise de possession par les hospitaliers de la maison du Temple de Toulouse (1313), Mémoire de la Société archéologique du Midi de la France*, xi (Toulouse, 1880), 172-85.

[15]   Du Bourg, *Histoire,* 10, 518.

Sergeac, Saint Naixent, Andrivaux, et cetera, and the Hospitals of Montguyard, Bonnefare, and Combarenches.[16]

His statement contains two errors: Saint Naixent was not Templar, but Hospitaller, as I have shown; and Bonnefare was not of the Hospital, but was, as I have said, the Templar house from which Bertrand of Got set out on his journey in 1304. Du Bourg would likely not have committed either of these errors had his book not come out a few years before the Vatican published the Register of Clement the Fifth – but it was, and remains forever, too late.

But then Clement's Register adds its own errors, naming Saint Naixent as 'Saint Maxent,' and these were soon repeated in the Delaville le Roux *Cartulaire général de l'Ordre des hospitaliers de Saint-Jean*, where the Hospital of Saint Naixent is listed not under Condat, but 'Condom.'[17] Another entry does list Saint Naixent correctly under Condat, but under the authority of La Cavalerie, in the arrondissement of Condom, in the Gers.[18] And La Cavalerie, according to Léonard, whose work we will soon consider, was a 'domus templi.'[19] And so it goes....

While Delaville le Roux was assembling his cartulary of the Hospital, A. Trudon des Ormes was composing his *Liste des maisons et de quelques dignitaires de l'Ordre du temple en Syrie, en Chypre et en France d'après les pièces du Procès*. The only Templar house in Périgord, according to Trudon des Ormes, was Saint Paul la Roche (circle 6 on the map, in the north) – which only serves to demonstrate that attempts to identify properties based on the evidence of the trials alone are bound to be misleading.[20]

In 1891, eight years after the publication of Du Bourg's book (which was reprinted in facsimile in 1978), a French edition of the *Annales historiques de la ville de Bergerac*, as reprinted in facsimile in 1976, contains a footnote to a reference to Saint Naixent in which we read: 'Commandery of the Order of the Temple, which passed in turn to the Order of the Hospitallers of Saint John of Jerusalem, later called knights of Rhodes and of Malta.'[21]

The tradition of this error has not died hard; it is still alive.

It would be comforting to be able to say that the historiography of the twentieth century has been more accurate and successful than that of the nineteenth – but such is far from being the case. After the publication in 1913 of the Marquis d'Albon's fragmentary *Cartulaire Général de l'Ordre du Temple, 1119?-1150*, in 1930 Emile Léonard published a book misleadingly titled *Introduction au Cartulaire Manuscrit du Temple (1150-1317) constitué par le Marquis d'Albon et conservé à la Bibliothèque nationale, suivie d'un tableau des maisons francaises du Temple et leurs précepteurs*, which ought to have resolved our problems of identification, but

---

[16]   Ibid., 506.

[17]   *Reg. Clem. V*, iii, no. 3389, 275; no. 3393, 277; *CH*, iv, no. 4749, 143; no. 4826, 195; ibid., iii, nos. 4034-5, 533-34.

[18]   *CH*, ii, 638.

[19]   E.G. Léonard, *Introduction au Cartulaire Manuscrit du Temple 1150-1317, constitué par le Marquis d'Albon* (Paris, 1930), 199.

[20]   In *Revue de l'Orient Latin*, v (1897-99), 528-29.

[21]   La Roque, *Annales*, 40.

which in fact only serves further to confuse and misguide us. We have already noted a problem raised by Léonard's work. And where does he get his data from? Not from the manuscript of the Marquis d'Albon, but from published secondary works such as those of Du Bourg and Trudon des Ormes, whose errors we have already seen. But now, for Périgord at least, Léonard adds an error of his own. There now appears a phantom Templar house of Pontarnaud, which Léonard, while identifying its location as the commune of Monsec, situates it in what is the commune of Monsac, arrondisement of Bergerac, canton of Beaumont – which is south of the river, in the region of the Hospital of Saint Naixent. But, as our map shows, the real Templar house of Pontarnaud was in the commune of Monsec, arrondisement of Nontron, canton of Mareuil, far to the north of the river, circle 3 on the map.[22]

Does modern scholarship rescue us from these dilemmas? On the contrary. In the municipal library of Bergerac there is a document, dated 1961, entitled *Préinventaire des Monuments du Moyen Age – Canton de Bergerac*. It contains this description of Saint Naixent:

> the church was part of the old castle-fort of the knights of Malta... A stone representing a Malta cross with an indecipherable inscription and encased on the exterior wall dates from this period ... (so far, so good; but then we read) ... approximately at the time of the First Crusade. Later, in the time of Saint Louis (thirteenth century), the castle and its church belonged to the Templars. But the Templars were soon dispossessed, a text of 1304 showing that they were already no longer the proprietors.[23]

And so fiction in the guise of fact displaces fact. Then Jean Secret, the most eminent regional scholar of Périgord, had this to say about Condat – without a shred of evidence – in 1966:

> The bourg of Condat ... was the site of a Templar commandery, at once a fortified house where they could withstand a siege, a tithe barn to store the harvests, a commander's residence, a pilgrims' hostel, and a hospital for the sick.[24]

No wonder, then, that when the Saint John Historical Society visited Condat in 1998, they were informed that it was originally Templar, and later passed to the Hospitallers.[25]

In conclusion, while it is clear that there is a crying need for a comprehensive and accurate summary of Templar and Hospitaller properties in all regions, it is also clear that such a summary could not simply be assembled from existing published sources such as the trials, papal registers, and cartularies. It is even clearer that the secondary material is a minefield of errors. As Malcolm Barber has said, citing Umberto Eco,

---

[22]   Léonard, 100.

[23]   F. Bernier, *Préinventaire des monuments du moyen-âge-canton de Bergerac* (Bergerac, 1961), 35-55.

[24]   J. Secret, *Le Périgord: Châteaux, manoirs et gentilhommières* (Périgueux, 1966), 221-22.

[25]   *St John Historical Society Proceedings*, x (1998), iv.

you can tell a lunatic 'by the fact that sooner or later he brings up the Templars.'[26] A carefully co-ordinated review of archives would have to be undertaken at the local level for each region. Such a project would not be quick or easy. For example: recently, I learned that the archives of the Dordogne at Périgueux had acquired a microfilm of the Condat archive, so I e-mailed the archivist to ask if I could obtain a copy. In her reply, the archivist said that the work is still in progress, and will require some 2,500 photographs. They are working back from the end, she said, and so far are still in the eighteenth century. Daunting indeed.

---

[26]   U. Eco, *Foucault's Pendulum* (London, 1988), cited in M. Barber, *The New Knighthood: A History of the Order of the Temple* (Cambridge, 1994), 334.

Chapter 19

The Battle of Tannenberg-Grunwald-Žalgiris (1410) as Reflected in Twentieth-Century Monuments

Sven Ekdahl

There are historical events that not only remain anchored in the consciousness of a people for centuries, they also still perform an important cultural and political function long after their occurrence. The Battle of Tannenberg in Teutonic Prussia, which took place on 15 July 1410, is one such. A Polish–Lithuanian army had succeeded in defeating the armed forces of the Teutonic Knights and, in so doing, had fundamentally changed the pattern of international relations in this part of Europe. As a result, an 'unhealable wound' had been inflicted on the *Ordenstaat* of the Teutonic Knights which, in the end, contributed to the decline of the order. Victorious Poland and Lithuania, allied in a union since 1385/86, replaced Prussia as the most powerful territorial body in east-central Europe.[1]

By way of departure, a brief look backward would not be out of place. On 16 September 1410, not more than three days before raising the unsuccessful siege of the order's main castle of Marienburg (Pol. *Malbork*), the Polish King Władysław II Jagiełło made his intentions clear in a letter to the bishop of Pomesania to have a Brigittine cloister and church built on the battlefield at Grünfelde, literally *in loco conflictus nostri, quem cum Cruciferis de Prusia habuimus, dicto Grunenvelt.*[2] The village of Grünfelde (*Grunenvelt*) was situated about 3 km south-west of Tannenberg.[3] One of the revelations of the Swedish St Bridget (1303-1373) was a vision predicting the crushing defeat of the *cruciferi.*[4] This vision, directed against the Teutonic Order, was well known in Poland, and Jagiełło wanted his forces'

---

[1]   S. Ekdahl, *Die Schlacht bei Tannenberg 1410. Quellenkritische Untersuchungen*, i: *Einführung und Quellenlage*, Berliner Historische Studien, viii (Berlin, 1982); S. M. Kuczyński, *Wielka Wojna z Zakonem Krzyżackim w latach 1409-1411* (5th edn., Warsaw, 1987); A. Nadolski, *Grunwald. Problemy wybrane*, Rozprawy i materiały Ośrodka Badań Naukowych im. Wojciecha Kętrzyńskiego, cxv (Olsztyn, 1990); M. Jučas, *Žalgirio mūšis* (Vilnius, 1999); W. Urban, *Tannenberg and After. Lithuania, Poland, and the Teutonic Order in Search of Immortality* (rev. edn., Chicago, 2003); S. Ekdahl, 'Tannenberg, Battle of (1410)', in *The Crusades. An Encyclopedia*, ed. A. V. Murray, 4 vols (Santa Barbara, Ca. 2006), iv, 1145-46.

[2]   Ekdahl, *Die Schlacht bei Tannenberg*, 134-35.

[3]   See the maps in ibid., Figures 37-40.

[4]   Ibid., 135-36.

Fig. 19.1   Tannenberg-Grunwald. Foundation walls of the Teutonic Order's
            Mary chapel of 1411, with the vestry in front. View from the north-
            east in the direction of Grunwald village (Grünfelde) (Photo S. Ekdahl,
            1985)

victory to be seen as a fulfilment of the prophecy.[5] As the military and political
events of autumn 1410 thwarted his plans for Grünfelde, the Brigittine cloister was
instead built some years later in Lublin.[6] The new Grand Master Henry of Plauen
however, in 1411 ordered a Mary Chapel to be built on another place, in the middle
of the triangle formed by Tannenberg, Grünfelde, and the village of Ludwigsdorf.[7]
He asked for, and one year later received, a bull from Pope John XXIII stating that
whoever visited the chapel on particular days would be granted indulgences.[8] While
the history of this chapel, from its foundation to its destruction in the eighteenth

---

[5]   Ibid. Also *Die Ermahnung des Carthäusers,* ed. Th. Hirsch, in *SRP*, iv (Leipzig,
1870), 448-65, at 461.
[6]   S. Ekdahl. 'Heliga Birgitta, slaget vid Tannenberg och grundandet av klostret
Triumphus Mariae in Lublin', in *Slavica Lundensia,* xxiii (2007) 1-23; id., 'St Birgitta of
Sweden, the Battle of Tannenberg (Grunwald), and the Foundation of the Cloister *Triumphus
Mariae* in Lublin', in *Festschrift* for Prof. K. A. Kuczyński (Płock, 2007), forthcoming. For
literature, also Ekdahl, *Die Schlacht bei Tannenberg,* 136 n. 37.
[7]   Ibid., 191-92, 325-26.
[8]   Ibid.

century, cannot be discussed here, it is worth noting that its foundation walls have been preserved to the present day (Figure 19.1).[9]

For all those who had fought on the side of the victors, the Poles and Lithuanians in particular, the decisive battle of Tannenberg–Grunwald–Žalgiris played an important role in establishing their identity in times of hardship.[10] In Lithuania, however, it was not the Polish King Jagiełło (Lithuanian *Jogaila*), but rather his cousin, the Lithuanian Grand Duke Vytautas (Pol. *Witold*), who came to be celebrated as the victorious national hero who determined the outcome of the battle.[11] In Lithuania the battle is known as the 'Battle at Žalgiris', a translation of the Polish *Grunwald*, meaning *Grunenvelt* or *Grünfelde*. Russians and Belorussians use the designation *Grjunval'd* or *Grünwald*. The Germans have retained the name Tannenberg as the place where the order's army had been deployed.[12]

The Year 1910

After the partitions of Poland towards the end of the eighteenth century and the humiliation it suffered as a result (the country disappeared from the map of Europe), the memory of this victory revived hopes of resurrecting the Polish–Lithuanian nation. In all areas of political and cultural life there raged a bitter struggle against Prussia/Germany. The great adversaries of the Poles among those involved in the struggle were Reichschancellor Otto von Bismarck and Kaiser William II.[13]

In 1901, on the two-hundredth anniversary of the founding of the Prussian monarchy, the Germans erected the first memorial of the twentieth century on the battlefield of 1410: a big stone in the centre of the ruins of Mary Chapel with an inscription to honour the fallen Grand Master Ulrich of Jungingen (Figure 19.2).[14]

---

[9]   [9] The Prussian gouvernment ordered the chapel to be pulled down in 1720. See S. Ekdahl, 'Denkmal und Geschichtsideologie im polnisch-preußischen Spannungsfeld', in *Jahrbuch für die Geschichte Mittel- und Ostdeutschlands*, xxxv (Berlin, 1986), 127-218, at 128-29, 190-92. Also published in *Zum Verständnis der polnischen Frage in Preußen und Deutschland 1772-1871*, ed. K. Zernack, Einzelveröffentlichungen der Historischen Kommission zu Berlin, lix (Berlin, 1987), with the same pagination. For other sources and literature on the chapel, S. Ekdahl, 'Pobojowisko Grunwaldzkie i okolica w XV i XVI stuleciu', in *Studia Grunwaldzkie*, iii (Olsztyn, 1994), 61-118, *passim*.

[10]   [10] Id., 'Tannenberg/Grunwald – ein politisches Symbol in Deutschland und Polen', *JBS*, xxii (1991), 271-324.

[11]   [11] A. Nikžentaitis, 'Der Vytautaskult in Litauen (15-20 Jahrhundert) und seine Widerspiegelung im Denkmal', in *Das Denkmal im nördlichen Ostmitteleuropa im 20 Jahrhundert. Politischer Kontext und nationale Funktion*, ed.. S. Ekdahl, *Nordost-Archiv*, vi (Lüneburg, 1997), 131-46.

[12]   [12] Ekdahl, 'Tannenberg/Grunwald', in *JBS*, 273.

[13]   [13] Ibid., 276-82. Also id., *Die Schlacht bei Tannenberg*, 19-21.

[14]   [14] Ibid., 21.

Fig. 19.2   Tannenberg-Grunwald. The German commemorative stone tablet of
1901. The inscription *Im Kampf für deutsches Wesen, deutsches Recht
starb hier der Hochmeister Ulrich von Jungingen am 15. Juli 1410
den Heldentod* was chiselled away in 1960 by order of a Communist
functionary. Cf. Figure 19.10 (Photo S. Ekdahl, 1977)

It was not this event, however, that sparked off the Polish Grunwald activities of 1902 and the great celebrations of 1910. It was rather the severely punished strike of Polish parents and students in Wreschen (Pol. *Września*) in 1901 against the sole use of the German language in teaching, together with the notorious speech William II delivered at the festival of the (Protestant) Prussian Order of St John (*Johanniterorden*) on 5 June 1902 at Marienburg.[15] In his speech, the German Kaiser invited an assembly of knights 'to take the sword of the order firmly in hand and bludgeon the Sarmatians, chasten their impertinence, exterminate them'.[16] It was at this point that the Poles decided to celebrate their victory over the Teutonic Knights in 1410 through the construction of memorials for the five-hundredth-year jubilee in 1910. Politically this event could only succeed in the Austrian part of Poland (Galicia). Since monuments to the battle itself were forbidden, other symbolic creative possibilities had to be thought of, such as the erection of statues of King Jagiełło. The symbolism was recognized by all Poles to be that of the victor of Grunwald.[17]

In 1910, according to the Polish journalist and historian Henryk Leśniowski, around 60 separate villages and cities, each boasting a Grunwald monument, existed in Galicia, within the Polish borders as they stand today.[18] Many of them were destroyed during the First or Second World War, and today they still live on only in the memories of the older generation residing in these places. Others either survived or were reconstructed in 1960.

One such monument is the one found in the town of Żywiec, destroyed in the Second World War and never rebuilt. Perched on its peak lay an eagle about to take flight as the symbol of Polish liberation. Other similar monuments, like those in Kańczuga, Błażowa, and Przeworsk are among the larger ones.[19]

The biggest and most significant of these monuments was unveiled in Kraków on 15 July 1910 upon the anniversary of the battle. It was a gift of the well-known pianist Ignacy Paderewski, representing King Jagiełło atop his steed (Figure 19.3). On the façade of the pedestal, just beneath the rider, stands the Lithuanian Grand Duke Vytautas/Witold holding a large sword pointed downwards and looking

---

[15]   J. Vietig, 'Die polnischen Grunwaldfeiern der Jahre 1902 und 1910', in *Berliner Historische Studien*, iv (Berlin, 1981), 237-62; Ekdahl, 'Tannenberg/Grunwald', in *JBS,* 281-82. See W. Wippermann, *Der Ordensstaat als Ideologie. Das Bild des Deutschen Ordens in der deutschen Geschichtsschreibung und Publizistik,* Einzelveröffentlichungen der Historischen Kommission zu Berlin, xxiv (Berlin, 1979), 185-209.

[16]   Vietig, 'Die polnischen Grunwaldfeiern', 244 n. 31, quoting B. von Bülow, *Denkwürdigkeiten,* i (Berlin, 1930), 569.

[17]   For the following, S. Ekdahl, 'Die Grunwald-Denkmäler in Polen. Politischer Kontext und nationale Funktion', in *Das Denkmal,* 75-107. Id., 'Tannenberg-Grunwald-Żalgiris: Eine mittelalterliche Schlacht im Spiegel deutscher, polnischer und litauischer Denkmäler', in *Zeitschrift für Geschichtswissenschaft,* l (2002), 103-18.

[18]   Ekdahl, 'Die Grunwald-Denkmäler', 76-79.

[19]   Ibid., 78-79.

contemplatively at the fallen Grand Master who lay beneath him. The sides of the pedestal are decorated with symbolic figures, inscriptions, and coats of arms.[20]

Fig. 19.3   Kraków: The rider statue of King Władyslaw Jagiełło (1910). (Polish pre-war postcard)

---

[20]   Ibid., 80-81. Also Ekdahl, *Die Schlacht bei Tannenberg*, 18-19, and id., 'Tannenberg/ Grunwald', in *JBS*, 282.

On the big artificial monument hill in Niepołomice, twenty kilometers east of Kraków, stands another monument constructed in 1910. Two Polish women are known to have carried soil from the distant battlefield at Grunwald to add it to the hill, while three students brought wheelbarrows full of soil from Silesia.[21]

The Interwar Period and the Second World War

Poland and Lithuania emerged from the First World War as victors and independent nations, while Germany ended up belonging to those who had had territory taken from them. Germany's strong resistance made itself felt in its reaction to the humiliating peace treaty of Versailles with its so-called 'war-guilt clause' 231. By 1924, a plan to build a Tannenberg national monument at Hohenstein (the Polish 'Olsztynek') in East Prussia was set in motion. Initiated three years later, it was meant to be not only a symbolic sign of victory over the Russians in 1914, but rather to serve as a warning to Poland. On 2 October 1935, on the anniversary of the birth of the deceased Field Marshall and President Paul of Hindenburg, the latter's remains were interred in a crypt under the Hindenburg Tower while the monument grounds were declared by Hitler to be a Reich memorial (*Reichsehrenmal*).[22] In 1999, a thorough account of the history of its architecture was published.[23]

The Poles' Grunwald monument in Kraków was completely destroyed by the Germans in November and December 1939,[24] and that of the Germans at Hohenstein, who were facing the onslaught of the Red Army in January 1945, was partially demolished by the Germans themselves.[25] Later, the German monument was razed to the ground and traces of it removed.[26] Some of the granite stones from the Hindenburg Crypt were used to build the monument to the Red Army in Olsztyn (Ger. Allenstein) in 1946, a Polish gesture thanking the Russians for their liberation.[27]

The interwar period witnessed not only tension between Germany and Poland and between Germany and Lithuania, but also between Poland and Lithuania.[28] A graphic example of this can be seen in the dedication of Vytautas the Great's statue on the five-hundredth anniversary of his death (1430) in Kaunas, the Lithuanian capital at the time. Standing on top of a high pedestal, the Grand Duke unambiguously

---

[21]   Id., 'Die Grunwald-Denkmäler', 83.

[22]   Id., *Die Schlacht bei Tannenberg*, 21-22; id., 'Tannenberg/Grunwald', in *JBS*, 283-84.

[23]   J. Tietz, *Das Tannenberg-Nationaldenkmal. Architektur, Geschichte, Kontext* (Berlin, 1999). Also E. Vogelsang, 'Aus der Geschichte des Reichsehrenmals Tannenberg', in *Zwischen den Weltkriegen*, ii, *Kultur im Preußenland der Jahre 1918 bis 1939,* ed. U. Arnold (Lüneburg, 1987), 73-122.

[24]   A. Urbańczyk, *Na chwałe narodu. Pomnik grunwaldzki w Krakowie 1910-1976* (Kraków, 1976), without pagination, but at [13-14]. Photos of the destruction at [36].

[25]   Tietz, 201.

[26]   Ekdahl, *Die Schlacht bei Tannenberg,* Figure 12; id., 'Die Grunwald-Denkmäler', 104.

[27]   Ibid. The monument still exists, but the place where it stands has now been converted into a car park.

[28]   See id., 'Tannenberg/Grunwald', in *JBS*, 284-86.

dominates four symbolic figures lying at his feet: a Russian, a Pole, a Tartar, and a defeated knight of the Teutonic Order holding a broken sword, a clear allusion to the order's defeat at Žalgiris (Tannenberg). The statue, originally standing in front of a military academy, was destroyed during the war and could only be re-erected after the reinstatement of the Republic of Lithuania on 11 March 1990, this time, however, in the centre of Kaunas on the Laisvės Alėja or Freedom Avenue.[29] (See Figure 19.4.)

Around the same time in July 1930, after a favourable vote taken in Warmia and Mazury (Ger. Ermland und Masuren) ten years earlier, the foundation stone for a monument to Jagiełło was laid in what had by then become the Polish city of Działdowo (Ger. Soldau). The unveiling took place four years later, on the five-hundredth anniversary of the king's death. The monument consisted of an obelisk crowned with a 'Jagiellonian' eagle; its mid-section showed a hand holding a sword. The monument was destroyed in the Second World War.[30]

Fig. 19.4   Kaunas: The statue of Vytautas the Great at its present site on Freedom
               Avenue (Photo S. Ekdahl, 1995)

---

[29]   Id., 'Die Grunwald-Denkmäler', 84; Nikžentaitis, 141.
[30]   Ekdahl, 'Die Grunwald-Denkmäler', 84.

Of perhaps greater political significance was the unveiling in Uzdowo (Ger. Usdau) of a Grunwald monument on 12 July 1931 by Rowmund Piłsudski, nephew of Jozef Piłsudski, the Marshall of Poland. Like Działdowo, Uzdowo had been chosen because the Polish-Lithuanian Armed Forces had marched through this town in 1410. In addition, on Germany's withdrawal from the area after the First World War, Uzdowo became Polish territory, close to the battlefield of Grunwald. The monument could be seen as a response to the Germans' Tannenberg National Memorial of 1927. The seal of this monument with its inscriptions formed a stylized eagle with two swords.[31]

After Germany's occupation of Poland in September 1939, the monument was razed to the ground. The heavy capital, with parts of the eagle, was secretly buried by the Poles not far from the square. In the spring of 1960 the remains were dug up again, and were furnished with an inscription tablet. In 1985, on the fortieth anniversary of 'the victory over Fascism', another monument was raised and placed beside it. It was an even larger stone monument, likewise furnished with an inscription tablet.[32] In 2006 a private organization took care of the restoration of the first monument of 1931; the unveiling ceremony was held on 12 August that year.

In Poland, towards the end of the 1930s, the rapidly worsening political relationship with Germany led to a resurfacing of Grunwald symbolism inspired by deep national and political sentiments. The reaction against the Germans was so strong that in World's Fair of 1939 in New York, a large bronze statue of a rider was erected in front of the Polish pavilion. The statue depicted King Jagiełło with two raised and crossed swords in the pose of a victor, an obvious allusion to his victory over the Teutonic Knights at Grunwald (Figure 19.5). At the end of the fair the statue was stored in a warehouse in New York until the Polish exiles handed it over to the city in 1945. The celebrated dedication of 'King Jagiello' at his new location in New York's Central Park followed on 15 July 1945. The monument, with its new granite pedestal, was over seven meters high. On the pedestal below was the name Wladyslaw Jagiello and the words 'Founder of a Free Union of the Peoples of East Central Europe, Victor over the Teutonic Aggressors at Grunwald, 15 July 1410'.[33] The Lithuanians too had placed a bronze statue of their national hero, Grand Duke Vytautas, in their pavilion during the same fair.[34] The artist was Vytautas Kašuba.

---

[31] Ibid., 84-85.
[32] Ibid., 85.
[33] Ibid., 88.
[34] K.R. Jurgėla, '1410.VII.15. Mūšis Eglijos Girioje. Įžanginis žodis', *Karys. Pasaulio Lietuvių Karių-Veteranų Mėnesinis Žurnalas. The Warrior. Magazine for the Veterans of Lithuanian Descent and for Lithuanians in the Wide World,* vi (1960), 162-200, photo at 163.

Fig. 19.5   New York: 'King Jagiello' with two raised and crossed swords at the
1939 World's Fair. The statue was later moved to Central Park

During the Second World War, as has already been indicated, monuments like these with a 'national content' were singled out and destroyed by the occupying German forces. The great rider statue of Jagiełło in Kraków was one classic example. The great propagandistic display carried out under the name of the 'Repatriation of the Flags (*Einholung der Fahnen*)' was another.[35] On this occasion. eighteen copies of the flags of the conquered Teutonic army of 1410 that were discovered in the Wawel Castle, were moved from the office of the Governor General Hans Frank in Kraków to Marienburg in 'Reichsgau Danzig/West Prussia' to be stored in the grand master's castle.[36]

The First Post-War Years

Following the end of the Second World War the Poles had the opportunity for the first time in their history to erect monuments on the battlefield of Grunwald itself. By 9 May 1945 celebrations were already taking place at the battlefield, and it appeared certain that the anniversary of the victory of 1410 would also be commemorated there. The otherwise modest monument was decorated with crosses and an outdoor Mass was celebrated. Later, during the Communist era, religious monuments and symbolism were banned. Informative materials about the appearance of this 1945 monument are today available in the form of films and photographs.[37]

A new and larger monument, with additional elements reflecting the political and social changes in post-war Poland, was inaugurated on this same site on 11 October 1953. Religious symbolism was absent; instead there was the memorialization not only of the Grunwald warriors but also of the ten-year existence of the (Communist) Polish People's Army.[38] In accord with the Soviet Government, on 15 July 1943, the First Infantry Division 'Tadeusz Kościuszko' was sworn in in the Soviet Union, and on 12 October that same year they had received their baptism of fire in the battle at Lenino.[39] Through the inauguration of the new monument on 11 October 1953, the two battles of Grunwald and Lenino were symbolically bound with each other. The powerful obelisk was furnished with a corresponding inscription on a stone tablet to which a shield and two swords were attached. In 1960, in the process of constructing the monument grounds, the obelisk was demolished and the inscription tablet and the bronze shield placed in a museum.[40]

---

[35] Ekdahl, 'Tannenberg/Grunwald', in *JBS*, 287-88, with the relevant literature.
[36] See Figures 13-16 in id., *Die Schlacht bei Tannenberg.*
[37] Id., 'Die Grunwald-Denkmäler', 90-91.
[38] Id., *Die Schlacht bei Tannenberg*, 27-28.
[39] J. Gutkowski, '15 lipca 1943 – Przysięga Kościuszkowców', in *Grunwald. 550 lat chwały,* ed. J.St. Kopczewski and M. Siuchniński (Warsaw, 1960), 324-29.
[40] Ekdahl, 'Die Grunwald-Denkmäler', 91.

The Monument Grounds of 1960

The political history of post-war Poland to 1990 was dominated by two constants: its dependence on the Soviet Union and its opposition to the Federal Republic of Germany. The latter, unlike the position assumed by the German Democratic Republic from 1950, officially declined to recognize the Oder-Neiße as Poland's definitive border. Recognition of this border by West Germany was first made in the Warsaw Treaty of 1970 and then definitively in 1990 by a reunited Germany. A strong national consciousness came to be intimately associated with the border question which, especially after the 'Polish October' of 1956, was promoted by Władysław Gomułka, First Secretary of the Central Committee. The party and the government henceforth endeavoured to channel such strong feelings of patriotism and exploit them for their political ends. The most obvious example of this was the erection of large monument grounds on the battlefield at Grunwald in 1960. In the background lay the overshadowing problem of the Oder-Neiße border.[41]

The history of the creation of these grounds will be discussed elsewhere. The winners of the competition to design and construct the grounds were the sculptor Bandura and the architect Cęckiewicz. Their project included several elements: an obelisk, a bundled prism of tall flagpoles, and a large sculptural map which allowed the visitor to contemplate the position of the armies before the battle (which Polish historians had surmised). The latter could then be seen from the elevated steps of an amphitheatre. Inside the amphitheatre there was a museum, a cinema, and a lecture hall. It was important that the place containing the remains of the chapel that the Teutonic Knights had built in 1411, lying nearly 500 meters to the south-west, be incorporated into the planning. In the less immediate area, the places where, according to Polish historians, Jagiełło and Vytautas had stayed during the different phases of the battle, were marked by flags on metal poles. In accordance with old Grunwald tradition, mounds had been piled up at these locations where the poles were placed. The so-called 'Jagiełło's mound' is an example of this.

The great monumentality of the grounds is visible from a long distance. The most prominent part is the obelisk, over ten metres high, made of Silesian granite and depicting the dark faces of two knights (Figure 19.6). Not far afield, eleven flagpoles, each thirty metres high, stand out very prominently. They carry the standards of the Polish and Lithuanian armies, symbolizing the battle standards planted after the victorious battle on conquered lands.

---

[41] For the following, id., *Die Schlacht bei Tannenberg*, 29-34; id., 'Tannenberg/ Grunwald', 92-100.

Fig. 19.6   Tannenberg-Grunwald: The obelisk of 1960 (Photo D. Heckmann, 2005)

The amphitheatre steps serve as a point from which the sculptured map, 18.5 by 23.5 metres, can be studied. On entering the museum, until some years ago, the visitor encountered a metal urn full of soil carried from 130 battlefields upon which Polish soldiers and partisans had fought against the Germans from 963 to 1945. Since 1960 the exhibition has had to undergo several changes to reflect the political landscape of Polish–German relations.[42]

It was not only at Grunwald that such monuments were erected in 1960. A similar monument stands before the Bishop's Palace in Wolbórz. It was here that the Polish army detachment from southern Poland had assembled from 24 to 26 June 1410 before marching off towards Prussia.[43]

In the Soviet Republic of Lithuania it was not possible to have similar celebrations organized: it was not in Soviet interests to promote Lithuanian national sentiments, to refresh the collective memory. As far as the battle of Tannenberg was concerned, it was above all important for Soviet historiography that the meaning of the aid troops provided by Russia in 1410 be explicitly emphasized as being of vital significance to the victory over the Teutonic Knights. Indeed remembrance celebrations took place in Moscow in 1960.[44] That year in the Lithuanian capital of Vilnius only a modest memorial stone with the inscription '1410' and the name of the battle in Lithuanian and Russian was allowed on the path leading to the castle of the Lithuanian Grand Dukes (Gediminas's Castle, the Upper Castle).[45] (See Figure 19.7.)

---

[42]   I am grateful to Mr Romuald Odoj, head of the Grunwald Museum, who has always provided me with whatever information I required.

[43]   Ekdahl, 'Die Grunwald-Denkmäler', 100.

[44]   Id., *Die Schlacht bei Tannenberg*, 33-34.

[45]   Id., 'Tannenberg/Grunwald', in *JBS*, 298-89. For more information on the history of monuments in the Baltic countries during the Soviet era, A. Butrimas, 'Denkmäler in Westlitauen: Errichtung (1928-1944), Zerstörung (1945-1954) und Wiederaufbau (1988-1991)', in *Das Denkmal*, 167-83; L. Bremša, 'Denkmäler des Ersten Weltkrieges und der Freiheitskämpfe in Lettland aus den Jahren 1920-1940', in ibid., 185-203; O. Spārītis, 'Politisches Handeln und die Frage des nationalen Bewußtseins bei Denkmälern russischer und deutscher Herkunft in Riga', in ibid., 205-40; K. Kodres, 'Restaurierung und das Problem der nationalen Identität. Paradoxa der sowjetischen Kulturpolitik in Estland', in ibid., 241-72; J. Maiste, 'Denkmalpflege in Estland. Die Suche nach Identität', in ibid., 273-320. Also S. Ekdahl, '"Nationale Identitäten in den baltischen Ländern im Spiegel der Kunst". Eine Tagung der Ostsee-Akademie vom 25.-27. August 1995 in Lübeck-Travemünde', in ibid., 351-68.

Fig. 19.7   Vilnius: Stone tablet commemorating the battle of Žalgiris-Grjunval'd, now lost. (Photo S. Ekdahl, 1991)

Three Decades of 'Grunwald' 1960-1990

The large, centrally organized Grunwald celebrations in Poland in 1960 reached their high point with the inauguration of the new monument grounds on Sunday, 17 July in the presence of high party and government officials, as well as delegates and representatives of the Soviet Union and other Eastern Block countries.[46](See Figure 19.8.) The events included mass demonstrations by youth, the army, and the air force (Figure 19.9). No costs were spared to demonstrate the 'unity, strength, and vigilance of the Polish people'. It was a clear attempt to achieve a domestic policy showing solidarity with the government by riding a wave of national sentiment. It was also an attempt to demonstrate a foreign policy showing national harmony and strength, and above all else to clarify the definitiveness of the western, i.e. the Oder-Neiße, border of the country. The religious symbolism which had earlier been so intimately bound with 'Grunwald' was allowed to fall by the wayside.

19.8   Tannenberg-Grunwald: Władysław Gomułka, First Secretary of the Polish United Workers Party, was the main personality during the Grunwald celebrations in 1960 (Courtesy Trybuna Ludu)

---

[46]   For literature, see n. 41 *supra*.

Fig. 19.9   Tannenberg-Grunwald: Sixteen Ilyushin bombers and 64 MIG fighters demonstrated Polish military effectiveness during the celebrations of 1960 (Courtesy Trybuna Ludu)

In a speech on the occasion of Poland's millennium celebrations in 1966, the minister for education and later chairman of the council of state, Henryk Jabłoński, stressed that the Grunwald anniversary six years earlier 'was aimed at evoking a public demonstration of national feelings':

> As previously indicated [he said], the Grunwald anniversary was conceived as a great national manifestation, commemorating a particular event of great historic significance, viewed against the wider background of history Applying the same standards to scientific research, we see this wider background extending to Polish-German relations in general, to the struggle for the western and northern borders of Poland, and to the efforts to preserve the Polish character of the territories held by Germany at various periods. Such an approach, fully shared by the authors of the programme of the celebrations, links these issues not only with the Grunwald anniversary, but also with the origins of Polish statehood, the history of the national liberation struggle, and also People's Poland as the state which enabled Poland to recover the territories seized by a foreign power.[47]

After the Grunwald festival that had brought the whole nation together, it took until 1973 before a new component was added to those monuments already existing on the battlefield. That year, near the amphitheater, the heirs of the war traditions of the First Kościuszko Division unveiled a memorial dedicated to the thirty-year existence of the division and to the 563-year-old victory lying further in the past.[48] In 1978 a tablet with another inscription was added.

Towards the end of the Second World War, it was decided to reconstruct the rider figure of Jagiełło in Kraków which the Germans had destroyed in 1939. These plans materialized in 1976. Since no cast or model of the old monument had survived, the figures had to be newly modelled by hand on available images of the original and then cast in bronze. The unveiling by the chairman of the council of state, Henryk Jabłoński, took place on 16 October 1976. The choice of date again symbolically bound together the victors of the 1410 battle of Grunwald and the Polish People's Army.

The Catholic Church did not participate in the celebrations, but to keep in line with tradition, it wished to contribute to the memory of 'Grunwald' and forestall both state and party. On Sunday, 10 October 1976, the archbishop of Kraków, Cardinal Karol Wojtyła, later Pope John Paul II, read a proclamation to all the churches of Kraków, stating that on 15 October, on the eve of the unveiling ceremony, Mass would be said on the occasion of the Grunwald festival at the Wawel cathedral. The cardinal himself celebrated the Mass and after the service delivered a sermon.[49]

In another symbolic gesture, the stones which had been preserved from the pedestal of the statue of Jagiełło were handed over by the 'Committee for the Construction of the Grunwald Monument' in Kraków to the province of Olsztyn.

---

[47]   H. Jabłoński, 'Poland's Millennium as Reflected in the Work of Polish Scientists', *The Review of the Polish Academy of Science*, xii (1967), 3, 1-13, at 6-7. See Ekdahl, 'Tannenberg/Grunwald', 290-91.

[48]   Id., *Die Schlacht bei Tannenberg*, 35.

[49]   Id., 'Die Grunwald-Denkmäler', 101. For more information on the monument, Urbańczyk (with several photos).

It was intended to 'bear witness to the eternal cult of national history' and to record the wishes of the monument's benefactor, Ignacy Paderewski. The stones were fashioned into an irregular obelisk, symbolizing 'a resurrection from the ashes'. An inscription recalls the history of the old monument and the stones. The monument was inaugurated on 17 October 1983, on the occasion of the fortieth anniversary of the birth of the People's Army.[50]

A year later, the 1901 German commemorative tablet of the fallen Grand Master Ulrich of Jungingen was laid, face down, into the ground outside the walls encircling the chapel ruins. Next to it lay a smaller tablet with an explanatory text.[51] (See Figure 19.10.)

Fig 19.10   Tannenberg-Grunwald: In 1984, the German memorial stone tablet of 1901 was laid, face down, outside the ruins of Mary chapel. Next to it lay a smaller tablet with an explanatory text.

In the 1990s, a new memorial in the form of a concrete frieze, 0.5 by 11 metres, was added. It had been submitted to a monument-design competition in 1959 but had failed to qualify. The frieze depicted the battle of Grunwald, with the middle section portraying cavalry battles between the victorious Poles and the Teutonic Knights. The knights are shown either being knocked off their horses or already fallen. Had

---

[50]   Ekdahl, 'Die Grunwald-Denkmäler', 101-102, with reference to other literature.

[51]   Ibid., 102. See id., *Die Schlacht bei Tannenberg*, 369; ibid., Figure 64 shows the stones stored on the battlefield, before they were arranged to form a monument.

the frieze been built according to the artist's vision, it would have been a colossal monument, 18 meters high and 220 meters long.[52]

Continuation and New Beginning after 1990

The monument grounds at Tannenberg–Grunwald–Žalgiris commemorate the victory of Poland and Lithuania over the Teutonic Order in 1410, but it can equally be claimed that they represent the country's struggle from 1945 to have the Oder-Neiße border recognized by the Germans. Within the framework of domestic politics, it represents a clear attempt to promote solidarity with the government and party of the People's Republic through the instrumentalization of symbols so deeply rooted in the conscience of the Polish people.

The great changes that the political landscape of Central and Eastern Europe had undergone after the break-up of both communism and the Soviet empire, together with Germany's recognition in 1990 of the Oder-Neiße as Poland's undisputed western border – all these had direct consequences on 'Grunwald'. The victory of 1410 would no longer be exploited as a political symbol, lest it hinders the chances of any genuine reconciliation between Poland and Germany.[53]

The annual Grunwald festivals organized at the battlefield have always been, and still are, seismographic indicators of the current state of Polish–German relations. In 1990, after decades of conspicuous absence, the church again made an appearance at the festival. That year the symbolism of Grunwald began to lose its true meaning. The plans for the expansion of the monument grounds, ratified by the 'All Polish Grunwald Committee' in 1986, were laid *ad acta* and the committee was dissolved.[54] No more funds flowed from the state, but solely from the province of Olsztyn and from certain sponsors like Polish Telecom.[55] The symbolically oriented formation of the museum now assumed a historical significance, where the visitor could appreciate the real facts concerning the events of 1410.[56]

---

[52] Id., 'Die Grunwald-Denkmäler', 102. A photo from 1977 in id., *Die Schlacht bei Tannenberg*, shows the tablet with the old German inscription chiselled away by order of communist authorities; and ibid., Figure 7.

[53] Id., 'Die Grunwald-Denkmäler', 107, with a photo at 106.

[54] Id., 'Tannenberg/Grunwald', in *JBS*, 295-98.

[55] Ibid.

[56] Polish and later French Telecom have sponsored the Grunwald Festivals with huge funds since 1998.

PART IV
Hospitallers

Chapter 20

The Decree of 1262: A Glimpse into the Economic Decision-Making of the Hospitallers

Judith Bronstein

Historians who have studied the international deployment of the military orders have not paid much attention to the influence which political and economic changes had on their houses in Europe, and to the implications these changes would have for their ability to support the convent in the Holy Land. The same is true for the strategies of policy-making and institutional changes adopted by their headquarters to face changing historical circumstances. Because the Hospitallers were an international order, it is very important to understand these links. The lack of evidence is the main obstacle in the way to studying the order's organizational functions. I believe, however, that there is a way to get around this lack of evidence by re-examining the circumstances, leading to the order's legislation of 1262, which, among other things, forbade the alienation of its property. In this way, it would be possible to reconstruct its process of policy making, which could give us a much better understanding of the ways the Hospital operated as an international order.[1]

The years leading to the 1262 chapter were years of adversity for the Hospitallers in the Latin East. In 1244, as a result of the defeat at the battle of La Forbie, they lost territory, including the castle of Ascalon, which they had refortified only that year, and suffered enormous casualties.[2] These losses were rapidly replaced with brothers shipped from Europe, who took part, only four years later, in the Egyptian crusade of St Louis. For this crusade, large sums of money were also required for the employment of mercenaries, the building of war machines, and the general maintenance of their forces.[3] Resources to take part in military campaigns and to rebuild the Hospitallers'

---

[1]   This article was written in 2000. Since then I have published *The Hospitallers and the Holy Land. Financing the Latin East, 1187–1274* (Woodbridge, Boydell & Brewer, 2005), which includes an expanded analysis of these events.

[2]   On the battle and its consequences, Salimbene de Adam, 'Cronica', *MGH SS*, xxxii, 17; Matthew Paris, *Chronica Maiora*, ed. H. R. Luard (Rolls Series 57, London 1871-83), iv, 307-11, 337-44. For an estimation of the order's casualties, J. Riley-Smith's commentary in *Ayyubids, Mamlukes and Crusaders. Selections from the Tarikh al-Duwal wa'l Muluk of Ibn al-Furat*, ed. J. Riley-Smith, trans. U and M. C. Lyon (Cambridge, 1971), 173 note 2 to page 5 (cited hereafter as Ibn al-Furat).

[3]   For the order's mobilization after La Forbie, J. Bronstein, 'The Mobilization of Hospitallers' Manpower from Europe to the Latin East in the Thirteenth century', in

economy in the East after La Forbie were needed, however, at a time when – so it seems – there was a decrease in their local income in the Holy Land. Their agricultural production was affected by continuous raids on their territories. In 1252 Turcomanes had raided the principality of Antioch and the surroundings of Crac des Chevaliers and Tripoli. A year later, Ayyubid forces pillaged the surroundings of Acre and destroyed the mills of the Templars and the Hospitallers at Doc and Recordane.[4] The Mongol incursions prevented the cultivation of the land. The shortage of food and its increasing prices forced the Christians in Syria to import foodstuff from abroad.[5] Many letters of appeal sent to the West emphasized their lack of weapons, men, provisions, and money.[6] The Mongol invasion and the civil war that was fought in Acre in the late 1250s, caused the decline of Acre and other Frankish coastal cities as centres of international trade.[7] These changes must also have affected the order's independent sources of income in the East from trading with expensive merchandise such as sugar, in the industrial production of which the Hospitallers seem to have been intensively involved throughout the thirteenth century.[8]

Out of consideration for the Hospitallers' financial strain, Pope Alexander IV granted them monies collected from the redemption of crusading vows in Europe.[9] In 1255 and 1256, Alexander also allowed the transfer to the Hospitallers of the abbey of Mt Thabor and the nunnery of St Lazarus of Bethany with all their assets, rights, and privileges.[10] These are important transactions aimed at enlarging the order's income in the East. St Lazarus owned extensive properties and land in the dioceses of Tyre, Tripoli, Valenia, and Gibelet. Mt Thabor's most important possessions, between Nazareth and the Sea of Galilee, constituted a large proportion of what little

---

International Mobility in the Military Orders, eds. H. J. Nicholson and J. Burgtorf (Cardiff, 2006), 29-30.On their participation in St Louis's crusade, John of Beaumont, 'Lettre à Geoffroi de la Chapelle sur la prise de Damiette', *AOL*, i, 389-90; Matthew Paris, vi, 192, 196-97.

⁴   Ibid., 205-07; *CH*, 2605, 3045; *Eracles*, 440-41.

⁵   Ibn al-Furat, 43.

⁶   See, for example, 'Menkonis Chronicon', *MGH SS*, xxiii, 547-49; *RRH*, 1288; 'Lettre à Charles d'Anjou sur les affaires de Terre Sainte', ed. C.V.Langlois, *Bibliotèque de L'École des Chartes*, lxxviii (1917), 487-90.

⁷   J. Riley-Smith, *The Feudal Nobility and the Kingdom of Jerusalem, 1174-1277* (London, 1973), 25, 215-17; id., *The Crusades: a Short History* (London and New Haven, 1987), 200-203; P. W. Edbury, *John of Ibelin and the Kingdom of Jerusalem* (Woodbridge, 1997), 61-62; R. Irwin, 'The Supply of Money and the Direction of Trade in the Thirteenth Century', *Coinage in the Latin East, The Fourth Oxford Symposium on Coinage and Monetary History*, eds. P. W. Edbury and D. M. Metcalf (British Archaeological Reports, series, 77) (Oxford , 1980), 73-84.

⁸   There is ample evidence for the involvement of the Hospitallers in the industrial production of sugar in, for example, casal Manueth and Cabor, in the vicinity of Acre and Boutoufarig (Bethorafig) in the county of Tripoli, which had sugar-cane plantations. See *CH*, 1383, 1991, 1996, 2200, 2875, 2915, 3106.

⁹   *CH*, 2772, 2906. For a similar grant to the Templars, *Malteser Urkunden und Regesten zur Geschichte der Tempelherren und der Johanniter*, ed. H.G. Prutz, (Munich, 1883), 60-61, no. 260. This privilege was first given to the orders by Innocent IV. See *CH*, 2462; M. Barber, *The New Knighthood* (Cambridge, 1994), 231-32.

¹⁰   *CH*, 2781, 2925, 2927, 2929, 2726-27.

agricultural land remained in the kingdom of Jerusalem.[11] In addition to these grants, the Hospitallers made great efforts to expand their holdings of agricultural lands in the East by acquiring a large number of *casalia*, mainly in Galilee, and by leasing and purchasing urban property in all the remaining Christian cities.[12]

To meet these expenditures in the East great pressure was put on their priories in Europe. A letter issued by Pope Innocent IV in May 1247 illustrates this point. Innocent forbade the prelates to demand from the houses of the Hospitallers and the Templars in Europe the money imposed on the church to support the Holy See. He explained that owing to the miserable state of the orders in the East, they were expecting immediate supplies from their houses overseas.[13] It is important to emphasize, however, that very little information has survived regarding the supplies sent to the East. We know that the priories were required to send *responsiones* first to Jerusalem, and after 1191 to Acre. From letters sent by the officers of the order in Acre to the West, we learn that they expected additional shipments of provisions and money in times of crisis.[14] And yet, no inventories or shipment lists have been found for the twelfth and thirteenth centuries.[15] Moreover, the material which has survived for the Hospitallers in Europe is to be found in cartularies of commanderies, which dealt only with local issues. They did not include any references to the connections of these houses to the order's headquarters in the East. Nevertheless, although we lack specific evidence, it is possible to assess the response of European priories to crises in the East by studying their economic activities, and I have assumed that the needs of the order in the East would have been reflected in its economic policy in the West.

Indeed, from the late 1240s on, in the years following La Forbie and St Louis's crusade, there was a sharp decline in the number of acts found in cartularies of 'French' commanderies – houses under the command of the priories of France, Auvergne, and St Gilles. This apparent decrease could be explained by a lack of

---

[11]   On the importance of St Lazarus of Bethany and Mt. Thabor, J. Riley-Smith, *The Knights of St John in Jerusalem and Cyprus, c.1050-1310* (London, 1967), 401-403, 415, 424-25, 427; B. Hamilton, *The Latin Church in the Crusader States* (London, 1980), 299-300.

[12]   *CH,* 2747-48, 2934, 2936, 3050-51, 3414. For the acquisition of lands and properties in the city and the surroundings of Acre, *RRH*, 1212, 1227; *CH*. 2661, 2732, 2753, 2865. For their expansion in the lordship of Caesarea, S. Tibble, *Monarchy and Lordships in the Latin Kingdom of Jerusalem*, 1099-1291 (Oxford, 1989), 132, 151; for the county of Tripoli, *CH*, 2875, 2915, 3106; J. Richard, 'Le comtè de Tripoli dans les chartes du fonds des Porcellet', *Bibliotèque de l'École des Chartes*, cxxx (1972), 360-82. For the acquisition of the lordships of Sidon and Arsur by the Templars and the Hospitallers in the 1260s, Barber, 243-44, 364, n. 65; Riley-Smith, *Feudal Nobility*, 32; and id., *The Knights of St John*, 133-34, 455-56.

[13]   *CH,* 2441.

[14]   In 1201, for example, the master wrote to the prior of England, asking for money; he explained that war in Sicily prevented the supply of food to the Holy Land.   *CH*, 1131

[15]   Although the rules of the order demanded that written accounts be sent from Europe together with the *responsiones*, and the commander of the vault, who was responsible for the warehouses of the order in Acre (appeared only in 1264) was supposed to have issued receipts; none of these have as yet been found. Riley-Smith, *The Knights of St John*, 308-12.

sources, as only few of the order's surviving cartularies cover the years beyond 1240.[16] Yet, even cartularies that include material for later years show a drastic decline in the number of charters. For the period between 1250 and 1260, the order's general cartulary includes only two acquisitions of property and two donations in France.[17] Although Delaville's cartulary is incomplete, other sources give similar indications. The cartulary of Fieffes includes only one acquisition of an annual rent of oats, while the cartulary of Eterpigny records only one purchase.[18]

This decline in the number of charters was typical not only of the Hospitallers, it was shared by other military orders.[19] It could mainly be explained as the result of economic changes leading to acute inflation in Europe.[20] This unstable situation seems to have affected regions which were central for the supply of *responsiones* to the East, such as Provence. The impoverishment of the nobility there caused a decline in the number of donations to religious houses, including the military orders.[21] These financial difficulties had to be faced at a time of increasing demands from the East, and resulted in the alienation of property in Europe. Malcolm Barber has already referred to the fact that the Templars were allowed by Innocent IV to sell property in Provence, England, and Aquitaine in order to cover the debts incurred during St Louis's crusade.[22] Some of the Hospitaller houses in Europe seem to have also been heavily in debt. In June 1257 Pope Alexander IV forbade the bishop of Orvieto from demanding money from the order. He stressed that 'the brothers run into heavy debts owing to the necessities they assigned to maintain the poor and support the Holy Land'.[23] To cover their debts the Hospitallers in Europe were also disposing of

---

[16] For example, the *Cartulaire du Prieuré de Saint Gilles de l'Hôpital de Saint Jean de Jérusalem (1129-1210)*, eds. D. Le Blevec and A. Venturini (Paris, 1997), and the *Cartulaire de Trinquetaille*, ed. P. A. Amarguier (Aix, 1972). See also D. Le Blevec and A. Venturini, 'Cartulaires des ordres militaires, XII-XIII siècles (Provence Occidentale, Basse Valle du Rhône)', *Les Cartulaires. Actes de la table ronde, organisée par l'École National des Chartes et le G.D.R 121 du C.N.R.S*, eds. O. Guyotjeannin, L. Morelle, and M. Parisse (Paris, 1993), 451-65.

[17] *CH*, 2544, 2648; 2690, 2965.

[18] Paris, Archives Nationales, Cartulaire de Fieffes, S5533, fols. 174v-175; Paris, BN, Cartulaire de Eterpigny, nouv. acq. lat. 927, fol. 59.

[19] A. Forey, *The Templars in the Corona de Aragón* (London, 1973), 60-61, 308-47; H. Nicholson, *Templars, Hospitallers and Teutonic Knight: Images of the Military Orders, 1128-1291* (Leicester, 1993), 65-8; D. Le Blevec, 'Les Hospitaliers de Saint Jean de Jérusalem en Bais-Vivarais: la commanderie de Trignan, XII-XIII siècles', *Religion et société en Ardèche et dans l'ancien pays de Vivarais, actes du 2 colloque*, ed. M. Riou (Privas, 1985), 22.

[20] G. Sivery, *L'économie du Royaume de France au siècle de Saint Louis* (Lille, 1984), 59-133; R. Fossier, *Le Moyen Âge, Le Temps des Crises, 1250-1520* (Paris, 1983), 24-27.

[21] P. Sigal, 'Une seigneurie ecclesiastique en Provence orientale au Moyen Âge: Le Commanderie de Ruou', *Provence Historique*, xv (1965), 129-33.

[22] *Les Registres d'Innocent IV*, ed. É. Berger (Paris, 1884-1921), nos. 6256, 6237. For additional evidence on the alienation of Templar property in Europe to support its activities in the East, see also 'Annales Monasterii de Burton, 1004-1263', ed. H. R. Luard, *Annales Monastici*, i, RS 36 (London, 1864), 491-95; Barber, 160-61.

[23] 'eorumdem fratrum gravamen indebitum sustinere, utpote quorum bona sustentationi pauperum et Terre Sancte subsidio sunt specialiter deputata'. *CH*, 2878.

property. In May 1257 Alexander instructed the head of the religious houses of St Etienne de Beaunne, in the diocese of Autun, to revoke alienation of property made by the Hospitaller priory of France. This letter was sent in response to an appeal to the pope, in which the Hospitallers explained that they had to sell or rent for life property incurring great losses.[24] After 1250, both the Hospitallers and the Templars in France appealed several times to the pope, asking for the annulment of their transactions.[25] Other regions, which were important for supplying the East, such as the order's houses in England, seem also to have been facing financial difficulties. In October 1256, Alexander IV forbade the alienation of Hospitaller property in England, which was made without the approval of their prior.[26] In March 1262, Urban IV wrote to the Hospitallers in this kingdom that letters, which had arrived at the curia, showed that they owed several sums to creditors. He, however, forbade the liquidation of the order's property to repay them.[27]

The disposal of property in Europe was a threat to the future abilities of these houses to send *responsiones* to the East. In 1262 the master Hugh Revel convened a general chapter, which in an attempt to overcome this crisis adopted a long-term economic policy. The chapter claimed that the commanders overseas had alienated property for which they received a large down payment and low rents; in a time of inflation such cash would lose its value very quickly. The chapter decreed, therefore, that the order's property should not be leased. Only in cases in which it would not be profitable, or in which it is not possible to keep the property, would it be leased for the largest rent that could be obtained. Strong measures were also taken to control the priors overseas, and they were ordered to keep a record of all their lands, vineyards, and meadows.[28]

The legislation of 1262 is one of the few surviving records of decrees legislated by the chapter regarding institutional international issues. Moreover, evidence for a definite policy also allows us to examine how institutional decisions were implemented and how successful the order was in this respect. It is particularly interesting to examine their ability to implement changes in policy in the 1260s and the 1270s, when the situation of the order in the East and its financial situation in Europe deteriorated rapidly. Ten years of unceasing Mamluk incursions caused the almost complete devastation of the order's military disposition and economy in the Levant. The Hospitallers lost all their castles except for Margat, and lost the major part of their agricultural lands, with a consequent loss of income from money rents

---

[24]   *CH*, 2873.

[25]   F. Reynaud, *La commanderie de l'Hôpital de Rhodes et de Malte à Manosque* (Gap, 1981), 49; *Malteser Urkunden*, no. 322.

[26]   *CH*, 2834-35. Decree no. 12 of the statutes of Margat, from 1206 (*CH*, 1193) forbade alienations of property, which had not been approved by Hospitaller officials and the central government. On restrictions imposed on the alienation of Church property, see *Dictionnaire de Droit Canonique*, ed. R. Naz (Paris, 1935-65), i, col. 403-415; ibid., ii, col. 377-80.

[27]   *CH*, 3016.

[28]   Ibid., 3039, clauses 15, 16, 23, 25. On the 1262 chapter, Riley-Smith, *The Knights of St John*, 346-47; also A. Luttrell, 'The Hospitallers' Early Written Records', *The Crusades and their Sources. Essays Presented to Bernard Hamilton*, eds. J. France and W. G. Zajac (Aldershot, 1998), 151.

and agricultural products. All their efforts to rehabilitate these lands were frustrated with each new Mamluk incursion. The Hospitallers and the Christian settlers in the East were besieged in a few towns along the coast and were completely dependent on supplies from Europe.[29] And yet, when help was most needed, some of the order's most important priories were unable to supply the East. They were faced not only with financial difficulties at home and increasing demands from the East. From the late 1260s, the Hospitallers' resources in Europe were diverted to support Charles of Anjou's campaigns in southern Italy.[30] In these circumstances the decree of 1262 became impractical. Short of cash, the priories kept alienating property.[31]

The main aim of the Hospitallers was charity and fighting for the Holy Land. To do that, they needed to create an economic structure. However, once created, this structure seems to have taken on a life of its own. Institutional decisions taken by the master and the chapter in the Holy Land, would, as in this case, clash with local economic policies. Practical policies implemented locally took precedence; the master failed to impose central economic decisions on the European priories.

---

[29]   The distressing situation of the Latin settlement was described in many letters of appeal sent to the West. See, for example, *RRH*, 1347-48; *Thesaurus novus anectdotorum*, eds. E. Martène and U. Durand (Paris, 1717, repr. Farnborough, 1968) i, col. 1013-14.

[30]   *CH*, 3308 (vol. iv). On the order's involvement in Charles's campaigns, see also *CH*, 3221; A. Forey, 'The Military Orders and the Holy War again Christians in the Thirteenth Century', *Military Orders and the Crusades* (Aldershot, 1994), essay number vii, 1-14.

[31]   See, for example, *CH*, 3492, 3539.

Chapter 21

The Hospitaller Order in Acre and Manueth: The Ceramic Evidence

Edna J. Stern

Historical sources reveal much about the wide range of activities the Hospitaller order performed during the second Latin Kingdom of Jerusalem; these include caring for the poor, the sick, and the pilgrims in the Holy Land, together with activities of a military and economic nature.

Archaeological excavations recently conducted in the northern part of Israel by the Israel Antiquities Authority have uncovered tangible evidence of the Hospitallers' material culture, allowing for a further investigation into their activities. Presented here are the ceramic finds from two sites already known to be connected with the Hospitaller order. The first site is the Hospitaller compound in the capital of the second Latin Kingdom of Jerusalem, Acre;[1] the second is a rural sugar production site lying in the agricultural hinterland of Acre, Manueth[2] (Figure 21.1).

Assigning ceramic types to a specific group of people is a very debatable practice. Since ceramic vessels were commonly used in everyday life – either for storing, preparing, and serving food, or for commercial and industrial purposes, the function usually dictated the shape of the vessel. Such functionally determined vessels may be used freely by different groups of people regardless of their traditions. It is thus usually difficult to identify an ethnic group solely on the basis of the ceramic vessels that they used. However, a specific shape and decoration of the vessels may hint at a certain ethnic group. The annals of archaeology record many such attempts. In biblical archaeology, the attempt to identify Philistine settlements through the ceramic remains is just one classic example.[3]

It is easier to try to associate pots with people during the thirteen century, the period we are dealing with here. The wealth and variety of historical sources from this period help to identify specific structures with the Hospitaller order with a fairly reasonable degree of accuracy. The finds in these identifiable structures allow researchers to examine the phenomenon of the connection of specific ceramic types

[1]   E. Stern, 'La Commanderie de l'Order des Hospitaliers à Acre', *Bulletin Monumental* clxiv, 1 (2006), 53–60.

[2]   E.J. Stern, 'Horbat Manot (Lower)', *Excavations and Surveys in Israel*, xviii (1998), 10–11; id., 'The Excavations at Lower Horbat Manot: A Medieval Sugar Production Site', *'Atiqot* xlii (2001), 277–308.

[3]   T. Dotan, 'Social Dislocation and Cultural Change in the 12th century B.C.E.', in *The Crisis Years: the 12th Century B.C. From Beyond the Danube to the Tigris*, ed. W.A. Ward and M. Sharp Joukowsky (Dubuque, Iowa, 1992), 93–98.

with the order. The ceramic assemblage from these sites may be compared to those from contemporaneous sites in the same geographical area in an endeavour to understand better the range and influence of the Hospital.

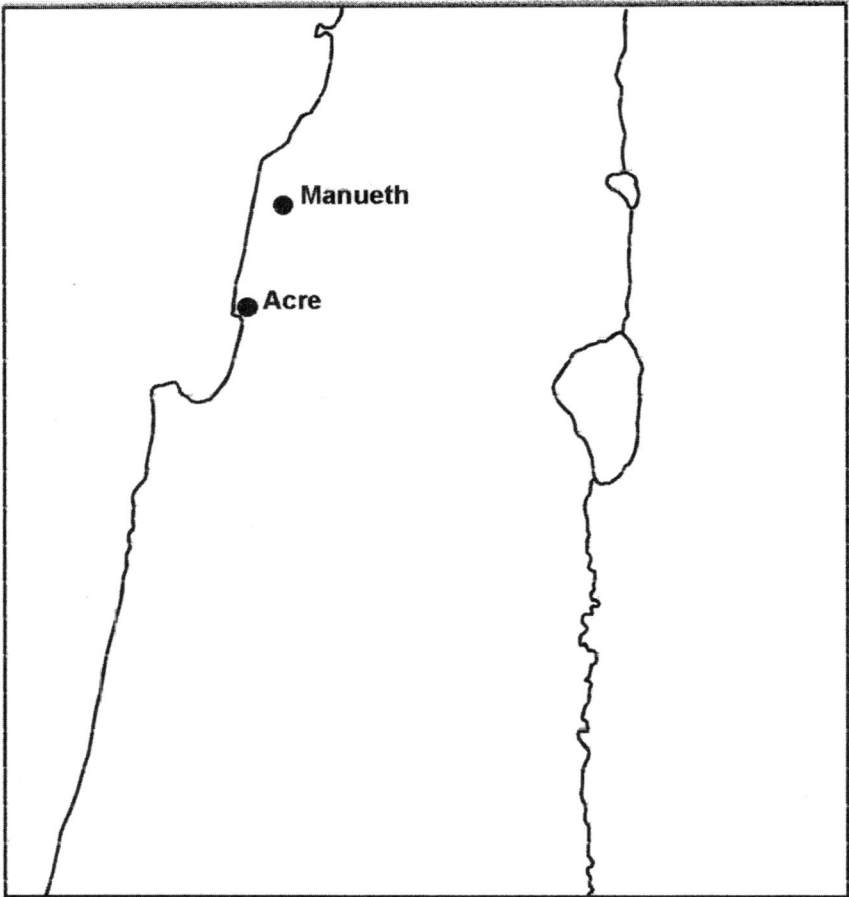

Fig. 21.1   Location of Acre and Manueth

The Hospitaller Compund of Acre

Large-scale excavations carried out by the Israel Antiquities Authority at the Hospitaller compound in Acre since the early 1990s have revealed a great variety of local and imported pottery types dating to the crusader period. The ceramic assemblage that has been found in the excavations of the Hospitaller compound is identical to those unearthed in other excavated locations in Acre.[4] It is also identical to assemblages uncovered at other Frankish towns, like 'Atlit,[5] Caesarea,[6] Tel Yoqne'am,[7] and other contemporary eastern Mediterranean sites.[8] However, the two types of vessel that will be discussed below appear in large quantities almost exclusively in the Hospitaller compound, and may thus be considered unique to this assemblage. It shall be posited that these two vessel types are directly connected with the activities of the Hospitaller order.

The ceramic assemblage from the Hospitaller compound consists in a variety of simple unglazed and glazed vessels.[9] The simple unglazed vessels are represented both by functional-shaped vessels, plates, bowls, basins, jugs, juglets, and jars, all made of local fabric common in the compound (Figure 21.2), and by transport amphorae imported from the eastern Mediterranean.

---

[4]   E.J. Stern, 'Excavation of the Courthouse Site at 'Akko: The Pottery of the Crusader and Ottoman Periods', *'Atiqot,* xxxi (1997), 35–70; D. Pringle, 'Excavations in Acre, 1974: The Pottery of the Crusader period from site D', *'Atiqot,* xxxi (1997), 137–56; D. Syon and A. Tatcher, 'Old 'Akko, The Kinghts' Parking', *Hadashot Arkheologiyot (Archaeological News)* cviii (1998), 17–24 (in Hebrew); E. Stern, 'Akko, The Old City', *Hadashot Arkheologiyot. Excavations and Surveys in Israel,* cix (1999), 10*-13*; H. Smithline and E. Stern ''Akko, Derekh Ha–Nof C', *Hadashot Arkheologiyot. Excavations and Surveys in Israel,* cx (1999), 12*–13*; E.J. Stern and M. Shalvi-Abbas, ''Akko, Ha-Gedud Ha-'Ivri Street', *Excavations and Surveys in Israel* 19 (1999), 10*–12*.

[5]   C. N. Johns, 'Excavations at Pilgrims Castle Atlit', *Quarterly of the Department of Antiquities of Palestine,* i (1932), 111–50; id., 'Medieval Slip Ware from Pilgrims Castle, Atlit (1930–1)', *Quarterly of the Department of Antiquities of Palestine,* iii (1934), 137–44; id., 'Excavations at Pilgrims Castle, 'Atlit (1932–3); Stables at the South-West of the Suburb', *Quarterly of the Department of Antiquities of Palestine,* v (1936), 31–74; D. Pringle, 'Some More Proto-Maiolica from 'Athlit (Pilgrims Castle) and a Discussion of its Distribution in the Levant', *Levant,* xiv (1982), 104–117.

[6]   N. Brosh, 'Pottery of the 8th–13th centuries C.E. strata 1–3', in *Excavations at Caesarea Maritima, 1975, 1976, 1979. Final Report (Qedem 21),* ed. L. I. Levine and E. Netzer (Jerusalem, 1986), 66–89; D. Pringle, 'Medieval Pottery from Caesarea: the Crusader Period', *Levant,* xvii (1985), 171–202; A. J. Boas, 'Islamic and Crusader pottery (c. 640–1265) from the Crusader city (Area P/4)', in *Caesarea Papers. Journal of Roman Archaeology Supplementary Series,* v (1992), 154–66; Y. Arnon, 'Islamic and Crusader pottery (area I, 1993–94)', in *Caesarea Papers 2. Journal of Roman Archaeology Supplementary Series,* xxxv (1999), 225–51.

[7]   M. Avissar, 'The Medieval Pottery', in *Yoqne'am I, The Late Periods (Qedem Reports 3),* A. Ben-Tor, M. Avissar and Y. Portogali (Jerusalem 1996), 75–172.

[8]   D. Pringle, 'Pottery as Evidence of Trade in the Crusader States', in *I Comuni Italiani nel Regno Crociato di Gerusalemme,* ed. G. Airaldi and B. Z Kedar (Genoa, 1986), 451–75.

[9]   For a detailed description and analytical study of the types of ceramic vessels from Acre, E.J Stern and S.Y. Waksman, 'Pottery from Crusader Acre: A Typological and Analytical Study', in *VIIe Congrès International sur la Céramique Médiévale en Méditerranée. Thessaloniki, 11-16 Octobre 1999,* ed. C. Bakirtzis (Athens, 2003), 167-80.

Fig. 21.2   Simple unglazed closed-shaped vessels and 'Acre Bowls' from the
             Hospitaller compound

The greater part of the cooking wares that have been discovered are local glazed
cooking vessels of two predominant shapes – closed globular cooking pots and open
shallow baking dishes. A recent analytical study reveals that the majority of these
cooking vessels were manufactured along the Levantine coast, most probably the
Lebanese littoral.[10] Other cooking vessels that were found in much smaller quantities
were imported into Acre. These included hand-made cooking pots from Cyprus, two
types of cooking vessels from Provence and Languedoc in southern France, and
shallow glazed baking dishes from Liguria in Italy.

Among the local glazed bowls are those with a green or yellow, low quality
glaze, with simple decorations in sgraffito, slip-painted, and reserved slip techniques.
Recent analytical study reveals that these bowls were likewise manufactured along
the Lebanese littoral.

Also unearthed were glazed vessels made of fritware and painted in black and/or
blue under a colourless alkaline glaze, originating from central Syria, and glazed
bowls with underglazed painting, coming from Egypt. Although these vessels were
produced in Islamic centres, they were nevertheless used by the Franks in Acre. It is
well known that the crusader kingdom had carried on a regular trade with its Muslim
neighbours despite the constant state of war between the two sides. These vessels
provide further supporting evidence of this commerce.

---

[10]   Ibid.

The imported glazed wares include such well-known types[11] as the 'Byzantine Fine Ware', the 'Aegean Wares', the 'Zeuxippus Ware' and sub-types of this family, the 'Cypriot thirteenth-century sgraffito and slip-painted wares', the 'Port St Symeon Ware', and 'Proto-maiolica Ware'.

The rare types of imported glazed wares include glazed vessels with a roulette decoration apparently produced in Venice at the end of the thirteenth century,[12] and the 'Cobalt and Manganese Ware' imported from Tunis.[13]

The most unique glazed bowls that have been found in Acre are the Chinese celadon bowls dated to the thirteenth century.[14] They are made of a fine stoneware and covered with a thick coat of shiny jade-coloured glaze. Acre was apparently a transit port for exporting the celadon to the West, mainly by Italian merchants. These bowls were found near what is thought to have been the refectory of the order, and it would appear that these luxury vessels were used by the Hospitallers.

The two vessel types also found in the Hospitaller compound and apparently indicative of the Hospitaller order are bowls and sugar vessels.

Large quantities of simple bowls of a uniform shape have been unearthed in the courtyard of the Hospitaller compound. The typical bowl has a short ledge rim, a hemispherical body, and a flat, string-cut base.[15] The fabric is coarse and gritty, and has a light coloured slip (Figure 21.2). This is a very simple bowl that seems to have been mass-produced. Over-fired wasters discovered in the Hospitaller compound and their scientific analysis indicate that they had been manufactured in Acre.[16] The same compound provided hundreds of examples of such bowls. Smaller quantities of the same type were found at all the other excavated sites within Acre, as well as in a number of rural sites in the close vicinity of Acre. They were not found, however, in other sites in Israel. It is precisely for this reason that they have been termed 'Acre bowls'.

Owing to the large amount that has been unearthed in the courtyard of the Hospitaller compound, I would like to suggest that these bowls were used to serve the pilgrims and the sick quartered at the hospice. It is possible that the Hospitallers themselves too ate from these bowls in their communal meals. It is therefore being proposed here that the 'Acre bowls' are indicative of the Hospitaller order and reflect some of their main activities, like their care of the sick, the poor, and the pilgrims in the Holy Land as well as their communal life in general.

The second type of ceramic vessel, found in large quantities in the compound, indicating a major economic activity of the Hospitallers, consisted of vessels employed in the production of sugar from sugar cane. These sugar pots, conical in shape with a hole at the tip, and the accompanying molasses jars, upon which

---

[11]   A.J. Boas, 'The Import of Western Ceramics to the Latin Kingdom of Jerusalem', *Israel Exploration Journal*, xliv (1994), 102–122.

[12]   S. Gelichi, 'Roulette Ware', *Medieval Ceramics*, viii (1984), 47–58.

[13]   Pringle, 'Ceasarea', 199 - 200, Fig. 16:90.

[14]   M. Medley, *The Chinese Potter. A Practical History of Chinese Pottery* (3rd edn., Oxford, 1989).

[15]   Stern, 'Pottery of the Courthouse site at 'Akko', 37–39, Fig. 4:1–9.

[16]   Stern and Waksman, 'Pottery from Crusader Acre'.

the sugar pots were placed, are well known from other sites in Israel and Cyprus[17] (Figure 21.3). In the excavation of two halls in the Hospitaller compound, these vessels were found shattered, lying as they were under a thick layer of stones and burnt debris, presumably a collapsed ceiling[18] (Figure 21.4). This layer of fallen stones is attributed to Ashraf el-Halil at the fall of Acre in 1291. The existence of hundreds of sugar vessels here suggests that this site must have been somehow related to sugar production. For ecological and environmental reasons, however, it is not likely that a sugar refinery was situated either in the Hospitaller centre or on the boundaries of the crusader city. The way the vessels were stacked, one upon the other in numerous rows, points to the fact that they were in storage. One of the possibilities is that the vessels were manufactured in Acre and were stored there prior to their distribution to the Hospitaller sugar-production centres lying on Acre's hinterland. From the historical sources, we know that the Hospitallers owned sugar-production sites during the second kingdom, and that these were one of their main sources of income during their stay in the Holy Land.[19] It is therefore suggested that these sugar vessels are characteristically Hospitaller and reflect the order's involvement in sugar production in the Holy Land.

---

[17]   Stern, 'A Medieval Sugar Production Site'; M–L. von Wartburg, 'The Medieval Cane Sugar Industry in Cyprus: Results of Recent Excavation', *Antiquaries Journal,* lxiii (1983), 298–314.

[18]   Stern, 'La Commanderie de l'Order des Hospitaliers à Acre'.

[19]   W.D. Jr. Phillips, 'Sugar Production and Trade in the Mediterranean at the Time of the Crusaders', in *The Meeting of Two Worlds. Cultural Exchange between East and West during the Period of the Crusades*, ed. V.P. Goss (Michigan, 1986), 393–406.

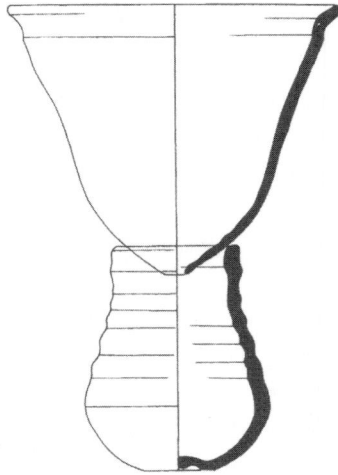

Fig. 21.3   A drawing of sugar vessels

Fig. 21.4   Sugar pots in storage in the Hospitaller compound at Acre

The Sugar-Production Site at Manureth

A small rescue excavation on behalf of the Israel Antiquities Authority at Lower H. Manot in 1995 revealed interesting finds.[20] The remains at the site consist of a large building, an aqueduct, and a base for a screw press hewn into the bedrock. The site is identified as crusader Manueth, which is well known from contemporary historical documentation. Manueth is mentioned in a document, dating from 1169, concerning sugar production under Godifedus Tortus.[21] Later, between 1212–1217, the site was sold to the Hospitaller order.[22] There is no doubt that these remains are those of a sugar refinery; their being dated to the thirteenth century place them squarely in the period of Hospitaller ownership. The larger part of the pottery found in the crusader phase consists of sugar vessels, similar to those found at the Hospitaller compound at Acre. 'Acre bowls' were discovered in relatively large quantities, compared to other types of glazed bowls or cooking and storing vessels. The pottery assemblage is typically Frankish, similar to that found at crusader Acre, suggesting that at least some of the people working on the sugar-production site were Franks who carried their material culture with them from Acre. The large quantity of 'Acre bowls', however, indicates that these people must have belonged to the Hospitaller order. The sugar vessels that were found at Maneuth underscore one of the economic activities that the order was engaged in on the Holy Land. Here again, a Hospitaller site provides convincing evidence of the dominance of types reflecting specific activities.

Conclusion

In this paper an attempt has been made to look at the Hospitaller order from a different angle. I have tried to examine what one can learn from the ceramic remains left by the order on two sites in the Holy Land in the thirteenth century. In the first place, it was shown that the general assemblage of pottery is similar to that of other Frankish sites in the Latin Kingdom. Secondly, two types of vessels that appeared in relatively large quantities on Hospitaller sites have been examined, indicating in particular some of the order's economic activities in the Holy Land.

The storage of sugar vessels in the order's headquarters in Acre suggests that here lay an organized management and distribution centre which supervised the rural production sites outside Acre as well. The second site, Manueth, is in fact one such production site, and here similar sugar vessels were unearthed.

The 'Acre bowls' provide an additional interesting insight. In the Hospitaller compound at Acre, they point to some of the main activities of the order – their care of the sick, the attention they offered to pilgrims, and aspects of its communal life. At Manueth, on the other hand, these bowls are not generally associated with any charitable or religious activity. Rather, they indicate that members of the Hospitaller institution were involved in sugar refining. It would appear that these brethren had

---

[20]   Stern, 'A Medieval Sugar Production Site'.
[21]   *RRH*, 123, no. 468.
[22]   *RRH Ad*, 858a; *RRH*, 240, No. 892; *RRH*, 268, no. 1027.

brought their material culture with them from Acre, including the 'Acre bowls' and imported glazed ware.

Chapter 22

Bioarchaeological Analysis of the Latrine Soil from the Thirteenth-Century Hospital of St John at Acre, Israel

Piers D. Mitchell, Jacqui P. Huntley, and Eliezer Stern

Introduction

Bioarchaeology is the study of living organisms in the past through the process of archaeological excavation. Classic finds of this type include human bones from cemeteries and seeds charred by the cooking fire. In recent years the concept has been greatly advanced by the use of microscopy and biotechnology to detect not only extremely small structures such as pollen grains and parasite eggs, but also the remains of certain organic substances such as blood. When they are correctly applied to a well-preserved archaeological context, these techniques have great potential to improve our understanding of what it was like to live in the past. The excavation of latrines in particular can tell us considerable amounts about daily life. It not only demonstrates what it was like to use the latrines themselves, but also shows which foods people were eating, which kinds of parasitic helminths infested the intestines of those using the facilities, and even the predominant vegetation in the surrounding countryside. In special situations such as hospitals, it may also be possible to assess evidence that may be obtained of medical treatment of the patients.[1] Luckily for the archaeologist, after several hundred years the contents of a latrine look and smell like any other soil, but still contain many of the more robust components of the material originally deposited there.

This is the first time the contents of a crusader-period latrine have been fully analysed. This means that much of the resulting information is invaluable in improving our understanding of Frankish life.

Method of Analysis

The latrines of the hospital of the Order of St John at Acre (now 'Akko) have been excavated by the Israel Antiquity Authority. They are located in the north-west of the complex and were built from stone at the end of the twelfth century, after the recovery of the city during the Third Crusade. The latrine block was constructed

---

[1]   P.D. Mitchell, *Medicine in the Crusades: Warfare, Wounds and the Medieval Surgeon* (Cambridge, 2004).

on four levels. Those using the facilities sat on stone seats, which were arranged in parallel rows on the ground and first floors. Rainwater was collected on the roof and used to wash the latrines through the complex system of channels that conveyed the waste into the basement hall, and out via a drain to the sea. The complex of St John was destroyed after the loss of Acre by the Franks in 1291, and the latrines were not used after that time. In consequence, human waste in the latrines should date from the hundred-year period from the 1190s to 1291. If the irrigation system was effective at washing through the system, then material from the later years should predominate in the samples. This has been conformed by the radiocarbon dates discussed below. The toilets were used only by those cared for in the Hospital of St John and the members of the order who looked after them. Three samples of latrine soil were taken. Small sub samples (1 gram) from each were processed, using standard techniques to remove mineral and unwanted plant debris from the samples.[2] The resulting material was examined microscopically for parasitic helminth ova and plant pollen. The remaining material, approximately 200g from each sample, was analysed using flotation techniques to separate out macroscopic organic structures of interest from the inorganic residues prior to the identification of the former.

The very nature of microscopic evidence raises problems that have to be carefully handled. For example, very small structures may move around in the soil, as water percolates through after rain, and so be washed into a layer of soil dating from a different archaeological time period. To reduce the risk of errors, the same analysis must be performed on samples from different areas and soil layers to ensure that the findings of interest are truly representative of the time period under study. Such control samples tested at this site were from eighteenth-century levels directly above the latrines and thirteenth-century halls elsewhere in the complex of St John. To further confirm the dates of the samples tested, AMS radiocarbon dating of organic remains was undertaken. This demonstrated that soil from upper layers of the basement hall dated from the Ottoman Period, and was probably washed in by rain after the latrine fell into disuse. However, samples from the base of the hall adjacent to its drain were dated to the late thirteenth century (1260–1310). This closely matches our understanding of the dates when the latrine was in use, based upon historical and archaeological evidence.

What It Was Like to Use the Latrines

A number of interesting finds help in our understanding of what it must have been like to use the latrines. Significant numbers of mineralized fly pupae were recorded (Figure 22.1), although none was present in either control sample. This confirms the presence of flies laying their eggs on the human waste and they may well have bothered people as they used the facilities. Stems of grasses and cereals were found in the latrine samples, but not in the control samples. Possible interpretations of this plant matter include the use of straw for personal hygiene after using the latrines, the

---

[2]   K. Faegri, J. Iversen, *A Textbook of Pollen Analysis*, 4th edn. (Chichester, 1989); P.J. Warnock, K.J. Reinhard, 'Methods for Extracting Pollen and Parasite Eggs from Latrine Soils', *Journal of Archaeological Science*, xix (1992), 261-64.

presence of straw on the floor of the latrine block, or perhaps both. The latrine samples also contained large amounts of lime, and it is possible that this was intermittently poured over the human waste to reduce the smell. The use of lime and materials for personal hygiene has been noted at a number of other latrines both in the Middle East and in medieval Europe.[3] Small mammal remains suggest the presence of vermin in the hospital complex. Humans using the latrines may well have shared the building with rats, mice, and other rodents.

Fig. 22.1   Fly Puparia from the Latrines (each approximately 2mm long)

---

[3]   J. Greig, 'The Investigation of a Medieval Barrel-latrine from Worcester', *Journal of Archaeological Science,* viii (1981), 265-82; J. Greig, 'Garderobes, Sewers, Cesspits and Latrines', *Current Archaeology,* viii (1982), 49-52; J. Cahill, K. Reinhard, D. Tarler, P. Warnock, 'Scientists Examine Remains of Ancient Bathroom', *Biblical Archaeology Review* (May/June 1991), 64-69.

Vegetation on Land Surrounding Acre

Latrine soil can also be used to determine the kinds of plants that surrounded Frankish settlements. Analysis of appropriate samples can determine if the local plants were crops, wasteland, or woodland, and can also identify the types of plant present. We found fine charcoal fragments representing wood from coniferous species of tree such as the cedar (*Cedrus*). A sample of this charcoal was radiocarbon-dated to 960–1020. This means that the trees from which this burnt wood originated must have been felled in the tenth or eleventh centuries. It seems most likely that the charcoal may represent ash from buildings constructed in the century before the crusaders arrived in the Levant, which were burnt down during the sack of the city in 1291. This confirms the presence of these species of tree in the region of Acre in the medieval period, at least in the eleventh century. Further evidence of indigenous flora comes from pollen analysis (Table 22.1). The outer coat of a pollen grain is very resistant to degradation in the soil and has many characteristic structures on its surface that often enable it to be identified to the genus and sometimes species of plant from among the many of the millions of different plants on earth. Unfortunately the pollen in the latrines' soil was neither abundant nor well preserved. Wind-borne pollen in the latrine samples suggests the dominance of grassland (Figure 22.2) rather than woodland in the immediate environs of Acre. Pollen types identified included cereals and wild grasses as well as dandelion, scabious, thistle, umbellifers, and goosefoot. Comparable use of this technique can be found in an excavation of a Mamluk courtyard building on the Red Sea coast of Egypt, dating from the same period as the complex of St John.[4]

The Diet of Those Using the Latrines

It is to be expected that research based on a latrine can be highly informative with regards to the diet of those using the facilities. However, the fact that the material deposited there has been chewed and digested does greatly limit the size of the fragments recovered. This is further compounded if foods are processed by grinding or cooking prior to their consumption. However, this technique does have the distinct advantage over analysis of farm buildings or harbour warehouses that we know the foods were actually eaten by humans, rather than fed to animals or further processed for their constituents. Analysis of dietary components from the latrines of St John is summarized in Table 22.2. We have identified many fragments of animal bone, but their small size makes identification of the species impossible. Fish bones and scales were also present, confirming their consumption in the diet. This ties in well with the presence of fish tapeworm ova noted in the same samples.[5] A range of seeds were

---

[4]   G.K.Kelso, I.L.Good, 'Quseir Al-Qadim, Egypt, and the Potential of Archaeological Pollen Analysis in the Near East', *Journal of Field Archaeology,* xxii (1995), 191-202.

[5]   P.D. Mitchell, E. Stern, 'Parasitic Intestinal Helminth Ova from the Latrines of the 13th Century Crusader Hospital of St John in Acre, Israel', in *Proceedings of the XIIIth European Meeting of the Paleopathology Association, Chieti, Italy,* ed. M. La Verghetta, L. Capasso (Teramo, 2001), 207-13.

recovered from the latrine samples, demonstrating the role of certain plants in the Frankish diet. Cereal grains and pollen confirmed the consumption of wheat, barley, rye, and oats (Figure 22.3). Before now it was not clear if the less palatable grains such as oats were merely fed to animals or actually eaten by humans too. Fruits were also represented in the remains by some fig seeds and fragments of cherry stone. A few small legumes recovered from the control samples from the thirteenth-century halls also suggest their use in Frankish diet, although none were recovered from the latrines themselves.

Fig. 22.2   Cutting meadow grass with a scythe. An illustration for June, from the calendar of an English psalter, c.1250–75 (parchment). Corpus Christi College, Oxford, UK/Bridgeman Art Library. MS CCC 285, fol.5v. (Reproduced by permission of the President and Fellows of Corpus Christi College, Oxford)

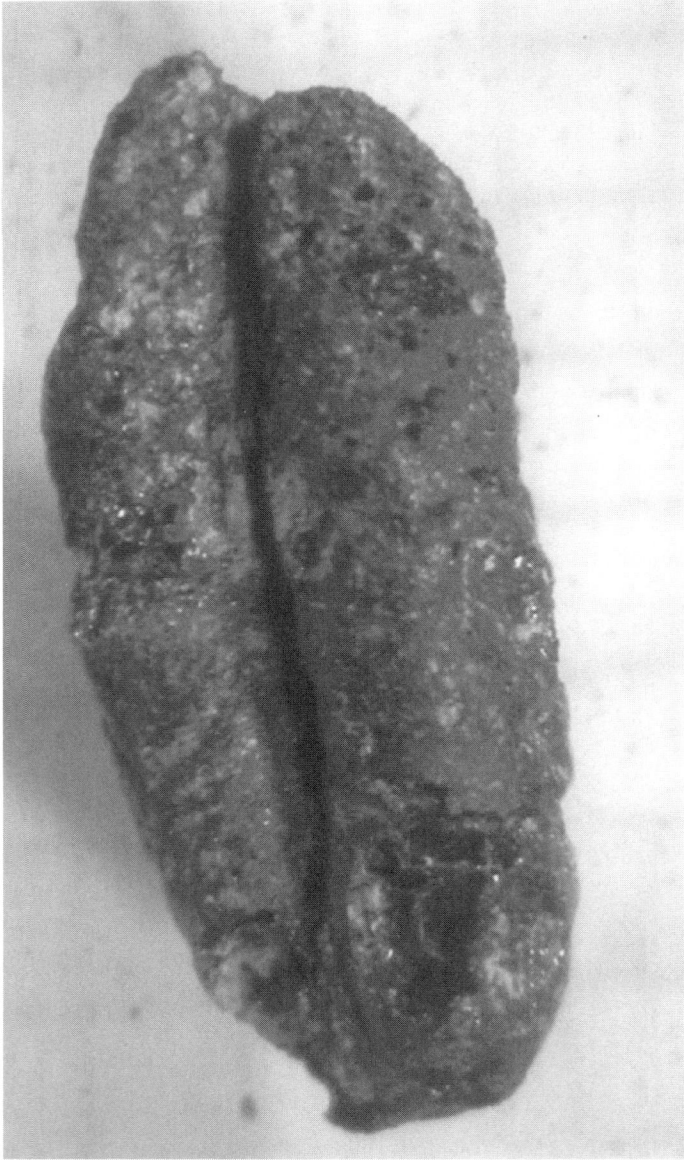

Fig. 22.3   Charred cereal grain, probably Triticum sp. (wheat). Left ventral view (7mm long)

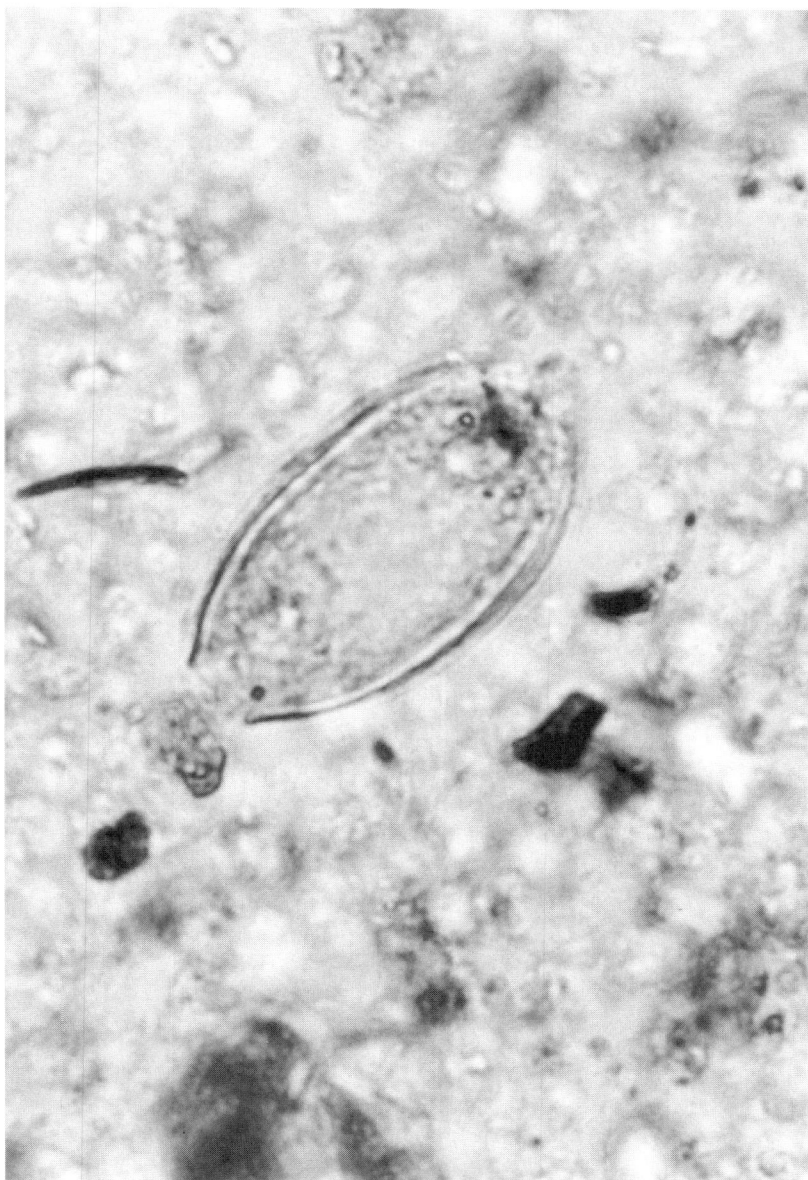

Fig. 22.4   Ova of whipworm (Trichuris trichuria) from the Latrines of St John's

A few excavations of Frankish sites have demonstrated the farming and processing of animal and plant foods. Animal bones from Belmont Castle,[6] Sumaqa,[7] and Caymont,[8] and plant remains from the Red Tower[9] have all been analysed. Large animals included sheep, goat, cattle, pig, donkey, camel, and deer; birds included chicken, pigeon, goose, and partridge; and fish were also eaten. Plant foods identified included cereals such as wheat and two-row hulled barley, broad beans, lentils, chickpeas, and the grass pea. Historical texts also mention details of foods eaten by the Frankish population. Export of food from Europe to the Latin States included processed animal products such as salt meat, fish, and cheese; livestock such as hens and pigs and plants foods such as wheat, barley, beans, chick peas, and other legumes, along with walnuts, wine, and oil.[10]

Parasitic Intestinal Helminths

Three types of parasitic worm eggs were identified in the latrine soil samples[11] (Figure 22.4). The most common type of ova present were those of the whipworm *(Trichuris trichuria)*; the next most common was the roundworm *(Ascaris lumbricoides)*; and the remainder were of the freshwater fish tapeworm *(Diphyllobothrium latum)*. The presence of these eggs shows that male and female adult worms were present in the intestines of the hosts. The whipworm and roundworm are indicators of poor hygiene, faecal contamination of food and ineffective cooking techniques, as these conditions are required before viable eggs can be inadvertently eaten by the next host. They were widespread in Europe and also the Middle East before the time of the crusades. The fish tapeworm shows that raw or smoked fish was being eaten by those using the toilets. This was widespread practice in medieval Northern Europe, as shown by the common finding of fish tapeworm eggs in latrines from this region.[12] Interestingly, the fish tapeworm has never been identified in the eastern Mediterranean prior to the crusader period, and it seems highly likely that crusaders brought the worms with

---

[6]   P. Croft, 'The Faunal Remains', in *Belmont Castle: the Excavation of a Crusader Stronghold in the Kingdom of Jerusalem*, ed. R.P. Harper, D. Pringle (Oxford, 2000), 173-94.

[7]   L.K. Horwitz, E. Dahan, 'Subsistence and Environment on Mount Carmel in the Roman-Byzantine and Mediaeval Periods: the Evidence from Kh. Sumaqa,' *Israel Exploration Journal*, xl (1990), 287-304.

[8]   L.K. Horwitz, E. Dahan, 'Animal Husbandry Practices during the Historic Periods,' in *Yoqne'am I. The Late Periods*, ed. A. Ben-Tor, M. Avissar, Y. Portugali (Jerusalem, 1996), 246-55.

[9]   R.N.L.B. Hubbard, J. McKay, 'Medieval Plant Remains,' in *The Red Tower*, ed. D. Pringle (London, 1986), 187-91.

[10]   J.H. Pryor, 'In Subsidium Terrae Sanctae: Export of Foodstuffs and Raw Materials from the Kingdom of Sicily to the Kingdom of Jerusalem, 1265-1284', *Asian and African Studies,* xxii (1988), 127-46.

[11]   P.D. Mitchell, E. Stern, 'Parasitic Intestinal Helminth Ova', 207-13.

[12]   B. Hermann, 'Parasite remains from medieval latrine deposits: an epidemiologic and ecologic approach,' in *Actes des 3emes Journees Anthropologiques*, Notes et Monographies Techniques no. xxiv (Paris, 1988), 135-42.

them in their intestines. Parasitic helminths in the intestines may have resulted in malnutrition in those Franks who were underfed due to sieges or crop failures. It is likely that people with a heavy worm load may have been more likely to die from starvation at times when food was short than those who had no parasites competing for their food.

A cesspool from crusader Acre has also been excavated recently.[13] Palaeoparasitological analysis of the latrine soil has identified the presence of whipworm, roundworm and also pork or beef tapeworm (*Taenia sp.*).[14] Unfortunately the onchospheres of these tapeworms cannot be differentiated by their appearance on light microscopy, as they look identical. This confirms that inhabitants of the city were eating undercooked meat from pigs or cattle, since thorough cooking kills off the tapeworm onchospheres.

Conclusion

The study of the soil from the latrines of the hospital of St John in thirteenth-century Acre has demonstrated a wealth of information that can be viewed from a number of levels. It seems that despite the irrigation system, the latrines were infested with flies and rodents, and lime was added to the human waste to lessen the stench, while grass and cereal stems may have been used for personal hygiene after using the latrines. Evidence obtained of the Frankish diet has shown the consumption of a range of cereals, fruit, meat, and fish. Three species of parasitic worms were to be found in the intestines of at least some of those patients and members of the order who used the latrines. At a yet wider level, it seems the dominant vegetation immediately around the city by the late thirteenth century was probably grassland and cereal crops, rather than woodland.

It is hoped that more widespread use of bioarchaeological techniques during the excavation of other Frankish sites will substantially improve our understanding of the lives of the inhabitants of the Latin states of the medieval eastern Mediterranean.

---

[13] D. Syon, E. Stern, P.D. Mitchell, 'Water installations at Crusader 'Akko', in *'Atiqot* (forthcoming).

[14] P.D. Mitchell, Y. Tepper, 'Intestinal parasitic worm eggs from a crusader period cesspool in the city of Acre (Israel)', *Levant* xxxix (2007) (in the press).

Table 22.1   Pollen analysis of samples from the latrines

Pollen Type	Pollen Counts from Each Sample				
	Latrine Samples			13th Century Control	18th Century Control
	1	2	3		
Pinus	-	2	3	-	4
Betula	1	-	-	-	-
Olea type?	-	-	-	-	1
Frangula alnus	-	1	-	-	2
Poaceae >40µ - Hordeum type	1	-	2	-	-
Poaceae >40µ - Avena-Triticum type	-	1	5	-	-
Poaceae >40µ - Secale cereale	-	-	1	-	-
Poaceae >40µ - undiff. pore	-	-	-	-	-
Poaceae >37µ - Glyceria type	-	-	2	-	-
Poaceae >27µ <37µ	1	5	13	2	1
Poaceae <26µ	-	4	1	-	-
Anthemis type	-	1	2	-	2
Aster type	-	-	1	-	7
Chenopodiaceae	1	1	7	-	1
Cruciferae	-	1	2	-	2
Apiaceae	1	-	11	-	-
Lactuceae	-	-	2	-	1
Cirsium type	-	-	2	-	-
Scabiosa type	-	-	1	-	-
Centaurea nigra type	-	-	2	-	-
Artemisia type	-	-	1	-	-

Key: Latrine sample 1 – hall under latrine seats / Latrine sample 2 – junction of hall with drain / Latrine sample 3 – latrine drain
13th-century control – storage halls elsewhere in complex of St John / 18th-century control – archaeological levels directly above the latrine block

Table 22.2   Dietary components recovered from the complex of St John.

Foodstuffs		Latrine Samples 1	2	3	13th Century Control	18th Century Control
Plant						
Pollen	wheat	-	4	4	-	-
	barley	4	-	4	-	-
	rye	-	-	4	-	-
Seeds	wheat	-	-	4	-	-
	unidentified cereal	-	-	4	4	-
	fig	4	4	4	-	-
	fruit stone (?cherry)	-	-	4	-	-
	legumes	-	-	-	4	-
Animal						
Fish	bone	-	4	4	4	-
	scale	-	4	4	-	-
Mammal bone		-	4	4	-	-

Chapter 23

The Hospitallers and the 'Peasants' Revolt' of 1381 Revisited

Helen J. Nicholson

On the evening of Thursday 13 June 1381, a large armed band broke into the Hospitallers' priory at Clerkenwell and set it and the many houses around it on fire, beheaded several people, and plundered documents, goods, and money from the house.[1] The leader of this band was one Thomas Farndon or Farringdon of London, one of the leaders of the rebels who had ridden down from Essex on the previous day after plundering and burning Temple Cressing and the house at Coggeshall of Sir John Sewale, sheriff of Essex (Figure 23.1). Earlier on that Thursday Farndon had led the rebels in an attack on the New Temple, London, which was burned; and on the Savoy Palace, the property of John of Gaunt, duke of Lancaster and uncle

---

[1]   For the sacking of Clerkenwell, see, for instance, TNA: PRO, KB 145/3/5/1 (5 Richard II): unnumbered folios: 'The jurors present that John Shakett ... on the Friday after Corpus Christi went to the house of Clerkenwell and the Savoy in a multitude of other *proditores* and there feloniously and treacherously burnt it. ... Ditto that Robert Gardiner of Middlesex ... went to the house at Clerkenwell with the other malefactors and there he feloniously, callously and treacherously decapitated seven men and also he took *a calite* at Clerkenwell, feloniously and treacherously, to the value of 100 *solidi*. ...' For Clerkenwell and Highbury, TNA: PRO, CP 40/490 (Trinity 7 Richard II) 1 dorse (the prior appeals against John Halingbury of Wandsworth), 333 recto (ditto). On Thomas Farndon, see the jurors' reports in TNA: PRO, KB 145/3/6/1, printed in André Reville, *Le Soulèvement des travailleurs d'Angleterre en 1381, études et documents publiés avec une introduction historique par Ch. Petit-Dutaillis*, Mémoires et Documents publiées par la Société de l'École des Chartes (Paris, 1898), ii, 194–95, no. 10; Charles Oman, *The Great Revolt of 1381*, new edn with an introduction by E. B. Fryde (Oxford, 1969), 211–12; and translated in R. B. Dobson, *The Peasants' Revolt of 1381* (Basingstoke, 1970, 1983), 218–19; and see TNA: PRO, KB 27/484 rex 3r. On the revolt, see also Rodney Hilton, *Bond Men Made Free: Medieval Peasant Movements and the English Rising of 1381* (London, 1973); E. B. Fryde, *The Great Revolt of 1381*, Historical Association Pamphlet (1981); *Studies towards a History of the Rising of 1381 in Norfolk*, ed. Barbara Cornford et al. (Great Yarmouth, 1984); *Essex and the Great Revolt of 1381: Lectures Celebrating the Six hundredth Anniversary*, ed. W. H. Liddell and R. G. Wood, Essex Record Office Publications, lxxxiv (1982); *The English Rising of 1381*, ed. R. H. Hilton and T. H. Aston, (Cambridge, 1984); Andrew Prescott, 'Judicial records of the rising of 1381' (Unpublished Ph.D. thesis, Bedford College, University of London, 1984); Nicholas Brooks, 'The Organisation and Achievements of the Peasants of Kent and Essex in 1381', *Studies in Medieval History Presented to R. H. C. Davis*, ed. Henry Mayr-Harting and R. I. Moore (London, 1985); David Crook, 'Derbyshire and the English Rising of 1381', *Bulletin of the Institute of Historical Research*, lx (1987); Herbert Eiden, 'Joint Action against 'Bad' Lordship: The Peasants' Revolt in Essex and Norfolk', *History*, lxxxiii (1998), 5–30.

of King Richard II. The Savoy had been plundered and then deliberately blown up with gunpowder. After sacking Clerkenwell priory, Farndon and other rebels spent the night drawing up a 'black list' of those in the government that they wanted dead. On Friday 14 June, Jack Straw and other rebels, including some of those who had attacked Clerkenwell, burned down Highbury Manor, the property of the prior of the Hospital in England, and looted it, taking from it and Clerkenwell 'rolls and other muniments and goods and chattels'. King Richard II (then aged fourteen) rode out to negotiate with the rebels at Mile End, where Thomas Farndon seized his bridle and declared: 'Avenge me on that false traitor the prior for my property which he falsely and fraudulently stole from me. Do me justice because otherwise I will get justice done myself.' The king agreed to do him justice. Farndon and his associates then went to the Tower of London. The chancellor of the kingdom, Archbishop Simon Sudbury of Canterbury, the treasurer Robert Hales prior of the Hospital in England, John Cavendish the chief justiciar, and other leading royal officials were cowering in the Tower – their attempted escape through the postern gate opening on to the River Thames had been foiled by a woman who was keeping guard on it. Farndon and his associates seized Sudbury, Hales, and the other leading royal officials, marched them out to Tower Hill and beheaded them.

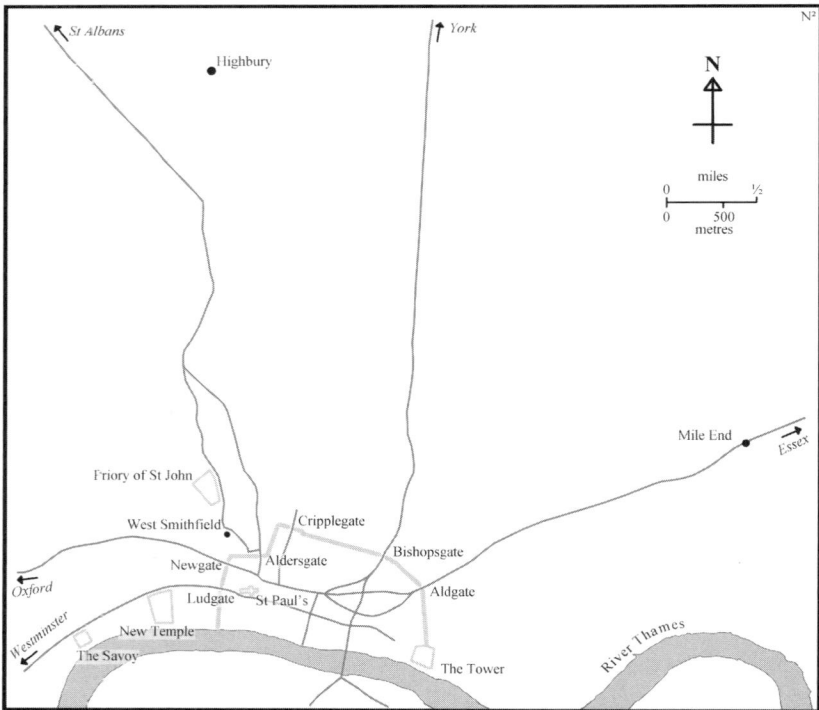

Fig. 23.1   The City of London and its environs in 1381.

The following day, the king met the rebels under Wat Tyler of Kent at West Smithfield. Wat Tyler was killed by the mayor of London, and the king assumed leadership of the rebels. The rebels then went home with the king's promise that their demands would be met. This was not done, and the legal investigations into the revolt occupied the king's bench for a long time afterwards. A large number of people were given pardons; only ringleaders of the revolt were executed. In March 1383 Thomas Farndon was given a personal royal pardon, which included both his surnames to ensure that there was no doubt over the matter.[2]

Robert Hales was not the first prior of the Hospital to die in the course of service for a secular sovereign; the prior of France had died at Crécy in 1346, fighting for the French king against the English king. Nor was he the last prior of England to be executed; Prior John Langstrother was executed on the orders of King Edward IV after the Battle of Tewkesbury in 1471. Yet whereas it is possible to see Prior Langstrother's support for the earl of Warwick as having been the best course of action to defend his order's interests in the face of King Edward IV's policies, Robert Hales could be regarded as acting less in his order's interests and more as an ambitious politician. Certainly contemporary observers had little sympathy for his fate: Thomas Walsingham spent much ink bewailing Archbishop Sudbury's death, which he saw as martyrdom, but merely listed the other executions, describing Hales as a very active knight: *miles strenuissimus*.[3] He said nothing about Hales as a religious.

Hales's fate was examined by Lionel Butler in an address to the St John Historical Society in 1981 – the year of the six-hundredth anniversary of the revolt. This is a useful study but it lacks references and bibliography, and its consideration of the revolt has been partly superseded by subsequent scholarship. Butler concluded that the treatment of the Hospital during the revolt indicated that it was not very popular in England at that time, and that Hales did not deserve such a humiliating and brutal death after strenuous service to the English monarchy and faithful service for the order in Rhodes, Corinth, Rome, and Alexandria.[4] The purpose of this article is to revisit the Hospitallers' place in the Great Revolt of 1381 and to ask whether events during the revolt did indicate that the order was unpopular, how far Robert Hales contributed personally towards his own fate, and how far he was a serious loss to his order.

---

[2]   This account is based largely on the account in the *Anonimalle Chronicle, 1333 to 1381: From a MS written at St Mary's York, and now in the possession of Lieut.-Col. Sir William Ingilby, Bart., Ripley Castle, Yorkshire*, ed. V. H. Galbraith (Manchester, 1927), 135–51. See also the chronology of the revolt in *Peasants' Revolt*, ed. Dobson, 39–40. For Farndon's royal pardon, TNA: PRO, KB 27/484 rex 3r.

[3]   *Chronica Monasterii S. Albani Thomae Walsingham quondam monachi S. Albani, Historia Anglicana*, ed. Henry Thomas Riley, 2 vols, Rolls Series xxviii (London, 1863–4), i, 459–61 on the death of Sudbury; on other executions, ibid., 462.

[4]   Lionel Butler, 'The Order of St John and the Peasants' Revolt of 1381', *St John Historical Society Pamphlet*, no. 1 (1982). I am very grateful to Dr Theresa Vann of the Monastic Manuscript Library, St John's University, Collegeville, Minnesota, for providing me with a copy of this pamphlet.

The first point to note is that most of the rebels were not peasants.[5] The rebels included innkeepers, alewives, labourers, craftsmen (such as carpenters), widows carrying on a business, and clerics. Most were landholders, and some held large holdings. Some held positions of responsibility in their locality: one was a hundred juror, another was a bailiff, and another was a reeve. Some of them were from the alderman class in London, including Thomas Farndon himself. They all had in common a grudge against the *status quo*. Christopher Dyer has pointed out that many rebels held by disadvantageous customary or servile tenures; while they themselves were moving up in the world, they were still restrained by age-old, out-dated laws that attempted to restrict their lives. Others felt that they had been mistreated by the law of the land.[6] The rebels did not want to overthrow the king; in fact they claimed to have his support and to be acting on his behalf.[7] This seems to have been a significant factor in the king's decision to pardon the great majority of the rebels.

Ecclesiastical estates in general were experiencing considerable difficulties in enforcing the payment of customary services at this period. An examination of the common pleas and pleas before the king's bench of the 1380s reveals a high level of violence against the possessions and employees of religious orders, some of which resulted from officers of religious orders trying to enforce customary services and being resisted by the tenants.[8] The Church suffered badly in the revolt: religious houses were sacked and their abbots and priors assaulted. The prior of the mighty Bury St Edmunds abbey was beheaded; the prior and canons of Breadsall priory in Derbyshire were imprisoned.[9] The rebels burned the court rolls of these religious houses, which recorded what services tenants owed and what they had refused to perform. The court rolls of secular landlords were also burned, but religious houses were clearly being singled out for destruction. It is clear that the rebels regarded the terms by which land was held from religious houses as particularly restrictive and oppressive, and had determined to destroy the records of these terms.

As a religious order, the Hospital came under attack for the same reason as other religious orders in England: because it was a landowner and many of its tenants held by unfavourable terms. Its house at Temple Cressing was singled out largely because it was the local administrative centre of the Hospital and held the order's manorial court records; it was also full of food and wine for the English priory's general chapter, which the rebels carried off with other goods, money, and animals,

---

[5] See Eiden, 10; H. E. P. Grieve, 'The Rebellion and the County Town', in *Essex and the Great Revolt*, 37–54; Christopher Dyer, 'The Causes of the Revolt in Rural Essex', in *Essex and the Great Revolt*, 21–36.

[6] Dyer, 'Causes of the Revolt', 29–35; Eiden, 29.

[7] See the rebels' password: 'With whom haldes yow?' – 'With King Richard and with the true commons': *Anonimalle Chronicle*, 139.

[8] For instance, compare TNA: PRO, CP 40/490 (Trinity 7 Richard II, i.e. June 1384) fols. 1r, 1d., 15d. 25d, 54d (was 53d), 94r (was 92r), 106d (was 104d), 132r (was 122r), 273d (was 257d), 333r: these all relate to violence against the Order of St John but not necessarily to the great revolt. In particular, 54d (was 53d), and 94r (was 92r), relate to violence which occurred when an official of the Order of St John attempted to levy services due *per consuetudinem et serviciis debitis*. See also Prescott, 73.

[9] Prescott, 141, 155, 169, 221–4, 226, 339.

pulling down the manor buildings and burning them.[10] The reasons why Essex was a centre of the revolt relate to the local social and economic situation and lie outside the scope of this article.

The Hospital was also attacked because of its association with royal government. The New Temple and Clerkenwell Hospital had long been used as depositories for government records and funds. The rebels destroyed the books, rolls, and memoranda at the New Temple. Here again an important factor in inspiring the rebels was the desire to destroy unfavourable legal terms.[11] But other records held at the New Temple were financial, in particular relating to the poll tax.

The poll tax was in theory assessed at the same rate on every person in England over the age of fifteen, whatever their income. Because of the financial problems of the English government, there had been three poll taxes in four years: 1377, 1379, and 1380/1. The 1377 tax was 4d. on each adult; the 1379 tax was graduated, so that those on higher incomes paid more; but in 1380, although the rich were asked to help the poor, there was no graduation and the rate was one shilling for each person over fifteen. In a poor family with adult children still dependent on their parents, the results could be financially crippling. Moreover, the collectors of the tax made enquiries at each community as to how many adults lived there, and caused much offence by the manner and detail of their investigations.

It was the opinion of the writer of the Anonimalle chronicle and of the Leicestershire chronicler Henry Knighton that it was the poll tax that prompted the revolt. The third poll tax had been decided at the Parliament of November 1380. The intention was to collect the tax quickly, two-thirds by January 1381, but opposition to the collectors meant that the money was slow coming in. On 1 February 1381, a new royal treasurer was appointed – Robert Hales, the prior of the Hospital in England. Thomas Walsingham remarked that Hales was a great-hearted and active knight, but that his promotion to treasurer would not please the community of the realm. He did not explain his remark.[12]

Robert of Hales was from the new gentry class: of a non-knightly family, but rising in social status. As such, he was typical of fourteenth-century English Hospitallers. Other examples are the Archer (L'archer) family, which supplied several prominent Hospitallers to the English tongue during the fourteenth century,[13] and Hildebrand Inge, a leading English Hospitaller in the last three decades of the fourteenth century: the Inges were landholders and were involved in the royal administration, but were not of knightly origin.[14] Hales's precise origins are unknown. The Brother Nicholas

---

[10]   *Anonimalle Chronicle*, 135.

[11]   Ibid., 139; *CPR Richard II (AD 1381-1385)* (London, 1895), p. 394.

[12]   *CPR, Richard II: AD 1377–1381* (London, 1895), 589; *Chronica Monasterii S. Albani Thomae Walsingham*, i, 449–50.

[13]   Peter Coss, 'Knights, Esquires and the Origins of Social Gradation in England', *Transactions of the Royal Historical Society*, 6th series, v (1995), 155–178: here 175 and note 95; see also Anthony Luttrell, 'English Contributions to the Hospitaller Castle at Bodrum in Turkey: 1407–1437', *MO*, ii, 163–72: here 164.

[14]   Paul Brand, *The Earliest English Law Reports*, 2, Seldon Society, cxii (1996), pp. lxi–lxv on William Inge (d. 1322). William Inge came from Bedfordshire. I am indebted to Professor Peter Coss for his help in tracing the origins of the Inge family. By the mid-

of Hales, who appears as prior of Clerkenwell from the 1330s to the 1350s, may have been a relation.[15] A 'Robert Hales of Norfolk' is mentioned in the Close Rolls in 1331 standing bail for a Brother Martin de Belton or Bolton of the Hospital, but is not himself called 'brother'. This Robert Hales is unlikely to have been our man – if he were still an active knight in 1381 he was hardly likely to have been over eighteen and eligible to stand bail for a man in 1331 – but he might have been a relative.[16]

Brother Robert Hales's career can be traced in part through the papal and Hospitaller archives. In February 1358, Robert Hales was on Rhodes when the chapter general of the order granted one Brother John Andaby the *bailies* of Eagle (in Lincolnshire), Bruer (in Lincolnshire), Beverley (Yorkshire), and Aslackby (Lincolnshire), with churches, manors, and mills. John de Pavely, prior of England, and Brother Robert Hales opposed this grant and claimed these properties from John Andaby. The matter was taken to the papal court.[17] By June 1358, Grand Master Roger des Pins (1355–65) was addressing Robert Hales as commander of Eagle, Sutton atte Hone (in Kent), and Bruer. He also granted him the *bailie* of Aslackby, which he was allowed to hold with the other three *bailies* by special dispensation of the convent. Later in the same year Robert was granted the commanderies or *bailies* of Sandford (in Oxfordshire) and Slebech (in south-west Wales), which had fallen vacant on the death of the previous incumbent (Brother Philip de Thame, prior of England until 1353) – and surrendered Eagle, Bruer, and Sutton in exchange. The Grand Master also gave him permission to return to England whenever he pleased.[18]

In July 1362 Robert Hales was back in England, and was admitted as one of the attorneys of the prior of England, John Pavely – his ally in 1358.[19] By 1365, however, he had returned to the East, as he was one of the hundred Hospitallers who went with four galleys and other vessels to accompany King Peter I of Cyprus in 1365 in his campaign to capture Alexandria. Later that year, Grand Master Raymond

---

fourteenth century some Inges had achieved knightly status: *CPR, Edward III*, xiii: *AD 1364–1367*, 211, 402. Hildebrand Inge first appears in 1372 as an attorney of the prior of England (Robert Hales): *CPR, Edward III*, xv: *AD 1370–1374*, 188. In 1392 he was made turcopolier of Rhodes, the highest office available to a brother of the English tongue on Rhodes (below the office of master): Malta, Cod. 326, fol. 108r. He was still turcopolier in 1394–5: Joseph Delaville le Roulx, *Les Hospitaliers à Rhodes (1310–1421)*, new edition with introduction by Anthony Luttrell (London, 1974), 302, n. 1. By 2 August 1396 he was dead, as Peter Holt was appointed turcopolier: Malta, Cod. 329, fol. 91r.

[15]   *The Knights Hospitallers in England: being the report of Prior Philip de Thame to the General Master Elyan de Villanova for AD 1338*, ed. L. B. Larking and J. M. Kemble, Camden Society 1st ser., lxv (London, 1857), 101; *CPR Edward III*, xiii: *AD 1364–1367*, 404; in 1358: Malta, Cod. 316, fols. 198r–v (was 199r–v); *The Cartulary of the Knights of St John of Jerusalem in England, Secunda Camera, Essex*, ed. Michael Gervers (Oxford, 1982), 565 n. 956.

[16]   *CCR, Edward III*, ii: *AD 1330–1333* (London, 1898), 385, 418.

[17]   *CEPRGI, Petitions to the Pope*, ed. W. H. Bliss, i: *AD 1342–1419* (London, 1896), 347. For the date of the general chapter, Delaville le Roulx, *Les Hospitaliers à Rhodes*, 136.

[18]   Malta, Cod. 316, fols. 198r (was 199r), 199 (was 200), 201r (was 202r), 202r (was 203r).

[19]   *CPR, Edward III*, xii: *AD 1361–1364*, 233.

Bereguer (1365–74) wrote to William of Middleton, turcopolier of the Order, and Robert Hales, whom he called his *socius* or personal aide, acknowledging their role in the campaign and their work on behalf of Christendom in the East, and granting Robert Hales the master's churches of Kirketon (Lincs.) and Donington (Lincs.) in the English priory.[20] Earlier in the year he had been confirmed as commander of Sandford, Slebech, and Upleadon (Bosbury in Herefords.), with Prene (Shrops.) and Kingsbury (Middx.).[21]

In spring 1366 the grand master wrote to Brother Richard of Overton, collector of responsions in the English priory, and John of Ycle, commander of Dalby, to have the English responsions ready to hand over to Brother Robert Hales, his *socius*.[22] Hales was in England again by November 1370, when he was appointed one of the attorneys of Prior John Pavely. By July 1372 he was prior himself. As prior, King Edward III expected him to contribute troops to the defence of England against possible French and Spanish invasion.[23] In 1375–76 he supported King Edward III in a bitter dispute with the grand master on Rhodes over the question of whether the Scottish priory of the Hospital was subject to the English prior; Edward III and Hales maintained that it was, and Grand Master Robert de Juillac (1374–77) was forced to concede the point.[24]

According to the sixteenth-century historian of the Order, Giacomo Bosio, the prior of England was in the Morea in 1377–78 trying unsuccessfully to secure the release of Grand Master Heredia, but Delaville le Roulx showed that this whole account is a myth. Heredia was in fact released, yet the prior of England was not one of the hostages; it was the English Brother Richard Overton, turcopolier of Rhodes, who went to the Morea with this mission in 1377–78. Hales was in the West throughout 1377 and 1378, playing a leading role in English political events. By 1 May 1377, before the death of Edward III, Hales had been appointed admiral

---

[20]   Malta, Cod. 319, fols. 177–178r (were 171–172r).

[21]   Malta, Cod. 319, fol. 175r (was 169r). Brother Thomas of Burley, prior of Dinmore, claimed that Upleadon was subject to Dinmore (Herefords.), but on investigation this was found not to be the case: ibid., fol. 176r (was 170r).

[22]   Ibid., fol. 179r (was 173r).

[23]   Charles Tipton, 'The English Hospitallers during the Great Schism', *Studies in Medieval and Renaissance History*, iv (1967), 91–124: here 96, 99–100; *CPR, Edward III*, xv: *AD 1370–1374*, 4, 8 (acting as attorney for Prior John Pavely, November 1370), 188 (as prior, July 1372); *CCR, Edward III*, xiii: *AD 1369–1374* (London, 1911), 568. I am grateful to Prof. Jürgen Sarnowsky for allowing me to see his biography of Robert Hales for the *Dictionary of National Biography* before publication.

[24]   On 5 June 1381 Grand Master Heredia (1377–96) confirmed to Hales that the English prior had authority over the Scottish priory: Malta, Cod. 321, fol. 145r (was 136r). For the dispute, see also Malta, Cod. 346, fols. 121r–v, 236r–v. See also: *CEPRGI, Papal Letters*, ed. W. H. Bliss *et al.*, iv: *AD 1362–1404* (London, 1902), 135, 140–2, 146, 205; *CCR, Edward III*, xiv: *AD 1374–1377*, 297–8, 330; Delaville le Roulx, *Les Hospitaliers à Rhodes*, 192–95; Charles Tipton, 'English and Scottish Hospitallers during the Great Schism', *Catholic Historical Review*, lii (1966), 240–45: here 241; *The Knights of St John of Jerusalem in Scotland*, ed. Ian B. Cowan, P. H. R. Mackay, and Alan Macquarrie, Scottish History Society, 4th ser., xix (Edinburgh, 1983), p. xxxiv.

of the fleet to the westward. After the old king's death he was made a member of the 'continual councils' governing for the young King Richard II. In December 1377 he was due to go overseas as admiral of the westward on the king's business, but had not yet departed; in May 1378 he was appointing attorneys for himself. He is recorded as being present at Parliament in 1378 and 1379.[25]

The government of the young Richard II presented an opportunity for a proven, able, and ambitious man of lesser birth to win wealth and power through taking on onerous and responsible but essential offices. The government was in financial crisis after years of war with France, which was currently going badly. But holding office under the child King Richard II was not a quick route to popularity. It was believed in the kingdom that the king was being badly advised by his ministers.[26]

As noted above, Thomas Walsingham reported that the appointment of Robert Hales as treasurer was not popular in the country. Walsingham's description of him as a great-hearted and active knight recalls his military career in the East, but gives no indication that he was a pious man. In the country his military reputation seems to have increased the distrust felt towards him: on 8 July 1381 the jurors at Hadleigh Castle in the Hundred of Rochford, Essex, presented that one John Buck had told the people of Great and Little Wakering and North Horbury that Robert Hales was coming with a hundred lances (i.e. a hundred men-at-arms) to kill all the people of the Hundred.[27] The fact that some of Hales' own servants (including one of his grooms) were among those who pillaged and burnt Highbury house and Clerkenwell priory and participated in his murder does not suggest that he was a well-loved master.[28] His behaviour during the revolt did not improve his popularity: he was blamed for preventing King Richard from going out to talk to the rebels when they first arrived in London, describing them as people without reason who did not know how to act sensibly.[29]

He may also have been disliked as a *parvenu*. Thomas Farndon was a member of a prominent and ancient London alderman family. The Farringdons or Farndons were goldsmiths. In 1313, 1320, and 1323 Nicholas Farringdon was mayor of London. A Thomas de Farndon was Member of Parliament for Middlesex in 1377; this may not be the Thomas Farndon involved in Hales' murder, but it may have been.[30] For Farndon, Hales was a 'new man' of no particular family who had, as Farndon told a

---

[25]   Delaville le Roulx, *Les Hospitaliers à Rhodes*, 203–206, esp. 204–205, n. 4; *CCR, Edward III*, xiv: *AD 1374–1377*, 495; *CPR, Richard II, AD 1377–81*, 75; Tipton, 'English Hospitallers', 96.

[26]   For the government of the young Richard, see Nigel Saul, *Richard II* (New Haven and London, 1997), 27–32, 44–52, 58.

[27]   TNA: PRO, KB 145/3/6/1, unnumbered membranes: hearings in Essex; Prescott, 115. A Hundred was an administrative division of a shire.

[28]   TNA: PRO, KB 145/3/5/1, unnumbered membranes: Richard Mory of Essex, *serviens* of the prior, John Webbe, *serviens* and *palefridarius* of the prior and Thomas Notman; Prescott, 207.

[29]   *Anonimalle Chronicle*, 139.

[30]   W. J. Loftie, *A History of London*, 2 vols, (2nd edn., London, 1884), i, 159, 201; ii, 308, 395; see also Reville, p. lxxii; Dobson, 213. Thomas Farndon's father was of illegitimate birth, and Thomas had recently lost two lawsuits 'one certainly, and the other possibly' because of

gathering of rebels in Essex, unjustly expelled him from his rightful inheritance. The details of this case are not known, but the fact that Farndon received an individual royal pardon for his actions against Hales is persuasive evidence that he was telling the truth. So far as Thomas Farndon was concerned, he had been deprived of his rights by a man who had come from nowhere, a man who misled the king, and a thief.

To conclude: the Hospital suffered in 1381 as a religious order and a landowner, alongside other religious orders and landowners. This is not surprising. It also suffered because of its role as a sort of government financial office. However, the Hospital itself was not disliked any more than any other religious order; it was its prior who was thoroughly hated. While it was known that Robert Hales was an active knight, he was not respected as a religious man but regarded as a danger to ordinary people, the sort of knight who would misuse armed power. His role as treasurer had given him a reputation for being greedy and power-hungry.

What of his order? Did it lament his death? The Hales who had served in Rhodes and was rewarded in 1365 for services at Alexandria (but had never gone to Rome or Corinth) had gone on to defy the grand master and convent in 1375–76 over the priory of Scotland. The grand master apparently made no comment on the death of Hales. A lieutenant-master was appointed by the English brothers: the experienced Hildebrand Inge, whose family was better than Hales's and had a long record of royal service. On 18 November 1381, John Radington was appointed prior of England by the grand master and convent. He had previously acted as turcopolier of Rhodes.[31] The Order did not insist on the punishment of the murderers of Hales. Perhaps the grand master and convent felt that for all his past service on Rhodes, in view of Hales's activity since he became prior of England, his death was no great loss to the Order.

---

this: Ruth Bird, *The Turbulent London of Richard II* (London, 1949), 54 and n. 3. Perhaps this was also the origin of his problems with the Hospital.

[31]   Malta, Cod. 321, fol. 145 (was 136); Tipton, 'English Hospitallers', 10.

Chapter 24

The Hospitallers and the Kings of Castile in the Fourteenth and Fifteenth Centuries

Carlos Barquero Goñi

In the twelfth and thirteenth centuries, the monarchy had been the great promoter of establishing and developing the Order of St John in the Crown of Castile, granting it several donations and privileges. During this period, the order, on its part, generally acted as an instrument of royal power in Castile. However, by the second half of the thirteenth century, it had gradually begun to lose this royal patronage.[1] It is precisely the purpose of the present paper to focus on the process of readjustment in the relations between the Hospitaller institution and the Castilian monarchy.[2]

Compared to the earlier two centuries, the fourteenth and fifteenth witness royal donations to the Hospital grinding practically to a halt. Indeed, I have come across only one such concession.[3] The monarchy's earlier interest in the changes in Hospitaller landownership is now limited to the management of two specific barters carried out by the Catholic Kings at the end of the fifteenth century.[4]

It would appear that in the later Middle Ages, the kings of Castile no longer desired any further growth of such property within their territories. The Castilian monarchy's consistent refusal in the fourteenth century, for example, to hand over old Templar possessions to the Hospital provides convincing evidence of this.[5] It is not unlikely that the Castilian monarchs aimed at limiting the size of the Hospitaller

[1]   C. Barquero Goñi, 'Los hospitalarios y la monarquía castellano-leonesa (siglos XII-XIII)', *Archivos Leoneses*, xcvii-xcviii (1995), 53-119. C. Estepa Díez, 'La Orden de San Juan y el poder regio. Castilla al norte del Duero. Siglos XII-XIV', in *Las Ordenes Militares en la Península Ibérica. Volumen I: Edad Media*, ed. R. Izquierdo Benito and F. Ruiz Gómez (Cuenca, 2000), 307-324. E. Rodríguez-Picavea Matilla, *Las Órdenes Militares y la Frontera. La contribución de las Órdenes a la delimitación de la jurisdicción territorial de Castilla en el siglo XII* (Madrid, 1994), 37-78.

[2]   C. Barquero Goñi, 'La Orden Militar del Hospital y la monarquía castellana durante la Baja Edad Media', *Meridies*, v-vi (2002), 141-154. P. Josserand, 'A l'épreuve d'une logique nationale: le prieuré castillan de l'Hôpital et Rhodes au XIVᵉ siècle', *Revue Mabillon*, xiv (2003), 115-38.

[3]   AHN OO.MM, carpeta 569, doc. 37.

[4]   *Archivo General de Simancas. Catálogo V. Patronato Real (834-1851)*, ed. A. Prieto Cantero, 2 vols (Valladolid, 1946-49), i, 138. *Documentos sobre relaciones internacionales de los Reyes Católicos*, ed. A. de la Torre, 6 vols (Barcelona, 1949-66), iii, 163.

[5]   C. Barquero Goñi, 'La Orden del Hospital y la recepción de los bienes templarios en la Península Ibérica', *Hispania Sacra*, li (1999), 547-55. C. Barquero Goñi, *Los caballeros hospitalarios durante la Edad Media en España* (Burgos, 2003), 55-66.

priory to be able to control it more easily. This does not necessarily imply that relations between the two had turned sour. On the contrary, Castilian monarchs in the fourteenth and fifteenth centuries endeavoured to maintain and preserve the privileges and possessions the order had already had by then. In the later Middle Ages, numerous royal documents were issued in favour of the Hospital, charters penned by earlier monarchs were ratified,[6] and privileges reconfirmed.[7] Certain documents that had not been originally issued by the monarchy were also validated in the interests of the Hospital.[8] Indeed, Castile did more than that. Not only, for example, did its monarchs recognize the Hospital as an exempt order;[9] it actively defended the Hospitallers' right to tax exemption[10] and the privilege of immunity enjoyed by their possessions.[11] Moreover, on several occasions in the fourteenth and fifteenth centuries, the Castilian monarchy is recorded to have protected Hospitaller property.[12] This is supported by various testimonies of numerous specific measures taken precisely for this purpose.[13]

On their part, the Hospitallers often offered military service to the kings and normally participated in their wars against the Muslims.[14] More often than not, it is the prior of the Order of St John in the kingdoms of Castile and Leon, who is identified in our sources as one of the components of the Castilian army during its campaigns against Islam. The prior's military contribution was specially underscored during the so-called 'Battle of the Strait' in the reign of Alfonso XI

---

[6]   *Libro de privilegios de la Orden de San Juan de Jerusalén en Castilla y León (siglos XII-XV)*, ed. C. de Ayala Martínez (Madrid, 1995), 656-58. J. M. Carmona Domínguez and A. J. López Gutiérrez, 'La encomienda de Tocina: nuevas aportaciones documentales. Siglos XII-XV', *Historia. Instituciones. Documentos*, xxiii (1996), 134-47, 149-50. AHN OO.MM, carpeta 569, doc. 35; carpeta 939, doc. 39; legajo 7746, doc. 2; Diversos, Colecciones, legajo 220. Archivo General de Palacio, Infante don Gabriel, Secretaría, legajo 760.

[7]   *Memorias del rey don Fernando IV de Castilla*, ed. A. Benavides (Madrid, 1860), ii, 385-87. AHN Diversos, Colecciones, legajo 220. P. Guerrero Ventas, *El gran priorato de San Juan en el Campo de La Mancha* (Toledo, 1969), 180.

[8]   *CH*, iv, 99-100. *Libro de privilegios de la Orden*, pp. 681-682.

[9]   AHN OO.MM, carpeta 569, doc. 33; Diversos, Colecciones, legajo 220. Carmona Domínguez and López Gutiérrez, 142-144. M. D. Rodríguez Brito, M. Canellas Anoz, J. M. Carmona Domínguez and A. López Gutiérrez, 'La encomienda de Tocina y Robayna de la Orden Militar de San Juan de Jerusalén. Fuentes bibliográficas y documentales (s. XIII-XVIII)', *Tocina. Estudios Locales*, ii (1990), 116, 122.

[10]   P. Rodríguez Campomanes, *Disertaciones históricas del Orden y Caballería de los templarios* (Madrid, 1747), 250-52.

[11]   AHN OO.MM, carpeta 569, doc. 34. Rodríguez Campomanes, 250-52.

[12]   AHN OO.MM, carpeta 939, doc. 39; Indice 175, fol. 76r, no. 128. *Libro de privilegios de la encomienda de Tocina 1242-1692*, ed. J. M. Carmona Domínguez (Seville, 1999), 78-80.

[13]   *Registro General del Sello*, 16 vols (Valladolid-Madrid, 1950-1992), v, 383; viii, 415, 510; xi, 537; xii, 573, 578; xiv, 178, 179, 286.

[14]   *Gran Crónica de Alfonso XI*, ed. D. Catalán, 2 vols (Madrid, 1976), ii, 37. J. Trenchs, 'Benedicto XII y las Órdenes Militares hispanas: regesta de los textos papales', *Anuario de Estudios Medievales*, xi (1981), 148.

(1312-50).[15] Later on, Hospitallers keep appearing in some of Castile's campaigns against the Muslim kingdom of Granada, though perhaps less frequently.[16] What is more striking, however, is the fact that Hospitaller priors are also recorded as having fought against other Christian kingdoms on mainland Spain under the command of the king of Castile. This occurred, for example, during the so-called 'War of the two Peters' (1356-69) between King Peter I of Castile and King Peter IV of Aragon.[17] The head of the Castilian Hospitallers participated actively too in their monarchs' warlike confrontations with Portugal.[18] Moreover, the members of the Order of St John and the prior in particular generally offered the monarchy military support in its frequent domestic conflicts. Throughout the civil war between King Peter I and his brother Henry of Trastamara, the order at first appeared to support the monarch.[19] However, the moment Henry II occupied the throne in 1366, the prior figured among his supporters until the end of the conflict.[20] In 1395 Henry III employed the prior's military forces to arrest his rebellious aunt Eleanor.[21]

During the reign of John II, in the first half of the fifteenth century, the prior of the Hospital appeared consistently among the bands supporting the monarch and his favourite Alvaro de Luna against the nobility's long series of rebellions.[22] The next reign witnesses an almost identical situation, with the prior of the Hospital in Castile extending his military assistance to Henry IV against the uprisings of the nobles.[23] The list of such instances can be extended. In 1475, for example, at the beginning of the reign of the Catholic Kings, the Hospitaller prior, Alvaro de Estuñiga, fought on the monarchy's side against the rebellious nobility.[24]

---

[15]   *Gran Crónica*, ii, 53, 260, 326, 343, 347, 368-70, 415-16. *Crónicas de los reyes de Castilla*, ed. C. Rosell, 3 vols (Madrid, 1953), i, 335, 343. *Colección de documentos para la historia del reino de Murcia*, vi: *Documentos de Alfonso XI*, ed. F. de A. Veas Arteseros (Murcia, 1997), 492-94.

[16]   Pero López de Ayala, *Crónica del Rey Don Pedro y del Rey Don Enrique, su hermano, hijos del rey don Alfonso Onceno*, ed. G. Orduna, 2 vols (Buenos Aires, 1994-97), ii, 45. *Crónicas de los reyes*, ii, 498, 636. M. A. Ladero Quesada, *Castilla y la conquista del reino de Granada* (Valladolid, 1967), 280-81.

[17]   Pero López de Ayala, i, 257, 279-80, 318, 320; ii, 103, 113.

[18]   *Crónicas de los reyes*, ii, 105. *Documentos referentes a las relaciones con Portugal durante el reinado de los Reyes Católicos*, ed. A. de la Torre and L. Suárez Fernández, 3 vols (Valladolid, 1958-63), i, 100-102.

[19]   Pero López de Ayala, ii, 11, 136.

[20]   Ibid., 145-46, 150, 160, 161, 227.

[21]   *Crónicas de los reyes*, ii, 232-33.

[22]   Ibid., 549, 628, 640. Pedro Carrillo de Huete, *Crónica del halconero de Juan II*, ed. J. de M. Carriazo (Madrid, 1946), 316.

[23]   Diego de Valera, *Memorial de diversas hazañas. Crónica de Enrique IV*, ed. J. de M. Carriazo (Madrid, 1941), 102. *Hechos del condestable don Miguel Lucas de Iranzo (Crónica del siglo XV)*, ed. J. de M. de Carriazo (Madrid, 1940), 313-18. Diego Enríquez del Castillo, *Crónica de Enrique IV*, ed. A. Sánchez Martín (Valladolid, 1994), 240-41.

[24]   Alonso de Palencia, *Crónica de Enrique IV*, ed. A. Paz y Meliá, 3 vols (Madrid, 1973-75), ii, 238.

In the fourteenth and fifteenth centuries the Hospitallers provided the Castilian kings with other services too, in addition to active military support.[25] The monarchy often appointed the prior of St John as its ambassador,[26] dispatching him on foreign missions, and choosing him to act as royal representative in domestic affairs.[27] On occasions, too, the prior held important positions within Castile's royal government, especially during the fourteenth century.[28] There is therefore ample evidence that, during the period under survey, the Hospital acted as an instrument of royal power, with the priors appearing as important figures very close to the monarch.[29]

On the other hand, instances of Hospitallers rebelling against the authority of the king of Castile during the later Middle Ages are remote and isolated.[30] The most outstanding example was perhaps that of 1328, when the prior, Fernan Rodriguez de Valbuena, took up arms against Alfonso XI.[31]

Cases like this were exceptionally rare, contrasting sharply as they do with the prevailing view that the Hospital had nearly always entertained very intimate relations with the Castilian monarchy. But on the whole the order's attitude was not very controversial; indeed, more often than not, it tended to place its resources at the service of the crown.

Hospitaller loyalty to Castile may perhaps be explained in terms of the pervasive influence the monarchy exercised over the priory, especially in matters of appointments and promotions. Castilian monarchs succeeded in influencing the choice of prior within their kingdom. The first known attempts date back to the fourteenth century.[32] However, it was not until the next century that the kings of Castile obtained from the pope the right to nominate a candidate when the post of prior in the priory of Castile became vacant.[33] In the history of the Hospitaller priory

[25]   P. Josserand, 'Les Ordres Militaires et le service curial dans le royaume de Castille (1252-1369)', in *Les serviteurs de l'État au Moyen Âge. Actes du XXIX congrès de la SHMESP (Pau, 1998)*, no editor (Paris, 1999), 75-83.

[26]   *Crónicas de los reyes*, i, 347, 368. L. Serrano, 'Alfonso XI y el Papa Clemente VI durante el cerco de Algeciras', *Escuela Española de Arqueología e Historia en Roma. Cuadernos de trabajos*, iii (1915), 26-32.

[27]   *Gran Crónica*, ii, 104-105. Pedro Carrillo de Huete, 300.

[28]   S. de Moxó, 'La sociedad política castellana en la época de Alfonso XI', *Cuadernos de Historia. Anexos de la revista Hispania*, vi (1975), 253, 301. L. V. Díaz Martín, *Los oficiales de Pedro I de Castilla*, (2nd edn.: Valladolid, 1987), 34-35.

[29]   *Gran Crónica*, i, 449, 451, 456, 460-61, 501-502. Pedro Carrillo de Huete, 231, 338, 347. Jerónimo Zurita, *Anales de la Corona de Aragón*, ed. A. Canellas López, 9 vols (Saragossa, 1967-85), vii, 51-52. Diego Enríquez del Castillo, 202.

[30]   *Gran Crónica*, ii, 84. *Crónicas de los reyes*, ii, 580. Diego de Valera, 180-82.

[31]   *Gran Crónica*, i, 422-27, 441-48. P. Josserand, 'Un maître politique: Fernán Rodríguez de Valbuena, prieur de l'Hôpital en Castille au début du XIVe siècle', in *IV Jornadas Luso-Espanholas de História Medieval. As relaçoes de fronteira no século de Alcanices. Actas*, no editor (Porto, 1998), ii, 1313-44.

[32]   *Gran Crónica*, i, 428, 450. *Bulas y cartas secretas de Inocencio VI (1352-1362)*, ed. J. Zunzunegui Aramburu (Rome, 1970), 204-205, 209-12, 225-26, 230-31, 253-54, 358-59. Pero López de Ayala, i, 278.

[33]   Archivo General de Palacio, Infante don Gabriel, Secretaría, legajo 760; Anexo, legajo 1.

of Castile, the fifteenth century was marked by a series of such royal protégés being chosen as priors.[34] This same right appears to have been extended to the nomination of Hospitaller commanders.[35] In an interesting correspondence between the Catholic Kings and the master of the order, the former openly express their desire to offer Hospitaller commanderies to persons of their choice.[36] In brief, ample documentary evidence supports Castile's influence in this matter.[37]

Castile's intrusion in the affairs of the order does not appear to have provoked great resistance. On the contrary, it is possible that such interference could have been considered a necessary evil, one that could have been, or indeed ought to have been, beneficial to the order. As the ultimate decision was always taken by the master on distant Rhodes, it was inevitable that the magistracy, in its own interest and in that of the order, had to count on the benevolence of the monarchy in the West to be able to exert some form of control on its estates in Castile. In such circumstances, accommodating the monarchy by appointing the priors and commanders of his choice was often unavoidable.

It is perhaps interesting to observe that in matters pertaining to the Hospital in Castile, it was the pope, rather than the master, who addressed the monarchy on behalf of the order.

This is hardly surprising. All the military orders originating in the twelfth and thirteenth centuries were armed branches of the Church, answerable to the pope and to him alone as their ultimate head.[38] In the case of the Hospital, its dependence on the papacy increased during the later Middle Ages, possibly because it was the only military order available for the pope's crusading plans in this period.[39] It is also possible that the convent's distance from the West determined the need for direct papal intervention in matters pertaining to the Hospital. Whatever the true reason, several were the occasions in the fourteenth and fifteenth centuries when the pope acted as the defender of the Hospitallers before the king of Castile.[40]

Towards the end of the fifteenth century, the Castilian monarchy began to show a renewed interest in the Order of St John. The Turks' westward drive and the pressure

---

[34]   *Crónica de don Alvaro de Luna*, ed. J. de M. Carriazo (Madrid, 1940), 70. Alfonso de Palencia, *Gesta Hispaniensia ex annalibus suorum dierum collecta*, ed. B. Tate and J. Lawrance, 2 vols (Madrid, 1998-1999), i, 150-52. J. Rius Serra, *Regesto ibérico de Calixto III*, 2 vols (Barcelona, 1948-58), ii, 364-65.

[35]   Biblioteca Nacional, Madrid, Manuscrito 6711, fol. 120.

[36]   *Documentos sobre relaciones*, iii, 357-58, 360; iv, 123-24, 543-44; v, 244-45; vi, 155-56.

[37]   *Registro General*, iii, 62, 66; vi, 141; viii, 47, 298; ix, 546.

[38]   A. Forey, *The Military Orders. From the Twelfth to the Early Fourteenth Centuries* (London, 1992), 169-70. L. García-Guijarro Ramos, *Papado, cruzadas y Ordenes Militares* (Madrid, 1995).

[39]   N. Housley, *The Avignon Papacy and the Crusades, 1305-1378* (Oxford, 1986), 281-92. A. Demurger, *Chevaliers du Christ. Les ordres religieux-militaires au Moyen Âge, XIe-XVIe siècle* (Paris, 2002), 248-50.

[40]   *Codice diplomatico del sacro militare ordine Gerosolimitano*, ed. S. Pauli, 2 vols (Lucca, 1733-37), ii, 118, 401. *Bulas y cartas*, 200-203. J. Delaville le Roulx, *Melanges sur l'Ordre de Saint Jean de Jérusalem* (Paris, 1910), item xvi, 3-4.

their advance created in the Mediterranean underscored the increasing relevance of the role the Hospitallers were playing from their base on Rhodes, the bulwark of Christianity in the eyes of the Catholic Kings.[41] This explains why, during these years, the Castilian monarchy increased its strong traditional patronage of the order.[42] It protected and promoted Castilian Hospitallers on the journeys they undertook on a regular basis to Rhodes, providing them with all necessary naval and military reinforcements,[43] and ensuring that all revenues earned from the order's estates in Castile in the form of *responsiones* were loyally dispatched to the master and convent.[44] It also explains why the order of St John in Castile, unlike the other military orders, was spared the fate of being incorporated into the Crown.[45] In the fourteenth and fifteenth centuries the Castilian monarchy had succeeded in tightening its grip on the order, perhaps to a degree sufficient to render integration superfluous.

---

[41]   L. Suárez Fernández, 'Política mediterránea de los Reyes Católicos', in *El Mediterráneo: hechos de relevancia histórico-militar y sus repercusiones en España. V Jornadas Nacionales de Historia Militar*, no editor (Seville, 1997), 386.

[42]   *El Tumbo de los Reyes Católicos del Concejo de Sevilla*, ed. R. Carande and J. de M. Carriazo, 5 vols (Seville, 1929-71), i, 189-90. AHN OO.MM, carpeta 569, doc. 38. L. Suárez Fernández, *Política internacional de Isabel la Católica. Estudio y documentos*, 5 vols (Valladolid, 1965-72), i, 484-89; iii, 121-22, 418-19. *Registro General*, iii, 38.

[43]   *Registro General*, iii, 64; xvi, 205.

[44]   Ibid., i, 170; ii, 316; x, 301.

[45]   C. de Ayala Martínez, 'La Corona de Castilla y la incorporación de los maestrazgos', *Militarium Ordinum Analecta*, i (1997), 257-90. C. de Ayala Martínez, *Las órdenes militares hispánicas en la Edad Media (siglos XII-XV)* (Madrid, 2003), 733-69.

Chapter 25

The Visit of the Emperor Manuel II Palaeologus at the Priory of St John in 1401

Julian Chrysostomides

It is perhaps appropriate to say a few words about the visit of the Emperor Manuel II Palaeologus, who six hundred years ago stayed in the Priory of the Hospital of St John at Clerkenwell. His visit casts light on the important role the Hospitallers played in the Mediterranean, and on the help they extended to the Emperor during his reign.[1]

Manuel had set out to visit Europe in December 1399 in the hope of eliciting help against the Turks, who since 1394 had laid siege to Constantinople. It was during these desperate years that the Emperor sought to arouse the conscience of the West against the Ottomans. As a result of his direct appeal to Charles VI of France, a small French force under Maréchal Jean de Boucicaut brought some relief to the hard-pressed city in the autumn of that year. It was at the suggestion of Boucicaut that the Emperor undertook this journey to appeal personally to western leaders.[2] He travelled through Italy, stopping at Venice, Padua, Vicenza, Pavia, Milan, probably Florence, and most likely Rome, where he was fêted with great honour.[3] But the highlights of his visit were France and England. In Paris, Manuel was received by King Charles VI with all the magnificence which France commanded. The two met

---

[1]   I would like to thank Professor Riley-Smith for inviting me to say a few words on the Emperor's visit to Clerkenwell.

[2]   Manuel II Palaeologus, *Funeral Oration on His Brother Theodore*, ed. J. Chrysostomides, Corpus Fontium Historiae Byzantinae, xxvi (Thessalonika, 1985), 7, 162; *Le livre des faicts du mareschal de Boucicaut*, ed. J.Fr. Michaud and J.J.F. Poujoulat, *Nouvelle collection des mémoires pour servir à l'histoire de France*, 1st series (Paris, 1836), ii, bk. 1. chs. 30–35, 247–54; *Le religieux de Saint Denys. Chronique contenant le règne de Charles VI (1380–1422)*, ed. and trans. L. Bellaguet (Paris, 1840)), ii, bk. 18, ch. 8, 558–61; ibid., bk. 20, ch. 3, 690-93. For Manuel's journey in general, J.W. Barker, *Manuel II Palaeologus (1391–1425). A Study in Late Byzantine Statemanship* (New Brunswick, N.J., 1969), 123–99.

[3]   ASV, *Maggior Consiglio, Libro Leona*, fol. 105ᵛ; Gio. Nicolo Doglioni, *Historia Venetiana* (Venice, 1598), 279; Marino Sanudo, *Vitae ducum venetorum*, Rerum Italicarum Scriptores, xxii (Milan, 1733), col. 789E; Andrea Gataro, *Istoria Padovana*, Rerum Italicarum Scriptores, xvii (Milan, 1730), 836D *et seq.*; *Annales Mediolanenses*, Rerum Italicarum Scriptores, xvi (Milan, 1730), col. 833C; Manuel II, *Funeral Oration*, 162 and n. 88; O. Halecki, 'Rome et Byzance au temps du grand schisme d'Occident', *Collectanea Theologica*, xviii (1937), 499 *et seq.* (also repr. in Variorum).

at the outskirts of Paris on 3 June 1400, and as a special honour the King offered him a white horse to ride, something that his father had refused to do for the German Emperor Charles VI some years before.[4]

Manuel II made a deep impression with his appearance. According to the French chronicle, *Le Religieux de Saint Denys*, he 'was a man of medium height, but with large chest and well-shaped limbs, with features full of nobility, whose long beard and white hair attracted all eyes'. He particularly delighted the Parisian crowd with his agility, when they watched him 'jump from one horse on to the other without condescending to touch the ground with his feet'. Later Charles led him to the Chateau de Louvre where he was to stay throughout his visit in that country. The King treated the Emperor with civility and courtesy during his entire sojourn in France, offering him a lavish allowance, as the chroniclers and the documents of the royal treasury attest.[5]

While in France, Manuel decided to seek help from Henry IV of England and began negotiations for his visit to that country, planned for September 1400. This, however, was delayed because of Henry's campaign against the Scots, and the Emperor was forced to remain in Calais until December.[6] Finally, after a rough crossing, he landed at Dover on 13 December, Saint Lucy's day. He was met by the King, Henry IV, at Blackheath on 21 December, the day of St Thomas the Apostle, and according to Walsingham 'gave him as he should the welcome of a hero. He escorted him to London and for many days he showed him honourable and sumptuous hospitality and offered him presents worthy of his supreme rank'. He spent Christmas with the King at Eltham and watched a tournament staged in his honour.[7] But unlike what had happened in France, his presence in England failed to arouse delight; instead it provoked reflections on the transience of power and glory, at least in the mind of the chronicler, Adam of Usk. 'I thought within myself,' he observed, 'what a grievous thing it was that this great Christian prince from the farther East, should perforce be driven by unbelievers to visit the distant lands of the West, to seek aid against them. My God! What dost thou ancient glory of Rome? Shorn is thy greatness of thine empire this day.'[8]

It was during his stay in London that Manuel was lodged in the Priory of St John. This is not surprising, since the person who arranged his visit to England with Henry IV was Peter Holt, Prior of the Hospital of St John of Jerusalem in Ireland.[9] In fact,

---

4   *Le Religieux de Saint-Denys*, bk. 21, ch. 1, 754-57; Christine de Pizan, *Le livre des faits et bonnes meurs du sage roy Charles*, ed. Michaud and Poujoulat, in *Nouvelle collection*, 102b-103a.

5   *Le Religieux de Saint-Denys*, bk. 21, ch. 1, 756-57; J. Berger de Xivrey, *Mémoire sur la vie et les ouvrages de l'empereur Manuel Paléologue*, Mémoires de l'Institut de France, Académie des inscriptions et Belles-Lettres, xix, 2 (Paris, 1853), 103–104, n. 1, 2.

6   On Manuel's stay in England, D.M. Nicol, 'A Byzantine Emperor in England: Manuel II's in England', *University of Birmingham Historical Journal*, xii (1970), 204–25.

7   Thomas Walsingham, *Historia Anglicana*, ed. H.T. Riley, Rolls ser. xxviii (London, 1864), ii, 247; Nicol, 213.

8   Adam of Usk, *Chronicon Adae de Usk (A.D. 1377–1421)*, ed. E.M. Thompson (2nd ed.: London, 1904), 57, 220.

9   For details, Nicol, 211 *et seq.*

the Emperor's links with the Order had begun a decade earlier in 1390, when he had sought their help to recover his throne during a brief civil war.[10] At the time, Manuel visited the Order in Rhodes, 'a community,' as he noted, 'composed of men who had vowed to the Saviour chastity, obedience and poverty, and who had also promised to fight those who strove against the Cross, and who bore the sign of the Cross on their clothes, their arms and banners.'[11] Manuel was able on that occasion to secure naval assistance, enabling him to recover his throne. But above all, he acquired friends. For, as he said, 'these men came to his rescue moved by a sense of honour and duty, and not of obligation.'[12]

It was this sense of trust that made his brother Theodore, the ruler of the Byzantine province in the Peloponnese, in consultation with Manuel and their mother Empress Helena, entrust the city of Corinth to the Hospitallers in 1396, and later some more of his lands, when he realized that he could not defend them against the Turks. Of the possibilities available to his brother, Manuel maintained that for several reasons 'the Hospitallers were the best'.[13] Referring to their military strength, he maintained:

> Let no one assume by looking at their few galleys stationed in Rhodes that the strength of the Hospitallers is weak and feeble. When they wish [to go to war to defend their lands], a great number of them can assemble from all over the world where they are scattered, for whom there is nothing more important than what is conducive to good courage, warfare and a noble spirit. To them [he continued] it is far better to die with glory [than to run away]. They also possess … wealth derived from revenues of the places given to them by God-loving men with the sole purpose to serving God, I mean by assisting their struggle against the infidel.[14]

But for Manuel military power was not their only asset. 'Above all,' he insisted, 'the Hospitallers possessed more enthusiasm in defending Christians than some who might be more powerful,' and in addition 'they had the reputation of not breaking their oaths.'[15]

Manuel's appreciation of the Order's vision and code of conduct transcended the theological differences that were so prominent at the time. The bonds of friendship and co-operation between the two, which remain paradigmatic, may have been further strengthened during his stay at Clerkenwell.

---

[10] Manuel II, *Funeral Oration*, 170-71.

[11] Ibid., 166-67.

[12] Ibid., 170-73.

[13] Ibid., 166-67.

[14] Ibid., 174-75.

[15] Ibid., 168-69.

Chapter 26

John Kaye, the 'Dread Turk', and the Siege of Rhodes

Theresa M. Vann

Guillaume Caoursin, the vicechancellor of the Order of the Hospital of St. John of Jerusalem in Rhodes, published the official Latin account of the victory of the Knights of St. John over the Ottoman Turks at Rhodes in 1480, the same year as the siege. The account, entitled *Obsidionis Rhodiae urbis descriptio* (hereafter referred to as *Descriptio)* was reprinted within two years and republished with Caoursin's collected historical writings in Ulm in 1496. As Caoursin's Latin text circulated throughout Europe, an English translation of it appeared in 1483, written by John Kay, who identified himself as Edward IV's poet laureate. This translation has enjoyed a long and active life. Two printed editions appeared before 1500.[1] Nineteenth- and twentieth-century reprinted editions attested to the continuing popularity of the text.[2] More recently, Kay's work has become available through facsimile and microfilm editions of early printed English books.[3]

Caoursin's Latin text has yet to appear in a modern edition, although facsimiles of the early printed editions have been published in Catalonia and in Denmark.[4] For the English-speaking world, Kay's translation is more accessible and thus a frequently-consulted source for the Turkish siege of Rhodes in 1480.[5] Most researchers do not assume that Kay's work is an exact translation of Caoursin. Kay, like other English translators of the period, took liberties with the original Latin text, translating for

---

[1]   *The Siege of Rhodes*, trans. John Kay (London, 1483). Id., *The Dylectable Newesse, and Tithynges of the Glorious Victorye of the Rhodyans Agaynst the Turkes, translated from the Latin of G. Caoursin by Johan Kaye (Poete Lawreate)* (Westminster, 1490).

[2]   See E. Gibbon, *Decline and Fall of the Roman Empire*, ed. A. Murray (London, 1870), ch. 57, 58, 59, 60, and 61. See also *Caoursin's account of the siege of Rhodes in 1480*, trans. John Kay, ed. H.W. Fincham, with an introduction by E.J. King (London, 1926 [1945]).

[3]   Facsimile editions of John Kay's translation of *The siege of Rhodes*: Gulielmus Caoursin, *The Siege of Rhodes* (1482). *The English Experience. Its Record in Early Printed Books published in   Facsimile*, Number 236 (New York, 1970). All subsequent citations refer to this edition. Idem, *The Siege of Rhodes (1482)*, trans. John Kaye (Delmar, NY, 1975).

[4]   M. López Serrano, 'Incunables españoles: *Obsidionis Rhodie descriptio* de Guillermo Caoursin,' *Revista Bibliográfica y Documental*, Suplemento No. 1, T. 1 (1947), 1-6, with facsimile of the 1481 Barcelona edn.; Guillaume Caoursin, *Beretning om belejringen af byen Rhodos*, ed. Jacob Isager (Odense, 1982). Facsimile of the Odense edn. of 1482.

[5]   See E. Brockman, *The Two Sieges of Rhodes: The Knights of St. John at War 1480-1522* (New York, 1995 [1969]).

the sense and not the exact meaning.[6] While remaining true to Caoursin's narrative, Kay presented his own interpretation of the siege. To support his interpretation, Kay altered portions of Caoursin's narrative, omitting some portions of his text and inserting miraculous elements. Importantly, Kay augmented Caoursin's sparse martial terminology and included details about weaponry in his account. A recent study by Malcolm Hebron compares Caoursin's and Kay's version of the siege and concludes that in contrast to Caoursin's dry, factual record, Kay's translation is a literary rendition of the Latin text, written to entertain an audience eager for chivalric literature.[7] Certainly Kay expanded upon Caoursin's concise Latin account to show the intervention of God in human affairs, but the type of changes Kay made to the Latin text shows that his work was not limited to literary embellishment alone. His efforts cannot, strictly speaking, be considered a translation.

Kay expanded and emended the *Descriptio*, producing a historical account that relied not only upon Caoursin but also upon other official accounts of the siege. Kay's preamble states his inspiration was the books he read and saw in Italy about the capture of Constantinople in 1453 and the taking of Negropont in 1470.[8] In particular, he mentions the Greek cardinal of Mycene's Latin letter on the fall of Constantinople, and how it inspired Balthasar to write a similar work in Italian on the taking of Negropont. These particular works are not readily identifiable, although the Greek cardinal Bessarion wrote a Latin letter on the taking of Negropont in 1470.[9] Textual analysis of Kay's military terminology shows that he also used Pierre d'Aubusson's official letters to Pope Sixtus IV and Emperor Frederick III, titled *Relatio obsidionis Rhodie* and printed in September 1480, to augment Caoursin's account of the siege.[10]

---

[6]   See T. W. Machan, 'Chaucer as Translator,' in *The Medieval Translator: The Theory and Practice of Translation in the Middle Ages*, ed. R. Ellis (Cambridge, 1989), 55-67.

[7]   M. Hebron, *The Medieval Siege: Theme and Image in Middle English Romance* (Oxford, 1997), 77-84.

[8]   Kay, *Siege of Rhodes*, fol. 1r-v.

[9]   J. Monfasani, 'Bessarion Latinus,' in *Byzantine Scholars in Renaissance Italy: Cardinal Bessarion and Other Emigrés* (London, 1995), 165-209.

[10]   Pierre d'Aubusson, *Relatio obsidionis Rhodie*; also titled *De obsidione urbis Rhodiae ad Fridericum imperatorem* (Mainz, Nürnberg, & Strasburg, 1480).

Table 26.1   The Siege of Rhodes (1480) in Caoursin, Kay, and d'Aubusson.

Event in the Siege	Caoursin	Kay	D'Aubusson
Makers of artillery	'machinarum viri periti'	'...many connying men in makyng of instrumens of werre, that is to saye Bombardes, gownes, culverynes, serpentines and such other.'	----------
Artillery carried in the Turkish ships to Rhodes	'machinarum & belli ingeniorum'	'...grete instumens of werre. That ys to say Bombardes, gownes, serpentynes with many other instrumens of werre...'	----------
Turkish artillery in the garden of St Anthony's Church	'...tres ingentes machinas...'	'...thre bombardes of grete vyolence...'	'tres ingentes bombardas...spherica novem palmarum torquebant'
Rhodian artillery	'...tria tormenta quae bombarde vocanter...'	'...thre grete bombardes...'	----------
Master George's report on the Turkish artillery	'...classem eam quam diximus machinas sexdecim ingentes devexisse quarum longitudinis dimensio palmorum duorum & viginti fertur: quae vehementissimo velocissimoque iactu globos saxeos rotunditatis palmorum novem plerosque undecim torquent.'	'...xvi grete bombardes everychon of xxii fote of lenght, of the whiche the lest casted stones every stone of ix spannes in compas aboute.'	(See report on Turkish artillery in garden of St Anthony's church and below, the attack on the Jewish quarter of Rhodes, for size of shot.)
D'Aubusson's defense of the harbor	'Disponuntur ea parte murorum urbis bombardae & tormenta quae triremes & turcorum navigia expugnent perfringantque.'	'...for in that part were ordeyned bombardes and other grete instrumentes casting grete stones for to breke the galeyes of the Turkes...'	'bombardis & saxis erant' 'vires [sic] & ingenium' 'machine saxa iaciunt milites gladiis stringunt, balistis fundis saxorum iactu ex turci & mole'
Turkish attack on the Jewish quarter of Rhodes	'Ante hos [sic] muros octo ingentes collocant...'	'...before the sayd walles they putted viii grete instrumentes...'	'viii ingentes grandissimasque bombardas comportant, saxa circuitus palmarum ix torquentes'

Turkish anti-personnel devices	'Collocat enim omni ex parte tormenta & mortaria...'	'...certayn instruments of werre the whyche ben called Slynges or Engynes.'	'tormenti genere, quo igneas pilas proiiciebant, ac sagittas ignitas ex balistas & catapultis torquebant, quo ignem in edificia iacerent'
The Turks attempt a landing by sea	'Nec turci impigri bombardis respondent: ignes iaciunt: sagittas impetuosissimas ex balistis & cathapultis torquent.'	'...the Turkes from thother banke manly and stoutely faughted and defended their people aforsayd wyth castyng to the cyte and toure grete stones of bombardes and of gonnes and wyld fire and arowes of bowes and balestres.'	----------
Rhodian anti-personnel devices	'colubrinis quoque ac serpentinis nostros'	----------	'colubrinis & serpentinis nostris...'
Turks bombard the walls	'lapides congere non cessant'	'grete bombardes, gunnes and serpentines'	----------
The Rhodians build a trebuchet	'machinam versilem quod tribuccum...'	'...an engine called Trebuke lyke a slynge'	----------

As a historian, Kay presents a different process of causation and a different context for the siege of Rhodes than Caoursin. Both men saw the siege of Rhodes as a natural consequence of the Ottoman capture of Constantinople, twenty-four years earlier. But they differed on why the Turks besieged Rhodes. Caoursin postulated that the siege of Rhodes was inevitable once Mehmet II, 'the Conqueror', had taken Constantinople.[11] This hypothesis justified past Hospitaller policy, traditionally attributed to Master d'Aubusson, to prepare the island of Rhodes for an Ottoman attack. D'Aubusson had warned of an Ottoman attack on Rhodes and prepared the city for a siege even before he became master in 1476. The order began intensive preparation for an imminent siege in 1479.[12] Although Caoursin was aware of the Ottomans' steady advance in the eastern Mediterranean (he was the probable author of Ursini's magisterial dispatch describing the taking of Negropont in 1470), he does not mention any Christian-Ottoman conflict occurring between the taking of Constantinople and the siege of Rhodes.[13] Instead, Caoursin describes the attempts of the Turks to force the Knights to pay tribute and ascribes the immediate cause

---

[11]   Guilelmus Caoursin, *Obsidionis Rhodiae urbis descriptio* (Venice, 1480), fol. 1r. All subsequent citations refer to this edition.

[12]   K. M. Setton, *The Papacy and the Levant (1204-1571)*, ii: *The Fifteenth Century* (Philadelphia, 1978), 346-48.

[13]   *Bulletin historique et philologique du comité des travaux historiques et scientifiques*, ed. F. Mollard (Paris, 1891), 65-8.

of the siege to Mehmet's wrath over the failure of the Hospitallers to acknowledge his overlordship.[14] Caoursin insists upon the knights' preparation, especially, the wisdom and foresight of the master, Pierre d'Aubusson, and the personal bravery of all the people of Rhodes.

Kay, like Caoursin, believes the taking of Constantinople triggered the siege of Rhodes, but he provides additional reasons that are absent from Caoursin's text. According to Kay, Mehmet besieged Rhodes to persecute and undermine the Christian faith, not to extend his sovereignty.[15] Kay introduces this motive for the siege to enhance the religious conflict between Christendom and Islam. His interpretation de-emphasizes the professionalism of the knightly fighting force on Rhodes and accentuates the role of piety in fighting the Turk. Kay's master remains astute and pious, but more reliant upon religious fervour to attain his ends. In Kay the defence of Rhodes was improvised, and its people succeeded against the perfidious Turk through divine intervention. Kay's intent was not to create a chivalric text, but to show how the victory of the knights at Rhodes was the beginning of the end of time, when the Turkish threat would be finally defeated and the Latin East reclaimed.

A comparison of Latin and English texts shows that Kay added blocks of prose to Caoursin's text in places where the idea of religious warfare could be emphasized. Caoursin reports that the master's brother, Anthony d'Aubusson, who was travelling to the Holy Sepulcher with a company of knights, stopped off at Rhodes and stayed to help fight the Turks.[16] In Kay, the master's brother stopped in Rhodes *en route* to the Holy Sepulcher to fight for the Christian faith, bringing with him an international army of English and French knights.[17] Not only did Anthony d'Aubusson assist in the siege, he did so on behalf of the struggle of all Christendom to keep the Turks from Rhodes. At the end of Caoursin's account of the siege, the knights unfurled banners depicting Christ and the Virgin, and St. John the Baptist.[18] The Turks thought they saw a vision in the sky, which threw them into terror. Kay recounts this event, then interprets the miraculous vision that the Turks saw, concluding by attributing the knights' victory to divine intervention rather than military action.[19] These interpolations support Kay's purpose, showing that the prayers and repentance of the pope, the cardinals, and all Christian people were sufficient to prevent Mehmet II, the Great Turk, from advancing further into Italy. Kay omitted from his text all of Caoursin's references to pagan achievements, including his description of the site of the Colossus of Rhodes and of the high quality of the ancient construction of walls, in order to focus on Christian accomplishments.[20]

In addition to the lengthy interpolations, Kay elaborates upon the perfidy of the Turks: their reliance upon spies, their attempts to poison the master, and their tactic of sneaking about and creating fear in the heart of the average Rhodian. These

---

[14]   Caoursin, *Descriptio*, fols. 1v-2r.
[15]   Kay, *Siege of Rhodes*, fol. 2r.
[16]   Caoursin, *Descriptio*, fol. 11v.
[17]   Kay, *Siege of Rhodes*, fols. 14v-15r.
[18]   Caoursin, *Descriptio*, fols. 16v-17r.
[19]   Kay, *Siege of Rhodes*, fols. 21v-22r.
[20]   Caoursin, *Descriptio*, fol. 5r.

changes reinforce Kay's interpretation, emphasizing divinely inspired amateur improvisation, as opposed to Caoursin's professional forces and brave, resourceful Rhodians. Thus a sortie against the Turks, which in Caoursin consisted of fifty young knights of the order, becomes in Kay a sortie of fifty young men who loved Jesus.[21] Caoursin describes how two mercenaries (*duo mercenarii*) were executed because they wanted to surrender to the Turks.[22] Kay translated the Latin word 'mercenary' as 'men', even though the word 'mercenary' had been known in English at the time of Chaucer.[23] The presence of mercenaries at Rhodes did not support Kay's concept of religious warfare.

Other changes show the millenial bent of Kay's thinking. Caoursin wrote that the Turks attacked the walls of the Jewish quarter of Rhodes.[24] Kay creates a Jewish garrison, under the command of the master, which fought the Turks.[25] The alliance of the Jews with the Latins, and their possible conversion once the Turkish enemy was defeated, was a sign of the end. Caoursin and Kay both assess the role of Greek Christians in the siege, but with a marked difference in emphasis. Caoursin says repeatedly that the Greeks formed part of the army, and that the native Rhodians cooperated with the knights in fighting the Turks. Kay briefly notes the Greek contribution but prefers to stress the deeds of Latin Christians. Kay's grand summation, which attributes the ultimate success of the siege to Pope Sixtus IV, shows an eschatological conclusion in which all of Christendom is united by the pope.

Kay made a valuable contribution to Caoursin's account of the siege by providing descriptive details on the ordnance used by the knights and the Turks. Caoursin, as befitted his pretensions to humanistic learning, used a classical Latin vocabulary to denote artillery. Classical Latin, unfortunately, had no words to describe gunpowder artillery. This terminological void has led some modern historians to conclude that pre-gunpowder artillery was the preponderate form of ordnance used at the siege of Rhodes.[26]

Caoursin's Latin vocabulary displays a strong preference for classicizing and a reluctance to use the vernacular names of gunpowder ordnance. Caoursin only used the word bombard or its variant four times, and speaks of mortars four times and *tormenta* (artillery) five times. He preferred the word *machina*, which he used in one form or another forty-eight times. *Machinarum* was an all-purpose word used since classical times to indicate artillery pieces. Caoursin used another classical word for artillery, *ingenio* or its variant, thirty-two times.

Kay does not merely translate the term *machina* into English. Instead, he specifies in each case the types of artillery pieces employed: 'bombard', 'gun', 'culvern', 'serpentine', or other artillery pieces. When Caoursin wrote of the weapons the Turks transported to Rhodes, he called them 'machines' and 'engines of war'. Kay

---

[21] Ibid., fol. 8v; Kay, *Siege of Rhodes*, fol. 11v..

[22] Caoursin, *Descriptio*, fol. 9v.

[23] *Oxford English Dictionary*, *sub voce* 'mercenary'.

[24] Caoursin, *Descriptio*, fol. 6v.

[25] Kay, *Siege of Rhodes*, fols. 9r-9v.

[26] See errors in L. Butler, *The Siege of Rhodes*, (London, n.d.), 7.

listed 'the great war artillery' of the Turks as 'bombards', 'guns', 'serpentines', and many other 'war engines'. When Caoursin wrote of the Turkish bombardment of the Tower of St. Nicholas, he made it clear that he was introducing new terminology that would be unfamiliar to his readers. The Turks used three *tormenta* (in classical Latin, 'torsion catapult' or 'artillery' in medieval Latin), which, he explains, are today called bombards. Even when Caoursin records the words of another, as when Master George reports the condition of the Turkish artillery, he once again uses the word 'machines' while Kay uses the word 'bombards'. Kay's account clarifies the extensive Turkish use of large calibre bombards at Rhodes, combined with torsion anti-personnel devices, and that the Rhodians built a trebuchet to defend walls too weak for gunpowder emplacements. (See Figure 26.1)

What can explain the detailed account of artillery found in Kay's text? Is this a case of literary licence, or did Kay derive his account of artillery from contemporary historical sources? D'Aubusson's official reports of the siege contained additional information about the artillery used at Rhodes. There has been a strong assumption that these reports were based on Caoursin's account. Based upon an analysis of the vocabulary, especially the use of rare and archaic words also found in the *Descriptio*, they probably were penned by Caoursin himself. In the matter of ordnance, however, these reports use the words 'bombards' and 'mortars', not 'engines' and 'machines'. D'Aubusson emphasizes, far more than Kay or Caoursin, the Turkish use of large-calibre bombards that threw balls that spanned nine palms (approximately forty-five inches). D'Aubusson also describes the lighter pieces of artillery, including lighted arrows hurled from balistas and catapults, colubrinos, and serpentines. The close parallel between Kay's description of artillery and that written by d'Aubusson suggests that Kay consulted either of d'Aubusson's letters while he was in Italy and based his account of the ordnance used at Rhodes on these sources. (See Table 26.1.)

Kay's account of the siege of Rhodes has been considered a mere translation of Caoursin's *Descriptio*. Kay's overarching theme of divine intervention, with its emphasis on the miraculous, has led scholars to emphasize the literary, rather than the historical, contribution made by Kay to the history of the siege of Rhodes. But Kay acted as a historian, not as a translator. Correctly interpreted, Kay's text provides evidence that the knights played a role in the divine plan for humanity, and did not, as some modern authors conclude, rely solely on miraculous intervention for their success.[27]

The siege of Rhodes in 1480 did not stop the inexorable advance of the Ottoman Turks across the Mediterranean. Rhodes fell to the Turks in 1522, only 42 years after the siege. But neither Caoursin nor Kay was to know that. The success of the knights, coupled with the death of Mehmet the Conqueror in 1481 and the subsequent dissent between his two sons, Jem Sultan and Bayazid II, may have seemed like the dawning of a new age. Although Caoursin's text looked to the classical past in the form of the humanistic revival, Kay's text is full of clues for the onset of the millennium: the end of time, when the Pope would unite all Christian peoples against a common foe and the Jews would join the Christians in the fight against the enemies of Christ.

---

[27]   See Setton, ii, 349.

The genre that inspired Kay was not the chivalric literature of *Tirant lo Blanc* that eventually drove Don Quixote insane; it was the torrents of Latin and vernacular treatises bewailing the fall of Constantinople and crying out for a renewal of the crusading ideal. Kay's work placed the knights of Rhodes in the forefront of that struggles.

Chapter 27

The Hospitaller Fraternity of St John at SS Johan and Cordula in Cologne

Klaus Militzer

On 20 December 1463 Hupert von Heinsberg, a Hospitaller priest, made a foundation for the celebration of mass in his commandery's chapel at Cologne. The foundation was probably linked to another – that of a fraternity in honour of St John the Baptist. Mass would be celebrated at an altar to be erected for the purpose.[1] The letter of confirmation which the *baiulus* of Mallorca, John de Cardona, as lieutenant of the grand master and visitor for Germany, had issued on 30 June 1463, provides evidence of this connection.[2] But the real date of the foundation charter is not known with any certainty. The day and month cannot be traced in the original. They can be identified in a copy found at the commandery's *copiarium*. Assuming that the foundation was genuine and that both the copyist and the brothers of St John are to be believed, it should also be assumed that discussions and negotiations must have preceeded the actual foundation of the fraternity, the altar, and the celebration of mass earlier than 20 December. Hupert von Heinsberg's project could not have been realized before it had been approved by his superior at the commandery at Cologne.

Hupert von Heinsberg, a Hospitaller priest and for the years 1469-99 commander of the house in Cologne, was the son of a furrier of Cologne, Volquin von Heinsberg, and his wife Margarete von Alpen.[3] Hupert's two sisters, Adelheid (Aleid), married to Heinrich Forßbach, a councillor and member of the furrier's *Gaffel*,[4] and Beatrix (Patza), married to Jakob von Brück, also a councillor and member of the same *Gaffel*, supported him, giving him funds to enable him to provide the necessary endowment for the foundation.[5] His two brothers-in-law may have been the first to join the new fraternity. But we do not know the names of either the charter members

[1]   *Quellen zur Geschichte der Kölner Laienbruderschaften*, ed. K. Militzer, ii, Publikationen der Gesellschaft für Rheinische Geschichtskunde lxxi (Düsseldorf, 1997), 685-90.

[2]   Ibid., 684.

[3]   K. Militzer, 'Die vermögenden Kölner 1417-1418', *Mitteilungen aus dem Stadtarchiv von Köln*, lxix (1981), 186. Historisches Archiv der Stadt Köln, Rechnung 28¹, fol. 52v.

[4]   *Gaffel* was a technical term for associations of merchants and guilds of craftmen. These associations had to elect the councillors and to control the council; see K. Militzer, 'Ursachen und Folgen der innerstädtischen Auseinandersetzungen in Köln in der zweiten Hälfte des 14. Jahrhunderts', *Veröffentlichungen des Kölnischen Geschichtsvereins*, xxxvi (1980), 231-35. K. Militzer, '"Gaffeln, Ämter, Zünfte". Handwerker und Handel vor 600 Jahren', *Jahrbuch des kölnischen Geschichtsvereins*, lxvii (1996), 41-59.

[5]   *Quellen Laienbruderschaften*, ii, 685-89.

or the first members. Hupert, Forßbach, and Brück came from the social surroundings of the furriers; the latter two belonged to families with members in the council of Cologne. They ranked among the leading group in that town.

The altar founded by the relatives of the Heinsberg family stood near the grave of the patron saint Cordula, second only to John the Baptist. The bones of St Cordula, a companion of St Ursula, were discovered in the vineyard of St Johan commandery in 1278. They were allegedly removed from the ground by Albertus Magnus and buried in the middle of the commandery's chapel. More bones were again found later in the same vineyard. They were placed with the relics of St Ursula and those of her companions, including St Constantia. In 1327 these relics were once more removed from where they had been interred and ceremoniously exhibited.[6] It was a rich collection, which kept increasing the following years with similar finds. In fact the discovery was hardly surprising. The commandery had been erected at the Johannisstrasse, an old Roman street leading from Cologne to Neuss along the Rhine river. The Romans buried their dead along such streets outside the city. It is no wonder, then, that in the commandery's vineyard itself lay a Roman cemetary, which the brethren of St Johan exploited in order to raise their renown and prestige. It was precisely next to the burial place of St Ursula's companion that the Heinsberg family erected the altar.

The brethern and benefactors of the Hospitaller commandery had originally built another altar in the chapel, near the tomb of St Cordula in the middle of the nave. But once the fraternity altar was erected, it was transferred to the newly built chapel of St John.[7] The *confratres* were probably half-brothers or *familiares*, who were not members of the fraternity. Both the *familiares* and benefactors of the order and the commandery had other functions to perform. They had to support the knights of St John in their struggle for the faith and in caring for the sick.

The Heinsberg family had reasons to believe that a fraternity with an altar dedicated to a well-known saint would prove successful. Indeed, the fraternity flourished, survived the turmoil of the Protestant Reformation without suffering apparently any harm at all, and lasted through the seventeenth century. In 1645, in a book on the miraculous grandeur of Cologne, Aegidius Gelenius referred to the fraternity as still existing.[8]

The founding family had backed the right horse. The members of the fraternity prayed for the founders and their ancestors, and payments for masses celebrated for the repose of their souls. At the altar next to the tomb of St Cordula, mass was celebrated daily in honour of the Holy Virgin Mary and once a week in honour of St John the Baptist. The Hospitaller priests were responsible for these masses,

---

    [6]   *Die Kunstdenkmäler der Stadt Köln, Ergänzungsband: Die ehemaligen Kirchen, Klöster, Hospitäler und Schulbauten der Stadt Köln*, ed. L. Arntz, H. Neu, H. Vogts (Düsseldorf, 1937), 117-18.

    [7]   *Quellen Laienbruderschaften*, ii, 690-91.

    [8]   A. Gelenius, *De admiranda sacra et civili magnitudine Coloniae Claudiae Agrippinensis Augustae Ubiorum urbis libri IV* (Cologne, 1645), 445; cf. *Quellen zur Geschichte der Kölner Laienbruderschaften*, ed. K. Militzer, iii: Publikationen der Gesellschaft für Rheinische Geschichtskunde, lxxi (Düsseldorf, 1999), xiv.

which were to be celebrated invariably regularly – even in times of interdict or excommunication. Penalties were contemplated for the commandery if this obligation was neglected capriciously. The fraternity had retained the right to have these masses said in another church and, indeed, to move the whole fraternity to another place.

The Hospitaller commandery in Cologne attracted the founders partly through the relatives who had joined the order, and partly through the offer extended to all fraternity members to share in all the good works, indulgences, and prayers of the whole order, as long as these members actively participated both in the celebration of the masses and in the prayers recited by the fraternity. The order of St John could offer a lot. As the knights of St John fought for the faith at the front, their treasure of mercy by God was great. Whoever could get a share of the treasure, could expect a merciful judgement in Doomsday and perhaps could save himself from the horrors of purgatory.

The benefits the fraternity could draw from its settling in the commandery were clear and plausible. What was not as clear, however, were the advantages the order could derive from its interest in the new fraternity. That Hupert von Heinsberg was a Hospitaller, one of the founding brothers, and indeed the prime mover does not say much. He was elected commander years later. Moreover, fraternity members were not obliged to offer alms in support of the order's fighting for the faith in the eastern Mediterrenean. In the foundation charter and other agreements, the struggle against the enemies of the Christian faith was never mentioned. Neither was care for the sick. There was a considerable difference between the fraternity and the *familiares*.

A subordinate clause in the foundation charter of 1463 indicates that the commander of the house in Cologne should not make it difficult for Hospitallers to become either masters or assessors of the fraternity. Indeed, it was pointed out that a Hospitaller priest residing at the commandery should be one of the fraternity's masters or one of its assessors. It is not unlikely that through the fraternity, the commandery aimed at gaining and strengthening its influence in the town. Could it be that the commandery treated the fraternity as a sponsoring club? With the Hospitaller priest at the head of the fraternity, the order had control over the activities of the fraternity members. For subsequent years, however, we have failed to find any supporting evidence for this. The masters we have identified were all lay masters and came from the leading social group of Cologne. They were members of the town council or relatives of councillors. But the councillors in the fraternity did not belong to the cream of this social group. Constantin von Lyskirchen, a fraternity master, was an exception. All the other masters were members of the *Gaffeln*[9] of the smiths,[10] the furriers,[11] the fishmongers,[12] the coopers,[13] the shoemakers,[14] the painters,[15] and the goldsmiths.[16]

[9]   K. Militzer, 'Die Kölner Gaffeln in der zweiten Hälfte des 14. und zu Beginn des 15. Jahrhunderts', in *Rheinische Vierteljahrsblätter* xlvii (1983), 124-43.
[10]   Heinrich von Engelskirchen: *Quellen Laienbruderschaften*, ii, 698.
[11]   Heinrich von Wickrath, in ibid., 701, 707.
[12]   Engelbert Moll, in ibid., 710.
[13]   Bernd Ys, in ibid., 715.
[14]   Johann Risholtz, in ibid., 717.
[15]   Hermann Penterlinck, in ibid., 720.
[16]   Karl Wolf, in ibid., 692.

Some belonged to the *Gaffeln Aren*[17] and *Himmelreich*.[18] Only a few had joined the Gaffeln Windeck[19] and Schwarzhaus,[20] which belonged to the merchants. Persons from outside Cologne could not be admitted into the fraternity, which was open not only to the highest strata of society, but also to the wealthiest families in the town.

---

[17]   Johann Ryndorp, in ibid., 712, 726; Wennemar Hack and Johann von Kerpen, in ibid., 714. The *Gaffel Aren* was the association of makers of leather straps.

[18]   Johann von Reven, in ibid., 689, 692; Johann Keye, in ibid., 692; Johann Risholtz, in ibid., 722; Hermann Pastoir, in ibid., 692. The *Gaffeln Himmelreich*, *Windeck*, and *Schwarhuas* were associations of merchants.

[19]   Heinrich Hach, in ibid., 692.

[20]   Dietrich von Linz, in ibid., 723.

Chapter 28

Hospitaller Commanderies in the Kingdom of Hungary (*c.1150–c.1330*)

Zsolt Hunyadi

The last scholarly Hungarian monograph on the Hospitallers was published in 1925-28 by Ede Reiszig.[1] Since then a small number of articles and other popular works have appeared in print; none of these have been the result of any further research on primary sources. In the 1980s Croatian scholars, including in particular Lelja Dobronić, endeavoured unsuccessfully to correct the conclusions of several earlier decades of work.[2] One of the fundamental problems with Reiszig's work lies with the one-sided picture she drew of the Order of St John. She studied the activity of the order in the region of present-day Croatia. This constituted only one half of the former Hungarian-Slavonian priory of the Hospital, which covered present-day Hungary, Croatia, Romania, and parts of Slovonia. There is no doubt that the territorial distribution of the commanderies indicates a certain preference for Slavonia from the fourteenth century onwards, but approaching the issue according to the borders of modern States would definitely be unhistorical. It is unfortunate that these works determined the limits of other secondary works written either in the region[3] or

---

[1]   E. Reiszig, *A jeruzsálemi Szent János lovagrend Magyarországon* [The Order of the Knights of St. John of Jerusalem in Hungary], 2 vols (Budapest, 1925–28).

[2]   L. Dobronić, *Posjedi i Sjedišta Templara, Ivanovaca i Sepulkralaca u Horvatskoj* [Estates and Residences of Templars, Hospitallers, and Canons Regular of the Holy Sepulchre of Jerusalem in Croatia] (Zagreb, 1984); ead., *Viteški redovi, Templari i Ivanovci u Hrvatskoj* [Knightly Orders, Templars, and Hospitallers in Croatia] (Zagreb, 1984, 2002); ead., 'The Military Orders in Croatia', in *The Meeting of Two Worlds: Cultural Exchange between East and West during the period of the Crusades*, ed. V. Goss, (Kalamazoo, 1986), 431-38.

[3]   L. Hársing and K. Kozák, 'A johanniták a középkori Magyarországon' [Hospitallers in Medieval Hungary], *Világosság*, 20 (1979), 692-99; K. Kozák, 'Constructions dans la Hongrie des XII–XVe siècles des ordres de chevalerie et d'Hospitaliers et leur influence', *Acta Archaelogica*, xxxiv (1982), 71–130; N. Budak, 'Ivan od Palizne, prior vranski, vitez sv. Ivana', *Historijski Zbornik*, xliv (1989), 57–70; id., 'John of Palisna, the Hospitaller Prior of Vrana', in *The Crusades and the Military Orders: Expanding the Frontiers of Medieval Latin Christianity*, ed. Zs. Hunyadi and J. Laszlovszky (Budapest, 2001), 283–90; J. Török and L. Legeza, *Máltaiak. Szerzetesrendek a Kárpát-medencében* [The Maltese Order. Religious Orders in the Carpathian Basin] (Budapest, 1999).

by Western scholars.[4] It is hardly possible to produce appropriate comparative works before a more accurate picture is drawn of the history of the commanderies and the Hospitallers in this part of Europe.

One problem with the early monographs (from Georgius Pray[5] to Ede Reiszig) is that they fail to meet modern scholarly standards, although many scientific works (especially the publication of archival source material) have stood the test of time. After eight whole decades since Ede Reiszig's work was published, it is necessary to revisit the history of the Hospitallers in Hungary. The discovery of new sources, the new insights they provide, and the application of new methods may not only yield more accurate results, they may also encourage young historians to aspire to higher levels of contemporary scholarship. Moreover, Hospitaller historiography has long been burdened with a serious conceptual problem. In contrast to the Western European context, Hungarian and many Central European (Latin) written sources often use the term *crucifer* for the more appropriate *frater hospitalis* or *miles Templi*, conceivably with reference to the cross depicted on the Hospitaller or Templar habit. This has led to confusion: several scholars have treated the houses and the landed properties of other orders (like the Order of St Anthony, the Order of the Holy Spirit, and others) as belonging to the Hospital, and vice versa. On the basis of this perception and by a close reading of primary sources as well as by the clarification of the notions and denominations applied in the primary sources, Karl-Georg Boroviczény, a German hematologist of Hungarian origin, discovered or, in fact, singled out (in the late 1960s), a formerly unknown religious institution, the Order of Hospitaller Canons Regular of St Stephen, founded by the Hungarian King Géza II (1142-62) around the mid-twelfth century.[6] The members of this order were also called *cruciferi* in contemporary sources – they even used this expression in the inscriptions of their own charters – but they had nothing in common with either the crusaders or with the Hospital of St John. Mainstream Hungarian scholarship accepted Boroviczény's ideas, but has failed to draw the necessary conclusion, namely, that the history (settling down, presence, activity, role) of the Hospitallers in the Hungarian kingdom should be fundamentally reconsidered.

---

[4]   K. Borchardt, 'Military Orders in East Central Europe: The First Hundred Years', in *Autour de la première Croisade*, Actes de Colloque de la Society for the Study of the Crusades and the Latin East, ed. M. Balard, *Byzantina Sorbonensia*, xiv (Paris, 1996), 247–57; A. Luttrell, 'Change and Conflict within the Hospitaller Province of Italy after 1291', in *Mendicants, Military Orders, and Regionalism in Medieval Europe*, ed. J. Sarnowsky (Aldershot, 1999), 185–99; id., 'The Hospitaller Province of *Alamania* to 1428', in *Ordines Militares – Colloquia Torunensia Historica VIII*, ed. Z. Nowak (Torun, 1995), 21–41; id., 'The Hospitallers in Hungary before 1418: Problems and Sources', in *The Crusades and the Military Orders: Expanding the Frontiers of Medieval Latin Christianity*, ed. Zs. Hunyadi and J. Laszlovszky (Budapest, 2001), 268–81.

[5]   *Dissertatio historico-critica de Prioratu Auranae in qua origo, progressus, et interitus, ex monumentis nondum editis, compendio a P. Georgio Pray e S. J. explicantur* (Viennae, 1773).

[6]   K.-G. Boroviczény, '*Cruciferi Sancti Regis Stephani*: Tanulmány a stefaniták, egy középkori magyar ispotályos rend történetéről', *Orvostörténeti Közlemények. Communicationes de Historiae Artis Medicinae*, cxxxiii-cxl (1991–92), 7–48.

The appearance of the Hospitaller Order in the Hungarian Kingdom can be traced back to the middle of the twelfth century. In contrast to recent historiography, the role of King Géza II's wife, Queen Euphrosyne (b.1130–†c.1193),[7] and that of Martyrius, archbishop of Esztergom, primate of Hungary (1151–1157), should be emphasized much more. Probably owing to their initiative, sometime around 1150 the members of the Hospital founded the first commandery in Székesfehérvár, dedicated its church to the first (holy) king of Hungary, St Stephen, who established the Hungarian section of the inland pilgrims' road towards the Holy Land after 1018.

Royal support proved to be long lasting. It began with Euphrosyne and continued with her son, Béla III (1172–1196), who, as a prince of Hungary, Dalmatia, and Croatia, granted the master of the Hospital a good sum of money in the first half of 1170.[8] In 1193 he also confirmed that his mother's gift extended to the first commandery of the Order in Hungary and included more than fifty pieces of landed property.[9] It resembled the Bohemian Prince Frederick's confirmation in 1186 of all former donations given to the Hospitallers in Bohemia.[10]

Székesfehérvár was not only the first commandery in Hungary; it became the 'mother' house of several commanderies established later[11] and founded in the Trans-Danubian region during the thirteenth century. Three additional establishments, which were not dependencies of Székesfehérvár, have been identified as commanderies from the second half of the twelfth century. The first of these, in 1166, was granted funds from a rare private donation and consisted of three predial lands and a church dedicated to St. Peter in Zala County.[12] Like contemporaneous grants that the Order received all over Europe, the charter mentions the poor and not the defenders of the Holy Land, even if it is known that in certain regions the number of '*pro defensione sancte terre*' donations increased remarkably in the middle of the twelfth century.[13] Since no commandery dedicated to St Peter is known from later sources, it is hopeless to try to identify its locality.

---

[7]   According to tradition, she had been buried in the church of the Székesfehérvár commandery: *in qua corpus regine Euphrosine* [...] *intumulatum est.* (4 April 1272). *Codex diplomaticus Hungariae ecclesiasticus ac civilis*, ed. G. Fejér, 11 vols. (Buda, 1829–44), ii, 184; v (1), 211–4; xi (1), 67-69.

[8]   Fejér CD, v (1), 284–88, *CH*, no. 309. On the dating of the charter, F. Makk, *The Árpáds and the Comneni. Political Relations between Hungary and Byzantium in the 12ᵗʰ Century* (Budapest, 1989), 106, 170-71.

[9]   [...] *hec igitur sunt nomina prediorum que a domina matre nostra prefato monasterio sunt collata* [...]. *Árpád-kori oklevelek, 1001–1096* [Charters from the Arpadian Age], ed. Gy. Györffy (Budapest, 1997), 93-96; Fejér CD, ii, 288; *CH*, no. 936. *Monumenta Ecclesiae Strigoniensis*, ed. F. Knauz, *et al*, 4 vols. (Esztergom–Budapest, 1874-1999), i, 142-47.

[10]   *Codex diplomaticus et epistolaris Moraviae*, ed. A. Boczek, *et al*, 15 vols. (Olomucii–Brunae, 1836-1903), i, 317; *CH*, no. 802.

[11]   Aracsa, Gyánt, Újudvar, Csurgó, and Varasd (Bonyhádvarasd).

[12]   Fejér CD, ii, 174–5; *CH*, no. 368; *Hazai Okmánytár. Codex diplomaticus patrius*, ed. I. Nagy, *et al.*, 8 vols. (Győr–Budapest, 1865-91), vii, 1–2.

[13]   Cf. Michael Gervers, '*Pro defensione sancte terre*: The Development and Exploitation of the Hospitallers' Landed Estate in Essex', in *MO*, i, 3-20.

The second establishment was located at Boisce on the Dalmatian coast. It is only known from a papal bull addressed to *Matheo rectori et fratribus cruciferariis (sic) hospitalis Sancti Petri Boisce.*[14] Since this papal letter and a charter from 1217 are the only extant documents, Boisce may have belonged to the Templars[15] or was perhaps run by another Hospitaller or military religious order which the term *crucifer* referred to. In 1247 Béla IV granted the order the Severin region,[16] including the city of Scardona on the Dalmatian coast, and emphasized that the purpose of the donation was to render the order's maritime travels easier. This implies that the Hospitallers had no direct access to the sea before 1247. By the second half of the fourteenth century, Boisce was held by the Hospitallers in the aftermath of their acquisition of Templar property.[17]

The existence of a third hospital in Pécs (Baranya county) has been deduced from the appearance in a charter of a certain Gilbert *magister hospitalis* as a witness to a transaction in 1181.[18] There are no additional grounds to prove that it belonged to the Hospital either at that time or later. It was apparently an episcopal hospital. This claim is reinforced by a charter of 1217, when the Hospitaller master of Pécs witnessed a transaction between the bishop and the canons of the cathedral chapter of Pécs, indicating that the hospital was under episcopal auspices.[19] Thus, a certain woman with the name of Froa made a grant to this hospital[20] rather than to the Order of the Hospital, though she later changed her mind and revoked the donation.[21]

As in the case of those commanderies that were the *membra* of Székesfehérvár, the landed properties of the Order may well indicate the stages they followed in settling down within the realm. As already indicated, the first private donation was made as early as 1166, but the charter did not restrict the purpose of the gift by applying, for instance, the increasingly common Western formula: *pro defensione sancte terre.*[22] Queen Euphrosyne's patronage in the second half of the twelfth century and that of Béla III in 1193 were followed by the dowry of Margaret, Béla III's sister in

---

[14]   *Árpádkori új okmánytár. Codex diplomaticus Arpadianus continuatus*, ed. G. Wenzel, 12 vols. (Pest, 1860-74), vi, 149.

[15]   Wenzel, vi, 390-91. A charter claims that the Templars owned a house in Boisce which may have been identical to the one mentioned. Pontius de Cruce stayed *in casa nostra in San Pietro de Boischie* in 1217. *Codex diplomaticus regni Croatiae, Dalmatiae ac Slavoniae, Diplomatički zbornik kraljevine Hrvatske, Dalmacije i Slavonije*, ed. M. Kostrenčić and T. Smičiklas, 18 vols. (Zagreb, 1904-90), iii, 165.

[16]   Fejér CD, iv (1), 447-54; *CH*, no. 2445; *Vetera Monumenta Historica Hungariam Sacram Illustrantia, 1216-1352*, ed. A. Theiner, 2 vols. (Romae, 1859–60), i, 208.

[17]   Fejér CD, ix (5), 496-97; Smičiklas, xvi, 190.

[18]   *III. Béla magyar király emlékezete* [Memory of King Béla III of Hungary], ed. Gy. Forster, (Budapest, 1900), 345.

[19]   Wenzel, xi, 153-54; L. Koszta, *A pécsi székeskáptalan hiteleshelyi tevékenysége (1214-1353)* [The Pécs cathedral chapter as a place of authentication, 1214–1353] (Pécs, 1998), 16, 183.

[20]   As has been thought by several scholars to date. *III. Béla emlékezete* [Memory of King Béla III], ed. Gy. Kristó and F. Makk ([Budapest], 1981), 107, 194.

[21]   Forster, *III. Béla emlékezete*, 245-46.

[22]   Gervers, 3-20.

1208.[23] Though indirectly, the continuous conflicts with several Hungarian bishops and Benedictine monasteries over tithes may also help us to locate the Hospitaller estates and commanderies in Hungary.

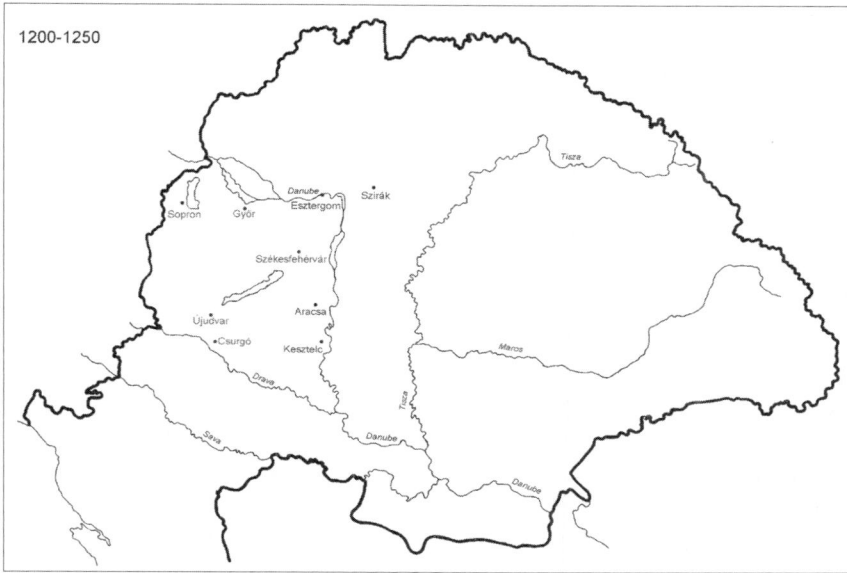

Fig. 28.1   Hospitaller commanderies in the Hungarian-Slavonian priory, 1200–1250

The first known conflict occurred as early as 1207, when the bishop of Vác was informed of the rights that the Hospitallers enjoyed over their landed property in his diocese.[24] Although it is not possible to identify with any certainty the houses referred to in Innocent III's bull, they might have been Szirák and Tolmács: these were already commanderies by the first third of the thirteenth century. The charter of 1207, issued by King Andrew II (1205–1235), provides further proofs to the existence of the house of Tolmács.[25] In 1209, a similar problem arose in the diocese of Győr.[26] However, it is not known whether the estates referred to in this case were close to Sopron or Győr, that is to the towns where commanderies were later established.

---

[23]   Fejér CD, iii (1), 56-57; *Veszprémi püspökség római oklevéltára, Monumenta romana episcopatus Wesprimiensis, 1103–1526*, ed. V. Fraknói, 3 vols. (Budapest, 1896-1907), i, 17; *CH*, no. 1302; M. Wertner, *Az Árpádok családi története* [A history of the Árpáds] (Nagy-Becskerek, 1892), 351-52.

[24]   Fejér CD, iii (1), 44.

[25]   [...] *eadem septem villarum concessimus in perpetuum gaudere libertate qua faventer ville templariorum et hospitalariorum*. Ibid., 42; Smičiklas, iii, 72.

[26]   Fejér CD, iii (1), 99-100.

Similarly, it is still doubtful whether the Hospital had owned any estates or houses in the diocese of Pécs in 1213, when the pope warned the Hospitallers not to abuse their privileges.[27] By 1216 a commandery appeared in Kesztelc[28] and by 1226 another in Aracsa,[29] and both were founded in the archdeaconry of Tolna, which belonged to the diocese of Pécs. The autonomy of these commanderies was short-lived as there is no further mention of them after 1226.

The most serious conflict, however, concerned the tithe levied in Somogy County by the Székesfehérvár commandery and the Benedictine convent of Pannonhalma.[30] The fact that the Hospitaller commandery had been added to the *Liber Censuum* in 1192[31] did not prevent the Benedictines from protesting against the exemption enjoyed by the Székesfehérvár commandery. Other Hospitaller commanderies in the region (Csurgó and Újudvar) found themselves equally involved later in several similar lawsuits processed by the judges delegate of the Holy See. The quarrel did not come to an end until the second half of the thirteenth century.[32]

Andrew II's donations, granted during his sojourn in the Holy Land[33] and confirmed by Honorius III in 1218,[34] should also to be considered. There is no doubt that the Hospitallers had seized the lands lying between Csurgó and the River Drava. However, one should question whether the king had in fact kept his promise of handing over the taxes paid out of the saltpans of Szalacs to the fortresses of Crac and Margat. Though the king himself reconfirmed his donation in 1225,[35] about four decades later, in 1258 and 1259,[36] Pope Alexander IV warned Béla IV (1235–1270), Andrew II's son, to fulfil his father's promise made in the Holy Land. It would appear that both *verba et scripta volant*.

Nevertheless, owing to the attitude of the Hungarian rulers – Béla III, Andrew II, Béla IV, and Stephen V (1270–1272) – and aided by papal exemptions, the development of the Hospitallers in Hungary was almost unbroken for several decades. Nine commanderies are known from the first half of the thirteenth century: Székesfehérvár apart, there are data concerning Kesztelc and Csurgó, Szirák, Aracsa and Esztergom, Újudvar, Sopron, and perhaps Győr. It is clear from the map that these commanderies were mostly located in the Trans-Danubian region or fairly

---

[27]   Ibid., 141-42.

[28]   Ibid., 179-80; *CH*, no. 1463; Wenzel, i, 222; *A pannonhalmi Szent-Benedek-rend története*, [History of the Benedictine Order of Pannonhalma], ed. L. Erdélyi and P. Sörös, 12 vols, (Budapest, 1902–16), i, 672-73; Fraknói, i, 70; Knauz, i, 260; Smičiklas, iii, 225; ibid., iv, 109, 276; ibid., v, 177.

[29]   Erdélyi, i, 672-73; Fraknói, i, 70; Knauz, i, 260, 278; Wenzel, i, 222-23.

[30]   E.g, *CH*, nos.1438, 1472, 1586, 1816; Erdélyi, i, 164, 638, 672-73; Wenzel, i, 146, 222-23; ibid., vi, 377-79; Fraknói, i, 36-37, 40, 65-66, 70; Fejér CD, iii (1), 228-30; ibid., iii (2), 38-41; Theiner, i, 8-9, 57-58; Knauz, i, 260.

[31]   Fejér CD, ii, 282; Knauz, i, 142.

[32]   Erdélyi, ii, 93, 313; Fraknói, i, 140; Wenzel, iii, 7.

[33]   Ibid., i, 140-42; Fejér CD, iii (1), 233-43; *CH*, no. 1590.

[34]   Fejér CD, iii (1), 244; Theiner, i, 14-15, 17; *CH*, nos. 1602, 1614; Wenzel, i, 156-57.

[35]   *CH*, no. 1803.

[36]   Fejér CD, iv (2), 466-69, 504-506; Wenzel, ii, 301-303; Theiner, i, 236-38; *CH*, nos. 2896, 2920; Knauz, i, 454.

close to it. The explanation for this phenomenon is manifold. Queen Euphrosyne's grant and its confirmation in 1193 can be regarded as the point of departure. The next substantial royal gift of land was made in 1238 and the Slavonian properties proved eventually significant, although most of the rest lay in different parts of the kingdom. There were various reasons for this. The consistent development of western Hungary was one; the increasing density of population was another; the third was the early prevalence of a money economy. Each of these parameters in a sense justifies the choice of location of the first donations. They do not, however, explain why the situation remained unchanged for so long. In the case of three other commanderies,[37] there is supporting evidence concerning the existence of baths and a hospice. Béla IV's charter of 1238 makes it clear that the baths had already existed at the time of the royal donation.[38] Since several of these commanderies had originally been estates of the Székesfehérvár commandery, they might have been affiliated with the first house.

By the end of the third decade of the thirteenth century, these commanderies constituted the so-called Hungarian–Slavonian priory. The Slavonian part covered the area between the rivers Drava and Sava and slightly further towards the south of the Sava. However, in its broader sense, from the beginning of the fourteenth century, it also included the Croatian commanderies. Though in Slavonia the order gained its first landed properties in 1238[39] and 1240,[40] the bulk of them were obtained only after the acquisition of the Templar possessions, thereby spreading over the river Drava.

During the 1230s and the beginning of the 1240s, the pace of the order's development began to slow down. Béla IV tried to regain a considerable part of the royal domain alienated by his father. This included Hospitaller landed property. The issue was solved in Rome. Pope Gregory IX warned Béla IV to restore the original status quo and nominated the bishops of Vác, Nyitra, and Bosnia to collaborate in the process of recovery.[41] The next blow came from the Mongol invasion of 1241–1242, during which both the order's lands and its serfs suffered. Although there is no direct evidence of the military help extended by the Hospitallers at this time, a number of brethren are believed to have accompanied Béla IV on his flight from the Mongols to *circa maritima*, that is to the Dalmatian coast.[42] In 1243 the first extant charter of the Székesfehérvár commandery recorded that *proprium sigillum nostrum erat*

---

[37]   Győr, Esztergom, and Sopron.

[38]   *Item concessimus eidem domui quedam balnea in Ieurino* {Győr} *sita* [...]; *quedam balnea communia in Strigonio* {Esztergom} *que fecit fieri avia nostra domina Anna secundum normam et libertatem a predecessoribus nostris eidem domui super hoc concessam.* Smičiklas, iv, 48-50; Fejér CD, iv (1), 104-111; ibid., ix (5), 153; Knauz, i, 326.

[39]   Smičiklas, iv, 48-50; Fejér CD, iv (1), 104-111, Knauz, i, 326.

[40]   Wenzel, xi, 313.

[41]   Fejér CD, iv (1), 33-36, Theiner, i, 143; *CH*, no. 2136.

[42]   Rogerius' information is not reliable as it reads (in its extant form): *... rex Bela marittimis de partibus per cruciferos de insula Rodi* [...] *de recessu Tartarorum in Hungariam venit.* ('Rogerii carmen miserabile', in *Scriptores Rerum Hungaricarum*, ed. E. Szentpétery, 2 vols. (Budapest, 1937-38, repr. 1999.), ii, 588.) It is an obvious interpolation of a later hand.

in maritima.[43] Rembald of Voczon, the prior of the Hungarian–Slavonian priory at the time, remained in Dalmatia until November 1243, when he acted as one of the witnesses to a legal case in Trau (Trogir).[44]

The aftermath of the Mongol devastation made Béla IV more cautious and prudent. In 1247 he entered into a contract with the Hospitallers, granting them the whole Severin, together with another 400 acres of land in an unidentified locality which led to Severin.[45] It was also at this time that the order received the town of Scardona (Skradin) on the Mediterranean coast. There is no plausible explanation of why the Hospitallers failed to establish any commandery or stronghold in the region (sc. Severin), or why they abandoned it shortly afterwards and providing the king with no explanation.[46] Nor is there any adequate justification for Béla IV's reaction towards the order, who introduced a form of mortmain. The king consented to the last will of a certain *comes* called Nána in 1256[47] and similarly in connection with another will, he stipulated that *cruciferis dumtaxat exceptis* (1260).[48]

In the second half of the thirteenth century, the Hospital owned some eighteen commanderies in Hungary.

A new pattern can be discerned in the distribution of the commanderies, namely that new administrative units appeared in the Trans-Drava region[49] well before the acquisition of Templar property. A new commandery was also established in Transylvania (at Torda), the easternmost part of the kingdom. At the same time, a number of houses had disappeared from the sources by the last quarter of the thirteenth century.[50] Three of them had been administered jointly with the Esztergom commandery during the first three decades of the century.

---

[43]   Wenzel, vii, 144-45; cf. Zs. Hunyadi, 'A székesfehérvári johannita konvent hiteleshelyi tevékenysége az Árpád-korban' [The Székesfehérvár commandery of the Order of St. John of Jerusalem in Hungary as a place of authentication in the Árpád Age], in *Capitulum I. Tanulmányok a középkori magyar egyház történetéből*, ed. L. Koszta (Szeged, 1998), 40-41.

[44]   *Testes sunt Rambaldus preceptor domus Hospitalis per totam Hungariam* [...]. Smičiklas, iv, 205-206.

[45]   Fejér CD, iv (1), 447-54; Theiner, i, 208; *Erdélyi okmánytár, Codex diplomaticus Transsylvaniae, 1023–1300*, ed. Zs. Jakó (Budapest, 1997), 191; *CH*, no. 2445. Since the donation is well-known even among Western scholars, there is no need to go into details.

[46]   Reiszig, i, 61-63; A. Forey, *The Military Orders from the Twelfth to the Early Fourteenth Centuries* (London, 1992), 38, 81; A. Luttrell, 'The Hospitallers in Hungary before 1418', 271-72.

[47]   [...] *quod domui Hospitalis terram unius aratri suffiecientem, et unum locum molendini supra Danubiam possit dare* [...] *et non ultra*. Fejér CD, iv (2), 377.

[48]   Ibid.; also ibid., iv (3), 44-45.

[49]   Dopsin, Pakrac, Bela, and Čiče.

[50]   Kesztelc, Szirák, Aracsa, Tolmács, and Szomolya.

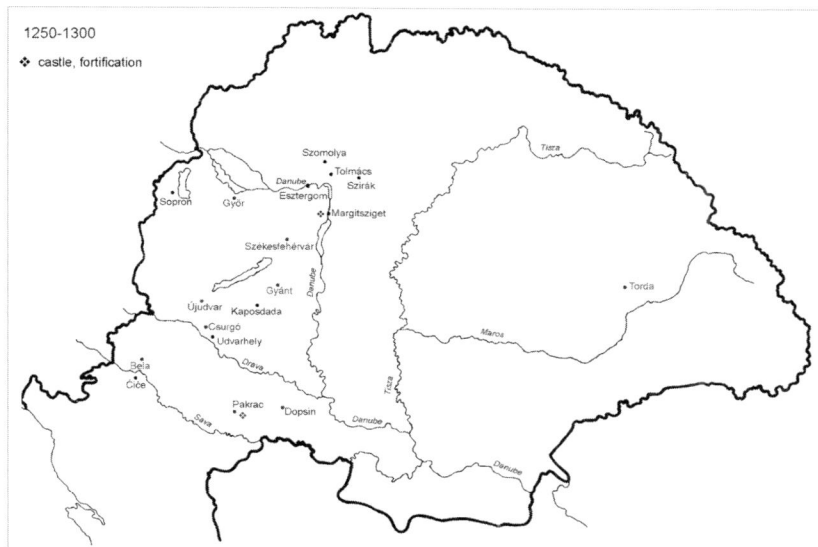

Fig. 28.2   Hospitaller commanderies in the Hungarian-Slavonian priory, 1250–1300

Although ample evidence supports the important role royal patronage played in the establishment of the commanderies, very little is known about the actual process of foundation of these houses, or their affiliation. It would appear that a circle of commanderies gradually became affiliated with Székesfehérvár and Esztergom, but the actual stages in the process itself are quite difficult to prove. On the other hand, the process of the disappearance of the commanderies is perhaps more evident. The smaller or less prosperous commanderies usually lost their autonomy first, and began to be administered either by the commander of another house or by the lieutenant prior of the Hungarian–Slavonian Priory. These commanderies sooner or later appeared as mere dependencies of another commandery, often that of Vrana from the fourteenth century onwards, or were either alienated or pledged.

At the dawn of the fourteenth century, one of the most significant events in the history of the military orders was no doubt the dissolution of the Templars and the acquisition of most of their houses and estates by the Hospital. This process, together with the disappearance of several 'northern' Hospitaller commanderies, basically altered the balance within the Hungarian–Slavonian Priory and transferred the centre of the order's authority to the opposite side of the river Drava, giving Vrana, the former Templar headquarters, and the coastal areas increased significance.

Between 1312/1314 and *c*.1340, at least eleven former Templar houses and several estates were taken over by the Hospitallers.[51]

Fig. 28.3   Hospitaller commanderies in the Hungarian-Slavonian priory, 1300–c.1350

Most of these units had vanished by the last quarter of the fourteenth century; many of them lost their autonomy and later became dependent upon the Priory of Vrana.

Loca credibilia

Contrary to the practice adopted by European public notaries, certain institutions in Hungary issued charters to record private legal transactions (e.g., conveyances) under their authentic seals upon the request of the parties concerned. The major collegiate and cathedral chapters were the first such institutions to start issuing charters. They were soon followed by the convents of the Benedictines, the Premonstratensians, the canons regular of St Stephen, and the Hospitallers, all acting as places of authentication (*loca credibilia*). Nine Hospitaller commanderies were involved in this activity. From the Árpád Age onwards, these were Székesfehérvár, Csurgó, Újudvar, Pakrac (Pekrec), Gyánt, Sopron, and Torda; with Bő and Dubica in the fourteenth century. The activity of the first four commanderies should be emphasized, especially that

---

[51]   These were at Hresztva (Hresno), Gora, Dubica, Našice-Martin, Szentmárton (Bo žjakovina), Lešnik, Okur (Szentlőrinc), Vrana, Keresztény (Christiana), Bő, and Szentiván (Ivanec).

of Székesfehérvár which, from the second half of the fourteenth century, enjoyed a nation-wide sphere of authority.[52] Although there are minor differences between the 'output' of each Hospitaller *scriptorium*, the formal features of the documents issued by them show that from the mid-fourteenth century onwards, the activities of these commanderies as places of authentication corresponded with other Hungarian ecclesiastical establishments.

Personnel of the commanderies

Owing chiefly to the charters issued by the Hospitallers, more than one hundred members of the order from the long years under survey (1186-1330s) are known individually by name. From the middle of the thirteenth century to the early 1370s, the officials of the Hungarian–Slavonian priory[53] and those of the commanderies were, with very few exceptions, of French and Italian origin. They bore such names as Gwyllerm,[54] Hugo,[55] Giacomo of Siena (Gora), and Lorenzo of Perugia (Sopron); Argellin, and John the Gallic (Székesfehérvár); Peter Ymberth;[56] and Marc of Bologna (Vrana). Brothers of local origin were not of course excluded. The list of names of members of the Sopron commandery included Rudewan (1274), Theoderic (1276), and Detric (1276), who might have well been local townsmen of German origin.[57] Commander Peter (1308–1321) was certainly of local origin, the son of a local burgher of higher social standing.[58] There were members of other commanderies who might have been of Hungarian origin, like Simon (Csurgó), Andrew (Dubica), John,[59] Robert, Benedict, or Michael (Székesfehérvár). At least one case from the period under review stands out: in 1339 Pierre (Peyre) Cornuti appointed a Hungarian

---

[52]   Cf. Hunyadi, 'A székesfehérvári johannita konvent', 61. Zs. Hunyadi, 'The *Locus Credibilis* in Hungarian Hospitaller Commanderies', in *La Commanderie: institution des ordres militaires dans l'Occident médiéval*, ed. Anthony Luttrell et Léon Pressouyre (Paris, 2002), 285–96.

[53]   On the priors and their lieutenants, Zs. Hunyadi, 'Hospitaller Officials of Foreign Origin in the Hungarian–Slavonian Priory: Thirteenth-Fourteenth centuries', in *International Mobility in the Military Orders (Twelfth to Fifteenth Centuries): Travelling on Christ's Business*, ed. H. J. Nicholson and J. Burgtorf (Cardiff, 2006), 142-54.

[54]   Bela, Čiče, Csurgó, Hresno, Székesfehérvár, and Újudvar.

[55]   Csurgó, Pakrac, Székesfehérvár, and Újudvar.

[56]   Szirák, Szomolya, and Tolmács.

[57]   *Urkunden des Cistercienser-Stiftes Heiligenkreuz im Wiener Walde. Fontes Rerum Austriacarum*. Abt. II, *Diplomataria et acta*, xi, ed. J. N. Weis (Wien–Graz–Köln, 1856), 188-89; *Sopron szabad királyi város története, Oklevelek* [A history of the royal exempt town of Sopron, Charters], ed. J. Házi, 2nd ser. (Sopron, 1921-43), i (1), 5-6; Nagy, *Hazai okmánytár*, iii, 24-25.

[58]   Házi, i (1), 34-35; *Urkundenbuch des Burgenlandes und der angrenzenden Gebiete der Komitate Wieselburg, Ödenburg und Eisenburg*, ed. H. Wagner and I. Lindeck-Pozza, 5 vols. (Graz–Köln–Wien, 1955-99), iii, 129-30.

[59]   Gora, Našice-Martin, and Újudvar.

layman as protector of the Csurgó commandery for three years.[60] The general trend or policy may also be observed in the case of the Székesfehérvár commandery. Towards the end of our period, the brethren of minor ranks (e.g., *clerici chori*) were Hungarians, while by the end of the fourteenth century the entire staff of the commandery was of local origin.[61]

One other observation must be made. The members of these Hospitaller places of authentication are very likely to have spoken the vernacular and to have studied customary law. Brethren performing service on the very spot of the legal case were obviously Hungarians and more or less familiar with the local or general customs of the realm. It is not known to what extent foreign members were involved in the everyday life of the commanderies. It can be shown, for example, how the highest officers on the priory acted in local affairs through native members of the Hospital. Master Rolando of Gragnana participated indirectly through chaplain Nicholas (1315);[62] so did the prior Filippo de Gragnana through one George, *presbyter, capellanus, et scriptor* (1325).[63]

To conclude: the Hospitallers settled in the medieval kingdom of Hungary during the second half of the twelfth century partly following the initiative of Queen Euphrosyne. Royal patronage of the order remained remarkable throughout the period under survey; it had almost entirely replaced private benevolence. Such patronage enabled the order not only to perform its usual Hospitaller activities; it also encouraged the Hospital to play an important role in the promotion of private legal literacy. Similarly to what happened to other European provinces, the dissolution of the Templars and the Hospital's acquisition of their estates fundamentally reshaped the Hungarian-Slavonian priory by the end of the 1330s.

---

[60]   [...] *fecimus et ordinamus* [...] *tutorem defensorem gubernatorem et protectorem preceptoris domus nostre de Chergo.* L. Solymosi, *A földesúri járadékok új rendszere a 13. századi Magyarországon* [The new system of manorial allowances during the thirteenth century in Hungary] (Budapest, 1998), 336-37.

[61]   Zs. Hunyadi, 'The Knights of St. John and the Hungarian Private Legal Literacy up to the Mid-Fourteenth Century', in *The Man of Many Devices, Who Wandered Full Many Ways*, Festschrift in Honour of János M. Bak, ed. B. Nagy and M. Sebők (Budapest, 1999), 514.

[62]   *Anjoukori Okmánytár, Codex diplomaticus Hungaricus Andegavensis*, ed. I. Nagy and Gy. Tasnádi Nagy, 7 vols. (Budapest, 1878-1920), i, 389-90.

[63]   National Archives of Hungary, *Collectio Antemohacsiana*, Dl.2337.

Chapter 29

Frisians and Foreigners in the Hospitaller House of Sneek: Origins and Careers

Johannes Adriaan Mol

Introduction

As a result of the massive participation of Frisians in the crusades, the military orders were able to acquire a considerable amount of property in the Frisian lands. Before the middle of the fourteenth century, the Order of St John and the Teutonic Order had no less than twenty-one houses in the long but narrow strip of coastal lands along the North Sea between the isle of Texel and the German Bight.[1] Most of these commanderies were convents that had begun as double monasteries, developing either into nunneries with a small number of priests and lay brothers, or into houses with a male population, including priest brethren active as pastors in dependent parishes. The present paper is thus about priests, parish ministers, sisters, and lay brothers.[2] From what regions had these originated? What do we know about their careers?

A study of the background and origin of the Frisian members of the Teutonic Order showed that their recruitment was a regional affair, at least up to the 1470s, when serious management troubles in the Frisian houses offered the provincial commander in Utrecht an opportunity to force a *reformatio* upon them. In the end this was secured by having these houses peopled with only non-native brethren.[3] By then, the policy of gradually replacing natives with foreigners in religious communities was not new. Reform congregations like those of Windesheim and the Order of the Crutched Friars had institutionalized the regular transfer of brethren, obviously to prevent their members from getting overly involved in regional, family-tied interests.[4] This led to a strengthening of the non-Frisian element in the population of the Frisian convents that joined them. As to the non-reformed houses

---

[1] J.A. Mol, 'The Beginnings of the Military Orders in Frisia', *MO* 2, 307. For the Hospitaller houses in the Frisian part of the county of Oldenburg, E. Koolman and U. Elert (eds), *Johanniter im Nordwesten* (Oldenburg, 1999), 23-32.

[2] The original extended version of this article, including an annex with all the names and data, has been published in Frisian under the title 'De Johanniters fan Snits: nammen, komôf en karrières', *Fryske Nammen*, x (1996), 117-55.

[3] J.A. Mol, *De Friese huizen van de Duitse Orde. Nes, Steenkerk en Schoten en hun plaats in het middeleeuwse Friese kloosterlandschap* (Leeuwarden, 1991), 117-8, 143-4, 318-24.

[4] Id., 'Kruisheren op de Friese zieleheilsmarkt in de vijftiende eeuw', *Tijdschrift voor Sociale Geschiedenis*, iv (1990), 345-47.

of the Hospitallers in Frisia, west of the Lauwers, one might suppose that the number of allochtonous brethren in them remained fairly low.

To corroborate this assumption, I gathered as many data as possible about the members of the Hospitaller house of Sneek. Since the scattered archive of this convent only contains deeds on the purchase and sale of land (in which hardly a brother is named), and since the archive of its mother house in Utrecht was destroyed by a fire in the early sixteenth century, I had to rely mainly upon such external sources as judicial archives, private charter collections, and so on, except of course for the visitation acts of 1495 and 1540. The harvest consisted of the names of, and data on, 168 brethren and one sister. After some onomastic identification work, this figure could be reduced to 127. Although statistically these figures may not look very impressive, they appear to be sufficiently numerous to be able to identify certain important trends or patterns. But before that, it would be useful to spend some time on the history of the Hospitaller commandery of Sneek and its place within the Order.

The Hospital of Sneek and its Relations with St Catherine's Convent of Utrecht

In the regional sources, the Hospitaller commandery of Sneek is simply called the *Hospitaal*.[5] The official name, *domus in monte Sancti Johannis prope Snekis* (house on the mount of St John), is perhaps more impressive, though in English it would be more accurate to spell 'mount' with a final 'd' instead of a 't', because the house had been founded on one of those artificially heightened sites with which the Frisians protected their low-lying land against sea floods before it was encircled with dykes. The name indicates that it was founded at an old place of residence, not *in* but *near* Sneek. Looking at the map, one can see that this was where the clay region of Westergo borders on an area with less fertile peat soils that were reclaimed in the High Middle Ages. Although the town of Sneek got its walls only in the fifteenth century, it had already been a market centre of some importance in the thirteenth. The parish church, dedicated to St Martin, was the *ecclesia matrix* of a whole series of village churches in the region.

The end of the commandery can be dated back to 31 March 1580, when the States of Friesland forbade the practice of the Catholic religion and subsequently confiscated nearly all monastic property. The beginning is shrouded in mystery. The first time the house is mentioned in a reliable document is in 1318. That it must have existed a long time before that becomes clear when we compare the Hospital of Sneek with the nearby commandery of the Teutonic Order of Nes, named 75 years earlier, in 1243. Sneek had acquired more churches, owned more property, and accounted for more brethren than Nes, which presupposes an earlier beginning.

Founded some time between 1220 and 1240, the house in Sneek was still newer than St Catherine's convent in Utrecht, already in existence before the end of the

---

⁵   Id., 'Deux commanderies de la Frise médiévale', in *Les ordres militaires: la vie rurale et le peuplement en Europe occidentale (XIIe-XVIIIe siècles)*, ed. Ch. Higounet (Auch, 1986), 241-54.

twelfth century.[6] This implies that Sneek must have been a *membrum* of Utrecht from the beginning. It is likely that the bishop of Utrecht had been involved in its early patronage, since research into the extent and location of the landed property of the Hospital shows that its core complex consisted of the glebe of St Martin's church, originally a proprietary church belonging to the bishop. He alone could have made possible its incorporation into the Hospital.

That the *Hospitaal* had to pay *responsiones* to the commander of St Catherine's convent is known from fourteenth-century charters and later visitation acts. However, the provincial commander could not determine the course of things in Sneek at will. In important matters, like the election of their commander, the brethren of the *Hospitaal* succeeded in obtaining a modicum of autonomous government, against the wishes of their direct superior. A charter from 1320, issued by the bailiff Jacob van Suden, claims that 11 individually identified brethren from Sneek expelled the commander whom Suden had appointed and had him replaced with a candidate they had themselves elected.[7] Van Suden, of course, strongly disapproved of this act as it defiantly infringed upon the statutes. In his additional function as suffragan of the bishop of Utrecht, he ordered all ecclesiastical dignitaries in the Frisian part of his diocese to compel the disobedient brethren of Sneek to rectify their errors. The outcome of the conflict is not clear, but it seems very unlikely that the Hospitallers of Sneek were eventually forced to submit. In the visitation act of 1540 it is explicitly stipulated that when their commander died, the bailiff had to confirm the candidate presented by the brethren.[8]

It can be assumed that they also probably decided on who was to be admitted to their community. In any case, their East Frisian fellow brethren had been successful in 1319 in obtaining the right, vis-à-vis the commander of Steinfurt, to recruit new brothers and sisters themselves, as the Teutonic brethren of Nes had done some thirty years later vis-à-vis their provincial commander in Utrecht.[9] Consequently recruitment must have probably been limited to the regions around Sneek or to the Frisian part of the Utrecht diocese, the present-day Dutch province of Friesland. No brothers are known to have been transferred to Sneek from St Catherine's convent, at least in the fourteenth century. The 11 names recorded in the charter of 1320 all have the dual form, typical of Germanic-Frisian names. It would therefore appear plausible to claim that the *fratres presbyteri* Boeno, Thibod, Ghalo, Zifrid, Focolf, and Wibrand, and the *fratres conversi* Reyner, Bocco, Benthet, Yppo, and Andolf probably were all Frisian by birth.

Sisters, Priest Brethren, and Lay Brothers

Since no Knights Hospitallers were to be found in Sneek, the *Hospitaal* appears to have been a convent of chaplains and serving brothers. From the second half of the

---

[6]   Id., 'Beginnings', 313.

[7]   Id., *Friese huizen*, 253-55.

[8]   J.M. van Winter, *Sources concerning the Hospitallers of St John in the Netherlands, 14th-18th Centuries* (Leiden/Boston/Cologne, 1998), 562.

[9]   Mol, 'Beginnings', 314-15.

fifteenth century, the community of Sneek consisted only of priest brethren and a few lay brothers under the direction of a prior and a priest commander. But there were sisters too. There are two indications that the convent on Mount St John, like so many other Frisian convents of diverse orders, had been a double monastery up to the beginning of the fifteenth century. The first indication is in the form of a notice in a seventeenth-century chronicle, claiming that four nuns had lost their lives in a city fire in 1286. This could be dismissed as an unreliable source. However, a charter from 1432 provides a second indication: a sizeable piece of land of a *soror ordinis Sancti Johannis* is allocated to the *monasterium* of the Order of St John in Sneek, where she resided.[10] The document was issued by three parish priests, acting as arbiters in a conflict over the ownership of the land between the commandery and the family of the sister. Hence the use of the revealing term monastery. That it was sister Eelke's intention not to join a male convent as *consoror* or *familiaris*, but to serve God as a choir nun in a female community, can be concluded not only from the size of her donation, but also from her statement to the arbiters – that she wished to renounce the world and live *in* the monastery, committing her goods, body, and soul to God and St John. By then the presupposed separate nunnery of the *Hospitaal* could not have been very populous. In 1495 the commandery did not house any sisters. So after 1432 the brethren must have allowed it to decline by not admitting any fresh novices.

The most important offices and functions with which the brethren of Sneek could be entrusted were those of commander and prior. Both were always priest brethren. The commander was the actual leader of the convent, to whom every member owed obedience. The prior seems to have been the supervisor of the priest brethren in the convent, responsible for the religious services. After 1507 he disappears from the documents, although the visitation acts do not provide evidence that the community of resident brethren had begun to grow smaller. In 1495 there were six priests, apart from the commander; in 1540 there were eight. It would appear that even in earlier times, the convent had never housed more than eight to ten resident *fratres* other than the lay brothers. As far as we know, the other three priest convents of the bailiwick of Utrecht (St Catherine's convent, Harderwijk, and Haarlem) had hardly ever housed more.[11]

Other offices in which priest brethren could make themselves useful for the convent were those of *cellerar* and *grangiarius*. These functions and titles were not very common in the order. They were probably derived from the Cistercian system of organization, imitated by most Frisian monasteries. This underlines the importance of what in German is called *Eigenwirtschaft* for the religious houses in these lands. The *grangiarii*, or grange masters, were the managers of the big farmsteads, kept in own exploitation until the middle of the fifteenth century. Before then most grange

---

[10]   Id., *Friese huizen*, 256-57.

[11]   Van Winter, 421, 439; T. van Bueren, *Tot lof van Haarlem. Het beleid van de stad Haarlem ten aanzien van de kunstwerken uit de geconfisqueerde geestelijke instellingen* (Hilversum, 1993), 89-90.

masters were lay brothers.[12] They were subservient to the *cellerar*, or the central manager, responsible for the financial administration and the one who supervised the production of the granges. He could have been a lay brother too. After 1500 he is no longer mentioned, indicating that the economic structure of the convent had changed. The leasing out of the lands had obviously simplified his task, so that it could be taken over by the commander himself.

By far most of the names that have survived belong to the brethren responsible for the care of souls in the ten parishes depending on the commandery. Very little is known about the acquisition of these churches. It has already been suggested that the church of St Martin in Sneek had passed into Hospitaller hands at an early date through a donation by the bishop. It is very well possible that this donation opened the way for the brethren to acquire patronage rights on some of the daughter churches of Sneek. The parishes with Hospitaller priests were those of Sneek, IJsbrechtum, Folsgare, Hommerts, Uitwellingerga, Oppenhuizen, and Olde Ouwer – all recorded in the visitation act of 1495. Not mentioned, however, in this document, but definitely ministered by the priest brethren of Sneek, were the village churches of Longerhouw and Boornzwaag, together with the important church of St Martin in the town of Bolsward, which was probably older than the church of Sneek.

Like most *personae* or parsons in the Frisian lands, Hospitaller parish priests were nearly always resident. In the small towns and in the big villages they gradually acquired the help of one or two secular curates, called *vicarii* or juniors. These were usually appointed by the church wardens in concert with the parson. In the towns of Sneek and Bolsward the city councils decided their nomination. Here, in the sixteenth century, the curates bore the title of second or third head priest, or second or third parson. It is worth noting that the commander of Sneek had nowhere succeeded in acquiring a say in their election. On the contrary, he had to allow the parishioners in Sneek and Bolsward to decide who among the Hospitaller priests of his convent was to be nominated their parson. For St Martin's church in Sneek, a charter from 1507 lays down the rules governing the election of the parish priest.[13] The Hospitallers of Sneek were not the only regulars in Frisia who had to reckon with election rights of the parishioners in their city churches. The parson of Leeuwarden, for example, was elected by the city council from among the community of canons of the Premonstratensian abbey in Mariëngaard. This can only be explained in terms of the few forces prevailing in the lordless Frisian society that could set limits to the emancipation of the expanding urban communities.

Second in rank after the priests were the lay brothers or *fratres conversi*. That five of them had been personally identified in the charter of 1320 as having participated in the election of a commander is an indication that they were accepted as full

---

[12]   See also the data for the Hospitaller houses in the present-day Dutch province of Groningen and the German 'Landschaft' Ostfriesland in G.F. Noordhuis, *De Johannieters in Stad en Lande* (Warffum, 1990), 72; E. Schöningh, *Der Johanniterorden in Ostfriesland* (Aurich, 1973), 23, 31, 43, 47.

[13]   A. Hallema, 'Over de collatie van het pastoors- en dekenofficie binnen de parochie Sneek in de aanvang der 16ᵉ eeuw', *Archief voor de geschiedenis van het Aartsbisdom Utrecht*, liii (1927), 225-47.

members of the order in Frisia, possibly as sergeant brothers.[14] It also underlines their role as the pillars supporting the conventual structure. Lay brothers were used by most Frisian monasteries until about 1400/1450 to manage the exploitation of their lands in the granges mentioned earlier. Originally the *Hospitaal* owned at least four granges, two of which were alienated before the middle of the fifteenth century. The other two, each having a small chapel attached to it, were apparently the most valuable ones, with demesnes of 120 and 180 acres respectively. In the sixteenth century their lands were leased out by the grange masters, who were by then no longer lay brothers but priest brethren. The last two *fratres conversi* we know by name, Bonno and Nicholaus, are mentioned in a charter from 1459.

Frisians and Foreigners

These last two names present the problem of onomastic regional identity. The Frisian lands did preserve their wealthy collection of Germanic personal names much longer than the neighbouring regions in the South.[15] Christian names became trendy relatively late, in the fifteenth and sixteenth centuries, but did not push aside the older ones. In theory this fact should help to identify the Frisian brethren on the basis of their first names or their patronyms, if their origin cannot already be deduced from the extensions with place names. In practice, however, the procedure is not that simple, as most sources are written in Latin. Until about 1400, clerical writers, when Latinizing dually-constructed Germanic names, limited themselves mostly to the adding of Latin endings. Later they did not hesitate to translate the Germanic Frisian names radically into proper, generally accepted Christian ones. In this way, Feiko or Fetza could be transformed into Fredericus, Dyurre into Theodericus, Rioerd into Reinerus, and even Buwe or Bentho into Bernardus. This means great caution is required when identifying the bearers of Latin names as non-Frisians, unless surnames or place names are given that betray their origin. One should also take into account that Frisians could bear Christian names in these days. *Petrus Petri de Bolswardia* was of course a Frisian.

With these and other reservations in mind, I grouped the 127 names that remained into four different categories, reflecting the origin of their bearers. These are: the 'West Frisia' category; the 'Frisia in general' category (consisting of West Frisia and its adjoining regions of Middle and East Frisia); the 'Not from Frisia' (and therefore allochtonous) category; and the 'Impossible to classify' category (See Table 29.1).

---

[14]   It is only at the end of the fifteenth century that objections were raised against the practice of giving these lay brothers the cross and admitting them to the chapter meetings. J.G.C. Joosting, 'Onuitgegeven pauselijke bullen verleend aan de Hospitaalbroeders', *Nederlandsch Archief voor Kerkgeschiedenis, nieuwe serie*, i (1902), 312-13.

[15]   R.A. Ebeling, *Voor- en familienamen in Nederland* (Groningen/'s-Gravenhage, 1993), 55-56.

Table 29.1   Frisians and Foreigners in the Hospitaller House of Sneek

Origin	Period			
	Before 1400	1400–1500	1500–1580	Total
West Frisia	1	4	16	21
Wider Frisia	13	14	18	45
Total Frisians	14	18	34	66
Not from Frisia	—	13	14	27
Unclassifiable	4	15	14	33
Total Non-Frisians and Unclassifiable	4	28	28	60
Total of all 4 Categories	18	48	61	127

The category of inconclusive names appears relatively large, *c*.26 per cent of the total. However, this should not effect our conclusions regarding the first period. It has already been argued that before 1400 only Frisians must have been admitted to the *Hospitaal*. In the fifteenth century a change gradually occurred. Most non-Frisians begin to appear after 1450 and reached a peak around 1495. Here the figures are distorted because most of the related dates are from the last decades of the century. In the first half, some non-native priest brethren had already formed part of the Hospitaller community, like *dominus* Simon of Enchuysen in Holland, who ministered the parish of Hommerts between 1427 and 1434.

The most striking result is that the number of Frisians in the sixteenth century comes out as far higher than that for foreigners. This may seem logical, but in several convents in Frisia it was the other way round. Any endeavour to interpret these figures is hampered by names that defy classification; but this does not necessarily mean that they originally belonged only to non-Frisians. Even if this were the case, the Frisians would still have been in the majority. Their ascendancy manifests itself most clearly in the list of commanders. At least five out of the eight known commanders after 1500 originated from Frisia, while only one, Adriaen Martensz van Geertruydenberghe, can definitely be classified as a foreigner.

Most of the time, therefore, the direction of the *Hospitaal* remained in Frisian hands. It would appear that Frisian superiors had a preference for family, friends, and fellow countrymen. The choice of the regular canon Geltet Harinxma is a classic example. In 1449 the brethren of Sneek asked him to become their commander on the grounds that he belonged to a noble and influential family and as such he was thought to be the right man to defend their interests. He is probably the one who brought the priest brother Hotse Harinxma, who died shortly before 1477, into the convent. Apart from this particular family connection, it becomes clear from their names of origin that most Frisian brethren came from places in the vicinity of Sneek.

It I difficult to say where the brethren of Sneek received their training. Most priest brethren in the convents of the Teutonic Order in the diocese of Utrecht began their careers as *choralis* or choirboys. As to the Hospitaller houses belonging to the bailiwick of Utrecht, the well-known visitation acts do not mention any *chorales* or *fratres-clerici* residing in the convents at Utrecht, Haarlem, Harderwijk, and Sneek. One would simply assume they were there. Otherwise it would not be possible to locate the several Hospitallers who appear in the early sixteenth-century ordaining lists preserved for the diocese of Utrecht.[16] Considering the fact that in the sixteenth century about 40 to 45 per cent of the Frisian clergy had received some form of academic training,[17] it is worth noting that the only university matriculation record that has been found belonged to one Frisian Hospitaller priest. This means that the brethren of Sneek had probably assumed responsibility for the intellectual prepartion of their novices and juniors within their own convent.

Another question concerns how the still-sizeable group of non-native brethren had found its way to Sneek. Taking into consideration the twenty known places of origin, one has to establish that they came both from within diverse regions of the present-day Netherlands and from places outside, like Westphalia and Brabant. No clear pattern emerges from this geographical dispersion. It is plausible to assume, however, that brethren proceeding from adjacent or neighbouring places, like Emmerich and Doetinchem in the eastern part of the Netherlands, had cultivated some form of relationship with one another. Once a brother had found a place in a Frisian monastery, he would have probably drawn the attention of his family, friends, and relatives to attractive vacant positions in his own convent or elsewhere in the neighbourhood.

It is perhaps strange that not one single non-Frisian brother of Sneek could be found in another house of the Utrecht bailiwick before their appearance in Frisia. That notwithstanding, it would be too risky to draw any definite conclusions from that, as very little research has hitherto been done on the careers and backgrounds of the brethren of St Catherine's convent and its dependent *membra*. On the scant evidence of a few name lists one can only claim that there were no relations between Sneek and the priest convents of Haarlem and Harderwijk. Since the middle of the fifteenth century, both had enjoyed a form of self-government.[18] They appear to have recruited their brethren from within an even narrower geographical circle surrounding their houses. As for St Catherine's, the mother-house of Sneek, no data on the exchange of personnel have survived. Nor is there any evidence to indicate that brethren were transferred from Utrecht to Sneek and vice versa. This can only imply that, unlike his Teutonic counterpart, the provincial commander of the Hospitaller bailiwick of

---

[16]   G. Brom, 'Naamlijst der priesters, die in het bisdom Utrecht gewijd zijn van 1505 tot 1518', *Archief voor de geschiedenis van het Aartsbisdom Utrecht*, xxiii (1896), 386-471; xxiv (1897), 1-40.

[17]   S. Zijlstra, *Het geleerde Friesland - Een mythe? Universiteit en maatschappij in Friesland en Stad en Lande ca. 1380-1650* (Leeuwarden, 1996), 105.

[18]   E.A. van Beresteyn, *Geschiedenis der Johanniter-orde in Nederland tot 1795* (Assen, 1934), *passim*.

Utrecht refrained from interfering in the admission policy adopted by the brethren in his Frisian daughter house.

Careers

Less problematic is the career pattern of the brethren of Sneek. First, it can be securely claimed that the *fratres* of Sneek had never turned up in any of the other houses of the Hospitaller bailiwick of Utrecht. Whoever worked his way through the parishes dependent upon the convent was never promoted to another important position in the bailiwick. In this respect, one can speak in terms of totally separated circuits.

The ideal career of a Hospitaller priest brother in Frisia can best be illustrated by the list of successive jobs that were held by the last commander, Gellius IJstanus. According to a late sixteenth-century chronicler, he was first parson of Oppenhuizen. In 1559 he appears to be parson of IJsbrechtum, was elected parson of Sneek in 1561, occupied the post of grange master of Osingahuizen in 1570, was active from 1570 to 1576 as parson of Bolsward, and in 1576 assumed the task of directing the commandery until it was dissolved in 1580. Apart from the grange mastership of Osingahuizen, the steps are clear and understandable. A priest brother, finishing his training in the convent, was most likely to begin his career in one of the five poor parsonages in the fenland district south of Sneek. From there, he would gradually be promoted to one of the two rich village parishes in the clay district west of Sneek, Folsgare and IJsbrechtum. Another good intermediary post was the priorship. When a Hospitaller had done well in one of these offices, he would become eligible for the city parsonages of Sneek and Bolsward. To reach that stage, however, he had to impress not only his commander, but the parish communities represented by the respective city councils, who had the last say in the election process. They could, of course, choose a young priest who had just made a start in a poor parish. But, more often than not, their choice fell on one of the more ambitious candidates who had already occupied one of the better positions as prior or parson of Folsgare or IJsbrechtum. In the case of Gellius Ilstanus, the parsonage of Bolsward proved to be a step higher on the scale than that of Sneek. If the community of Bolsward called upon the Hospitaller parish priest of Sneek to become their new parson, they must have probably known the man would accept their nomination.

The *sinecures* of the Osingahuizen and Eemswoude granges were understandably sought-after positions for brethren who had already been active elsewhere as parish priests. Peter of Tongerlo had been parson of Folsgare before he became grange master of Osingahuizen. Apart from saying Mass every day in the chapel, he seems to have had no other obligations. The leisure associated with the posts may have very well been part of the incentive; however, it would appear that the main attraction of the grange mastership was that it was well paid. It is hardly surprising that the parishes in the fertile clay district could offer their parsons a better income than those in the fenlands.

Thus, income as well as prestige played an important role in the careers of the Hospitaller priest brethren of Sneek. This may sound strange for clerics who had taken the holy vow of poverty on entering the order. Most of them led a non-communal life as parish priests and had therefore to build up their own households, for which they needed property and income. That regular parish priests did not behave very differently from their secular colleagues may be concluded from an issue appearing in a charter from 1477: upon his death, *frater* Hotse Harinxma left two children for whom the convent did not wish to be held responsible.[19]

Conclusiom

As a convent dedicated entirely to the care of souls, the Hospitaller house on Mount St John near Sneek, although belonging to a centrally-led order, hardly differed from the monasteries in the neighbourhood, peopled by Benedictines, Augustinian canons, or Premonstratensians. The brethren elected their own superiors who themselves decided on the admission of new members. This resulted in an autochtonous Frisian-speaking population. As they did not undermine the convent's own autonomy through mismanagement, no need was felt to have reform imposed upon them from above; this would have probably led to a strong inflow of foreign *fratres*.

It would appear the results of the present onomastic analysis tend to confirm the view that in the non-reformed monasteries in Frisia, where most priest brethren were active as parish ministers, the native brethren were, and indeed remained, in the majority throughout the fifteenth and sixteenth centuries. However, the number of foreigners in Sneek during the same period need not be considered to have been small. How they succeeded in finding their way into Frisia remains unclear until further research is carried out into the other Hospitaller brethren of the bailiwick of Utrecht.

---

[19]   P. Sipma (ed.), *Oudfriesche oorkonden*, i ('s-Gravenhage, 1927).

Chapter 30

Hospitaller Baroque Culture: The Order of St John's Legacy to Early Modern Malta

Victor Mallia-Milanes

It has only been fairly recently that the significance of the term 'baroque' has begun to assume proportions much wider than those attributed to it traditionally to define seventeenth-century art and literature in all their stylistic manifestations.[1] Initially inspired by an overwhelming Counter-Reformation sensibility and expressing the emotional aspirations of the Catholic church, today the term is used to denote a social reality, to comprehend the development of a whole society, a collective and individual way of life which spread from the Mediterranean to far beyond its shores. It reached maturity during the general crisis of the seventeenth century, when society was dominated by a strong sense of fear and instability.[2] Indeed, crisis was the quintessence of the European scene. Chaos, claims Pierre Chaunu,[3] had been let loose. On both the collective and individual levels, the age was marked by conflict whose intensity and wide diffusion had been decisive in transforming contemporary thought and action. On the first level, the clash of political and religious ideas and ideals, the spread and continuity of war, the growth of social antagonism, revolution, and not least 'the resentful disposition behind issues of precedence in daily ritual – administrative or ecclesiastical' – all were among the turbulent features of the epoch.

On the other level, the peculiarity of the 'baroque conflict', observes Rosario Víllari, is not so much to be found in the contrast between diverse individuals or social groups, as in 'the presence of apparently incompatible or evidently contradictory attitudes within the same person':

> Traditionalism and the search for the novel; conservatism and rebellion; the love of truth and the cult of disguise; wisdom and folly; sensuality and mysticism; superstition and

---

[1]   See, for example, the introduction to *L'Uomo Barocco*, ed. Rosario Víllari (Rome-Bari, 1991), vii-xv.

[2]   For the general crisis of the seventeenth century, T. Aston (ed.), *Crisis in Europe 1560-1660* (London, 1965); G. Parker and L.M. Smith (eds.), *The General Crisis of the Seventeenth Century* (London, 1978). See also P. Clark (ed.), *The European Crisis of the 1590s: Essays in Comparative History* (London, 1985).

[3]   *L'Uomo Barocco*, ix.

rationality; austerity and consumerism; the affirmation of natural rights and the exaltation of absolute power.[4]

This is precisely what Víllari means by 'the cohabitation of opposites', an appropriate qualification of the inherently conflicting cohesion of baroque culture, a projection of the new aesthetic beauty that emerged from the heterogeneity of Gian Lorenzo Bernini's *bel composto*. Renaissance art had focused 'on pleasing a small, wealthy, cultural élite'. Baroque would appeal to the senses in a way that would 'touch the soul and kindle the faith' of the common man, of the 'ordinary churchgoer', and at the same time 'proclaim the power and confidence of the reformed Catholic church'. This was the culture of a declining Mediterranean. 'Perhaps the extravagance of a civilization,' points out Fernand Braudel, 'is a sign of its economic failure.'[5] Cultural peaks are often reached in moments of decline. Can a similar claim be made for the Order of St John on early modern Malta?

At one time I was inclined to believe that the Hospital's resort to the full effervescence of baroque culture was a tendency to detach itself from reality, its only chosen alternative to escape temporarily the trauma of its own irreversible decline and conceal its symptoms from itself and the rest of the outside world. Today I view the crisis, which had begun with the Ottoman conquest of Damascus (Syria) and Egypt in 1516-17, not so much a manifestation of decadence and decline as that of 'an agitated interlude', however unsettled and unsettling. Notwithstanding the Rhodian crisis, notwithstanding the consequences of the Reformation, the Dissolution of the Monasteries, and the suppression of the Langue of England, which sapped the Hospitaller institution of much of its financial strength, there was a fairly rapid recovery after the 'defensive victory' of 1565 when 'a new stasis' gradually set in, metaphorically 'followed by a long spell of warmer weather, whose good harvests fed an ever-increasing population'.[6] The evidences of this, I am now prepared to admit, were visible in every single branch of the order's activity. This is sufficient testimony to the claim that the Order of the Hospital had retained 'a great deal of its original vitality'.

A medieval charitable institution born and bred in the true spirit of the Mediterranean, the religious military Order of St John settled on Malta at the very moment when Charles V's German mercenaries, with their horrendous sack of Rome (May 1527) and Florence (1530), eclipsed almost completely the Renaissance and unwittingly ignited the creative explosion of the baroque after a brief mannerist interlude.[7] The Knights, still struggling through their worst crisis, would break late

---

⁴   Ibid., ix-x.

⁵   F. Braudel, *The Mediterranean and the Mediterranean World in the Age of Philip II* (London, 1972-73), 826-35. On the phenomenon of decline, J.K.J. Thomson, *Decline in History: The European Experience* (Oxford, 1998).

⁶   The quote belongs to Gregory Hanlon.

⁷   Braudel, 828ff. On the origins of the Order of St John, J. Riley Smith, *The Knights of St John in Jerusalem and Cyprus, c.1050-1310* (London, 1967). There is no standard modern history of the Knights on Rhodes, but Anthony T. Luttrell's three books of collected research papers in the Variorum edition (*The* Hospitaller *State on Rhodes and its Western Provinces, 1306-1462*; *The Hospitallers in Cyprus, Rhodes, Greece, and the West 1291*-1440; and *The*

medieval Malta's isolation – splendid or unfortunate – and steer the island through momentous changes, breathing fresh life into it.[8] The inevitable cultural shock of the initial encounter between them and the local population was short-lived. The natives were essentially peaceable, their confidence fairly quickly gained. The Knights' restrained and tranquil approach to them at the outset contained the seeds of subsequent harmony. There is no denying, however, that the arrival of Grand Master L'Isle Adam at the Grand Harbour in October 1530 and his solemn entry later in Mdina, the ancient capital, with all the splendour of Hospitaller pomp and ceremony, magnificently attired, was meant to demonstrate that his presence, and that of his brethern, had brought to the island a new and final authority.

This unique moment in the Hospitallers' characteristic propensity to display status and taste – as much part of aristocratic culture as of post-Tridentine Catholic rites, ritual, and religion – was years later captured on canvas by Antoine Favray. Evoking awe and admiration, the demeanour they adopted, intended to leave a lasting impression on the natives and ensure their respect, achieved its desired effect. During the Turkish siege of 1565, both sides 'stood firm together with a new mutual respect and loyalty'.[9] For nearly four months Malta turned into a theatre of valour. By the standards of late medieval Malta, the Knights were provocatively rich and powerful with embarrassingly clever and wide-ranging links with all the royal courts of Catholic Europe. They offered the local inhabitants security, greater opportunities for employment, and better conditions of work. A large proportion of their resources was invested on the island. The mild élitist consternation and discomfort, and the consequent tensions which had originally marked the earlier years of this régime, gradually 'gave way to genuine harmony and mutual trust'.[10] From the current state of our scholarship, it would appear that the Maltese lived through most of these long

---

Hospitallers of Rhodes and their Mediterranean World) provide very valuable insights. And so does Kenneth M. Setton, *The Papacy and the Levant 1204-1571*, 4 vols (Philadelphia, 1976-84). On the coming of the Knights to Malta in 1530, V. Mallia-Milanes, 'Emperor Charles V's Donation of Malta to the Knights of St John', *Peregrinationes: Acta et Documenta: Carlo V e Mercurino di Gattinara suo Gran Cancelliere*, ii, 2 (2001), 23-33. Also R. Valentini, 'I Cavalieri di S. Giovanni da Rodi a Malta: Trattative Diplomatiche', *Archivum Melitense*, ix, 4 (1935), 3-103. On the sack of Rome and Florence, Mallia-Milanes, 'Emperor Charles V's Donation', 31; Setton, iii, ch. 8. See also National Library of Malta, Archive 84, fol.33r.

[8] On the history of Malta before 1530, the latest work is Charles Dalli, *Malta; The Medieval Millennium* (Malta, Midsea Books, 2006); but see also Anthony Luttrell, *The Making of Christian Malta: From the Early Middle Ages to 1530*. Variorum Collected Studies Series (London, Variorum, 2002); and *Medieval Malta: Studies on Malta before the Knights*, ed. A.T. Luttrell (London, 1975).

[9] L. Butler, 'The Order of St John in Malta: An Historical Sketch', in Council of Europe, *The Order of St John in Malta with an exhibition of paintings by Mattia Preti Painter and Knight* (Malta, 1970), 28. On the historical significance of the siege, V. Mallia-Milanes, 'The Birgu Phase in Hospitaller History', in *Birgu: A Maltese Maritime City*, ed. L. Bugeja, M. Buhagiar, and S. Fiorini (Malta, 1993); id., 'Introduction to Hospitaller Malta', in *Hospitaller Malta 1530-1798: Studies on Early Modern Malta and the Order of St John of Jerusalem*, ed. V. Mallia-Milanes (Malta, 1993), 1-42, esp. 10-12.

[10] Butler, 40.

years of paternalist government 'relatively happ[il]y'.[11] It was essentially through this experience, baroque by any other name, indeed through its ability to diffuse its culture, 'its ways of thinking and living', that the Hospital succeeded in reshaping most of Maltese society, too small and primitive to offer any resolute resistance, Europeanizing it to a degree far more singularly solid and permanent than the Normans had ever hoped to achieve centuries earlier.[12]

The cultural habits of Hospitaller society had left an indelible mark on the culture of early modern Malta, its customs, its traditional religious beliefs and values, its archaic economy, and not least on the locally widespread splendour of its native tongue, however incomprehensible this might have very well been to the outsider. To these may be added art and architecture, rural and urban planning, music and printmaking, religious sermons and entertainment - all bear the mark (more or less) of the pervasive spirit of the Hospitallers who, along with the triumphant Tridentine church (of which they formed part), acted as powerful catalysts of change. These are merely a few of the means by which the historian can interpret such influence. There are others: the natives' idea of war and death; their habits of courtship; the way they reacted to pleasure and sorrow; the food they ate and the way they prepared it; their drink; their work; their trades, skills, and techniques; indeed, the depths of their feeling into which ironically no historian can genuinely peer. None of these means, however, had ever been an isolated and individual expression. They were constituent ingredients of a complex historical continuum, a spiritual whole encompassing an attitude of mind which in turn inspired the native inhabitants' entire way of life. To extract one element is to distort the whole. The *objets d'art*, for example, which the Knights had brought over with them in 1530, and which formed the theme of a 1989 exhibition in Malta, did not of themselves constitute, as has been claimed, the order's early legacy in Malta.[13] At best, they were small, worthy souvenirs of their Rhodian past.

What has for long been sustained as 'Maltese baroque' should, in the present writer's opinion, be more accurately identified as a Hospitaller phenomenon, one originally inspired by the order's needs and aspirations, and essentially determined by its historic mission of permanent war with Islam, its personality, its great moments of prosperity, its inherent or recurrent problems - very much the same way that these had been in a sense conditioned by the highly restricted insular world around them, the ceaseless constraints imposed upon the régime by the geography of the island, the nature of the barely 243 square kilometers of barren land, the character of the people. The order had been the first patron, long before the local church and the wealthier sectors of Maltese society.

Behind the inception of Malta's Hospitaller baroque experience lay three significant developments. The first concerned the frigid manner with which European politics began to value the relevance of crusading ideals to the 'unsparing realism' of its capitalist exigencies. By the end of the sixteenth century, the Order

---

[11] Ibid.

[12] On Norman Malta, Dalli, passim; and Luttrell, *Medieval Malta, passim*.

[13] See the exhibition catalogue, *The Order's Early Legacy in Malta*, ed. J. Azzopardi (Malta, 1989).

of St John had long become an embarrassment to Europe's vital interests, political and economic. Earlier, in 1534, an unholy alliance with France, the order's greatest patron, offered the Ottoman Empire an anti-Habsburg striking base at Toulon in Provence. Gradually, a growing cordiality began to develop between traditionally rival States, like France and Spain, Venice and Naples, each acknowledging the value of entering into bilateral agreements both with the Ottoman Porte in the East and with each of its satellite Barbary Regencies in North Africa. The second concerned the process of secularization of the magistracy. The history of the order's coinage provides just one classic example of the trend. In the last decades of the sixteenth century, Grand Master Verdalle 'introduced the ducal coronet and the cardinal's hat surmounting the arms of the grand master and the order on the obverse of most of the silver and copper coins. The ducal coronet remained until 1741, when Pinto introduced the closed crown.'[14] A comparison between the pictorial representation of the Blessed Gerard and Favray's grand portrait of Emanuel Pinto de Fonseca, invested with the attributes of royalty and lordly arrogance, provides a particularly poignant statement of this social and personal reality, so explicit, so unambiguous, so eloquent. The less reminiscent the Hospital became of its 'cloister' mentality, the more it visibly distanced itself from its traditional, medieval aspirations, and the faster it allowed itself, deliberately, to be absorbed with the trend which the rising tide of autocracy and royal absolutism unfurled upon post-Reformation Europe, East and West. The third development was the order's sudden release, towards the end of the sixteenth century, from the austerity of former years. The disappearance from the local scene, and from its wider Mediterranean context, of the anxieties, the rigidity, and the tensions which had disturbed the greater part of the century, fostered, by way of inevitable contrast, a sense of relaxation and a spirit of affluence. It was in part these three developments which in turn exposed, through 'a natural outburst of creative energy', Maltese society and its entire environment – physical, moral, and all – to the onrush of the Hospitaller baroque.

There is no doubt of course that what constituted this impressive Hospitaller phenomenon was an unconscious act of borrowing. For nearly eight whole years (not to go back beyond the siege of Rhodes), the Hospital had lived through the turmoil and tension of this distinctive development at the very heart of Rome, from where it probably had its first intoxicating impulse. It was a process of re-interpreting, as Braudel would call it – of adopting, of assimilating. In the end, like any other precious Rhodian icon, the order had it gently and safely transported to Malta on its strong galleys. The process needed time to mature. This it did through various channels, including the recruitment of leading artists, architects, and military engineers from abroad; the ambitions, inclinations, and wealth of the magistracy and its princely court; the ideas and pronounced tastes for luxury of the individual members of the Hospital living in priories and on commanderies overseas, generally among the high, the moneyed, and the mighty; and a host of other 'anonymous carriers', including the Common Treasury's disposition to invest lavishly on the island. In the Hospitaller context, this act of cultural borrowing was as much one of

---

[14] Joseph C. Sammut, 'The Coinage of the Order of St John in Malta', in *The Order of St John in Malta*, 48.

receiving, thereby allowing itself unconsciously to be imperceptibly transformed, as it was of diffusing it into others, conquering *them* in turn. 'He who gives,' says Braudel, 'dominates.' The stream of influences which has been over the centuries naturally imbued in the Maltese identity embodies a powerful Hospitaller-European, indeed universal, imprint – a clear reflection of the great order's civilizing process. After the siege of 1565, Malta was never quite the same as it had been before. It was 'the natural outcome of a long process.' Malta's social and artistic manifestations were and still are, like anybody else's, rooted in the past.

Indeed, if I may be allowed to resort to the term 'despotism' to define the order's rule over Malta, in the same way as the term 'dictatorship' has been used to describe the pontificate of Urban VIII (1623-44),[15] then it would appear that the Hospitallers' overriding quality – their autocratic style of government – (as with the case of Urban VIII) was more rigid and inflexible than one has hitherto been prepared to admit. This is evidenced in the extent and immensity of Hospitaller influence on Maltese society in general, on Malta's urban life in particular, and on the collective Maltese psyche – an influence at once profound, deep, and pervasive. By the time the ambitious French General had cast his eyes on the island-principality, and indeed much earlier, Malta's urban society had become 'largely indistinguishable in outlook' from that of other European urban centres. There were moments in the second half of the eighteenth century when resident political observers complained that certain commodity prices and the cost of living on the island were as high as at any other major city in Europe.[16]

From several artists' impressions and the visual insights these provide into the state of Maltese society,[17] and from the convincing evidence detailed in travellers' accounts,[18] it would appear that the Maltese townspeople's economic services and activities, their wine-shop and tavern sociability, their bustle and the vast array of goods on offer at their daily market, their splendid festivities, and the revelry and noise of their religious processions – all compared as favourably to southern European levels and practices, as did their general social tranquillity and relative prosperity.[19] 'Their level of education, their style of clothing, ... their houses and home life ... their musical tastes and other leanings,' we are told, 'were probably also much the same.'[20] The 'standard of living', a rather complex phenomenon, is much more difficult to determine. A recent historian of early modern Italy suggests quite rightly that an extensive analysis of post-mortem inventories is necessary for

---

[15]   Giovanni Careri, 'L'Artista', in *L'Uomo Barocco*, 340.

[16]   See Mallia-Milanes, 'Introduction to Hospitaller Malta', 26.

[17]   On art as historical evidence, Theodore K. Rabb and Jonathan Brown, 'The Evidence of Art: Images and Meaning in History', in *Art and History: Images and their Meaning*, ed. R.I. Rotberg and T.K. Rabb (Cambridge, 1986), 1-6.

[18]   For a short bibliography on such accounts, P. Xuereb, *Melitensia* (Malta, 1974), entries 422-572; and C. Cuschieri, *Index Historicus* (Malta, 1979), section xxvi, 105-107.

[19]   See, for example, Antoine Favray, 'Visit to a Maltese House', Museum of Fine Arts, Valletta.

[20]   G. Wettinger, 'Aspects of Maltese Life', in *Maltese Baroque*, ed. G. Mangion (Malta, 1989), 60-62.

an objective assessment, together with more studies on infant mortality.[21] However, considering the order's medical knowledge, its long traditional expertise in rigid quarantine practices and public hygiene, the Europe-wide reputation enjoyed by the Holy Infirmary,[22] and the state of the other hospitals on the island,[23] life expectancy was as reasonable in Malta as it was in other urban centres in Europe.

Comfortably enclosed within a line of fortifications[24] which were allowed to grow increasingly baroque over the years through progressive details of sophistication and a passion for ornamentation, the newly built city of Valletta[25] emerged from the devastation which the Turks had left behind. It set the tone of the Order of St John's baroque legacy to early modern Malta and held up the example of the refinements of civilized life.

The most important public buildings, sacred and profane, began to rise in the centre of Valletta as rapidly as the fortified walls had done a few years earlier. The magistral palace, begun under Del Monte around 1572, was at first little more than a converted 'wooden structure, with a dry stone wall on the outside to shelter it from the sun.' During La Cassière's and later magistracies, this *casetta*, as Bosio defines it, was to develop into one of the most magnificent palaces of Valletta, henceforth to serve as the official residence of the grandmasters. ... The conventual church of St John was built between 1573 and 1577. The soberness of its exterior, severe, yellowish, and cold, almost forbidding, yet so reconcilable with the austerity of the fortress at the heart of which it stood, earned it Giacomo Capello's epithet of elegance. Presumably, the unadorned architectural simplicity of its façade contrasted sharply with the Gothic delicacy and rich flow of colour and marble with the Venetian writer was so accustomed in his native city. Each of the seven auberges, or community 'palaces' where the knights lived, was erected, as in Rhodes, in the vicinity of the fortified post which the respective langue was expected to defend. At the southeastern side of the city, facing St Lazarus curtain, stood the holy infirmary. In his description, Capello rightly avoided the term *bel* he had used for the Jesuits' college and the Dominican convent. The 'vast structure' of this 'magnificent hospital' was, like the conventual church, unpretentious, although by the time he was writing in 1716 it had already undergone various modifications. These were perhaps the most outstanding public edifices. There were others – the treasury, the chancery, the castellania, the customs house.

---

[21]   Gregory Henlon, *Early Modern Italy, 1550-1800: Three Seasons in European History* (London, 2000), 339.

[22]   On the Order of St John's medical experience, its Holy Infirmary, and other charitable institutions, see the relevant bibliographical section respectively in F. de Hellwald, *Bibliographie méthodique de l'Ordre Souv[erain] de St. Jean de Jérusalem* (Rome, 1885); E. Rossi, *Aggiunta alla Bibliographie méthodique de l'Ordre Souverain de St. Jean de Jérusalem di Ferdinand de Hellwald* (Rome, 1924); and J. Mizzi, 'A Bibliography of the Order of St. John of Jerusalem (1925-1969)', in Council of Europe, *The Order of St. John in Malta with an exhibition of paintings by Mattia Preti Painter and Knight* (Malta, 1970), 108-204.

[23]   See in particular P. Cassar, *A Medical History of Malta* (Malta, 1964), and S. Fiorini, *Santo Spirito Hospital at Rabat, Malta: The Early Years to 1575* (Malta, 1989).

[24]   On the fortification of Valletta and the whole harbour area, A. Hoppen, *The Fortification of Malta by the Order of St John, 1530-1798* (Edinburgh, 1979); id., 'Military Priorities and Social Realities in the Early Modern Mediterranean: Malta and its Fortifications', in *Hospitaller Malta*, 399-428.

[25]   See, for example, E. De Giorgio, *A City by an Order* (Malta, 1985).

... Alongside these palatial buildings and sacred temples, and adjoining these commodious structures which provided private and communal residence to the celibate sons of the noblest European families, grew others, as sumptuous and as imposing, belonging to the wealthier sectors of Maltese society. Others still, ranging from shops, slave prisons, and monasteries to stores and flour mills and homes for charitable institutions were among the buildings of late sixteenth-century Valletta.[26]

Under the Knights, Valletta was destined to play several roles at once – those of a fortress and a formidable base of operations for the order's naval forces to fight for the faith and blunt the military might of Islam; a palatial convent, where the grand master 'lodged' and held his sumptuous princely court 'more ... commodiously' than any other ruling monarch in Europe;[27] a temple, whose austere and uncompromising simplicity was later reconciled with the most fashionable styles current overseas; a theatre, creating one great urban space for spectacle, drama, and 'self-presentation'; a hospital, faithful to the order's original raison d'être, to care for 'Our Lords the Sick', the 'holy poor', and the wounded; a widely renowned slave market; and a flourishing centre for entrepôt trade. Each of these roles was played to its own special type of music, ranging from the martial to the sacred and liturgical, from the chamber and the funerary to the light, comic, and entertaining - most of them accompanied by choirs, dance, and fireworks. Carnival was yet another role, when, in moments of 'folly and impunity', social barriers were temporarily lifted. The theatricality of social life was punctuated by regular periods of active combat either in formal war or in inconsequential skirmishes. It was, however, the city's embellishment which took on an expansionary form, impressively reinforced by all the major architectural and sculptural niceties of the new art, which was the striking mark of the baroque qualities of the Capital. Ramon Perellos had set a pattern of intensive building programmes to convert Malta, which Manoel de Vilhena was all too content to follow up with equal vigour.[28] From a cloister-citadel of the Late Renaissance and mannerist phase, it grew into a port city during the seventeenth and eighteenth centuries, integrating the two harbours on either side of the peninsula and the heart of the city into a functional whole. Space was used to blend everything together in a total baroque environment.

Valletta constituted what has been termed 'a massive injection of European high design', which soon spread with barely any restraint to the rural towns and villages, except for persistent traits of the traditional vernacular architecture. It was indeed an intrusive style, but on the whole the old integrated neatly with the new and vice

---

[26]   The extract is taken from V. Mallia-Milanes, *Valletta 1566-1798: An Epitome of Europe* (Malta, 1988). For a critical edition of Giacomo Capello's account on early eighteenth-century Malta, see the *Descrittione di Malta, Anno 1716: A Venetian Account*, ed. V. Mallia-Milanes (Malta, 1988).

[27]   P. Brydone, *A tour through Sicily and Malta in a series of letters to William Beckford Esq.* (London, 1773), Letter xv, Malta, 5 June 1770.

[28]   See Denis De Lucca, *Carapecchia: Master of Baroque Architecture in Early Eighteenth-Century Malta* (Malta, 1999).

versa.[29] There was overlapping, but there was also sharing. Demographic growth, the sense of security and political stability, economic prosperity and the human instinct of emulation, confirmed and further expanded the old established centres. In the countryside, especially in the rural parishes, a spectacular amount of new building, as lavish and as grandiose as in Valletta, was undertaken by members of the order, the church, and the wealthier sectors of society. The village environment became definitely church-dominated in more than one sense.

The order, the Tridentine church in Malta, and the Holy Inquisition collectively generated a surge of religious energy and fervour under the guise of various manifestations. There was a phenomenal increase, for example, in the number of religious confraternities.[30] Though it is admittedly difficult too to gauge and assess levels of piety and religiosity, it would be plausible to assume that in such circumstances the religious culture of the native population grew stronger in the seventeenth and eighteenth centuries. Not only did the vast majority become more religious; they would have embraced a purer Catholicism. This may be attributed to several factors, notably: the Society of Jesus's settlement on Malta shortly after the siege, in the 1570s;[31] a more systematic diffusion of religious instruction;[32] the greater moral authority of better-educated priests, having been trained either at the Jesuits' college in Valletta or later at the seminary in Mdina, or indeed, abroad;[33] the permanent presence on the island of the Roman Inquisition and its 'confessionalization' of the inhabitants – natives, foreign residents, or visiting sailors and traders;[34] and the coercive power of a Catholic religious State.[35] In perfect harmony with baroque taste, religious beliefs and practices began to assume a 'decorative exuberance'. New gathering places for daily prayer were built on a larger scale than before, and old ones remodelled or rebuilt in city, town, or village. Their dimensions were purposely augmented, not only to offer greater space for all

---

[29]   See Jo Tonna, 'The Ramified Route', in *Maltese Baroque*, 25-31, which provides extremely interesting insights.

[30]   David Rossi has done very valuable research on the subject, both locally and in foreign archives. See his 'Charity and Confraternal Piety in Malta and Sicily from the Sixteenth to the Eighteenth Century' (Unpublished MA dissertation, University of Malta, 2002).

[31]   See P. Pecchiai, 'Il Collegio dei Gesuiti in Malta', *Archivio storico di Malta*, n.s., ix, 2 (1938), 129-202; 3(1938), 273-325; R. Valentini, 'Scuole, Seminario, e Collegio dei Gesuiti in Malta, 1467-1591', ibid., n.s., viii, 1 (1936-37), 18-32; A. Leanza, 'La Compagnia di Gesu e la Sacra Milizia gerosolimitana in Malta', ibid., n.s., x, 1 (1938-39), 17-47; P. Pecchiai, 'La sommossa dei Cavalieri di Malta contro i Gesuiti nel carnevale del 1639', ibid., n.s., ix, 4 (1938), 429-32.

[32]   See, for example, V. Borg, 'Developments in Education outside the Jesuit *Collegium Melitense*', *Melita Historica*, vi, 3 (1974), 215-54.

[33]   On the clergy in Malta in medieval times, Stanley Fiorini, 'The Clergy of Malta, 1244 to 1460', *Melita Historica*, xiii, 2 (2001), 165-208.

[34]   For a brief account on the Inquisition in Malta, A. Vella, *The Tribunal of the Inquisition in Malta* (Malta, 1964); also Alex. Bonnici, *Il-Maltin u l-Inkizizzjoni f 'nofs is-seklu sbatax* (Malta, 1977).

[35]   For example, A. Koster, 'The Knights' State (1530-1798): a Regular Regime', *Melita Historica*, viii, 4 (1983).

the religious services that filled the liturgical calendar, but also to accommodate the faithful crowds that increasingly attended such functions. Ritual became more elaborate; there was more drama in it, more theatre. It was a necessary medium as it was believed to convey ideas to the community. And so was the religious sermon;[36] indeed, the art of sacred oratory appealed more to the emotions than to the intellect – in a sense, an Augustinian quality carried over from the Middle Ages. Not only did such services, processions, festive parades, and decorations faithfully reflect post-Tridentine practices; they anticipated the village-saints *festa* of later years, which can claim baroque qualities as any sculptured fountain adorning the city, or any painted ceiling, then as now.

The years 1530-1798 had witnessed the gradual metamorphosis of an early modern central-Mediterranean island into a Hospitaller microcosm. Malta of the days of La Valette and Suleyman disappeared from view. Almost. The pace and depth of change were, of course, uneven. Certain realities appear to have been more enduring than others, like Dingli cliffs, the barren rock, and the surrounding sea, more resistant to persistent pressure. Elements of vernacular architecture, for instance, remained adamant. They can be 'isolated and recognized'. The 'timeless peasantry', tied to the 'barren ground' in the semblance of relative poverty, remote and insular, and the traditional humble fisherman, wrinkled in the face by sun and sea spray, proud of his sturdy lively-coloured boat, are just two other classic instances where distinct Moorish or Maghribi features appear to have persisted to the present day. Similarly, emotional prejudices against the 'Turk', born of genuine, deep-rooted fear, may have very well been sharpened over the centuries. Today they still nourish the disposition of a cross-section of Maltese society towards certain non-European races, by deed if not by word. And so with the native language. All seem indestructible, 'moving through time,' Carlo Levi would say, 'without change.'[37] They are illusions of permanence. The late medieval *Cantilena*, for example, had been composed in a dialect which was probably already unrecognizable by the seventeenth or eighteenth century. Social reality tells a different story.

---

[36]   See J. Zammit Ciantar, 'Il-Prietki bil-Malti ta' Ignazio Saverio Mifsud: Edizzjoni Kummentata bi Studju Kritiku' (Unpublished Ph.D. thesis, University of Malta, 2005).

[37]   Carlo Levi, *Christ Stopped at Eboli* (Penguin Books, 1982 edn), 253.

Select Bibliography

A.-M. Legras, *Les Commanderies des Templiers et Hospitaliers de Saint-Jean de Jerusalem en Saintonge et en Aunis* (Paris, 1983)

Agnello, G., 'I cavalieri di Malta a Siracusa: Convento e chiesa di S. Francesco. La chiesa di S. Leonardo. Il Messale dell'Ordine', *Per l'Arte Sacra* (May-August, 1936), 27-33.

Avonto, L., *I Templari in Piemonte* (Vercelli, 1982).

Ayala Martínez, C. de, 'La Corona de Castilla y la incorporación de los maestrazgos', *Militarium Ordinum Analecta*, i (1997), 257-90.

Ayala Martínez, C. de, *Las órdenes militares hispánicas en la Edad Media (siglos XII-XV)* (Madrid, 2003).

Barber, M., *The New Knighthood. A History of the Order of the Temple* (Cambridge, 1994).

Barber, M., *The Trial of the Templars* (Cambridge, 1978).

Barquero Goñi, C., 'La Orden del Hospital y la recepción de los bienes templarios en la Península Ibérica', *Hispania Sacra*, li (1999), 531-56.

Barquero Goñi, C., 'La Orden Militar del Hospital y la monarquía castellana durante la Baja Edad Media', *Meridies*, v-vi (2002), 141-54.

Barquero Goñi, C., 'Los hospitalarios y la monarquía castellano-leonesa (siglos XII-XIII)', *Archivos Leoneses*, xcvii-xcviii(1995), 53-119.

Barquero Goñi, C., *Los caballeros hospitalarios durante la Edad Media en España* (Burgos, 2003).

Belabre, Baron de, *Rhodes of the Knights* (Oxford, 1908).

Bini, T., 'Dei Templari in Lucca', Reale Accademia Lucchese, 27 August, 1838 (repr. Latina, 1992).

Bonneaud, P., *Le Prieuré de Catalogne, le Couvent de Rhodes et la Couronne d'Aragon: 1415–1447* (Millau, 2004).

Boockmann, H., 'Über Ablaß-"Medien"', *Geschichte in Wissenschaft und Unterricht*, xxxiv (1983), 709-21.

Boockmann, H., *Der Deutsche Orden: Zwölf Kapitel aus seiner Geschichte*, 4th edn (Munich, 1994).

Borchardt, K., 'Die Johanniter in Schlesien (12. bis 18. Jahrhundert)', in *Jahrbuch der Schlesischen Friedrich-Wilhelms-Universität zu Breslau*, xxxviii-xxxix (1997/98), 161-80.

Borchardt, K., 'Military Orders in East Central Europe: The First Hundred Years', in *Autour de la première Croisade*, Actes de Colloque de la Society for the Study of the Crusades and the Latin East, ed. Michel Balard, Byzantina Sorbonensia, xiv (Paris, 1996), 247-57.

Borchardt, K., 'The Hospitallers, Bohemia, and the Empire, 1250-1330', in *Mendicants, Military Orders, and Regionalism in Medieval Europe,* ed. J. Sarnowsky (Aldershot, 1999), 201-31.

Borchardt, K., 'The Hospitallers, Bohemia, and the Empire, 1250-1330', in *Mendicants, Military Orders, and Regionalism in Medieval Europe*, ed. J. Sarnowsky (Aldershot, 1999), 201-31.

Boroviczény, Karl-Georg. '*Cruciferi Sancti Regis Stephani*: Tanulmány a stefaniták, egy középkori magyar ispotályos rend történetéről', *Orvostörténeti Közlemények. Communicationes de Historiae Artis Medicinae*, cxxxiii-cxl (1991–92), 7-48.

Bosio, G., *Dell'Istoria della Sacra Religione et Illustrissima Militia di S. Giovanni Gierosolimitano,* ii (Venice, 1695).

Bramato, F., *Storia dell'Ordine dei Templari in Italia* (Rome, 1991).

Braudel, F., *The Mediterranean and the Mediterranean World in the Age of Philip II* , trans. S. Reynolds (London, 1972-73).

Breycha-Vauthier de Baillamont, A. C., 'L'Ordre au Concile de Trente', *Annales de l'Ordre Souverain Militaire de Malte*, xx (1962), 82-4.

Brockman, E., *The Two Sieges of Rhodes: The Knights of St. John at War 1480-1522* (New York, 1995 [1969]).

Bronstein, J., *The Hospitallers and the Holy Land. Financing the Latin East, 1187-1274* (Woodbridge, Boydell & Brewer, 2005).

Bruce, G. and P. Marshall (eds.), *The Place of the Dead: Death and Remembrance in late Medieval and Early Modern Europe* (Cambridge, 2000).

Budak, Neven. 'John of Palisna, the Hospitaller Prior of Vrana', in *The Crusades and the Military Orders: Expanding the Frontiers of Medieval Latin Christianity*, ed. József Laszlovszky and Zsolt Hunyadi (Budapest, 2001), 283-90.

Butler, L., 'The Siege of Rhodes,' Order of St. John Historical Pamphlets, ix (London, n.d.).

Capone, B., *I Templari in Italia* (Milan, 1977).

Capone, B., *Vestigia Templari in Italia* (Rome, 1979).

Chartier, R., 'Les arts de mourir 1450-1600', *Annales ESC*, xxxi (Paris, 1976), 51-75.

Cole, P. J., *The Preaching of the Crusade in the Holy Land 1095-1270* (Cambridge, Mass., 1991).

Courtenay, W.J., 'Between Pope and King: the Parisian Letters of Adhesion of 1303,' *Speculum*, lxxi (1996), 580–84.

Dalli, C., *Malta; The Medieval Millennium* (Malta, Midsea Books, 2006).

Delaville Le Roulx, J., *Les Hospitaliers à Rhodes jusqu' à la mort de Philibert de Naillac, 1310-1421* (Paris, 1913).

Delaville Le Roulx, J., *Mélanges sur l'Ordre de S. Jean de Jérusalem* (Paris, 1910).

Demurger, A.: *Chevaliers du Christ. Les ordres religieux-militaires au Moyen Âge, XIᵉ-XVIᵉ siècle* (París, 2002).

Dobronić, L., 'The Military Orders in Croatia', in *The Meeting of Two Worlds: Cultural Exchange between East and West during the period of the Crusades*, ed. Vladimir P. Goss (Kalamazoo, 1986), 431-38.

Dobronić, L., *Posjedi i Sjedišta Templara, Ivanovaca i Sepulkralaca u Horvatskoj* [Estates and Residences of Templars, Hospitallers, and Canons Regular of the Holy Sepulchre of Jerusalem in Croatia] (Zagreb, 1984).

Dobronić, L., *Viteški redovi, Templari i Ivanovci u Hrvatskoj* [Knightly Orders, Templars and Hospitallers in Croatia] (Zagreb, 1984).

Dondi, C., 'Hospitaller Liturgical Manuscripts and Early Printed Books', *Revue Mabillon*, n.s., xiv (2003), 225-56.

Dondi, C., *The Liturgy of the Canons Regular of the Holy Sepulchre of Jerusalem: A Study and a Catalogue of the Manuscript Sources,* Bibliotheca Victorina, xvi (Turnhout, 2004).

Dygo, M., 'The political role of the cult of the Virgin Mary in Teutonic Prussia in the fourteenth and fifteenth centuries', *Journal of Medieval History*, xv (1989), 63-81.

Edgington, S., 'Medical Care in the Hospital of St. John in Jerusalem', in *MO*, ii, 27-33.

Edgington, S., 'The Hospital of St. John in Jerusalem', in *Medicine in Jerusalem Throughout the Ages*, ed. Z. Amar, E. Lev, J. Schwartz (Tel Aviv, 1999), ix-xxv.

Ehlers, A., 'The Crusade of the Teutonic Knights against Lithuania Reconsidered', in *Crusade and Conversion on the Baltic Frontier, 1140-1500*, ed. A. V. Murray (Aldershot, 2001), 21-44.

Engel, P., 'The Estates of the Hospitallers in Hungary at the end of the Middle Ages', in *The Crusades and the Military Orders: Expanding the Frontiers of Medieval Latin Christianity*, ed. József Laszlovszky and Zsolt Hunyadi. (Budapest, 2001), 291–302.

Estepa Díez, C., 'La Orden de San Juan y el poder regio. Castilla al norte del Duero. Siglos XII-XIV', in *Las Ordenes Militares en la Península Ibérica. Volumen I: Edad Media*, ed. R. Izquierdo Benito and F. Ruiz Gómez (Cuenca, 2000), 307-24.

Filla, L. de, *et al.* (eds.), *La Chiesa di San Giovanni in Jerusalem alla Magione di Poggibonsi* (Siena, 1986).

Finke, H., *Papsttum und Untergang des Templerordens,* 2 vols (Münster, 1907).

Forey, A. J., 'Ex-Templars in England', *Journal of Ecclesiastical History*, liii (2002), 18-37.

Forey, A. J., 'Literacy and Learning in the Military Orders during the Twelfth and Thirteenth Centuries', *MO*, ii, 185-206.

Forey, A. J., *The Fall of the Templars in the Crown of Aragon* (Aldershot, 2001).

Forey, A. J., *The Templars in the Corona de Aragón* (London, 1973)

Forey, A.J., *The Military Orders: From the Twelfth to the Early Fourteenth Centuries*, New Studies in Medieval History (Basingstoke, 1992).

Gabriel, A., *La Cité de Rhodes I, Architecture Militaire* (Paris, 1921).

Gabriel, A., *La Cité de Rhodes II, Architecture Civile et Religieuse* (Paris, 1923).

Galbreath, D.L., *Papal Heraldry*, rev. edn. G. Briggs (London, 1972).

García-Guijarro Ramos, L., *Papado, cruzadas y Ordenes Militares* (Madrid, 1995).

Gerola, G., 'Gli Stemmi Superstiti nei Monumenti delle Sporadi Appartenute ai Cavalieri di Rodi', in *Rivista di Studi Araldici* (1913).

Gerrard, C., 'Opposing Identity: Muslims, Christians, and the Military Orders in Rural Aragon,' *Medieval Archaeology*, xliii (1999).

Gervers, Michael. '*Pro defensione sancte terre*: the Development and Exploitation of the Hospitallers' Landed Estate in Essex', in *MO*, i, 3-20.

Gilmour-Bryson, A. (ed. & trans.), *The Trial of the Templars in Cyprus* (Leiden, 1998).

Gilmour-Bryson, A., 'Sodomy and the Knights Templar', *Journal of the History of Sexuality*, vii, 2 (October, 1996), 151-83.

Guerrero Ventas, P., *El gran priorato de San Juan en el Campo de La Mancha* (Toledo, 1969).

Hársing, L. and Károly Kozák. 'A Johanniták a középkori Magyarországon' [Hospitallers in the medieval Hungary], *Világosság*, xx (1979), 692-99.

Hasluck, F. W., 'Heraldry of the Rhodian Knights Formerly in Smyrna Castle', in *Annual of the British School at Athens* (1910-11).

Hebron, M.., *The Medieval Siege: Theme and Image in Middle English Romance* (Oxford, 1997).

Hellwald, F. H. de, *Bibliographie méthodique de l'Ordre Souverain de St. Jean de Jerusalem* (Rome, 1885).

Housley, N., *The Avignon Papacy and the Crusades, 1305-1378* (Oxford, 1986).

Housley, N., *The Later Crusades: From Lyons to Alcazar, 1274-1580* (Oxford, 1992).

Hunyadi, Z., 'A székesfehérvári johannita konvent hiteleshelyi tevékenysége az Árpád-korban' [The Székesfehérvár commandery of the Order of St John of Jerusalem in Hungary as a place of authentication in the Árpád Age], in *Capitulum I. Tanulmányok a középkori magyar egyház történetéből*, ed. László Koszta (Szeged, 1998), 33-65.

Hunyadi, Z., 'Hospitaller Officials of Foreign Origin in the Hungarian–Slavonian Priory: thirteenth–fourteenth century', in *International Mobility in the Military Orders (twelfth–fifteenth centuries)*, ed. H. J. Nicholson and J. Burgtorf (Cardiff, 2004).

Hunyadi, Z., 'The Knights of St. John and the Hungarian Private Legal Literacy up to the Mid-Fourteenth Century', in *The Man of Many Devices, Who Wandered Full Many Ways*, Festschrift in Honour of János M. Bak, ed. Balázs Nagy and Marcell Sebők (Budapest, 1999), 507-19.

Hunyadi, Z., 'The *Locus Credibilis* in Hungarian Hospitaller Commanderies', in *La Commanderie: institution des ordres militaires dans l'Occident médiéval*, ed. Anthony Luttrell and Léon Pressouyre (Paris, 2002), 285-96.

Jan, L., and V. Jesenský, 'Hospitaller and Templar Commanderies in Bohemia and Moravia: their Structure and Architectural Form', in *MO*, ii, 235-49.

Jones, M. H., *Le Théatre national en France de 1800 à 1830* (Paris, 1975).

Josserand, P., 'A l'épreuve d'une logique nationale: le prieuré castillan de l'Hôpital et Rhodes au XIVe siècle', *Revue Mabillon*, xiv (2003), 115-38.

Josserand, P., 'Les Ordres Militaires et le service curial dans le royaume de Castille (1252-1369)', in *Les serviteurs de l'État au Moyen Âge. Actes du XXIXe congrès de la SHMESP (Pau, 1998)*, [no ed.] (Paris, 1999), 75-83.

Josserand, P., 'Un maître politique: Fernán Rodríguez de Valbuena, prieur de l'Hôpital en Castille au début du XIVe siècle', in *IV Jornadas Luso-Espanholas de História Medieval. As relaçoes de fronteira no século de Alcanices. Actas*, [no ed.] (Porto, 1998), ii, 1313-344.

Kasdagli, A. M., 'Katalogos ton Thyreon tes Rodou', in *Archaiologikon Deltion* xlviii-xlix (1994-95), *Meletes* (Athens, 1998).

Kasdagli, A. M., 'Ta Rhoditika Oikosema. Merikes paratereseis gia te semasia tous', in *Istoria kai problemata syntereses tes mesaionikes poles tes Rodou* (Athens, 1992).

Kollias, E., *The Medieval City of Rhodes and the Palace of the Grand Master*, 2nd edn. (Athens, 1998).

Kozák, K., 'Constructions dans la Hongrie des XII–XV siècles des ordres de chevalerie et d'Hospitaliers et leur influence', *Acta Archaelogica*, xxxiv (1982), 71-130.

Kurrild-Klitgaard, P., *Knights of Fantasy: an Overview, History and Critique of the Self-styled 'Orders' called 'of Saint John' or 'of Malta', in Denmark and other Nordic Countries* (Turku, 2002).

Lamattina, G., *I Templari nella Storia* (Rome, 1981).

Laurence, C. (ed.), *The Western Medical Tradition 800 BC to 1800* (Cambridge, 1995).

Le Blevec, D., 'Les Hospitaliers de Saint Jean de Jérusalem en Bais-Vivarais: la commanderie de Trignan, XII-XIII siècles', *Religion et société en Ardèche et dans l'ancien pays de Vivarais, actes du 2 colloque*, ed. M. Riou (Privas, 1985).

Léonard, E. G., *Introduction au cartulaire manuscrit du Temple du Marquis d'Albon* (Paris, 1930).

Libro de privilegios de la encomienda de Tocina 1242-1692, ed. J. M. Carmona Domínguez (Seville, 1999).

Libro de privilegios de la Orden de San Juan de Jerusalén en Castilla y León (siglos XII-XV), ed. C. de Ayala Martínez (Madrid, 1995).

Lojacono, P., 'Il Palazzo del Gran Maestro in Rodi', in *Clara Rhodos*, viii (1936).

Lojacono, P., 'La Chiesa Conventuale di S. Giovanni dei Cavalieri in Rodi', in *Clara Rhodos*, viii (1936).

Luttrell, A.T. (ed.), *Medieval Malta: Studies on Malta before the Knights* (London, 1975).

Luttrell, A.T., 'Change and Conflict within the Hospitaller Province of Italy after 1291', in *Mendicants, Military Orders, and Reginalism in Medieval Europe*, ed. Jürgen Sarnowsky (Aldershot, 1999), 185-99.

Luttrell, A.T., 'Gli Ospedalieri italiani: Storia e Storiografia,' *Studi Melitensi*, vi (1998).

Luttrell, A.T., 'Hospitaller Birgu: 1530–1536,' *Crusades*, ii (2003).

Luttrell, A.T., 'Iconography and Historiography : the Italian Hospitallers before 1530,' *Sacra Militia*, iii (2002).

Luttrell, A.T., 'The Hospitaller Province of *Alamania* to 1428', in *The Hospitaller State on Rhodes and its Western Provinces, 1306-1462*, Variorum Collected Studies Series (Aldershot, 1999), XII, 21-41.

Luttrell, A.T., 'The Hospitaller Province of *Alamania* to 1428', in *Ordines Militares – Colloquia Torunensia Historica VIII*, ed. Zenon Nowak (Torun, 1995), 21–41.

Luttrell, A.T., 'The Hospitallers in Hungary before 1418: Problems and Sources', in *The Crusades and the Military Orders: Expanding the Frontiers of Medieval Latin Christianity*, ed. József Laszlovszky and Zsolt Hunyadi (Budapest, 2001), 269-81.

Luttrell, A.T., 'The Hospitallers' Historical Activities: 1530-1630', *Annales de l'Ordre Souverain Militaire de Malte*, xxvi (1968), 57-69.

Luttrell, A.T., and L. Pressouyre (eds.), *La Commanderie: Institution des Ordres Militaires dans l'Occident Médiéval* (Paris, 2002).

Luttrell, A.T., *Latin Greece, the Hospitallers and the Crusades 1291-1440* (London, 1982).

Luttrell, A.T., *Rhodes Town: 1306–1356* (Rhodes, 2003).

Luttrell, A.T., *The Hospitallers in Cyprus, Rhodes, Greece and the West, 1291-1440* (London, 1978).

Luttrell, A.T., *The Hospitallers of Rhodes and their Mediterranean World* (London, 1992).

Luttrell, A.T., *The Making of Christian Malta: From the Early Middle Ages to 1530*. Variorum Collected Studies Series (Aldershot, 2002).

Machan, T. W., 'Chaucer as Translator,' in *The Medieval Translator: The Theory and Practice of Translation in the Middle Ages*, ed. R. Ellis (Cambridge, 1989).

Maclean, I., 'Murder, Debt and Retribution in the Italico-Franco-Spanish Book Trade: the Beraud-Michel-Ruiz affair, 1586-91', in *Fairs, Markets & the Itinerant Book Trade*, ed. R. Myers, M. Harris, and G. Mandelbrote (London, 2007).

Maier, C., *Preaching the Crusades: Mendicant Friars and the Cross in the Thirteenth Century*, Cambridge Studies in Medieval Life and Thought, 4th ser., xxviii (Cambridge, 1994).

Maiuri, A., 'I Castelli dei Cavalieri di Rodi a Cos e a Bodrum (Alecarnasso)', in *Annuario della R. Scuola Archeologica di Atene* (1921-22).

Makk, F., *The Árpáds and the Comneni. Political Relations between Hungary and Byzantium in the 12 century* (Budapest, 1989).

Mallia-Milanes, V.(ed.), *Hospitaller Malta 1530-1798: Studies on Early Modern Malta and the Order of St John of Jerusalem* (Malta, Mireva, 1993).

Mallia-Milanes, V., 'Emperor Charles V's Donation of Malta to the Knights of St John', *Peregrinationes: Acta et Documenta: Carlo V e Mercurino di Gattinara suo Gran Cancelliere*, ii, 2 (2001), 23-33.

Mallia-Milanes, V., 'The Birgu Phase in Hospitaller History', in *Birgu: A Maltese Maritime City*, ed. L. Bugeja, M. Buhagiar, and S. Fiorini (Malta, 1993).

Mallia-Milanes, V., *Valletta 1566-1798: An Epitome of Europe* (Malta, BOV, 1988).

Maschke, E., 'Nikolaus von Cusa und der Deutsche Orden', *Zeitschrift für Kirchengeschichte*, xlix (1930), 413-42.

Masiá de Ros, A., *La Corona de Aragón y los estados del Norte de Africa* (Barcelona, 1951).

Mercati, A., 'Interrogatorio di Templari a Barcellona (1311)', *Spanische Forschungen der Görresgesellschaft: Gesammelte Aufsätze zur Kulturgeschichte Spaniens*, vi (1937), 240-51.

Miguet, M., *Templiers et Hospitaliers en Normandie* (Paris, 1995).

Miret y Sans, J., *Les cases de Templers y Hospitalers en Catalunya* (Barcelona, 1910).

Mitchell, P.D., and E. Stern, 'Parasitic Intestinal Helminth Ova from the Latrines of the 13th Century Crusader Hospital of St. John in Acre, Israel', in *Proceedings of the XIIIth European Meeting of the Paleopathology Association, Chieti, Italy*, ed. M. La Verghetta and L. Capasso (Teramo, 2001), 207-13.

Mitchell, P.D., *Medicine in the Crusades: Warfare, Wounds and the Medieval Surgeon* (Cambridge, 2004).

Monfasani, J., 'Bessarion Latinus,' in *Byzantine Scholars in Renaissance Italy: Cardinal Bessarion and Other Emigrés* (London, 1995), 165-209.

Monumens historiques relatifs à la condamnation des chevaliers de l'Ordre du Temple et à l'abolition de leur ordre (Paris, 1813).

Nicholson, H., *Templars, Hospitallers and Teutonic Knight: Images of the Military Orders, 1128-1291* (Leicester, 1993).

Nowakowski, A., 'Some Remarks about Weapons stored in the Arsenals of the Teutonic Order's Castles in Prussia by the end of the fourteenth and early fifteenth centuries', in *Das Kriegswesen der Ritterorden im Mittelalter*, ed. Z. H. Nowak (Toruń, 1991), 75-88.

Pauli, S., *Codice diplomatico del sacro militare ordine Gerosolimitano*, 2 vols (Lucca, 1733-37).

Procès des Templiers, ed. J. Michelet, 2 vols (Paris, 1841-51).

Prutz, H., *Entwicklung und Untergang des Tempelherrenordens* (Berlin, 1888).

Pryor, J.H., 'In Subsidium Terrae Sanctae: Export of Foodstuffs and Raw Materials from the Kingdom of Sicily to the Kingdom of Jerusalem, 1265-1284', *Asian and African Studies*, xxii (1988), 127-46.

Purcell, M., 'Papal Crusading Policy, 1244-1291: The Chief Instruments of Papal Crusading Policy and Crusade to the Holy Land from the Final Loss of Jerusalem to the Fall of Acre', *Studies in the History of Christian Thought*, xi (Leiden, 1975).

Raynouard, F.J.M., *Les Templiers, Tragédie en cinq actes* (Paris, 1805) (repr. Nîmes, Lacour éditeur, 1997).

Reiszig, E., *A jeruzsálemi Szent János lovagrend Magyarországon* [The Order of the Knights of St. John of Jerusalem in Hungary], 2 vols (Budapest, 1925-28).

Ricardi di Netro, T., and L. Gentile (eds.), *'Gentilhuomini Christiani e Religiosi Cavalieri': Nove Secoli dell'Ordine di Malta in Piemonte* (Milan, 2000).

Rieder, K., *Der Gottesfreund vom Oberland: Eine Erfindung des Straßburger Johanniterbruders Nikolaus von Löwen* (Innsbruck, 1905).

Riley-Smith, J., 'The Templars and the Teutonic Knights in Cilician Armenia', in *The Cilician Kingdom of Armenia*, ed. T.S.R. Boase (Edinburgh, 1978), 92-117.

Riley-Smith, J., *The Crusades: A Short History* (London, 1987).

Riley-Smith, J., *The Knights of St John in Jerusalem and Cyprus, c.1050-1310* (London, 1967).

Rödel, W. G., *Das Großpriorat Deutschland des Johanniter-Ordens im Übergang vom Mittelalter zur Reformation,* 2nd edn. (Köln, 1972).

Rodríguez Brito, M. D., M. Canellas Anoz, J.M. Carmona Domínguez, and A. López Gutiérrez, 'La encomienda de Tocina y Robayna de la Orden Militar de San Juan de Jerusalém. Fuentes bibliográficas y documentales (s. XIII-XVIII)', *Tocina. Estudios Locales*, ii (1990), 53-127.

Rodríguez Campomanes, P., *Disertaciones históricas del Orden y Caballería de los templarios* (Madrid, 1747).

Rodríguez-Picavea Matilla, E., *Las Órdenes Militares y la frontera. La contribución de las Órdenes a la delimitación de jurisdicción territorial de Castilla en el siglo XII* (Madrid, 1994).

Roncetti, M., *et al.* (ed.), *Templari e Ospitalieri in Italia: la Chiesa di San Bevignate a Perugia* (Perugia, 1987).

Rossi, E., 'Memorie dei Cavalieri di Rodi a Costantinopoli', in *Annuario della R. Scuola Archeologica di Atene* (1925-26).

Sans i Travé, J. M., 'Recull de cartes de fra Ramon de Saguàrdia durant el setge de Miravet (Novembre 1307-Desembre 1308)', in *Miscellània en honor del Doctor Casimir Martí* (Barcelona, 1994), 417-47.

Setton, K.M., *The Papacy and the Levant 1204-1571*, 4 vols (Philadelphia, Pa., 1976-84).

Sire, H., *The Knights of Malta* (New Haven, 1994).

Skinner, P., H*ealth and Medicine in Early Medieval Southern Italy* (Leiden, 1997).

Sloane, B., G. Malcolm, *Excavations at the Priory of the Order of the Hospital of St John of Jerusalem, Clerkenwell, London* (London, 2004).

Sommi-Picenardi, F. G., *Itinéraire d'un chevalier de Saint-Jean de Jérusalem dans l'Ile de Rhodes* (Lille, 1900).

Starnawska, M., 'Die mittelalterliche Bibliothek der Johanniter in Breslau', in *Die Spiritualität der Ritterorden im Mittelalter,* ed. Z. H. Nowak, Ordines Militares: Colloquia Torunensia Historica, vii (Toruń, 1993), 241-52.

Starnawska, M., 'Kocioly zakonów krzyowych na lsku jako orodki odpustowe', in *Peregrinationes: Pielgrzymki w kulturze dawnej Europy*, ed. H. Manikowska and H. Zaremska, Colloquia Mediaevalia Varsoviensia, ii (Warsaw, 1995), 313-18.

Stern, E., 'Excavations in Crusader Acre (1990-1999)', in *Il Cammino I Gerusalemme*, ed. M.S. Calò Mariani (Bari, 2002).

Suárez Fernández, L., 'Política mediterránea de los Reyes Católicos', in *El Mediterráneo: hechos de relevancia histórico-militar y sus repercusiones en España. V Jornadas Nacionales de Historia Militar*, [no ed.] (Seville, 1997), 385-92.

Szcześniak, B., *The Knights Hospitallers in Poland and Lithuania* (The Hague, 1969)

The Order of St. John in Malta, ed. Government of Malta and Council of Europe (Malta, 1970).

Thomson, J.K.J., *Decline in History: The European Experience* (Oxford, 1998).

Tommasi, F., 'L'ordine dei Templari in Perugia' in *Bollettino della Deputazione di Storia Patria per l'Umbria*, lxxviii (1981).

Török, J., László Legeza, *Máltaiak. Szerzetesrendek a Kárpát-medencében* [The Maltese Order. Religious Orders in the Carpathian Basin] (Budapest, 1999).

Trenchs, J.: 'Benedicto XII y las Órdenes Militares hispanas: regesta de los textos papales', *Anuario de Estudios Medievales*, xi (1981), 139-50.

Trendel, G., 'Les commanderies des chevaliers de St-Jean de Jérusalem en Alsace', in *Recherches médiévales* ii/iii (Reichstett, 1983).

Tyerman, C., *The Invention of the Crusades* (Basingstoke, 1998).

Upton-Ward, J. (ed. & trans.), *The Rule of the Templars* (Woodbridge, 1992).

Urban, W., *Tannenberg and After. Lithuania, Poland, and the Teutonic Order in Search of Immortality*, rev. edn. (Chicago, 2003).

Vaivre, J.-B. de, 'Les tombeaux des grands maîtres des Hospitaliers de Saint-Jean de Jérusalem a Rhodes', in *Monuments et Mémoires*, lxxvi (Vendôme, 1998), 35-88.

Valentini, E., *I Templari a Civitavecchia* (Latina, 1992).

Valentini, E., *Santa Maria in Carbonara, chiesa templare a Viterbo* (Latina, 1993).

Vatin, N., *L'Ordre de Saint-Jean-de-Jérusalem, l'Empire ottoman et la Méditerranée orientale entre les deux Sièges de Rhodes: 1480–1522* (Louvain, 1994)

Verdon, L., *La terre et les hommes en Roussillon aux XIIe et XIIIe siècles. Structures seigneuriales, rente et société d'après les sources templières* (Aix-en-Provence, 2001).

Villari, L., *I Templari in Sicilia* (Latina, 1993).

Weislinger, J. N., *Catalogus librorum impressorum in bibliotheca eminentissimi ordinis Sancti Johannis Hierosolymitani asservatorum Argentorati* (Strasburg, 1749).

Williams, A., *Servants of the Sick: The Convent of the Order of St John in Rhodes and Malta 1421-1631*, forthcoming.

Winter, J.M. Van, *Sources concerning the Hospitallers of St John in the Netherlands 14th-18th centuries*, Studies in the History of Christian Thought, lxxx (Leiden/Boston/Cologne, 1998).

Witler, J.J., *Catalogus codicum manuscriptorum in bibliotheca Sacri Ordinis Hierosolymitani Argentorati asservatorum* (Strasburg, 1746).

Index

Acre, 4, 14, 69, 73, 157, 161, 198, 199; ceramic evidence of Hospitallers' stay in, 203–11; diet at St John's hospital, 216–20; Hospitaller compound of, 204–8; St John's hospital at, 213–23; use of latrines at St John's hospital, 214–15; vegetation on land surrounding, 216

Adam of Usk, chronicler, 242

Alamania, Hospitaller priory of, 74

Albenga, 96, 98

Albon, Marquis d', historian, 171, 172

Alexander I, emperor of Russia (1801–25), 89

Alexander III, pope (1159–81), 98, 99, 156, 158, 159, 160, 163

Alexander IV, pope (1254–61), 142, 198, 200, 201, 262

Alexandria, 227, 230, 233

Alfaro, Inigo d', Spanish Hospitaller, 85

Alfonso I, king of Aragon (1104–34), 34

Alfonso XI, king of Castile (1312–50), 236–37, 238

Allemagna, Domenico d', Hospitaller admiral, 85

Ambel, Aragonese Hospitaller commandery at, 5

Amboise, Emery d', Hospitaller master (1503–12), 57, 67, 68

Amouda, Teutonic castle of, 131–37 *passim*

Amposta, Hospitaller Castellany of, 36

Anavarza, Teutonic fortress, 133–35

Andrew II, king of Hungary (1205–35), 261, 262

Ángel Ladero, Miguel, historian, 40

Antioch, 69, 160, 198

Apostolic See, *see* papacy

Aquitaine, 200

Aracsa, Hospitaller commandery of, 262

Aragon, 29, 107, 112, 113

architecture, Armenian military, 133–34; of military orders in Poland, 21–22

archives, of Dordogne, Périgueux, 173; of Haut-Garonne, Toulouse, 170 ; of Pyrénées-Atlantiques, Pau, 168, 169; of the Gironde, Bordeaux, 169; Templar, at Barcelona, 163; Vatican, 170

Arles, 70

Armenia, Cilician, 131–37

Assailly, Gilbert d', Hospitaller master (1163–70), 158, 159

Asti, 6, 105

auberges, 57, 285

Aubusson, Anthony d', 249

Aubusson, Pierre d', Hospitaller Cardinal master (1476–1503), 66, 67, 246, 248, 249; death of, 57; illness of, 56–57; popular reaction to death of, 57

Augustinian Hermits, 120, 121

Augustinians, 278

Auvergne, Hospitaller priories of, 199

Avignon, 153

Ayala Matrínez, Carlos de, historian, 25, 27, 29–30, 31–32, 33, 40, 41

Baldwin I, king of Jerusalem (1100–1118), 100

Baldwin III, king of Jerusalem (1143–62), 158

Banyas, 160, 162, 164

Barbarossa, Frederick, Holy Roman Emperor (1155–90), 98, 99

Barbary Regencies, 283

Barber, Malcolm, historian, 34, 115, 172–73, 200

Barcelona, 35, 38; Templar archives at, 163

baroque, 279–88

Barquero Goñi, Carlos, historian, 33–34, 40

Basel, 64

Bavaria, Louis of, Holy Roman Emperor, (1328–47), 74

Béla III, king of Hungary (1172–96), 260

Béla IV, king of Hungary (1235–70), 260, 262, 263, 264
Benedictines, 43, 74, 167, 261, 262, 266, 278
Bérenger, Raymond de, Hospitaller master (1365–74), 230–31
Bergamo, 96, 97
Bergerac, municipal library of, 172
Beriat, Antonius, 69
Bernard, of Clairvaux, 157, 162
Bernini, Gian Lorenzo, Italian architect, sculptor, and artist, 280
Bessarion, Greek cardinal, 246
bibliographies, Spanish, 24–25
bioarchaeology, xii, 213–23
Birgu, on Malta, 9, 57, 59
Bishop Albert, of Livonia, 147–53 passim
Bismarck, Otto von, 177
Blanchefort, Bernard de, Templar master (1156–69), 158
Blanchefort, Guy de, Hospitaller prior of Auvergne and d'Aubusson's Lieutenant, 57
Bodrum, xii, 4, 85
Bohemia, 259; Hospitaller priory of, 74
Boisce, on Dalmatian coast, 260
Bonet Donato, María, historian, 36–37
Boniface VIII, pope (1294–1303), 116, 122, 241–42
Bonneaud, Pierre, historian, 36
Bookmann, Hartmut, historian, 140
Borchardt, Karl, historian, 149
Bordeaux, archives of the Gironde at, 169
Borovoczény, Karl–Georg, 258
Bosio, Giacomo, sixteenth–century Hospitaller historiographer, 9, 231, 285; on Giovanni Battista Orsini's illness, 56
Bourg, Antoine du, historian, 170–71
Braudel, Fernand, historian, 39, 280, 283, 284
Braunsberg, Konrad von, Hospitaller prior of Alemania, 74, 75
Breslau, 78
breviaries, 63–71 passim,
Brigetines, 78
British Library, 66
Bubikon, Swiss Hospitaller commandery of, 5
Burns, Robert Ignatius, historian, 37–38

Butler, Lionel, historian, xi, 227
Byzantine empire, 131

Cagliostro, 91
Canelli family, 102–105
Caoursin, Guillaume, Hospitaller vicechancellor and historiographer, 245–52
Capello, Giacomo, 285
Capuchins, 60, 61, 70
Caravaggio, Michelangelo Merisi da, 5
Carmelites, 61, 69, 120, 121
carnival, in Valletta, 286
Carretto, Fabricius del, Hospitaller master (1513–21), 57
Carthusians, 78
cartularies, 199–200
Cassière, Jean l'Evêque de la, Hospitaller master (1572–81), 61, 62, 285
Castile, 235–40 passim; Hospitaller prior of, 235–39; the Hospitallers and the monarchy of, 235–40
castles, Teutonic, 131–37
Castro, Américo, historian, 24, 38–39
Catalonia, 29, 107, 112, 113; Hospitaller priory of, 36
Catherine II, the Great of Russia (1762–96), 89
Celestine III, pope (1191–98), 147, 150
Celestinians, 78
Centre Larzac Templier et Hospitalier, 6, 10
chapter general, Hospitaller (1262), 197–202 passim; (1510), 68–69
Charles V, Holy Roman Emperor (1519–56), 57, 58, 280
Charles VI, Holy Roman Emperor (1711–40), 242
Charles VI, king of France (1380–1422), 241–42
Chaunsu, Pierre, historian, 279
Chieri, 96, 100
Chigi, Fabio, Roman Inquisitor on Malta, 60
China, 89
chivalry, imagery and themes of, 87–92
chronicles, 139, 150, 158, 277; Anonimalle, 229; Armenian, 134; English, 163; French, 242; Leicestershire, 229; Muslim, 136
Cilicia, 131–37
Cirey, Jean de, abbot of Citeaux, 64

Cistercians, 19, 32, 43, 64, 120, 147, 149, 156, 272
Clairvaux, 157
Clement III, pope (1187–91), 147, 150, 156
Clement V, pope (1305–1314), 115, 117, 169, 171
Clement VII, pope (1523–34), 77
Clement VIII, pope (1592–1605), 71
Clerkenwell, Hospitaller priory at, xi, 5, 225, 226, 229, 232, 243; excavations at, 7; Emperor Manuel II Palaeologus's visit to Hospitaller priory at, 241–43;
Clermont, 157
coinage, Hospitaller, 283
Cole, Penny, historian, 156
collachio, collachium, 57, 59, 80
Cologne, 78; SS Johan and Cordula, 253–56
commanderies, 4, 6, 7, 14, 40, 164, 199, 239, 269, 272, 283; Cologne, 253 ; in Hungary, 257–68; of Alcañiz, 34; of Aracsa, 262; of Condat, 170–71;of Grünenwörth, 74–78; of Kesztelc, 262; of Montalbán, 34;of Saragossa, 36; of Sneek, 269–78; of SS Johann and Cordula, 78; of Strasburg, 73; of Székesfehérvár, 259; of Ulldecona, 37; Sainte-Eulalie de Larzac, 6
Compostela, 169
conferences, history, in Spain, 26–27; on military orders, xi
Constance, 76
Constantinople, 69, 85, 100, 134, 241, 246, 248, 249, 252
Corinth, 227, 233, 243
Corral Val, Luis, historian, 41–42
Cotoner, Nicolas, Hospitaller master (1663–80), 62
Cotoner, Raphael, Hospitaller master (1660–63), 62
Coulommiers, French Hospitaller commandery at, 6
Courtenay, William, historian, 116
Coveti, Vitale, Florentine sculptor, 62
Crac des Chevaliers, 198
Crécy (1346), 227
Cresson, 160
Croatia, 257

crusade, crusaders, xi, 92, 97, 98, 141, 142, 143, 147, 148, 149, 150, 151, 153, 155–65 passim, 197, 198, 199, 200, 216, 220, 252, 269, 282
Culant, Pierre, lieutenant to Hospitaller Master Juan Fernandez de Heredia, 85
Cusanus, Nicolaus, 144–45
Cyprus, 4, 69, 206, 208, 230

Daftary, Farhad, historian, 90
Damascus, 157, 280
death, of Hospitaller masters, secular aspects, 55–56
Del Monte, Pietro, Hospitaller master (1568–72), 285
Delaveille Le Roulx, J., historian, xi, 11, 171, 200, 231
Demurger, Alain, historian, 34
Denmark, Hospitaller houses in, 148, 151
Die Söhne des Thales, by Zacharias Werner, 91
diet, at St John's hospital, Acre, 216–220
Długosz, Jan, Polish chronicler, 17
Dobronić, Lelja, historian, 257
Dobrzyń, Knights of, 13–14, 19, 20
Docwra, Thomas, xii
Dola, Kazimierz, historian, 20
Dominicans, 60, 61, 120, 121, 143
Dusburg, Peter of, Polish chronicler, 18
Dyer, Christopher, historian, 228
Dygo, Marian, historian, 17

Eco, Umberto, 172
Edessa, fall of, 160
Edward III, king of England (1327–77), 231
Edward IV, king of England (1461–70, 1471–83), 227, 245
Edwards, Robert, archaeologist, 133, 134
Eger (Cheb), 144
Egypt, 89, 90, 157, 161, 207, 216, 280
Emilia, 96
England, 160, 227, 228, 230, 231, 200, 241, 242
Enlightenment, 87
Essex, 225, 229, 233
Estonia, 148, 151, 152
Estuñiga, Alvaro de, Hospitaller prior of Castile, 237

Eugenius III, pope (1145–53), 155, 157, 158, 162
Europe, xi, 73, 78, 87, 89, 92, 97, 160, 175, 197, 198, 200, 201, 202, 220, 241, 259, 279, 283, 285, 286
exhibitions, 3–11 *passim*

Faciens misericordia, papal bull (1308), 105
False Orders Committee, 4; *see also* Orders
Farndon, Thomas, leader of Peasants' Revolt (1381), 225, 226, 227, 228, 232, 233
Fascism, 183
Favray, Antoine de, eighteenth-century French artist, 281, 283
feudalism, 23–43 *passim*
Fifth Crusade (1217–21), 161
Florence, Council of (1439), 59–60; sack of (1530), 280
Fluvian, Anton, Hospitaller master (1421–37), 80, 81
Foray, Alan, historian, xi, 31, 35, 36, 37
Fort Saint Angelo, on Malta, 5
fortifications, on Rhodes, 79–86 *passim*
Fourth Crusade (1202–1204), 100
France, xi, 6, 19, 108, 115–22 *passim*, 159, 160, 207, 232, 241, 242, 283; Hospitaller priories of, 199, 201
Francigena, via, 97, 99
Franciscans, 120, 121
Franco, General Francisco (1939–73), Francoism, 24, 28, 29, 37, 42–43
Frederick III, Holy Roman Emperor (1452–93), 246
Freemasonry, 87, 92
Freiburg, 76; University Library of, 67
French Revolution (1789), 89
Frisia, 270–78
Frisians, in Hospitaller comandery of Sneek, 269–78

García Larragueta, Santos, historian, 34, 36
Garrigans, James of, Templar, 107–114
Garzes, Martin, Hospitaller master (1595–1601), 62
general crisis of the seventeenth century, 279
Genoa, 85, 96–97
Gerald, the Blessed, 156, 283

Germany, 3, 4, 7, 64, 74, 135, 147, 148, 150, 151, 181, 183, 186, 192, 194
Géza II, king of Hungary (1142–62), 258, 259
Gieysztor, Aleksander, historian, 13
Glandeurs, Claude de, Hospitaller grand commander, 58
Goñi Gaztambide, José, historian, 24
Górski, Karol, historian, 16
Granada, 237
grand masters, Hospitaller, 79–80; death of Hospitaller, 55–62; illnesses and funerary rites of Hospitaller, 55–62
Graz, Teutonic church at, 144
Gregory VIII, pope (October – December 1187), 155, 157, 159
Gregory IX, pope (1227–41), 142, 263
Gregory XI, pope (1370–78), 77
Grünenwörth, Hospitaller commandery, 74–78
Grünfelde, 175, 176
Grunwald, 175–94 *passim*
Gui, Bernard, inquisitor, 115
Guinot Rodriguez, Enric, historian, 38

Hadrian IV, pope (1154–59), 158, 159, 162, 164
Hales, Robert, Hospitaller prior of England, 226, 227, 229–33
Halle, Teutonic property at, 140, 144
Harunia, Teutonic castle of, 132–37 *passim*
Hattin, battle of (1187), 157, 160, 164
Hauziński, Jerzy, historian, 13
Hebron, Malcolm, historian, 246
Heggenzer, Johann, Hospitaller grand bailiff of Rhodes, 67
Heinsberg, Hupert von, Hospitaller, 253–56
Hellenkemper, Hansgerd, archaeologist, 133, 134
Hellinga, Lotte, 64
helminths, parasitic intestinal, 220–21
Henry II, king of Castile (1369–79), 237
Henry III, king of Castile (1390–1406), 237
Henry IV, German emperor (1084–1105), 136
Henry IV, king of England (1399–1413), 242
Henry the Lion, 147, 149
heraldry, in medieval Rhodes, 79–86

Heredia, Juan Fernández de, Hospitaller master (1377–96), 85, 231
Heredia, Juan Fernández de, historian, 36
heresies, historical, 3–11 *passim*
heritage, 3–11 *passim*
Hethoum I, king of Armenia (1226–70), 132–33, 136–37
Hethoum II, king of Armenia (1289–1307), 135
Hieronymites, 78
Hill Monastic, Manuscript Library, Collegeville, Minnesota, 10
Hippocratic / Galenic tradition, 56
Hirsch, Rudolph, 64
historians, Spanish, of the military orders, 23–43
historiography, xii; Hospitaller, 3–11, 258; on military orders in Poland, 13–22; on military orders in Spain, 23–43; Templar, 95–96
Holt, Peter, Hospitaller prior, 242
Holy Infirmary, Hospitaller, 285
Holy Land, 69, 70, 73, 103, 119, 131, 135, 142, 147, 148, 149, 157, 159, 160, 164, 197, 198, 200, 202, 203, 208, 210, 259, 262
Holy See, *see* Papacy
Holy Sepulchre, of Jerusalem, 66, 68, 69
Homedes, Juan d', Hospitaller master (1536–53), 58, 62
Honorius III, pope (1216–27), 161–62
Hospitallers, *passim*
hospitals, 21, 73, 77; Hospitaller, in northwestern Italy, 103; of St John, Acre, 213–23; Templar, in Pavia, 101; *see also* Acre
Housley, Norman, historian, 141
Hungary, Hospitaller commanderies in, 257–68; *see also* commanderies

illnesses, of Hospitaller masters, medical aspects, 55
Imbroll, Salvatore, Hospitaller conventual prior, 60
indulgences, 139–45, 147
Innocent III, pope (1198–1216), 100, 147–53, 155, 160, 161
Innocent IV, pope (1243–54), 141, 142, 143, 155, 199, 200

Innocent VIII, pope (1484–92), 67–68
Inquisition, 287
Istanbul, *see* Constantinople
Italians, and restoration on Rhodes, 4–5
Italy, xi, 8, 10, 84, 95–106 *passim*, 207, 241, 246, 284

Jacques of Thérines, Templar, 119, 120, 121
James II, king of Aragon (1291–1327), 108, 109, 110, 111, 112, 113
James of Garrigans, Templar, 107–114
Jerusalem, 4, 7, 66, 98, 141, 160, 164, 199, 203
Jesuits, 60, 61, 287
Johanniter-Orden, 3, 4
John II, king of Castile (1406–54), 237
John of Pouilly, 121
John of St Victor, 115
John Paul II, pope (1978–2005), 192
Judin, Teutonic Galilean fortress of, 135
Juilly, Robert de, Hospitaller master (1374–77), 231

Kaunas, Lithuanian fortress, 139
Kaye, John, and the Ottoman siege of Rhodes (1480), 245–52
Kehr, Paul, historian, 162
Kesztelc, Hospitaller commandery at, 262
Kienig, Erhardus, Hospitaller, 67
knighthood, imagery and themes of, 87–92
Knighton, Henry, English chronicler, 229
Kolossi, 4
Konrad von Braunsberg, prior, 78
Konrad, duke of Mazovia, 14, 17
Kujot, Stanislaw, historian, 19
Kwiatkowski, Stefan, historian, 17

L'Isle Adam, Philippe Villiers de, Hospitaller master (1521–34), 281; death and burial of, 57–58, 62
La Forbie, battle of, 197, 198, 199
Ladero Quesada, Miguel Ángel, historian, 27, 29–30
Langstrother, John, Hospitaller prior of England, 227
Languedoc, 207
Lascaris Castellar, Jean de, Hospitaller master (1636–57), 62

Lastic, Jean de, Hospitaller master (1437–54), 80, 81

latrine, bioarchaeological analysis of, soil, 213–23; use of, at St John's hospital, Acre, 214–15

Ledesma Rubio, María Luisa, historian, 35–36

legacy, Hospitaller, to Malta, 279–88

legislation, Hospitaller, of 1262, 197–202 *passim*

Leon II, king of Armenia (1198–1219), 131–37 *passim*

Léonard, Emile, historian, 171–72

Les Templiers, a tragedy, 46–52 *passim*

Leśniowski, Henryk, historian, 179

Levi, Carlo, 288

Liguria, 10

Lithuania, 14. 139, 141, 142, 175, 177, 181, 182. 194

liturgy, xii, 63–71

Livonia (Latvia), 19, 142, 147–53

Lomax, Derek, historian, xi, 25, 29–30, 39, 40

Lombardy, 96, 97

Louis VII, king of France (1131–80), 162

Löwen, Nikolaus von, Hospitaller mystic, 76–77

Loyola, St Ignatius, 60; his *Spiritual Exercises*, 60

Lucius III, pope (1181–85), 156, 163

Luttrell, Anthony T., historian, xi, 36

Lyons, 65; Council of (1274), 59–60

Madrid, 10, 38

Mainz, 65

Majorca, *see* Mallorca

Malbork, in Prussia, 14, 18

Małeki, Antoni, historian, 20

Mallorca, 29, 107, 253

Malta, xi, xii, 5, 7, 9, 55, 57, 70, 89; Hospitaller archives at, 162; Hospitaller baroque culture in, 279–88; Hospitaller legacy to, 279–88; Ottoman siege of (1565), 58, 281, 284

Manteuffel, Tadeusz, historian, 19

Manuel II Palaeologus, Byzantine emperor (1391–1425), 241–43

Manueth, ceramic evidence of the Hospitallers in, 203–11; Manueth, sugar production site in, 210

Manuscript found in Saragossa, by Count Jan Potocki, 88–92

Marburg, Wigand von, German chronicler, 139

Margat, Hospitaller castle, 201

Marienburg, 139

Martin Rodriguez, José Luis, historian, 40

Martínez Díez, Gonzalo, historian, 35

Martinez, Peter, 110

Mdina, Malta's medieval capital city, 281

Mediterranean, 25, 32, 33, 36, 89, 97, 106, 205, 220, 221, 240, 241, 248, 255, 264, 279, 280, 283, 288

Mehmed II, the Conqueror, Ottoman sultan (1444–46, 1451–81), 248, 249, 251

Mendicants, 156

Merswin, Rulman, 74–76, 78

Messina, 62, 163

Milan, 63, 96, 97, 104, 241

military orders, *see* Orders

Militia Christi, Livonia, 150, 151, 152, 153

Minnesota, 10

Miravet, 108, 109, 110, 111

Miret i Sans, historian, 34

missals, Hospitaller, 63–71 *passim*,

Molitor, Mathias, Hospitaller, 69

monastic reform, 64

Montecassino, 64

Montfort, Teutonic Galilean fortress of, 135

monuments, 3–11 *passim*, 175–94

Morea, 231

Moulins, Roger des, Hospitaller master, 159, 160

mysticism, 73–78 *passim*

Nadolski, Andrzej, historian, 15

Naillac, Philibert de, Hospitaller master (1396–1421), 75–76, 85

Naples, 29, 283

Napoleon Bonaparte, 89, 284

Negropont, 246, 248

Netherlands, 276

Nicholas IV, pope (1288–92), 161

Nicholas of San Clemente, 110

Normandy, 6

Normans, 282

North Africa, 283
Norway, Hospitaller houses in, 148
Notre Dame, cathedral of, 116
Nowak, Z.H., historian, 149
Nowakowski, Andrzej, historian, 15
nuns, Hospitaller, of Sigena, 66
Nyberg, Tore, historian, 148

O'Callaghan, Joseph, historian, 39–40
Obsidionis Rhodiae urbis descriptio, by
    Guillaume Caoursin, 245; Kahn
    Kaye's translation of, 245–52
Oration, by Andrew Michael Ramsey, 92
Orders: of Alcántara, 33, 41–42; of Ca-
    latrava, 13–14, 20, 26, 27, 33, 34,
    39, 40, 41; of Christ, *see* Dobrzyń,
    Knights of; of Crutched Friars,
    269; of the Golden Fleece, 87–88;
    of Holy Sepulcher, 27; of the Holy
    Spirit, 258; of Montesa, 33, 34, 37,
    38; of San Jorge de Alfama, 37; of
    San Marcos, 32; of Santa Maria de
    España, 32–33; of Santiago, xi, 27,
    33, 34, 39, 40, 41; of St Anthony,
    Order of, 258; of the Hospital,
    passim; of the Hospitaller Canons
    Regular of St Stephen, 258, 266; of
    the Sword Brothers, xii, 19, 147–53;
    of the Temple, *see* Templars; of
    the Teutonic Knights, *see* Teutonic
    Knights; Malteser-Orden, 4; Malte-
    ser Hilfdienst, 3; military, *passim*
Orsini, Giovanni Battista, Hospitaller master
    (1467–76), 56
Our Lady of Victories, church of, Valletta,
    59, 62

Padua, 241,
Palacios Martin, Bonifacio, historian, 41
Palestine, 96
papacy, Apostolic See, Holy See, xii, 41, 42,
    152, 153, 239
papal letters, pattern of, 155–65 *pasim*
Paravicini, Werner, historian, 143
Paris, 10, 46–52 *passim*, 90, 241, 242; the
    trial of the Templars and the Univer-
    sity of, 115–22
Pascal II, pope (1099–1118), 156
patronage, 235–40 *passim*

Pau, archives of Pyrénées-Atlantiques at,
    168, 169
Paul I, Russian Tsar (1796–1801), 89
Paule, Antoine de, Hospitaller master
    (1623–36), 57; death and burial of,
    60–61, 62
Paulus, Nikolaus, historian, 140
Pavia, 97, 241; Templar hospital at, 101
Peasants' Revolt (1381), composition of
    rebels, 228; the Church and the, 228;
    the Hospitallers and the, 225–33
Pécs, 260, 262
Peninsular War (1808–1814), 41
Perellos y Roccaful, Ramon de, Hospitaller
    master (1697–1720), 62, 286
Périgord, Hospitaller houses of, 167–73;
    Templar houses of, 167–73
Périgueux, archives of Dordogne at, 173;
    see also archives
Persia, 90
Perugia, 6, 10
Peter I, king of Castile (1350–69), 237
Peter I, king of Cyprus (1361–68), 230
Peter IV, king of Aragon (1336–87), 237
Philip II, king of Spain (1556–98), 59
Philip IV, the Fair, king of France (1285–
    1314), 106, 115–22 *passim*
Piacenza, Templar hospital in, 101
piety, 78, 145, 249
pilgrims, pilgrimage, 148, 149, 153, 157,
    169
Pins, Roger des, Hospitaller master
    (1355–65), 230
Pinto de Fonseca, Emanuel, Hospitaller
    master (1741–73), 89, 91, 283
pirates, 100
Pius IV, pope (1559–65), 70
Pius V, pope (1566–72), 70
Poggibonsi, Hospitaller commandery build-
    ings at, 6
Polak, Wojciech, historian, 17
Poland, xi, 13–22 *passim*, 51, 89, 92, 175–
    94 *passim*; Hospitaller grand priory
    of, 89, 90; partitions of, 89, 177
Polejowski, Karol, historian, 18–19
Polkowska-Markowska, Wanda, historian,
    19
Pomerania, 14, 20

Ponte, Pietro del, Hospitaller master
      (1535–36), 58, 62
Portugal, 25, 237
Postumia, via, 97
Potocki, Count Jan, 88–92 *passim*
poverty, Hospitaller vow of, 80
Prague, 139, 144
Pray, Georgius, historian, 258
Preti, Mattia, 62
printing press, 63–71 *passim*
priories, Hospitaller, in Europe, 199, 202
propaganda, papal crusading, 155–65
Provence, 200, 207
Prussia, xi, xii, 14, 18, 139, 141, 142, 143,
      144, 149, 175, 181
Pruthenia, 17, 18, 19, 21

Ramsey, Adrew Michael, 92
rationalism, 87
Raymond of Guardia, Templar, 108, 111,
      112
Raynouard, Just-François-Marie, historian,
      and his works on the Templars,
      46–52
Reconquista, 24, 42
Red Army, 181
Red Sea, 216
Redin, Martin de, Hospitaller master
      (1657–60), 62
reform, Hospitaller, 73–78 *passim*
Reformation, Counter-, 279; Protestant, 254,
      280
Reginai, via, 97
Reiszig, Ede, historian, 257, 258
relics, 100, 254
Renaissance, 280, 286–87
Resplus, Matthew, Dominican, 61
responsiones, 199, 200, 201, 240, 271
restoration, in Western Europe, 5; on Malta,
      5; on Rhodes, 3–4
Revel, Hugh, Hospitaller master (1258–77),
      201
Rhodes, xi, xii, 4–5, 7, 36, 55, 56, 59, 62,
      67, 68, 69, 70, 78, 79–86 *passim,*
      227, 230, 231, 233, 239, 240, 243,
      285 ; conquest of, 73; Ottoman siege
      of (1480), 245–52; Ottoman siege of
      (1522), 283

Richard II, king of England (1377–99), 226,
      227, 232
Riley-Smith, Jonathan, historian, 141
Rodriguez-Picavea Matilla, Enrique, histo-
      rian, 40, 41
Rojas Portalrubei, Martin, Hospitaller at
      Council of Trent, 70
Romania, 257
Romanticism, 88
Rome, 10, 59, 60, 62, 107, 144, 159, 161,
      227, 233, 241; sack of (1527), 280
Roussillon, 107
Ruano, Eloy Benito, historian, 39
Rule, Hospitaller, 8; Templar, 150, 152
Runciman, Sir Steven, historian, 34
Russia, 89, 92

Sáez Sánchez, Emilio, historian, 34, 37
Saint-Amand, Odo de, Templar master
      (1171–80), 159
Saint-Gilles, Hospitaller grand priory of,
      168, 170, 199
Sáinz de la Maza, Regina, historian, 37
Saladin, 157
Sallelles, Sebastian, Jesuit, 61
Samsonowicz, Henryk, historian, 18
San Bevignate church, Perugia, 6
Sánchez Albornoz, Claudio, historian, 24,
      38–39
Sans i Travé, Josep Maria, historian, 27,
      34–35
Santo Stefano, Templar hospital of, in
      Reggio, 99
Saragossa, 27, 65
Sardinia, 29
Sarnowsky, Jürgen, historian, 9
Saxony, Templar houses in, 149
Scandinavia, 148
Schiaparelli, Luigi, historian, 162
Schüpferling, M, historian, 148–49
Schwerin, Ursula, historian, 155, 156
Scott, Sir Walter, 9
Second Crusade (1145–49), 157, 158, 162,
      165
Secret, Jean, historian, 172
secularization, of Hospitaller magistracy,
      283
Seljuk Turks, 131, 132, 136, 137

Sengle, Claude de la, Hospitaller master (1553–57), death of, 58, 62
Sicily, 29, 60, 61, 105
Sigena, Hospitaller nuns of, 66
Silesia, 14, 21, 140
Siracusa, Sicily, 70
Sixtus IV, pope (1471–84), 246, 250
Slavonia, 257, 263
Smail, R. C., historian, xi
Sneek, Hospitaller commandery of, 269–78
Society for the Study of the Crusades and the Latin East, 23
soil, *see* latrine soil
Solano, Emma, historian, 40–41
Solomon, Temple of, 115
Spain, xi, 6, 8, 23, 89, 159, 160, 235–40 *passim*, 283; state of historiography in, 23–43
Speier, 65
SS Johan and Cordula, Cologne, the Hospitallers at, 253–56
St Angelo, fort, Malta, 57, 62
St Catherine's convent, Utrecht, 270–71, 272, 276
St Cordula, 254
St Costantia, 254
St Egidius, Templar hospital of, at Testona, 99, 101
St George, chapel of, on Rhodes, 85
Saint Jaille, Didier de, Hospitaller master (1535–36), 58
St Johan, 254
St John Historical Society, 227
St John the Baptist, feast of, 56
St John the Baptist, *passim*
St John, conventual church of, in Valletta, 60, 61–62, 285
St John's Ambulance Brigade, 3
St Lawrence, church of, in Birgu, 57
St Lazarus, nunnery, at Bethany, 198
St Louis IX, king of France (1236–70), 157
St Panthaleon, feast of, 67–68
St Paul, Hermits of, 78
St Stephen, king of Hungary (1000/1–1038), 259
St Ursula, 254
Starnawska, Maria, historian, 140
Starograd, Hospitaller estates in, 20
Stephen V, king of Hungary (1246–72), 262

Strasburg, 64, 65, 73–78 *passim*
Subiaco, 64
sugar, production and trade, 198, 203, 208, 210–11
Suleyman the Magnificent, Ottoman sultan (152–66), 288
Sweden, Hospitaller houses in, 148
Syria, 90, 96, 132, 157, 160, 198, 207, 280
Székesfehérvár, Hospitaller commandery of, 259

Tagliavia, Giorgio, rector of Jesuit College, Malta, 61
Tannenberg, 175–94 *passim*
Tannenberg-Grunwald-Žalgiris, battle of, 175–94
Taranto, 10
Templars, xi, xii, 46–52, 73, 260, 263, 264, 265, 266, 268; in north-western Italy, 95–106; in Poland, 20–21; in Spain, 34, 35, 36, 37, 38; trial of the, 103, 105–106, 107, 108, 112, 115–22
Temple Crossing, 5
Teutonic Knights, xi, xii, 13–19, 139–45, 175–94 *passim*, 269, 270, 271, 276; in Cilicia, 131–37
theatre and history, 46–52 *passim*
Thiergarten, Johannes Prüss zum, 67
Third Crusade (1189–92), 159, 165, 213
Third Lateran Council (1179), 160
Thuringia, 144
tombstones, Hospitaller, on Rhodes, 79–86 *passim*
Torroja, Arnold de, Templar master (1181–84), 160
Tortona, Templar hospital in, 101
Toruń, University of, 14, 15
Toulon, 283
Toulouse, archives of Haut-Garonne at, 170 ; grand priory of, 170–71
tourism, heritage and, 3–11 *passim*
Tower of London, 226
Trent, Council of (1545–63), 59, 60, 63, 70–71
Trial of the Templars, by Malcolm Barber, 115
Trier, 143, 144
Trionfo, Augustine, 120–21

Tripoli, 58, 160
Trudon des Ormes, A., historian, 171, 172
Tsirpanlis, Zacharias, historian, 9
Tunis, 89, 207
Turin, 8
Turkey, 4
Tymawa (East Pomerania), Knights of Cala-
   trava's estates in, 20
Tyre, William of, 158

Ulldecona, Hospitaller commandery of, 37
Ulm, 245
University of Paris, and the trial of the Tem-
   plars, 115–22
Urban III, pope (1185–87), 156, 159
Urban IV, pope (1261–64), 201
Urban VI, pope (1378–89), 77
Urban VIII, pope (1623–44), 60, 71, 284
Utrecht, 269, 270, 271, 272, 276, 277, 278

Valbuena, Fernan Rodriguez de, Hospitaller
   prior of Castile, 238
Valencia, 37, 107
Valette, Jean de la, Hospitaller master
   (1557–68), 56, 57, 288; illness and
   death of, 58–59, 61–62
Valletta Rehabilitation Project, 5
Valletta, Malta, 7, 59, 61, 62, 285, 286
Vasconcellos, Luiz Mendez de, Hospitaller
   master (1622–23), 61, 62
Vatican Archives, see archives
Vatin, Nicolas, historian, 9
vegetation, on land surrounding Acre, 216
Venice, 8, 14, 63, 100, 207, 241, 283
Vercelli, 96
Verdalle, Hugh Loubenx de, Hospitaller

master (1582–95), 62, 283
Verona, 160
Versailles, peace treaty of (1919), 181
Vicens-Vives, Jaume, historian, 38–39
Vicenza, 241
Victor IV, antipope (1159–64), 98
Vienne, Council of (1311–12), 115, 120, 121
Vilhena, Antonio Manoel de, Hospitaller
   master (1722–36), 286
Villaret, Fulk de, Hospitaller master
   (1304/1305, deposed 1317), 169
Villari, Rosario, historian, 279–80
Vilnius, 188
Visitation Books, 40
Viterbo, 162
Vittoriosa, see Birgu

Warsaw, 90
Werdenberg, Rudolf Graf von, Hospitaller
   prior of Germany, 66, 67, 68
Werner, Zacharias, 91
Wignacourt, Alof de, Hospitaller master
   (1601–22), 62
Willbrand of Oldenburg, German traveller,
   135–36
William II, Kaiser (1888–1918), 177, 179
William of Nogaret, councillor and keeper
   of the seal to Philip IV of France,
   115–16
wine, 169
Władysław II Jagiełło, king of Poland
   (1386–1434), 175–94 passim
Wojtyła, Karol, see John Paul II
World War I (1914–18), 179, 181, 183
World War II (1939–45), 179, 181, 182, 185